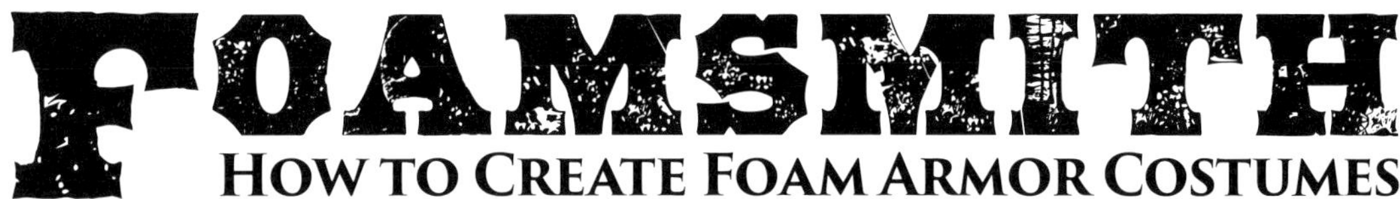

Bill Doran

Foamsmith: How to Create Foam Armor Costumes
by Bill Doran
Find Bill on the web at PunishedProps.com

Photography by Bill Doran
Editor and Layout Ninja: Brittany Doran

Printed in Canada

ACKNOWLEDGEMENTS

I could not have done this alone. The prop and costume making community has been an amazing, positive force in my life. Whether I'm looking for personal support or help with a technical problem, scores of amazing individuals have risen up to give me the push I need to improve my craft and my life.

When it comes to sussing out the technical aspects of foam fabrication, I have a handful of extraordinary friends whose brains I can always count on for picking. A gigantic thank you goes out to Will Morgan, Harrison Krix, Svetlana Quindt, Benjamin Schwarz, Evil Ted Smith, David Carpenter, and Eric Jarman. You guys rule!

Also thank you to my amazing wife Brittany. None of this happens, nor is it worth doing, without you.

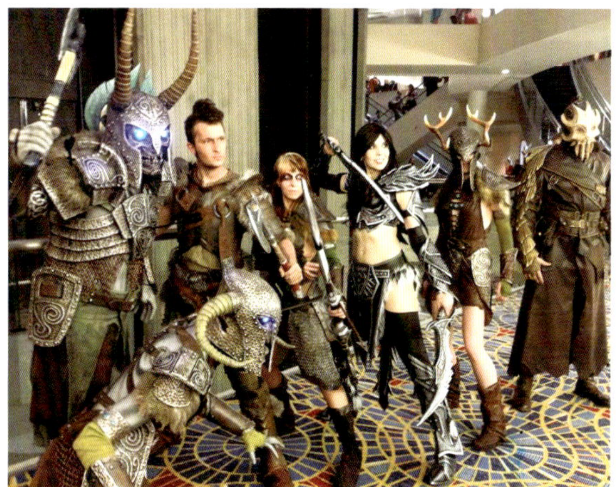

About the Author

Greetings! I'm Bill Doran and I build space guns, fantasy weapons, and elaborate sets of armor as my full-time living. It's a lot of hard work, and seldom glorified, but it's a whole lot of fun and I wouldn't trade it for any career in the world.

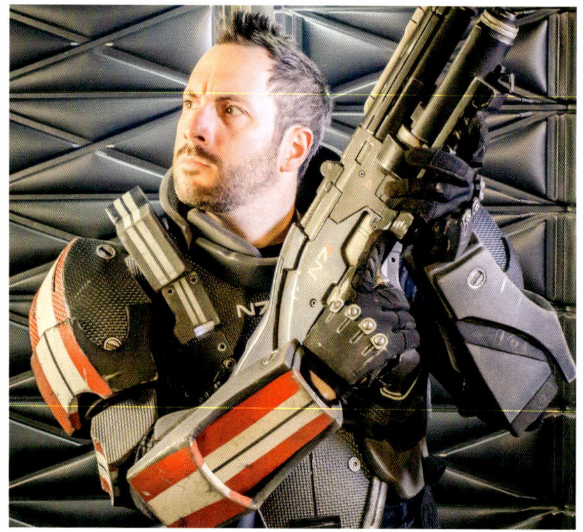

I started making props and costumes with my friends in 2009. Back then, we decided to try out cosplaying for a local fan convention. After that fateful event, I was totally hooked. Before I knew it I was buying more tools, building props for my friends, and traveling around the country to attend more and more fan expos.

The hobby consumed my life. I knew I needed to make a change, so in 2012 I quit my 9 to 5 day job and opened my own business: Punished Props. Since then I've been building high-quality replica props for clients all around the world!

As I picked up experience from my trial and error learning process, I started sharing what I knew with the quickly growing maker and cosplay communities. I've been documenting my builds and techniques so that others might glean some of my insight. My goal is to lower the barrier to entry for this amazing craft, inspire newcomers to join our growing ranks, and to help people learn the techniques they'll need to make their props and costumes stand out from the crowd.

My dedication to passing on my knowledge has turned into a major facet of my business. I've done many panels and presentations on the craft of prop making at popular fan conventions. To top it off, my eBook, A Beginner's Guide to Making Mind Blowing Props, has made its way into the hands of thousands of new makers!

Thank you for taking the time to see what I'm all about. I look forward to seeing what we can build together!

-Bill Doran
PunishedProps.com

WELCOME!

Welcome to the Foamsmith book!

The goal of this book is to help you create stunning, comfortable pieces of armor as painlessly and cheaply as possible. The book is split up into three parts.

Part 1: Design, Templating, & Fabrication
I will teach you all about the tools, materials, and skills you'll need to design, plan, and fabricate extraordinary pieces of costume armor!

Part 2: Finishing & Painting
We'll go over the painting and finishing procedures you'll need to turn your foam into true works of wearable art!

Part 3: Undersuits, Straps, & Lights
You'll learn the tips, tricks, and techniques to make a fantastic undersuit, strap up your armor, and add incredible lighting effects to your foam armor!

Contents

Part 3: Undersuits, Straps, & Lights

Part 1
Design, Templating, & Fabrication

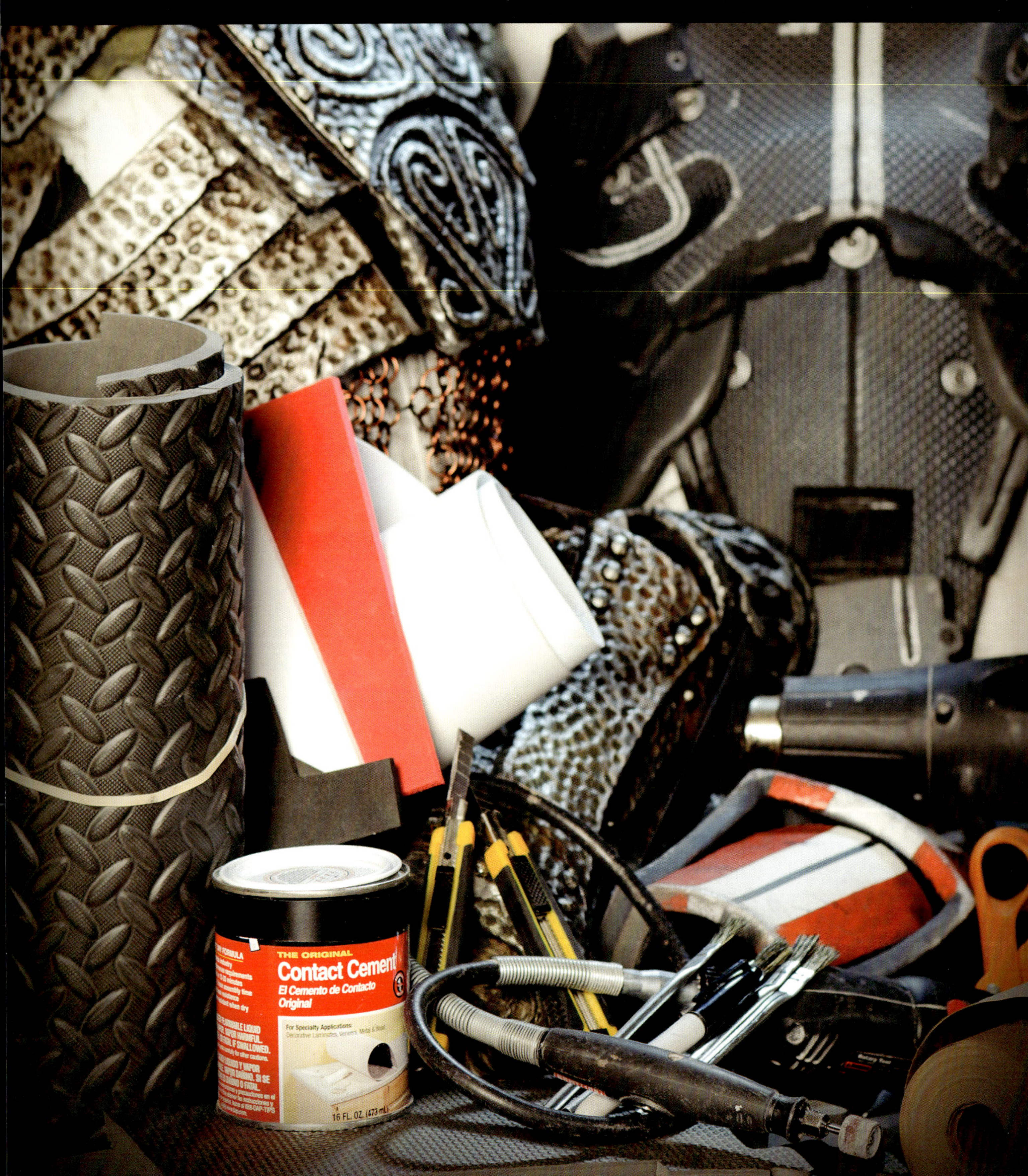

Is this stuff safe?

Compared to many other armor-building techniques, foam is relatively safe. There are, however, several concerns that should be accounted for.

Not only are sharp knives dangerous, but dull knives are even more so. Keep your knives razor sharp, use a metal straight edge, and handle them with care. It's unlikely that you'll lose a limb to an X-Acto cut, but you may bleed on your armor. That would ruin your project!

Heat guns are extremely useful, but as the name suggests, they get rather hot. Be wary of what, and whom, you set your gun on after using it. Sturdy work gloves are also useful when handling hot EVA foam. Seriously, that stuff can match temperatures at the surface of the sun.

One of the best things about working with foam is that you don't need a full shop to do so. Provided that you have a decently sized, flat surface to do your cutting, you could build foam armor in a closet.

The only real considerations are ventilation and dust. When using contact cement, you don't want to gas yourself with its toxic smell. Working in an open room near a window with a fan is the best case scenario. Also, a respirator is a must. As far as dust, any work with a rotary tool or belt sander is going to create a lot of foam dust. You certainly don't want to breathe it in and might not want it to get all over your living room.

Stay safe,
don't rush,
and have fun!

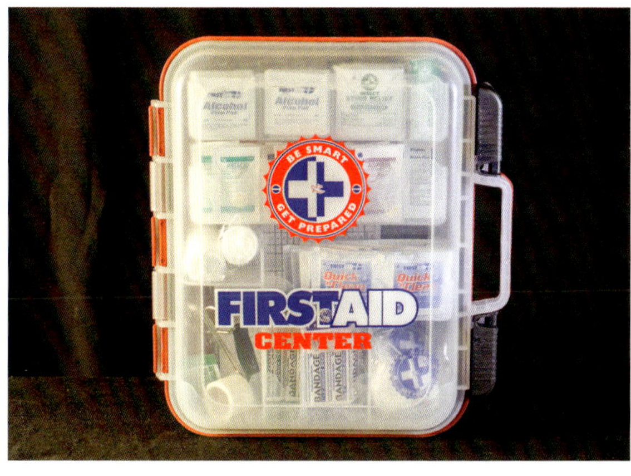

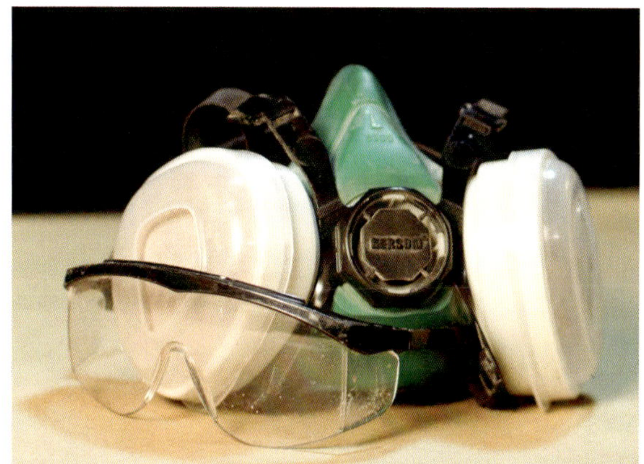

So, why foam?

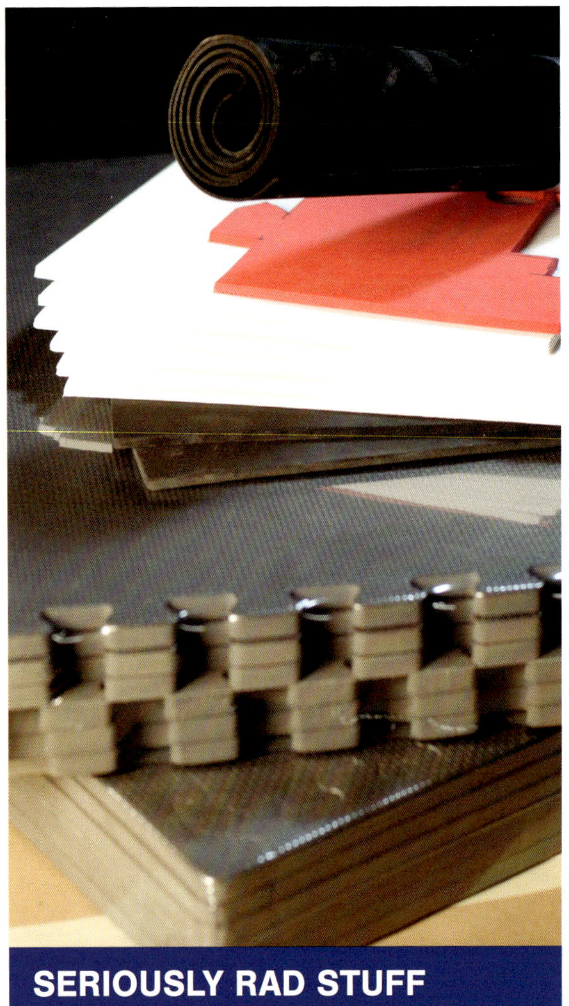

SERIOUSLY RAD STUFF

There is no one perfect material for making everything. The same holds true for making costume armor. Nearly every set turns into a mixed-media project. However, the case can be made that EVA foam is currently one of the best and most versatile materials for making your fictional outfits a reality.

It's cheap. Like, wicked cheap. This means two things: first, you can build a whole set of armor for less than you pay for a month of cable TV. Second, you can afford to mess up a lot. Especially when you're coming up with your own new set of templates, it pays to not worry about expensive material stock during that trial and error process. Plus it's readily available at many retail outlets and online stores, so you'll never run out!

Foam is extremely easy to work with. Unlike working with wood, metal, and rigid plastics, there are no super expensive power tools that you need to buy. Just a handful of inexpensive tools are all it takes to cut and shape your armor pieces. The durability and flexibility of EVA foam makes it a breeze to shape and form.

It's lightweight. A full set of steel armor sounds like a great idea until you need to walk around a convention floor wearing it for 12 hours straight. A full set of EVA foam armor can weigh as little as just a couple of pounds. This makes you nimble on your feet and able to endure wearing it for an extended period of time. It also makes it much easier to ship and transport your creation.

Finally, it stands up to abuse. If you, like me, travel with your costumes a lot, you know how valuable it is to be able to fit your costume into a suitcase. Sometimes you need to get rough with the pieces to fit them in. That, plus the inevitable abuse the armor will see on the con floor, makes the durability of EVA foam a huge boon. Plus, when the occasional foam damage does occur, repairs are generally trivial.

WHAT TYPES OF ARMOR COULD I MAKE FROM FOAM?

- Leather
- Metal
- Carbon Fiber
- Polycarbonate
- Alien Flesh
- Bone/Shell/Carapace/Exoskeleton
- Dragon Scales
- Wood
- Padded/Quilted Cloth Armor

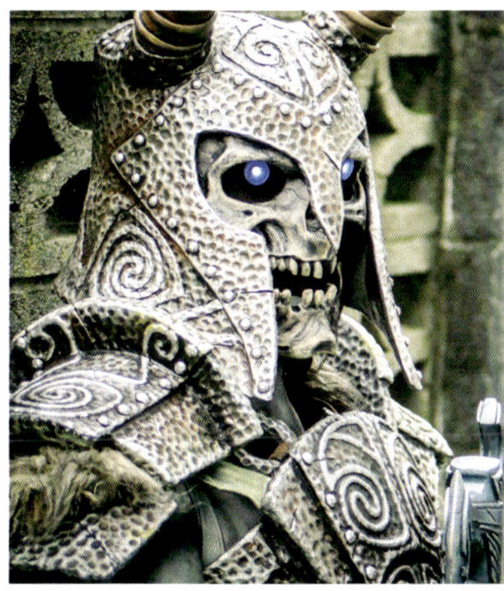

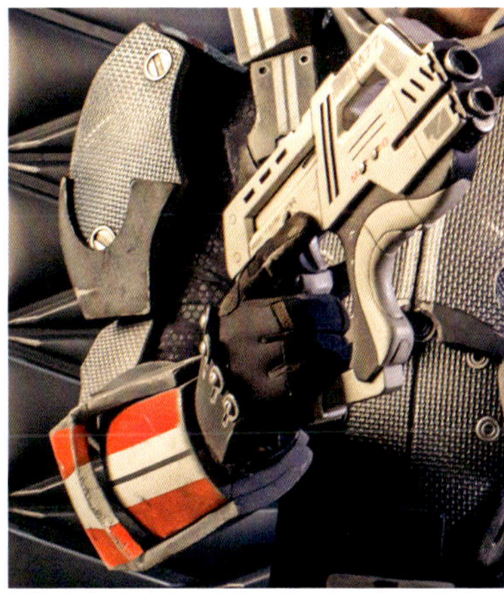

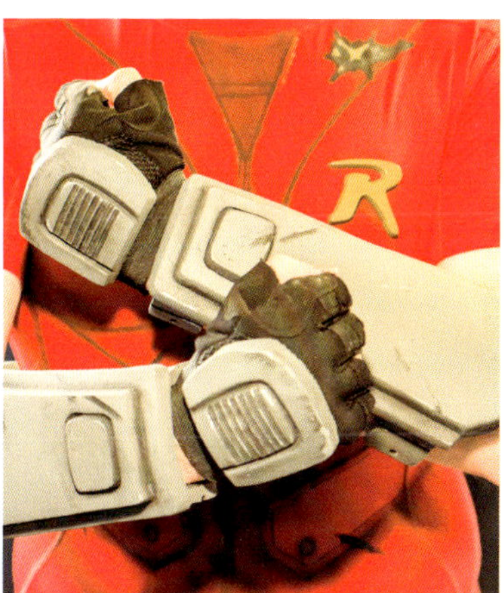

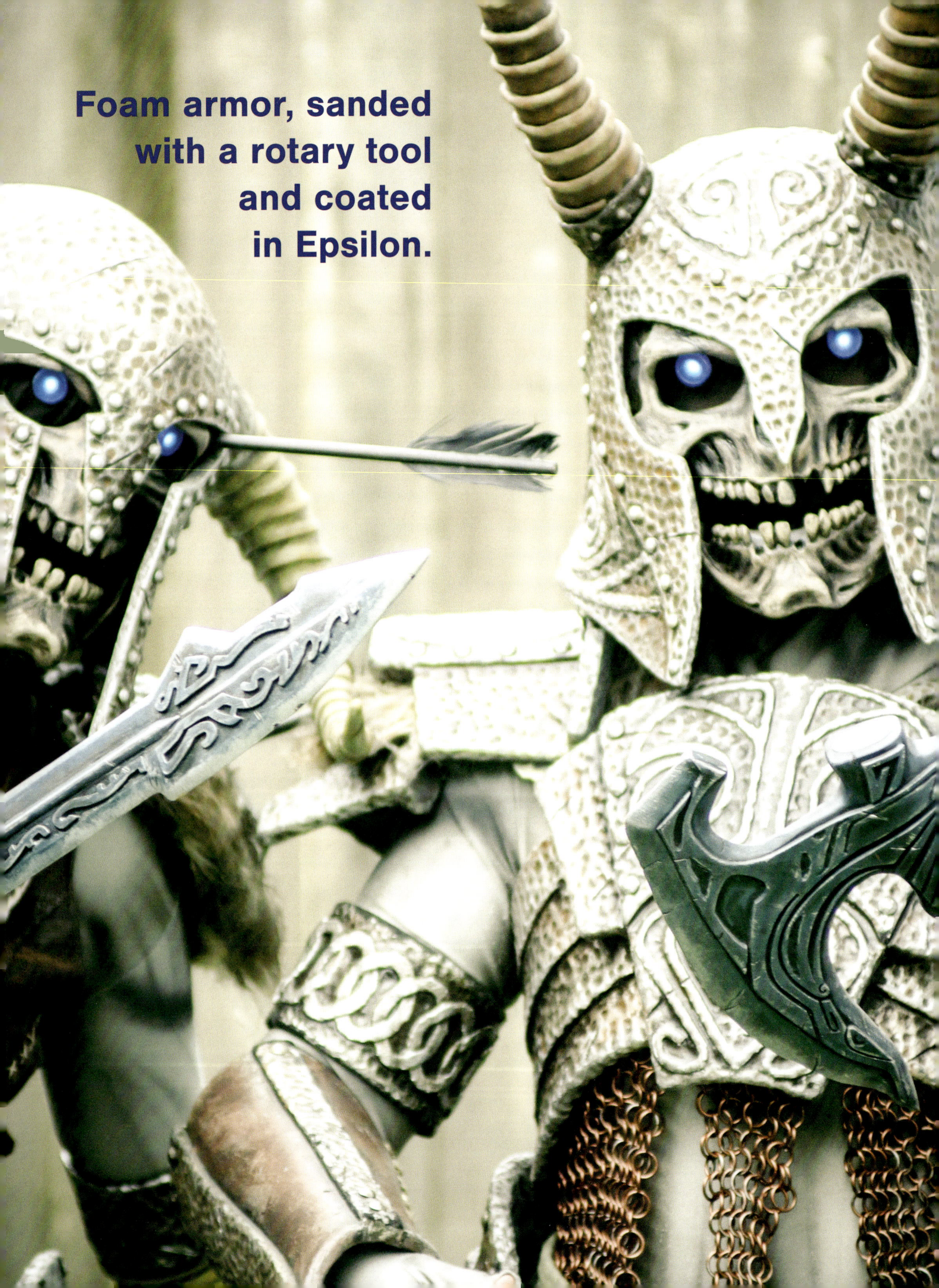

Foam armor, sanded with a rotary tool and coated in Epsilon.

OK Bill, you've sold me on foam, where do I get it?

Ethylene-vinyl acetate (EVA) foam is commonly found throughout the world in the shape of interlocking floor mats and colorful play materials for children. It comes in many sizes, shapes, and thicknesses for your convenience.

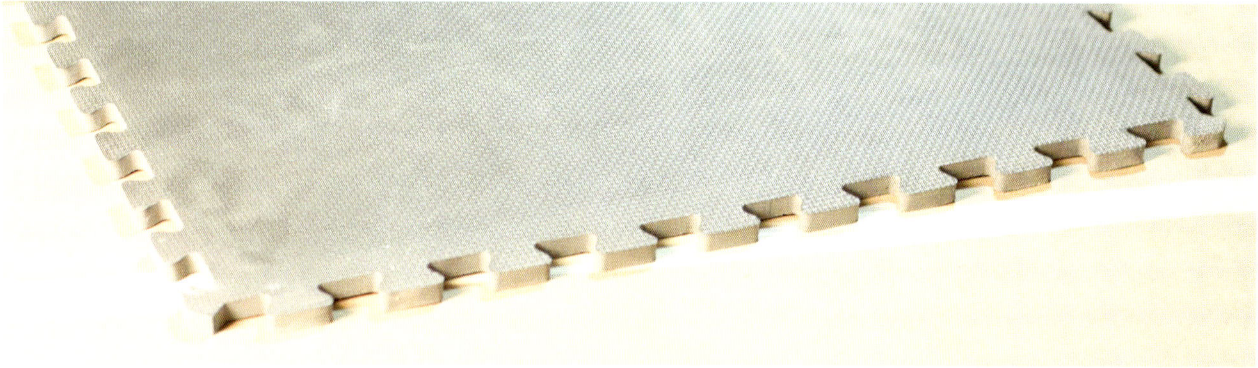

For the most part, you'll find your floor mats in half inch thick, two foot by two foot sections with jigsaw puzzle-piece edges for connecting them together. These can be found at most hardware stores and range in price from less than $10 for a pack of four and up to $20-$30 for a pack of 6.

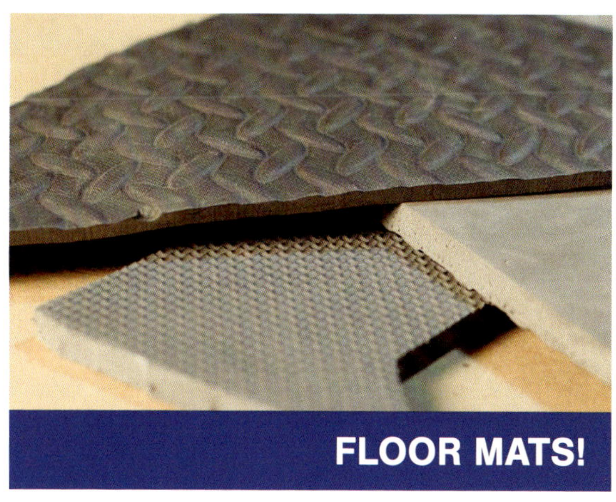

FLOOR MATS!

The sheets usually have one side that is smooth, with the other side being textured in some manner. Consider what your application will be when picking out the texture. You may want to use the texture in some way or remove it entirely via mechanical means (sanding). Also be on the lookout for bubbles in the smooth side. While not a deal breaker, not all EVA foam is created equal and you want to get the most bang for your buck.

Though less common, the foam floor mats also come in a thinner, quarter inch thickness. These are usually sold in sheets that are about two feet wide and several feet long. Because of the length, they are usually sold in rolls.

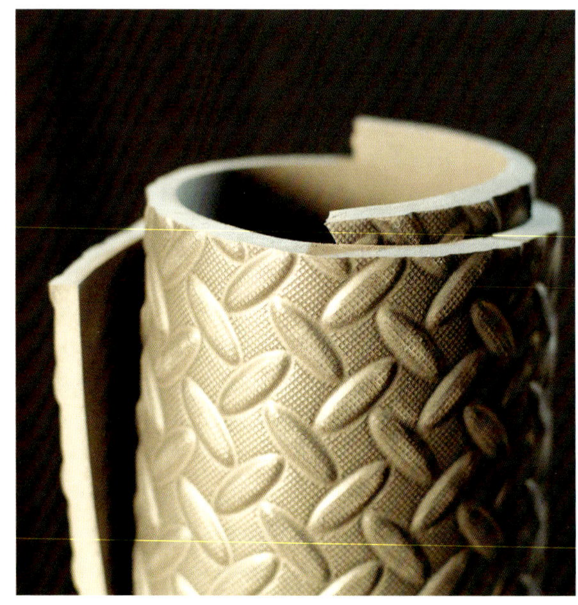

For thinner detail pieces on your armor, it's hard to beat "fun" foam from your local craft store. I know this stuff is designed for children's projects, but it's a miracle material for cosplay. It usually comes in both 2mm and 6mm thicknesses and in a myriad of colors.

Most of the time you'll find them in small page-sized sheets, but the 2mm stuff can also be picked up in large rolls. This is handy for when you're cutting out big pieces. If you need bigger pieces in the 6mm range, you might try and find some of the rolled up, quarter inch floor mats that I mentioned earlier.

FUN FOAM!

"I know this stuff is designed for children's projects, but it's a miracle material for cosplay."

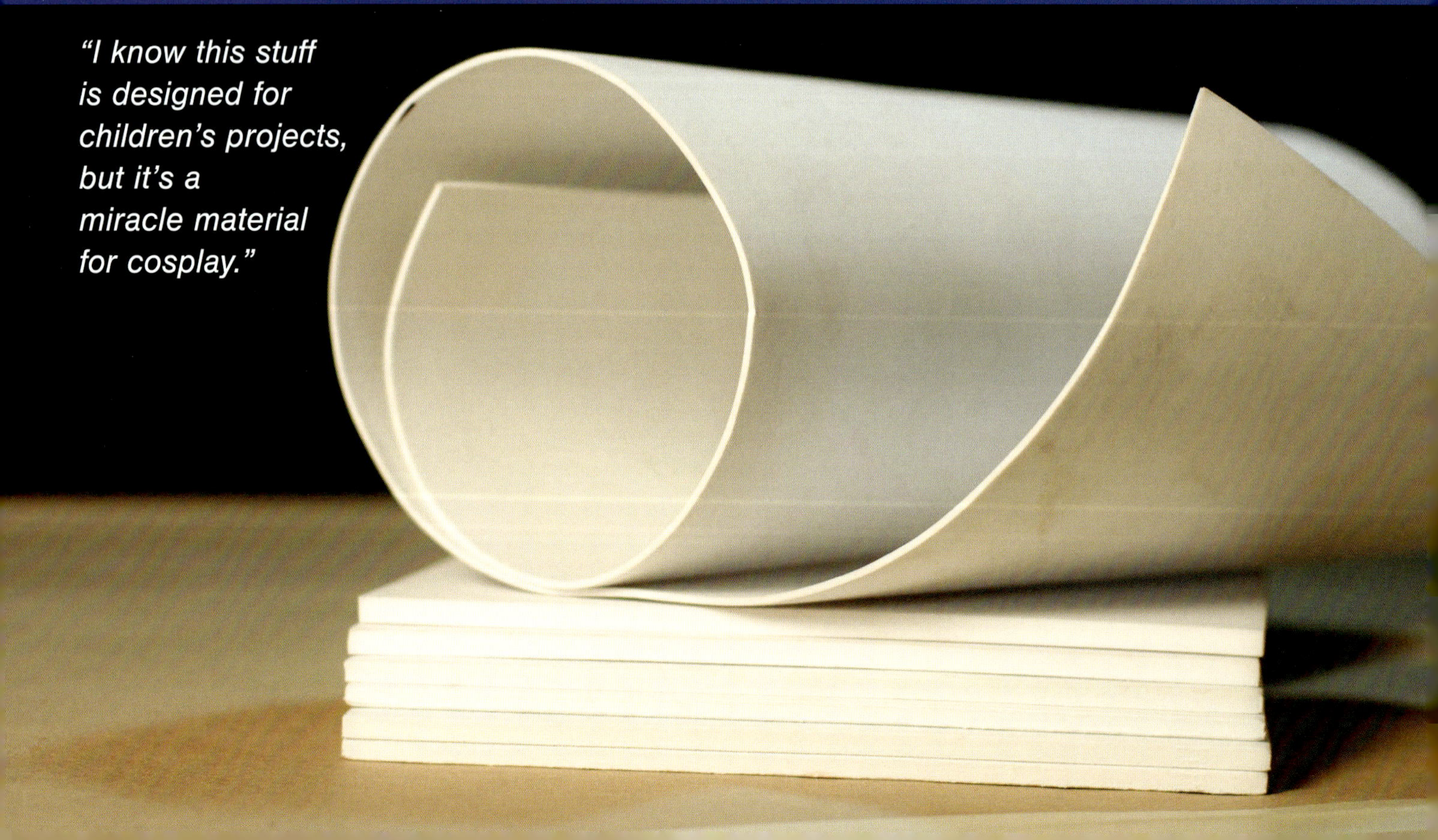

HOW MIGHT I STICK ALL THIS FOAM TOGETHER?

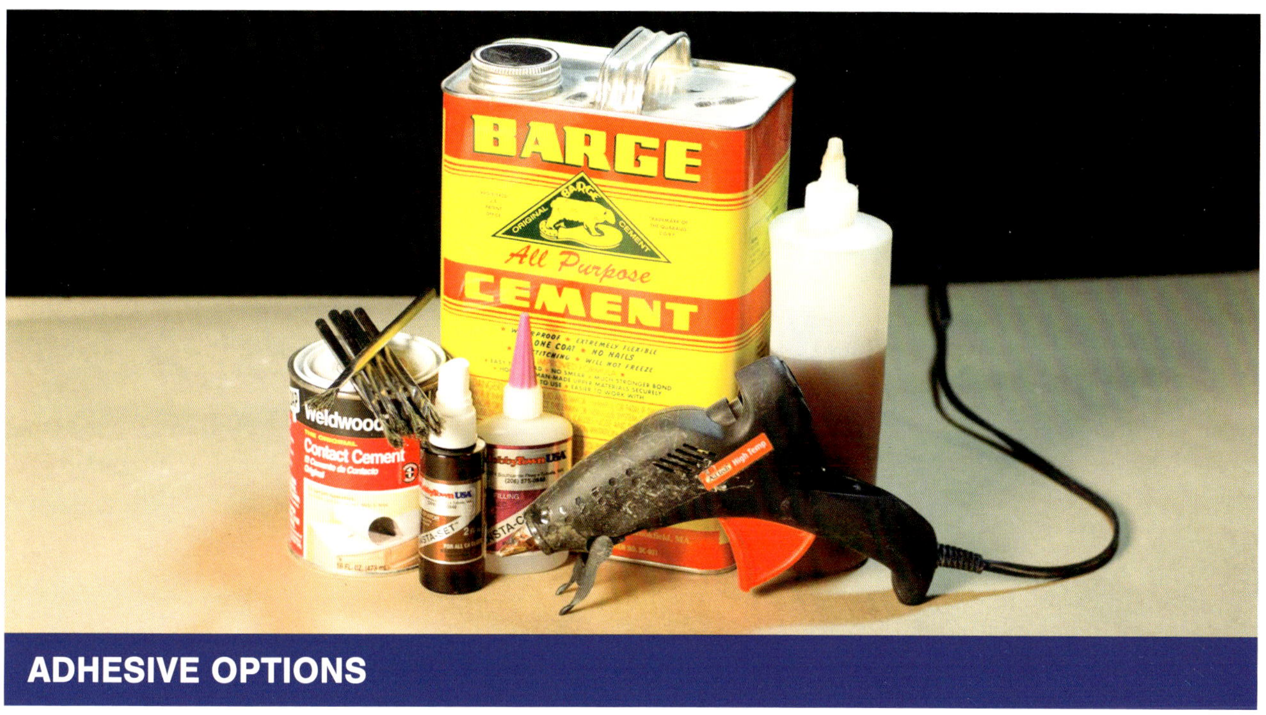

ADHESIVE OPTIONS

Much like the base materials, there is no one perfect, all-purpose solution for adhering foam together. There is, however, one that does most of the heavy lifting in my shop. That would be contact cement! This glorious goo is available at every hardware store. It's frequently used for putting shoes together, so you know it means business.

Most maker's favorite brand of contact adhesive is Barge. It is truly amazing stuff, but it is generally harder to come by than other generic brands. If you have a leatherworking supply store nearby, give them a holler to see if they carry it. If you do get the gigantic can of Barge, do yourself a favor and also get a squeeze bottle to put some of it in for application. This way you aren't trying to pour it out of a giant can each time you use it.

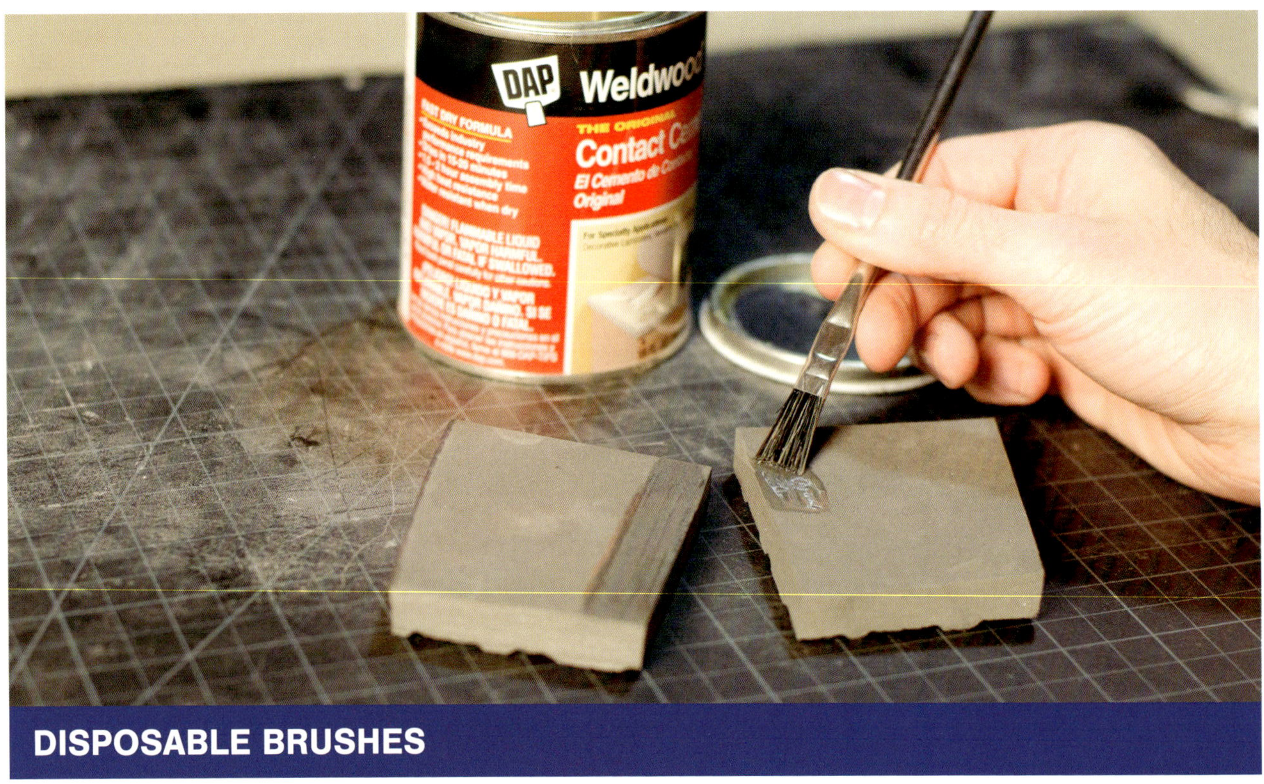

DISPOSABLE BRUSHES

Contact adhesives work differently than other, normal glues. You start by smearing or brushing the goo onto both surfaces that you intend to stick together. Make sure you put on a nice, consistent, even layer of goo. You don't need too much. Your foam may soak up all of it, in which case, brush on another layer after a couple of minutes.

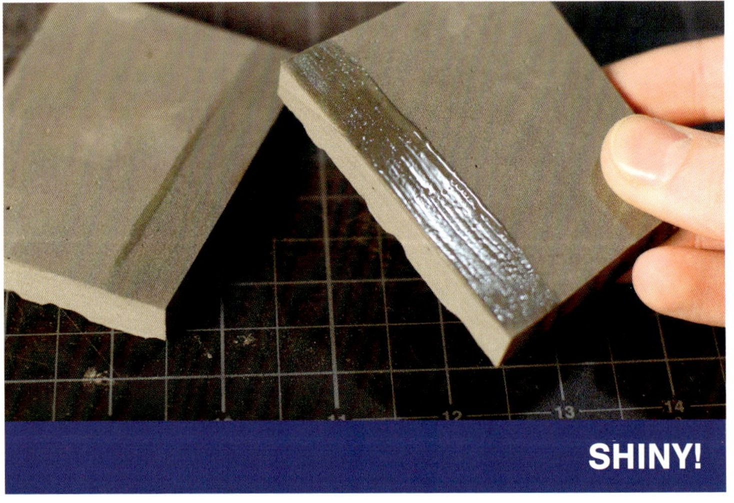

SHINY!

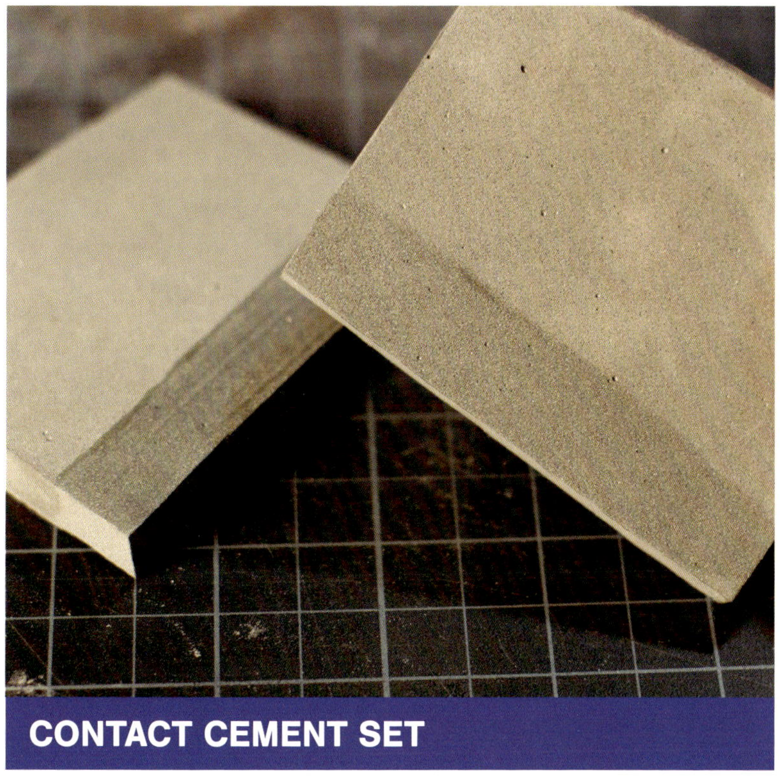

CONTACT CEMENT SET

Then you wait for it to set up. This usually takes only five to ten minutes. Once the adhesive loses its shine, you can touch the two surfaces together and they will bond immediately. This is really amazing since you don't have to hold two pieces together while the glue dries, as you would with a normal adhesive. This is especially useful when lining up seams between two pieces of foam.

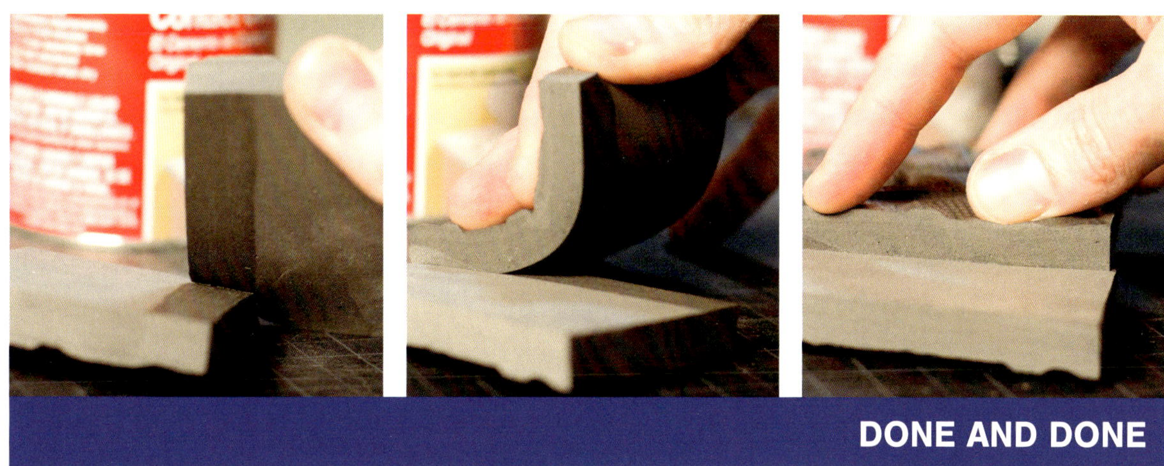

DONE AND DONE

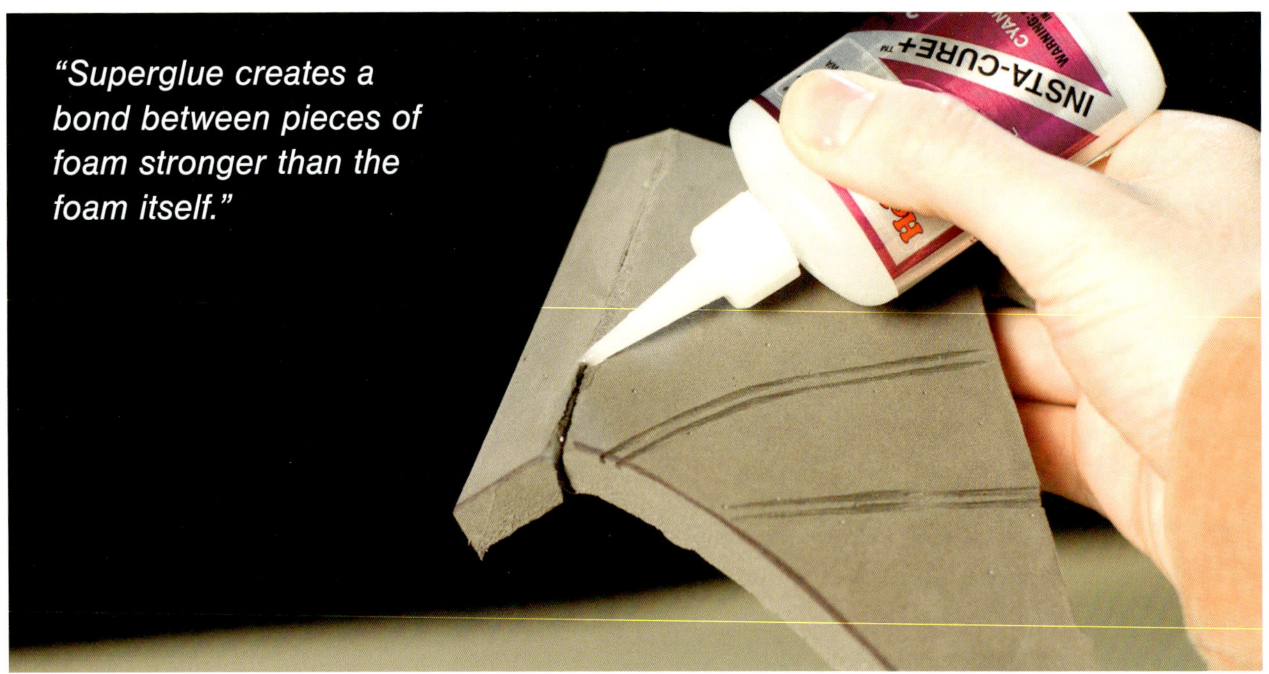

Contact cement is a real wonder tool, but it isn't the only adhesive that I use on my foam creations. For sticking on tiny detail pieces, I like good old cyanoacrylate. That's right, superglue! Available at hobby stores across the planet, superglue creates a bond between pieces of foam stronger than the foam itself. Most brands of CA glue come with a spray accelerant that will cure the glue instantly. This can be extremely useful.

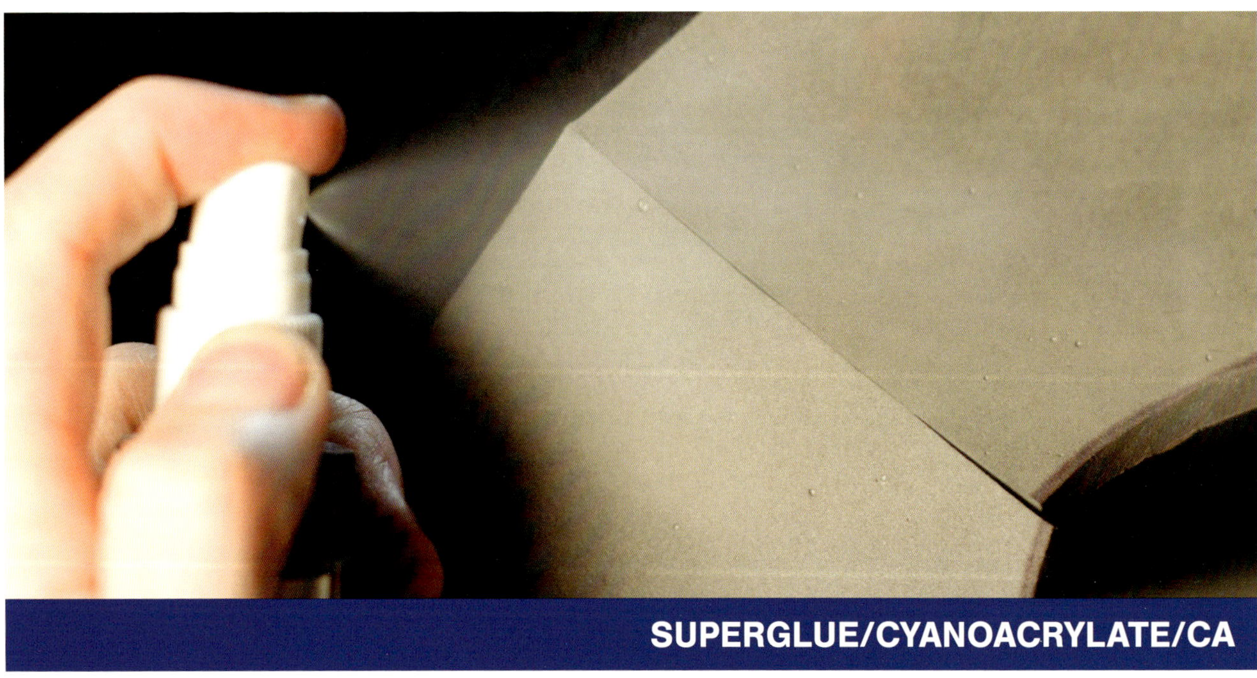

SUPERGLUE/CYANOACRYLATE/CA

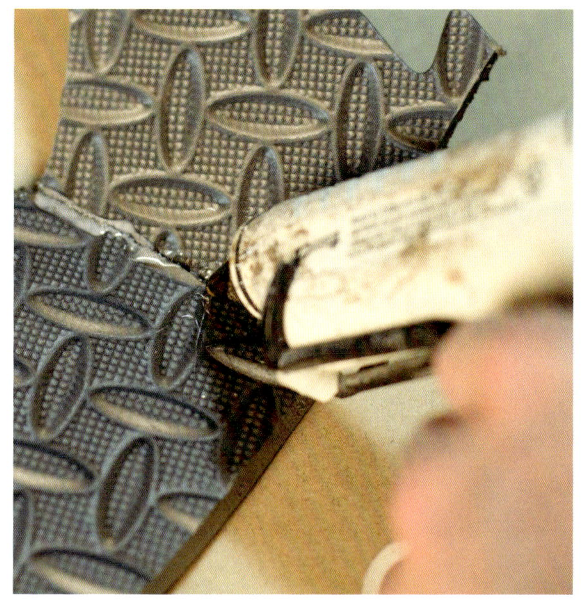

Another honorable mention is hot glue. I mostly use this for attaching straps to my armor pieces (which will be covered in Part 3). If a high stress point on your armor needs a little bit more structure behind the scenes, a bead of hot glue can literally make or break your creation. It can also be used to create faux weld lines on your armor that will look super legit when painted!

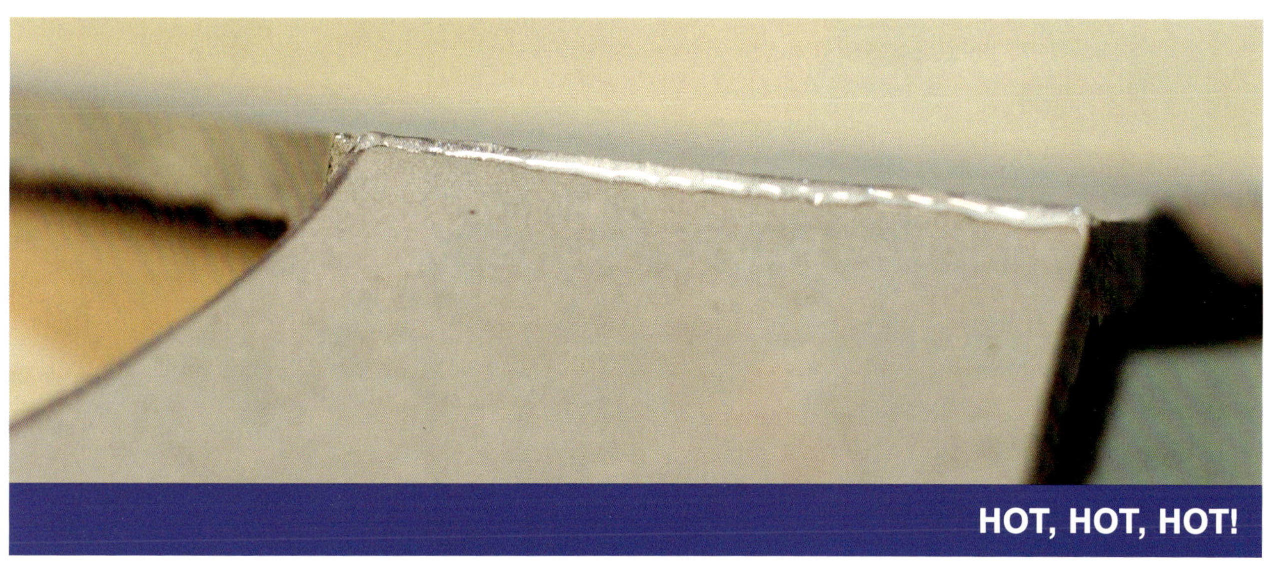

HOT, HOT, HOT!

Bill's Super Rad List of Foamsmithing Tools

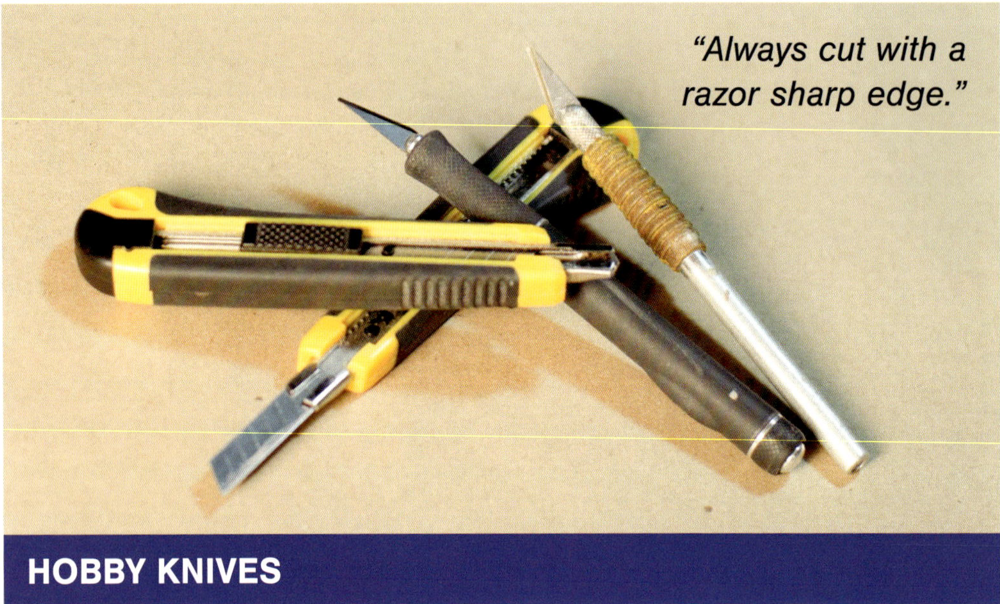

HOBBY KNIVES

One of the main reasons I like EVA foam so much is that the tools are crazy cheap to pick up. While some power tools do speed up the process, they are in no way necessary to build amazing armor.

Hobby knives come in all shapes and sizes. The most important feature is that you get really good at using whichever one you prefer. I really like the super cheap ones that click out a long blade with break marks along the length. Always cut with a razor sharp edge. Foam dulls a knife with surprising economy, so keep a sharpener handy and a bunch of replacement blades.

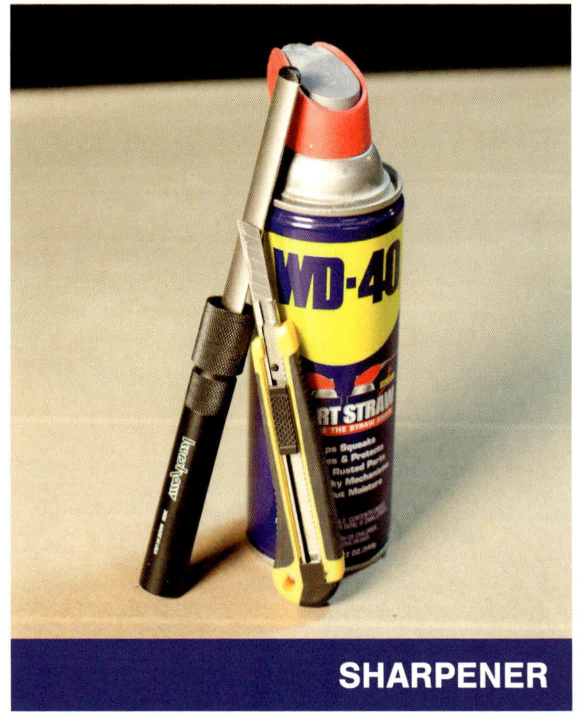

SHARPENER

When your knives dull, a good sharpener will extend their life tenfold. Mine is made by Kershaw and cost a cool $30; well worth the ticket price. You'll also want to pick up something to lubricate the blade. Some good old fashioned WD-40 will suit you just fine.

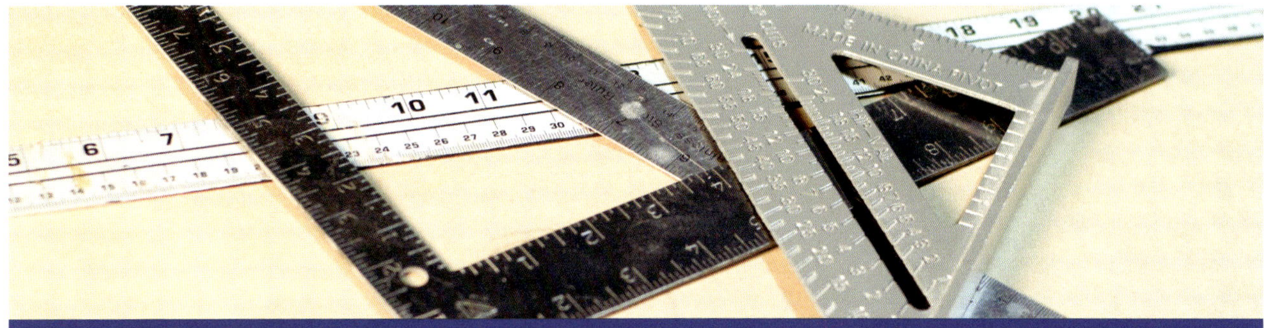

METAL RULERS

Used for measuring, drawing, and cutting, a good metal ruler will treat you properly for a lifetime. You can even pick them up in various lengths and shapes. An engineer's square won't hurt either.

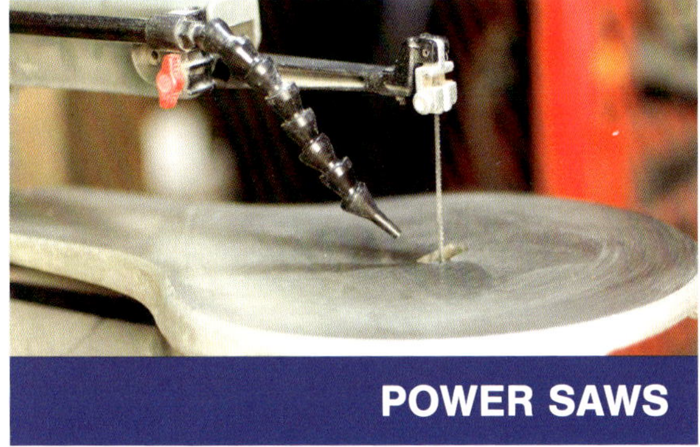

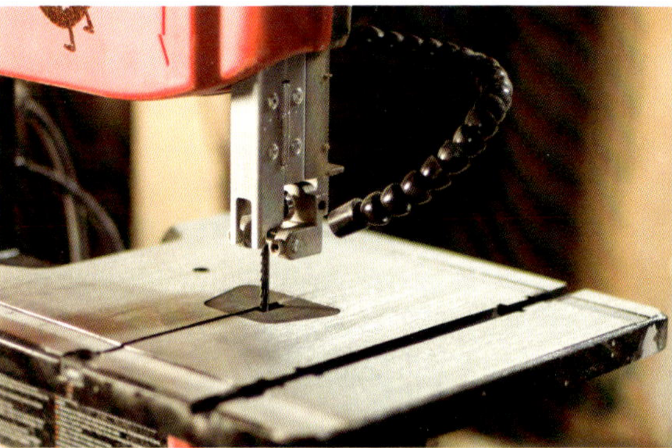

POWER SAWS

While not necessary in the slightest, having a band saw, scroll saw, or both in your shop is extremely handy. Making cuts at a perfect, consistent angle has proven useful to me time andtime again.

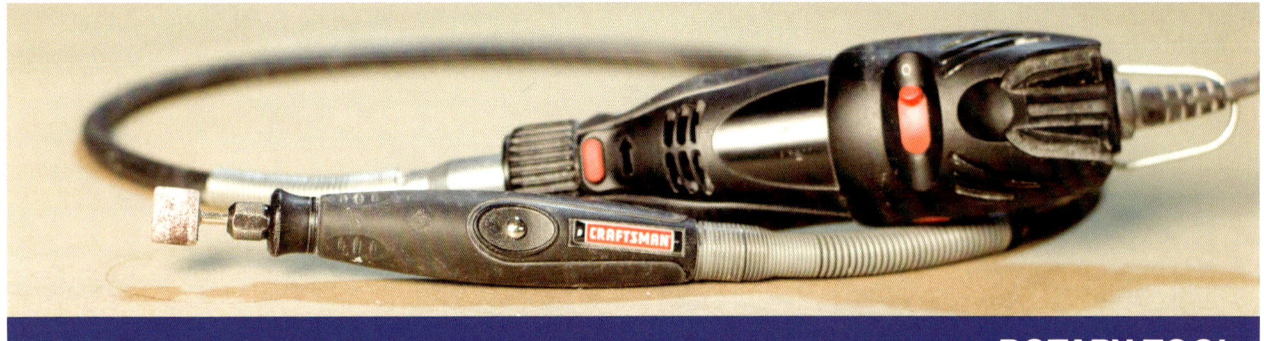

ROTARY TOOL

Your Dremel tool (or in my case, Craftsman rotary tool) will be the workhorse of your foam fabrication adventure. It would be very hard to get by without one. You can use it to sand and clean up cut edges, cut detail grooves, and create perfect circular embellishments. I highly recommend getting the extended flexible shaft attachment. It's one of my favorite things.

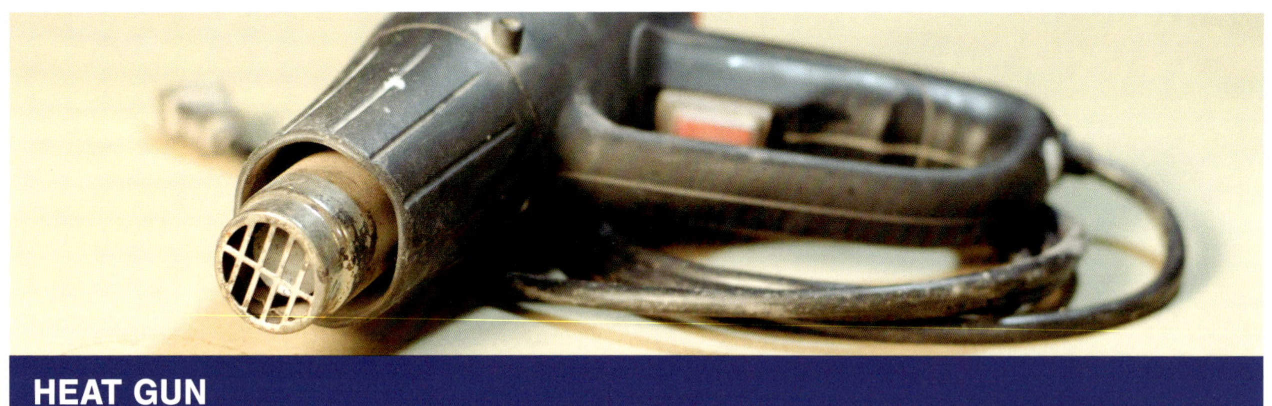

HEAT GUN

I've had my $12 heat gun from Harbor Freight for about 5 years now and it refuses to die. Just about any heat gun will make forming your foam armor pieces much easier.

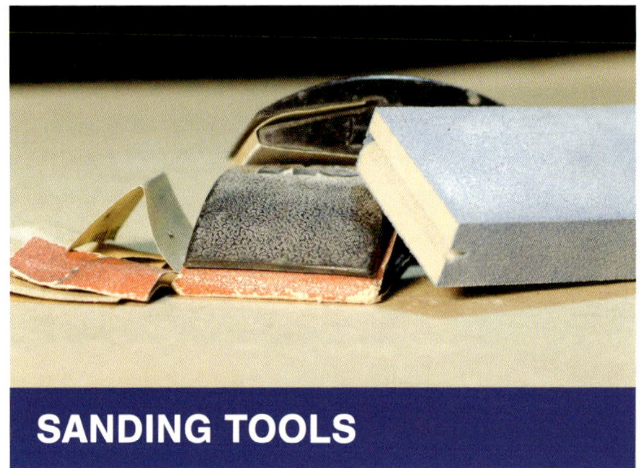

SANDING TOOLS

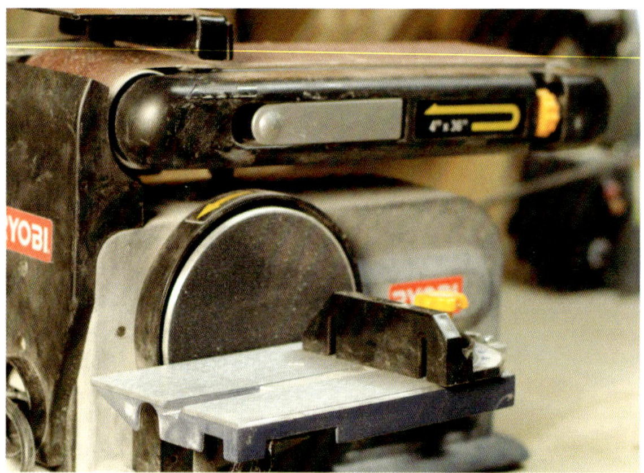

You may need to clean up some of your cut edges. This can be done with a hand sander, but a bench top belt or disc sander is really the way to go. You can use the rounded part of the belt sander to do some cleaning and a little bit of shaping, or use a cheap drum sanding bit clamped into a drill press.

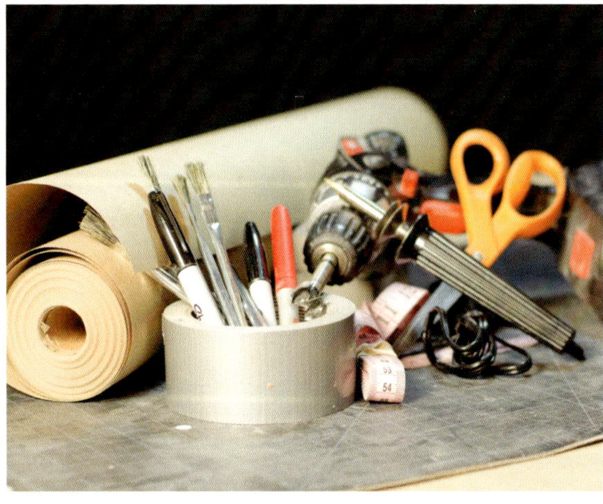

Other useful foam tools:

- Permanent Markers
- Throw Away Brushes
- Duct Tape
- Cutting Mat
- Scissors
- Craft Masking Paper
- Tape Measure Ribbon
- Hot Knife
- Power Drill
- Hot Glue Gun

I'VE GOT ALL THIS STUFF, NOW WHAT?

It's nearly time to start building, but don't start carving hunks of foam just yet! Most of the really difficult thinking is done before knife meets material. You need to plan out your entire build first. If you're building a set of armor from your favorite video game, that means scouring Google Image Search for as many high resolution images, from as many angles as possible.

If you're building your own design completely from scratch, this means drawing lots of concept sketches. As you do this, try and build up your forms with the seams in mind. Try to figure out how you'll be turning flat materials into the three dimensional forms in your drawings.

Bear in mind that foam can be painted to look like any type of armor you desire. Whether you want crazy organic looking, magical fantasy armor, weathered and rusted plate maile, space-faring future armor, a gigantic humanoid robot, or even contemporary military ballistics protection, you can do it in foam. Let your imagination run wild as you design your duds.

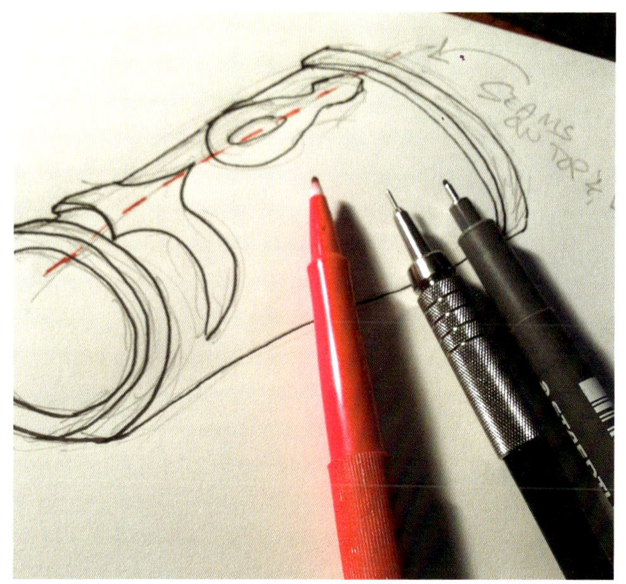

"Google Image Search for as many high resolution images, from as many angles as possible."

WHAT SORT OF DESIGN CONSIDERATIONS SHOULD I MAKE?

Here are some things you'll want to keep in mind when designing your armor construction. Many of these considerations are ignored in the source material, especially from video games, so you're going to have to do some clever design-fu to solve these problems.

WHERE DOES MY STUFF GO?

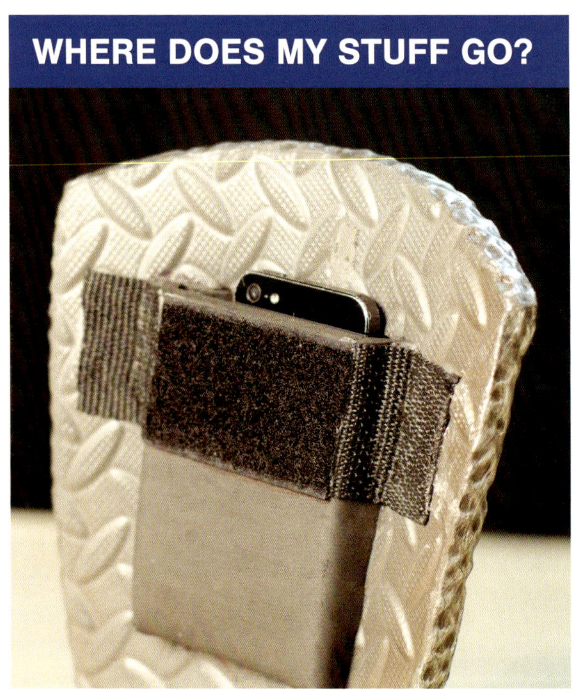

Sometimes video game designers tend to think their characters never need to carry a wallet or cell phone and thus omit pockets or pouches from many of their costume designs.

Where on your armor can you add a small pocket to slide a cell phone? How about behind a piece of hip or forearm armor?

Is there any place where the addition of a pocket or pouch won't ruin the aesthetic of the original artwork?

Is there a piece of armor that you could turn into a backpack? A jetpack perhaps? Heck, you could fit a whole lot of beverages into a jetpack!

CAN I BEND MY JOINTS?

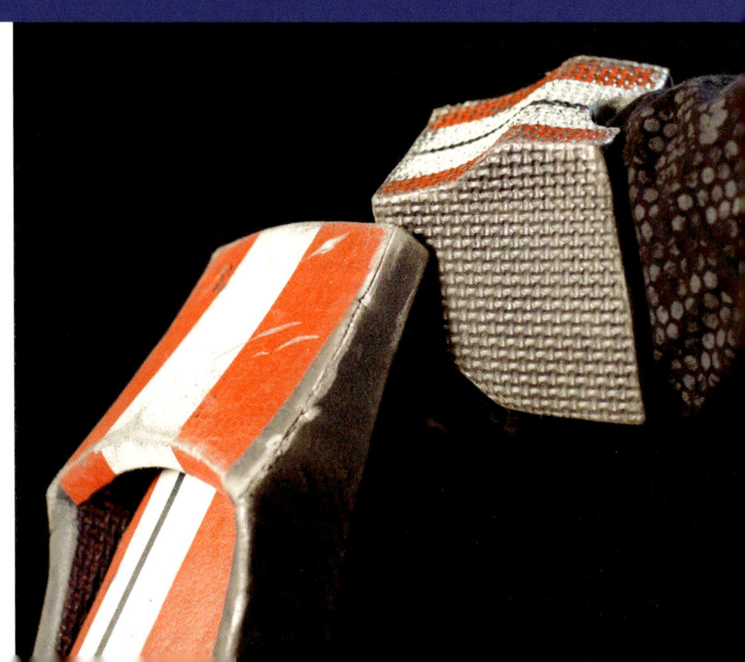

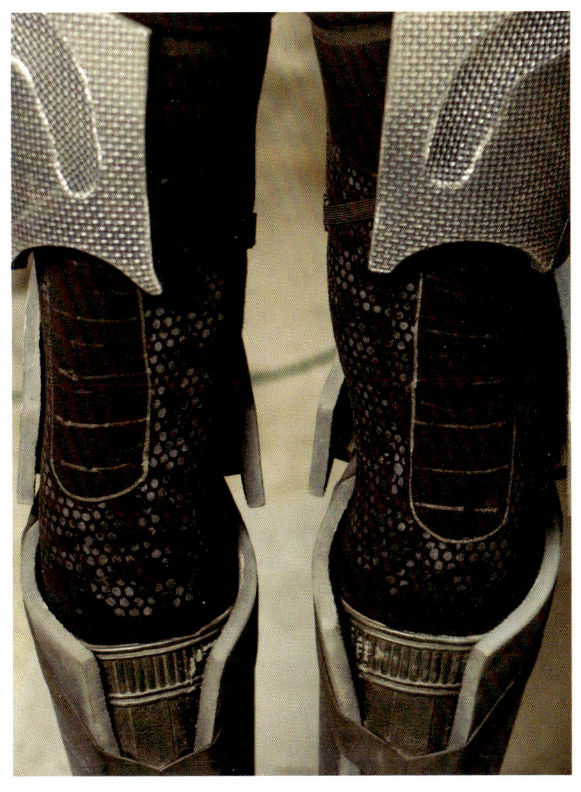

Video game characters don't really need to worry about whether or not their forearm armor will intersect with their biceps armor. Nor do they need to worry about their outlandish pauldrons accidentally putting out their own eye. Us non-magical humans, on the other hand, do need to worry about these annoyances.

Can the elbow joints be altered to give a more freeing range of motion without totally ruining the look of the original design? Could you maybe attach the bicep piece to the forearm piece with doll joints (explained later in the book)?

Are there any places that might make the EVA foam flex too much? Foam does have some give, but excessive flexing can cause any paint you've put down to chip off.

Would the knee pit look good enough if you simply painted the complicated knee mechanics on a cloth undersuit between the thigh and calf pieces?

Do you *really* need to bend your arms?

We really have no idea how Commander Shepard gets out of his space armor. Sometimes armor pieces from video games have no seams, buckles, or gaps where you would assume the character could escape their armor tombs.

Where can you add seams that would allow a piece to come apart? Can the torso come apart completely so that you can fit it into your luggage? Are you going to need someone's help during dress-up? Will your head fit through the neck hole?

How do you feel about just gluing this armor right around your body and wearing it forever?

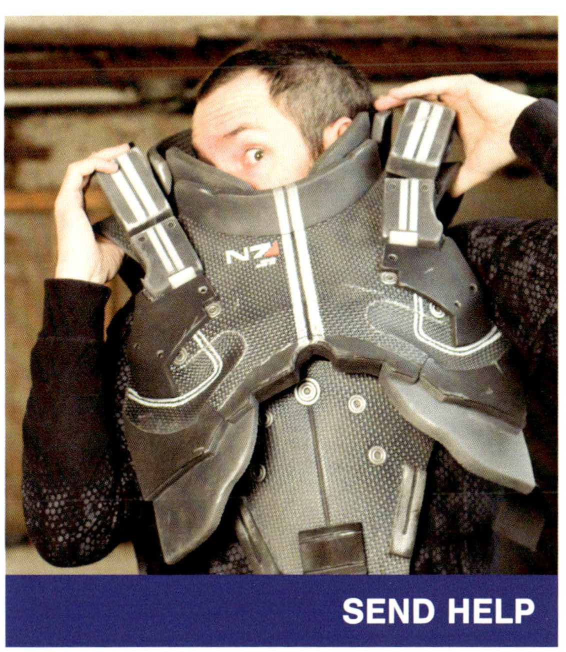

SEND HELP

You might think "Oh it's OK, I'll just stand all day.", but believe me, by midday at a convention, you'll want the option to sit down. Many fictional armor designs do a fantastic job of protecting the protagonist's posterior, but give little consideration as to what the hero might do when sitting time approaches.

How can you alter the design so that it still looks good, but allows for ninety degrees of hip motion and won't get crushed when you lean back in a chair?

How do the lower back and abdomen pieces move when you hunch or lean? Can they be designed in a way that lets them slide into the upper torso?

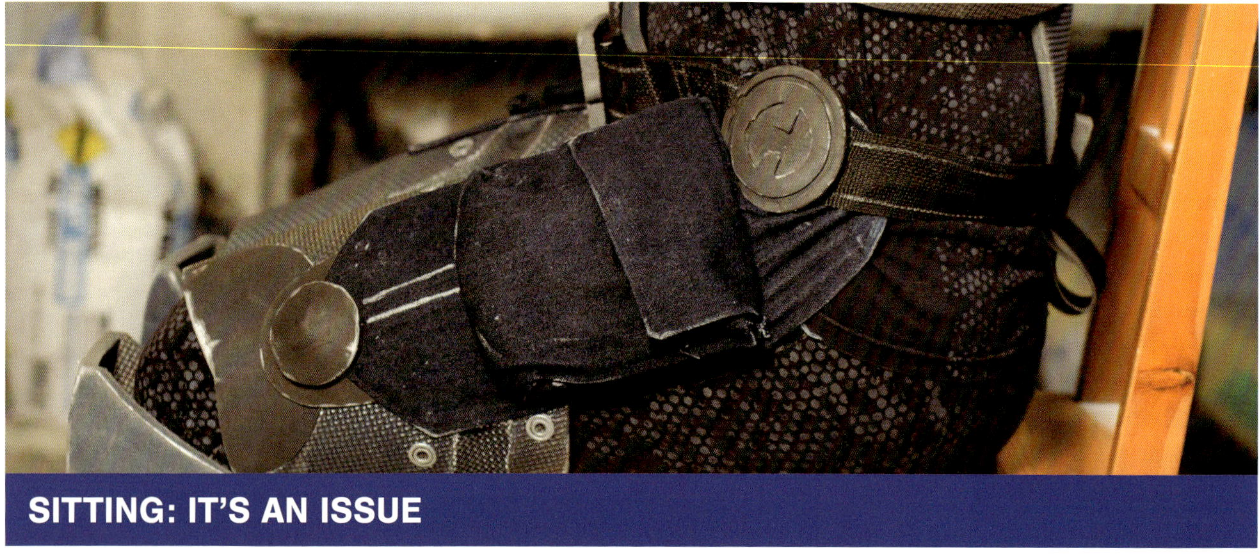

SITTING: IT'S AN ISSUE

Are we led to believe that Commander Shepard never used the bathroom while out on a mission? I mean, there's a restroom on the Normandy, for sure, but when he's planetside, gunning down Geth soldiers in his space armor, how did he take a leak?

Is keeping the perfect visual aesthetic matched to the original artwork really worth peeing yourself in the atrium of the Marriott? You may need to alter the design a bit to accommodate your… functions.

What is the simplest way to get parts off in a timely fashion? Will you need someone else's help getting out of this thing? How well do you REALLY know your friends? How long can you hold it?

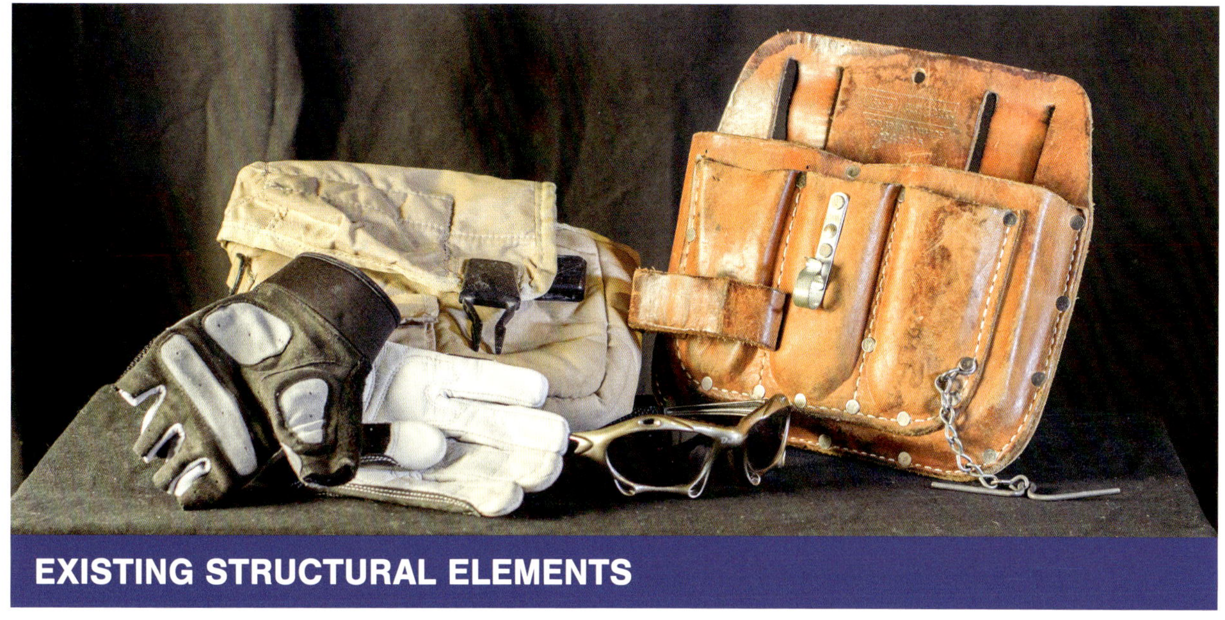

EXISTING STRUCTURAL ELEMENTS

More often than you might think, some kind of garment or sporting equipment already exists that can serve as a sturdy, comfortable, structural piece to build your armor on top of. This will save you a lot of time and frustration.

How can you turn those old sneakers or boots into a sweet pair of foam greaves? Can you replace the laces with elastic so that they can be slipped on and off easily?

How will you attach that whacky shoulder armor to your torso? Are there some football shoulder pads that already exist? I mean, heck, athletic shoulder pads are basically shoulder armor anyway!

What if you picked up an existing motorcycle helmet and glued foam to the outside of it? It would fit perfectly and comfortably and you could make it look however you like with your sweet foam fabrication skills! The same goes for paintball masks.

HOW BIG SHOULD ALL OF THE PIECES BE?

Once you have a good idea of what you'll be building, you need to figure out the size of all the pieces. Scaling can be one of the most frustrating part of the design process. Most of the time, the super hero scaled armor that you're trying to emulate from a video game will be dramatically disproportionate to your own body type. I know this is true for me. I'd like to think I'm built like the Dragonborn, but I know it just ain't in the cards.

Scaling armor references to your own body can be tricky, but it isn't impossible. If you're a Photoshop wizard, this becomes much easier. A free alternative to Photoshop can be found at Pixlr.com. Get a friend to take a photo of you in a similar pose to one of your armor reference images. It's also super helpful to get a large ruler or tape measure in your photo.

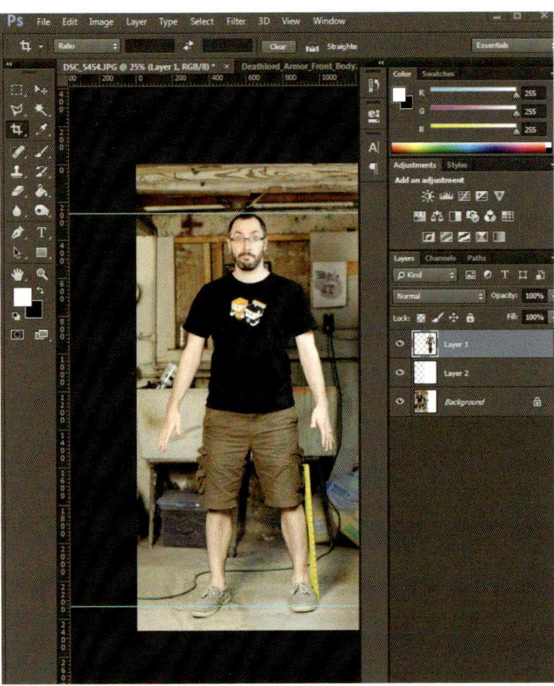

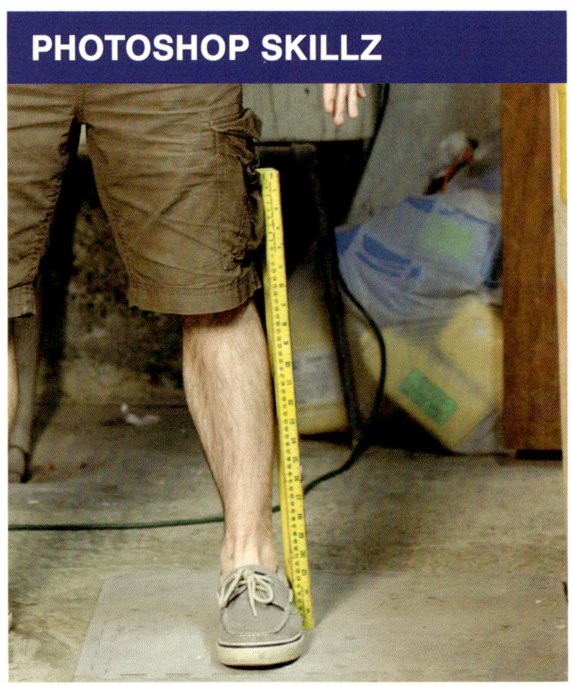

PHOTOSHOP SKILLZ

Then, in your photo editing software of choice, line up your reference image next to the photo of your body and scale them so that they are pretty close to the same size. Now you can take a look at the ruler in the photo and compare that to the armor in the reference to start getting an idea about what size each piece will be.

This will get you a ballpark figure to start from. It is by no means your final dimensions. You will still do plenty of scaling and alterations once you start putting together your armor bits.

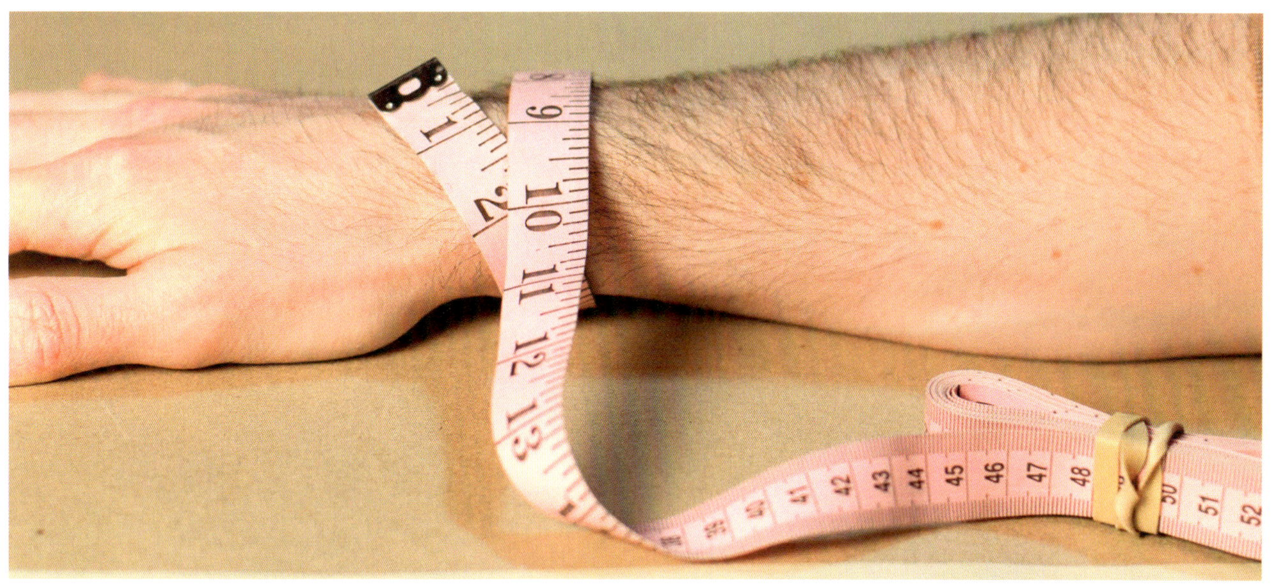

Other dimensions, like the circumference of your limbs, can be measured using a tape measure ribbon. Just bear in mind that the armor will rest outside of your body and you're measuring what will be the inside face of the armor. This is where a home made foam ruler can be really handy! That way your measurements will take the thickness into account. The outside surface of the armor will have to be larger to get the appropriate size and shape. Again, trial and error are your friends here.

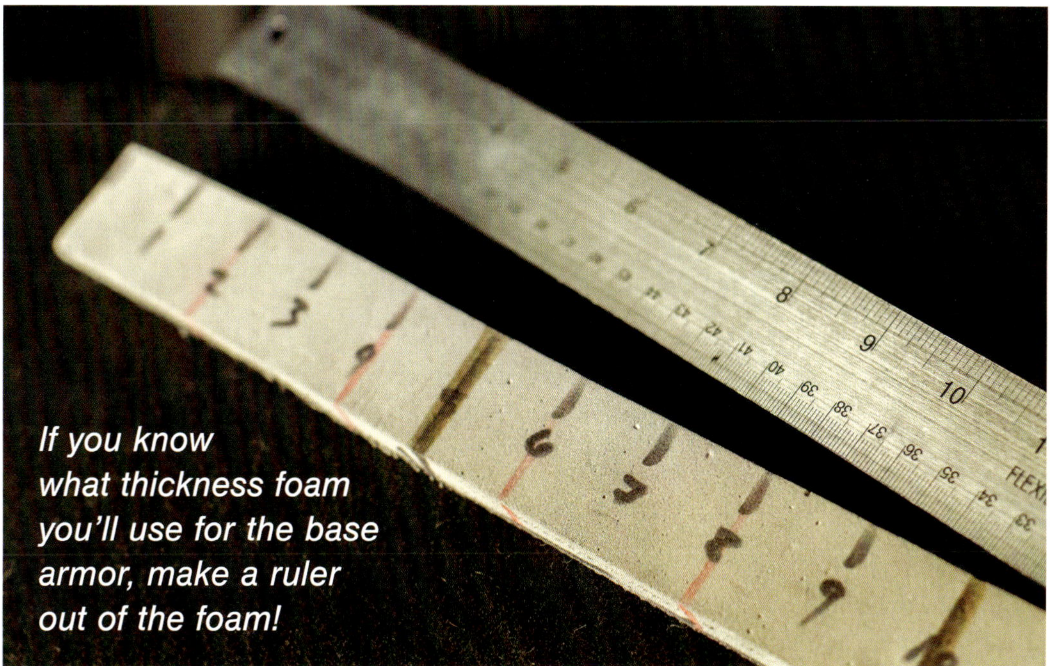

If you know what thickness foam you'll use for the base armor, make a ruler out of the foam!

ALL OF THESE FLOOR MATS ARE FLAT... AND MY ARMOR IS NOT

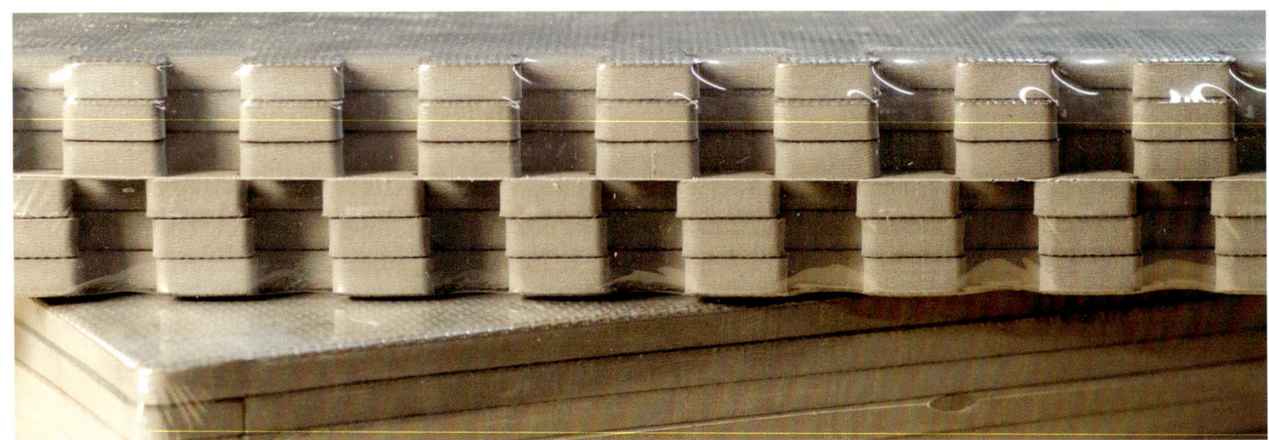

Translating your 3D designs to a 2D medium that's meant to be transformed back into a 3D form can be tricky and frustrating. You will need to draw up your own templates. Then, once you try and build those pieces, you'll probably have to re-draw some new templates. This is the sort of thing that's hard to get on the first try.

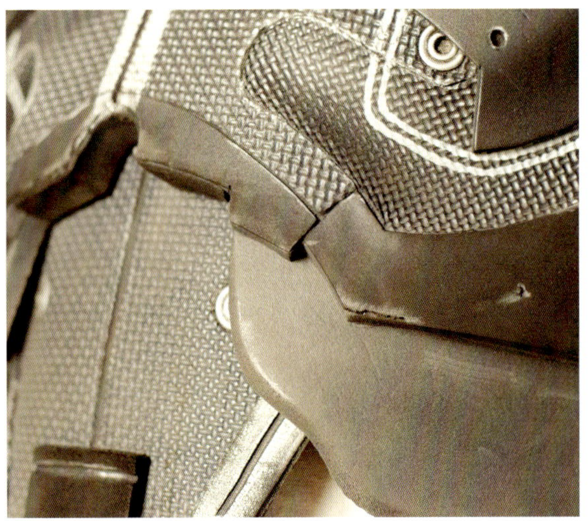

Consider the textured side of the EVA foam floor mats. You may end up using just the smooth side, but many futuristic looking armor pieces have textures that may look appropriate if you use the built in texture on your foam. Keeping that in mind, when you lay out your templates on the stock foam pieces, think about the direction the texture is facing and what it will look like when glued to other pieces. Lining up textures at seams is no small task, so be patient. This may mean that you will have to waste some foam by not tightly packing the templates onto a single sheet, but foam is cheap and you gotta look good!

Here are the default humanoid body parts and some extremely basic template shapes. I'm not going to give you scaling or dimension info. Chances are the armor you're building will be way different than anything I'm thinking of. These template shapes will give you an idea of the type of form you'll get when it's put together. You can start from there and alter them to your own scale and design to come up with a platform to construct your fancy looking armor details.

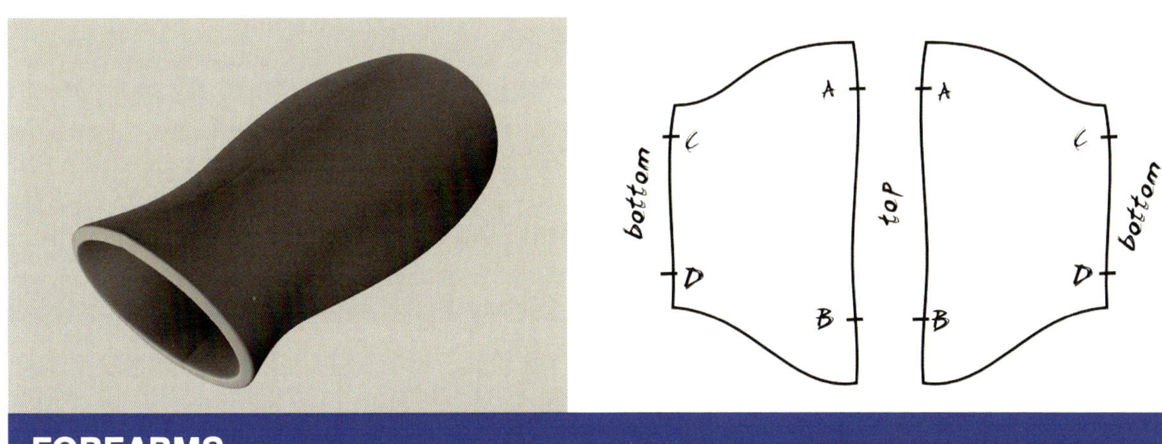

FOREARMS

I would start out by experimenting on a forearm piece. They're basically just tapered cylinders and shouldn't waste too much foam if you totally mess them up. You'll want to measure the circumference of your hand at the widest part for the diameter of the wrist end. Your whole hand has to make its way through the wrist when you're putting this on. Unless, of course, the forearm armor doesn't fully engulf your arm and simply buckles on.

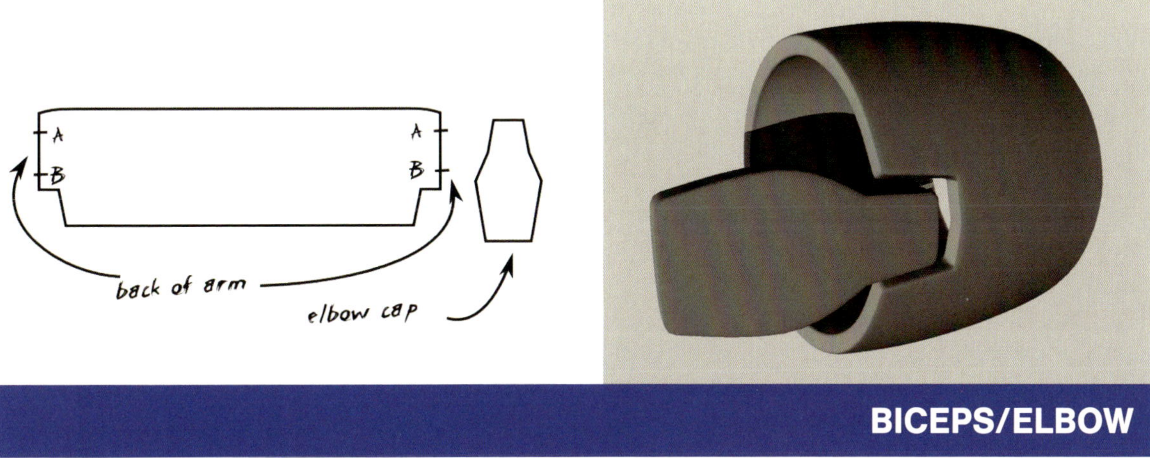

BICEPS/ELBOW

Frequently, biceps armor is just a cylinder, which would make your template a long rectangle. Even if the biceps armor is more elaborate, it's useful to build a cylinder form and then attach more decorative elements to it.

Elbow armor pieces tend to be single, small pieces. I've found that either attaching them to the forearm or biceps armor pieces with a flexible piece of foam or elastic is the best way to retain mobility in your arm.

Attaching your forearm armor to your biceps armor with a functional hinge can be done, but it's very tricky. Make sure you use very strong hinges and allow room for your wrist to rotate at the hand end of your forearm armor. I usually just skip the functional hinge and have armor pieces overlap, creating the illusion that they are connected, when they are not.

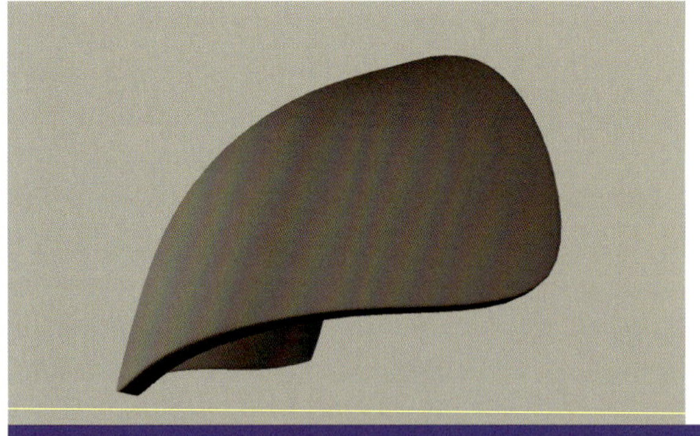

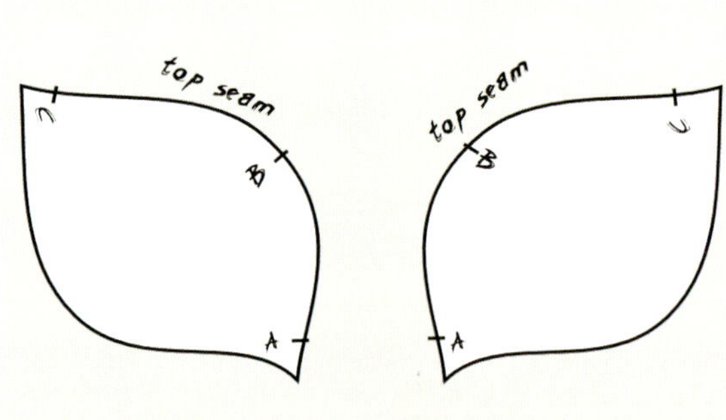

SHOULDERS

The basic form of shoulder armor pieces is very similar to a bowl. In fact, you could even heat form a piece of foam inside a bowl to achieve a very similar shape! If you'd like to build something similar from a template, follow my basic template. Again this form is very simple, but can be used as a structural base for a more elaborate design.

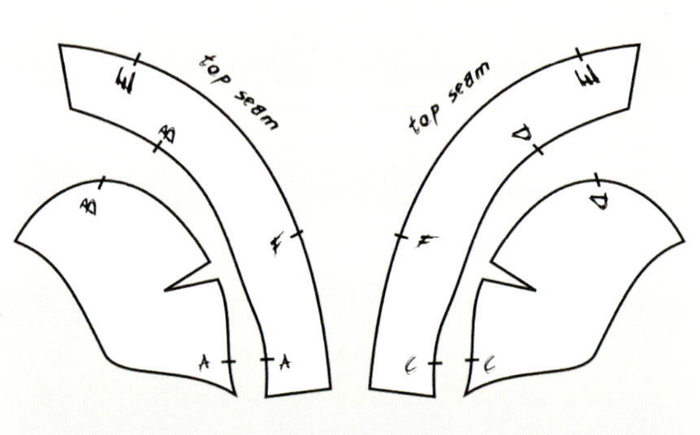

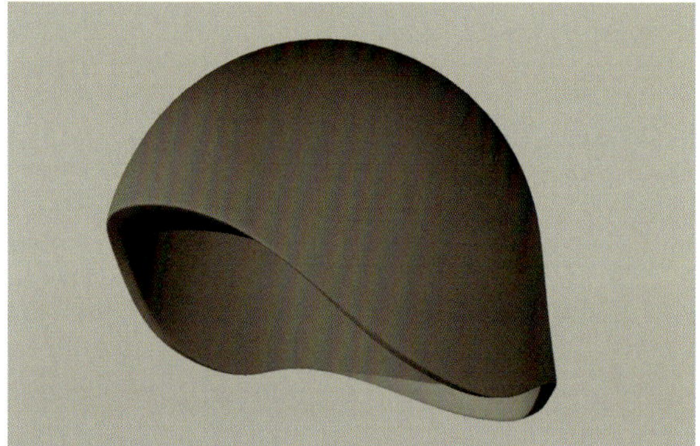

HELMET

Everybody loves a good brain bucket! If you only end up making one piece of armor, make a helmet. They're super fun to wear at parties. That is, if you go to the kind of parties I go to (the best kind).

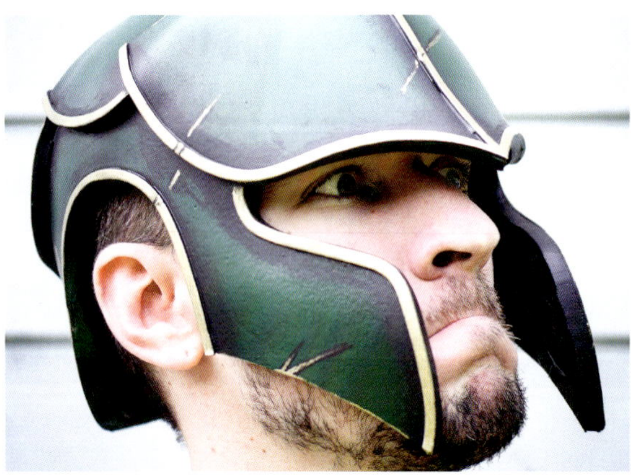

Like I said earlier, building a helmet on top of an existing, pre-made helmet may be your easiest option. However, if your design is extremely custom, that may not be an option, so you'll have to build it from the ground up. If you have a life cast of your own noggin, templating these pieces is much easier, otherwise you'll have to do a whole bunch of sizing trials to get it to fit nicely, starting with my basic shapes.

Again, these shapes will provide you with a base structure that you can add on to or take away from. You might need to remove material around the ears or change up the rim around the face a whole bunch. Once you have the base form down, adding a visor or mouth covering piece is a fairly straightforward bit of engineering.

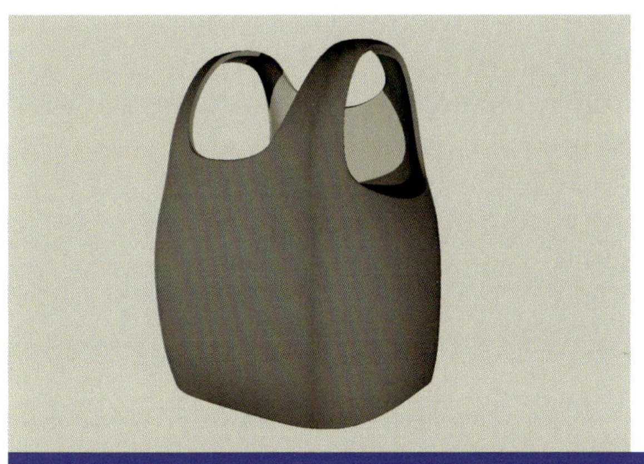

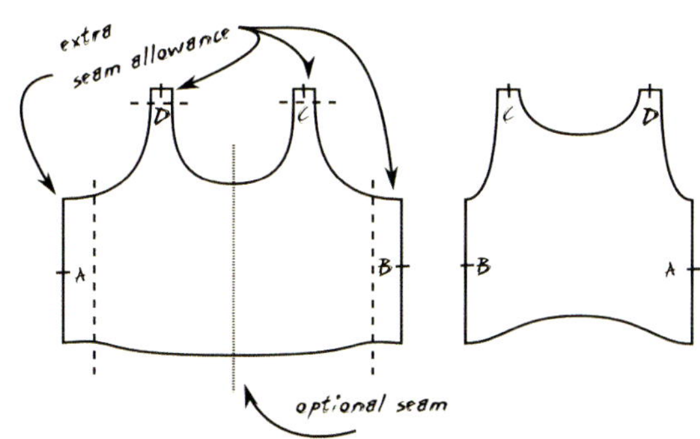

TORSO

Ahhhh the torso. The human body's Pandora's box. Not one of us is shaped quite the same and it's no more apparent than in the torso. My basic template will really only get you halfway there. If you'd like to bend over or turn around without using your feet, you'll need to do some serious modifications.

If you can get a plaster bandage life cast or make a "duct tape dummy" of your torso, I highly recommend it. There are dozens of video tutorials on YouTube that will help you out. Plaster bandages are super cheap and so long as you have some handy, trustworthy friends, you can make a copy of your body in no time and have a solid base to design your templates.

Many designs favor separating the lower abdomen from the chest/upper back area. These pieces can be attached from the back using nylon webbing (explained in depth in Part 3), so bear that in mind when planning how these pieces will fit together.

Also consider the seams where the back of the torso meets the front along the tops of your shoulders and down the sides of your body under your armpits. When drawing the template, I like to keep a couple extra inches of material on those places. That way, you can form the shapes and trim those down to meet flush once the parts are assembled enough that you can try them on.

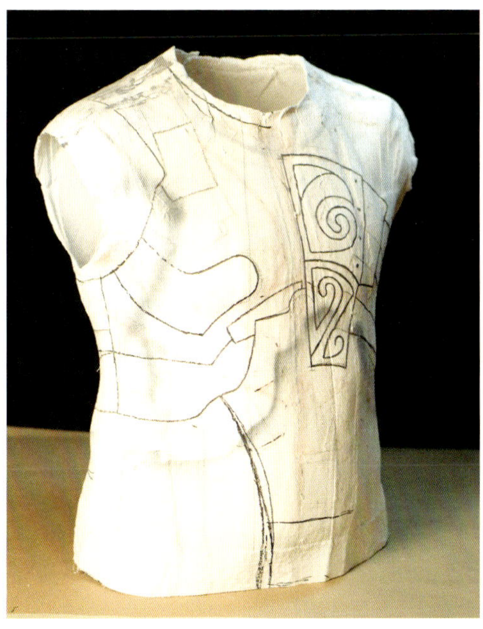

"Get a plaster bandage life cast or make a 'duct tape dummy' of your torso."

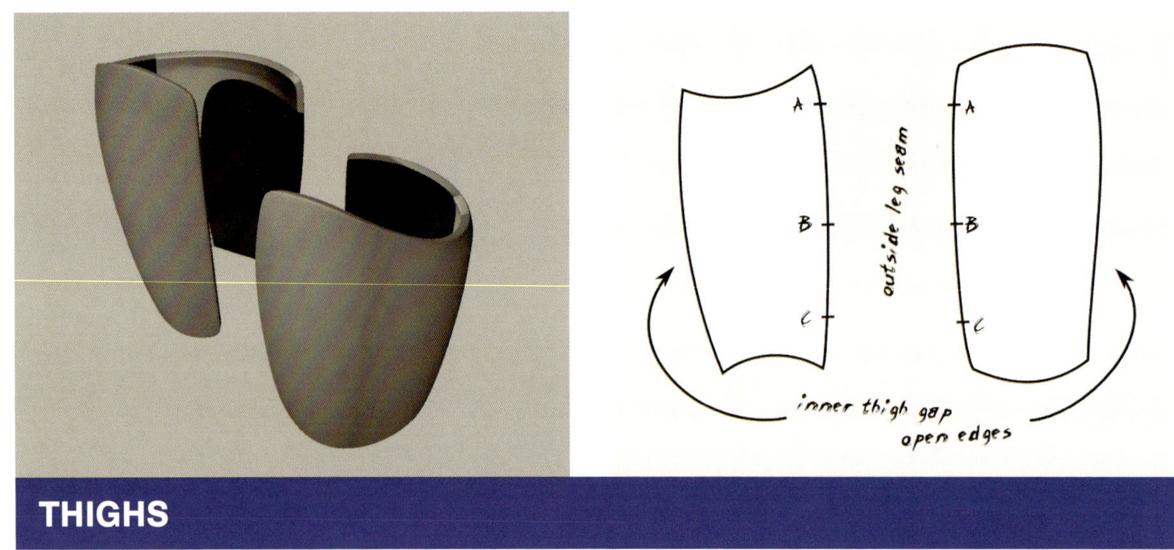

THIGHS

Thigh pieces are usually pretty basic tube-like forms, much like the forearms. Frequently in video game designs, the armor wraps around the entirety of the leg. I recommend altering the template so that the insides of your thighs are free from this obstruction. You'll be a much happier and more comfortable cosplayer.

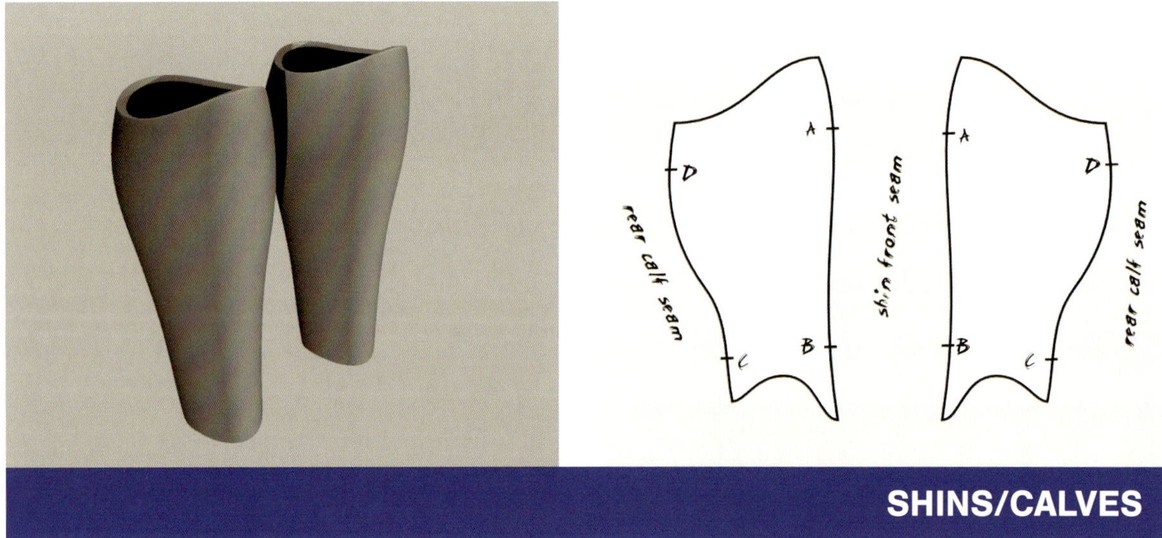

SHINS/CALVES

Whenever possible, I design my calf pieces to be attached directly to a tall boot. Cheap, rubber concrete boots from the hardware store are really fantastic for these. You can even trim the tall shin part down to suit your needs. Also, when possible, I like to attach the kneecaps directly to the shin area. A strap or elastic around the back of the knee will keep it tight to your leg as you walk and flex your leg.

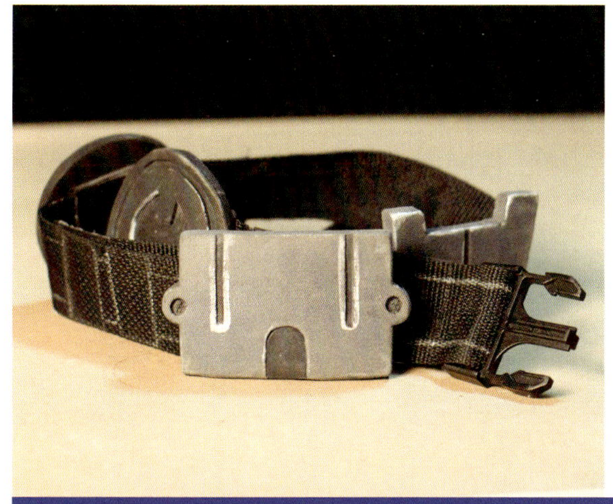

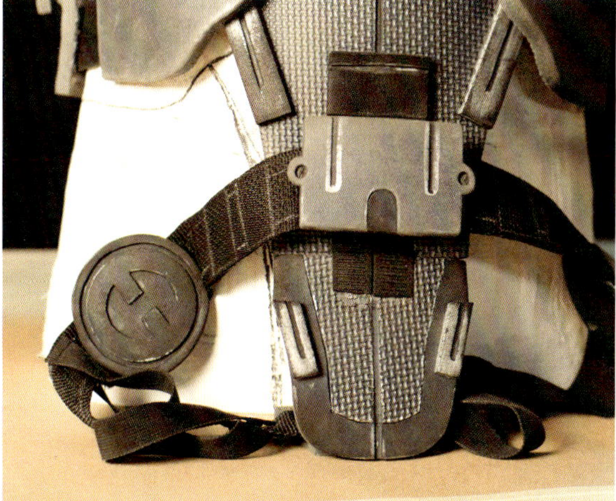

BELTS 'N' BITS

It's not all too necessary to work from a default template for the belt. For the most part, if your armor has an armored belt, you will likely be attaching smaller bits of foam to an existing belt or nylon strap or daisy chaining a bunch of segmented foam bits together. The same goes for a crotch. Codpieces come in all shapes and sizes, so play it by ear.

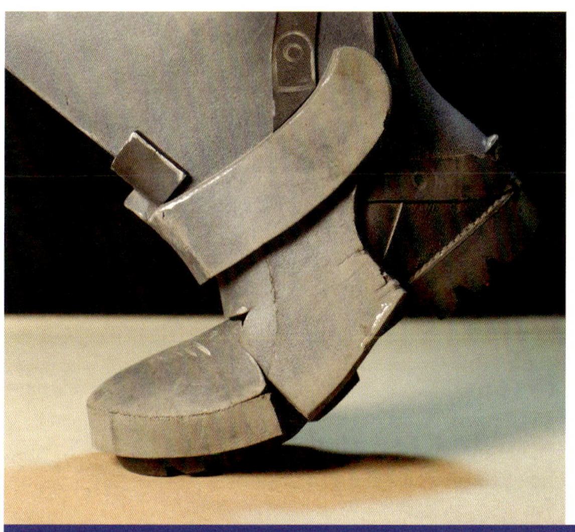

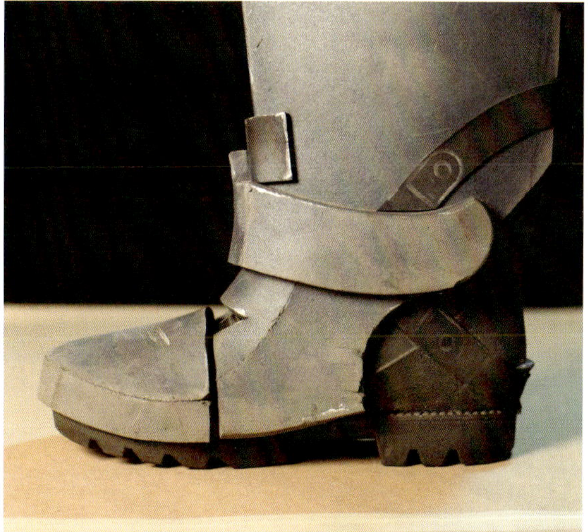

SHOES

Unless I'm building my shin and foot armor onto the same, large boot base, I prefer to keep my feet and shin parts apart from each other. The extra articulation achieved at your ankle will be much appreciated. Also, as mentioned before, building armor pieces directly onto a shoe or boot will make your life much easier. You can even design your armored shoe coverings to be removable, in case you don't want to ruin your nice shoes. Shoe covering designs will vary wildly, so working from a base template would be futile.

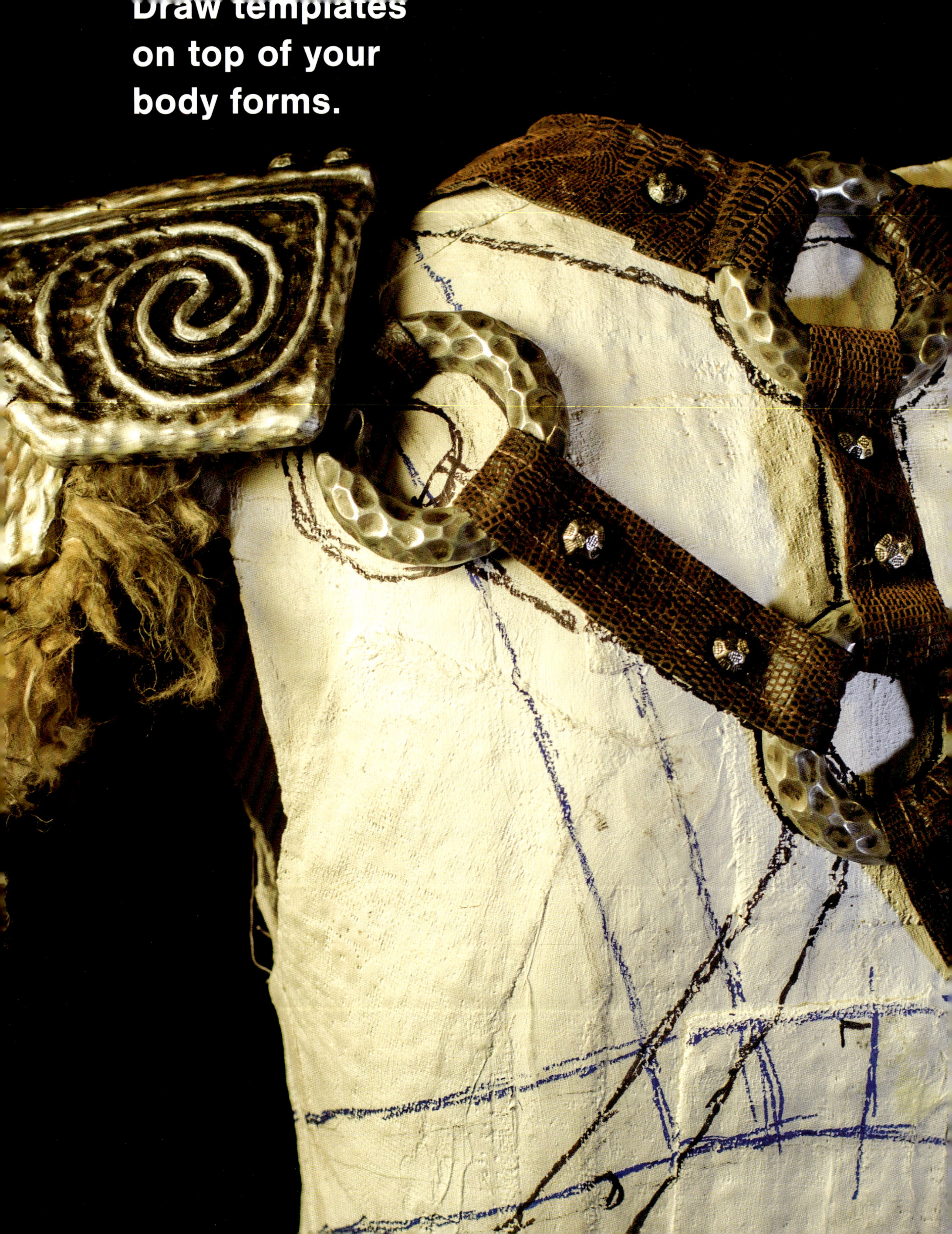

Draw templates on top of your body forms.

How might one cut out these pretty templates?

It's almost a statistical certainty that your first template will not be the right size or shape. That's OK. You're making a prototype here and sacrifices must be made. To mitigate your waste and loss of sanity, I highly recommend trying to make the first attempt much larger than you think it needs to be. That way, you can just carve away at it a little bit at a time until it's just right, rather than cutting out a whole new piece.

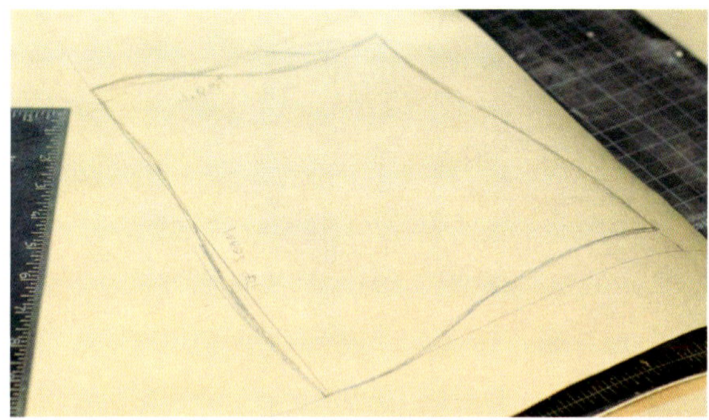

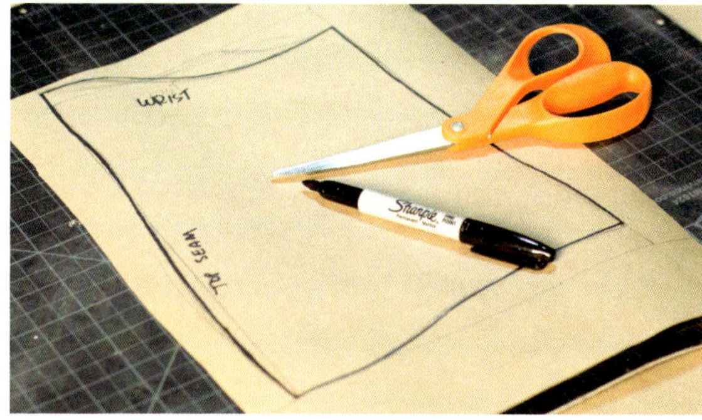

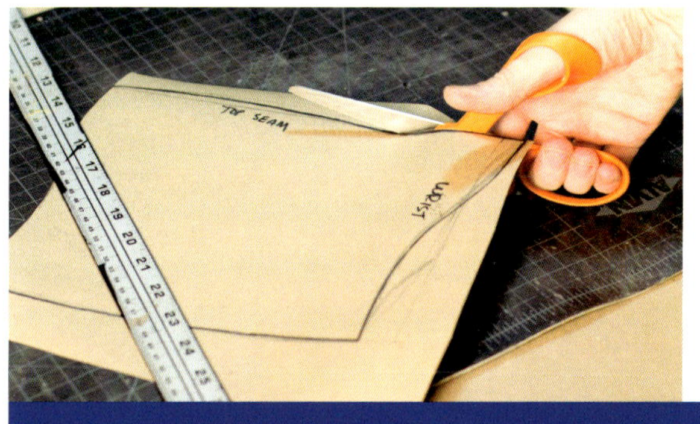

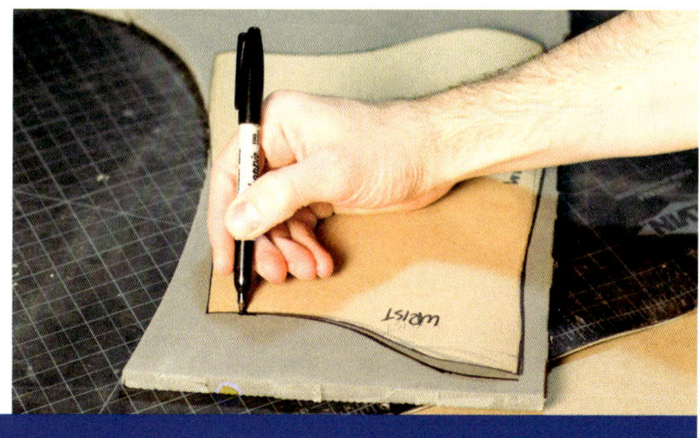

HALF OF FOREARM TRACED TWICE

"Put a date on your template pieces and keep them!"

This is where drawing out your templates onto a sturdy piece of masking paper or card stock becomes hugely beneficial. Draw out your patterns with a nice, bold Sharpie marker and cut it out using scissors or your hobby knife. Then trace out the pattern onto your foam sheets. If you've made any relevant notes on your template, transfer them to the foam too. Also, if any of your template pieces are meant to be used twice for each side of the piece, make sure you flip the template over to mirror the piece when drawing it onto the foam.

Even if you're planning on having the texture side facing out, it's much easier to see lines on the smooth side. Just be sure to flip your pattern piece over so that your part doesn't end up backwards.

Put a date on your template pieces and keep them! You will end up altering them a bunch and probably taking notes on them. Later on down the road you may find that you need to completely rebuild a part and having all of your templates stored and organized in a folder will do wonders for your blood pressure.

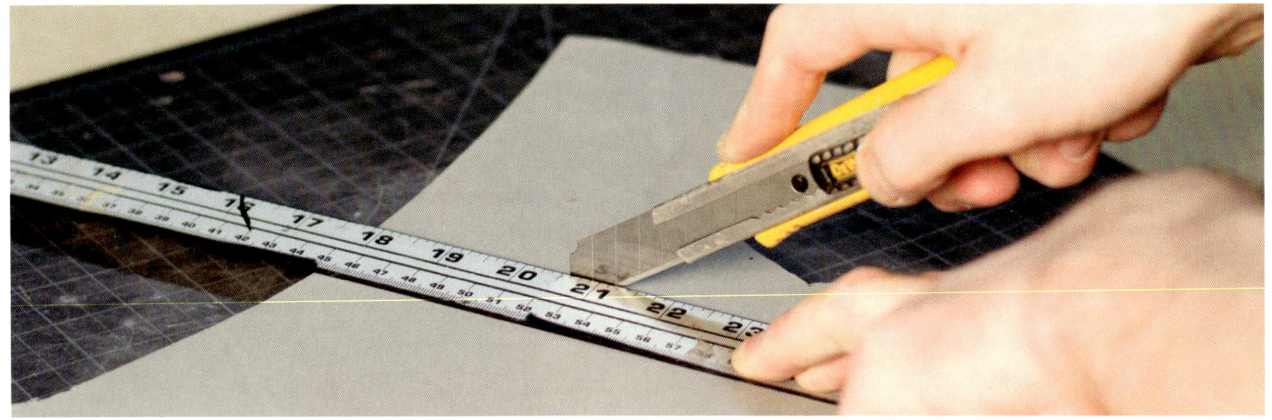

Now it's cutting time! Finally! I would recommend going through this whole process on a simple piece, like a forearm, to get the knack of it. Also, before making a series of cuts, test out your knife blade on a scrap of foam. If it doesn't make a perfect cut, give it a sharpen.

In fact, for all of your cuts, it doesn't hurt to do some practicing on some scrap pieces. Pretty soon you'll have more foam scraps than you know what to do with.

For straight lines, it couldn't be easier. Lay down your metal straightedge on the side of the line that you want to keep. This way, if the blade wanders, it will go into the scrap side and not the part that you want to keep. Then, using a smooth, consistent stroke, pull the blade through the foam along the straightedge. Keep the tip of the blade in contact with your cutting surface for the duration of the cut. Unless you're trying to angle the cut on purpose, make sure the blade stays perpendicular to the surface of the foam.

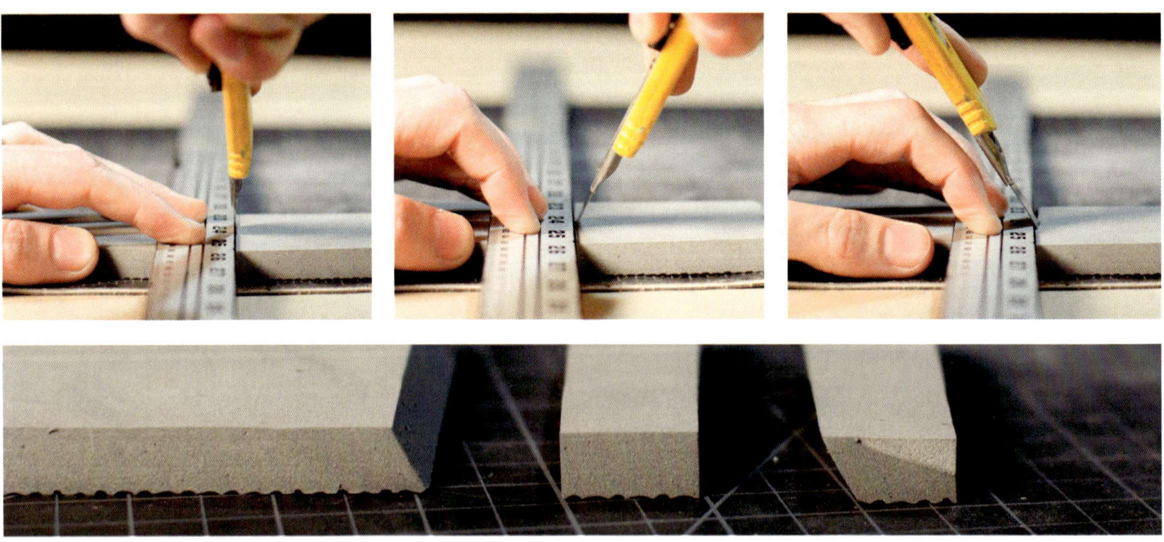

If you DO want to have an angled cut, simply hold the knife at your preferred angle next to the straight edge and pull it through the foam in a consistent stroke. This isn't easy at first, but keep practicing!

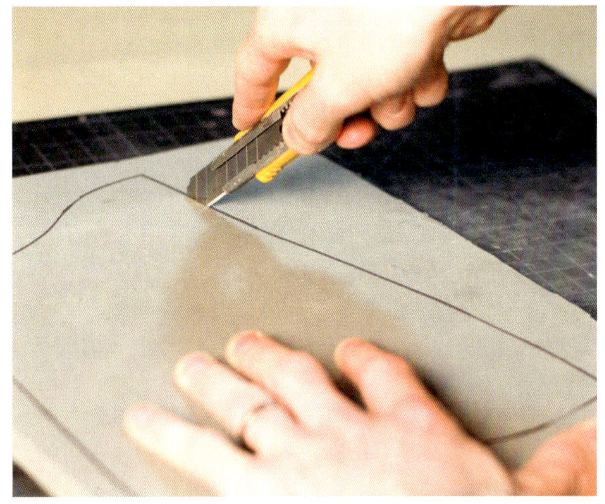

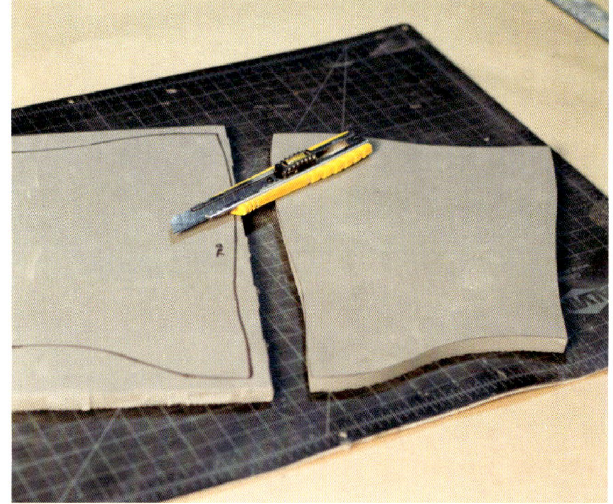

Curves can be quite a bit trickier, especially if they're super tight. You probably won't have a perfect metal edge guide that matches your curve, so you're going to have to cut it totally by hand. The most important factor here is blade sharpness. If your blade is dull, you'll get snags along the cut that will have to be cleaned up later with a sanding bit on your rotary tool. Save yourself lots of time and effort by keeping that blade sharp!

Make your curved cuts slowly and with a smooth, even stroke. Keeping the blade perpendicular to the surface can be quite a bit trickier here, so keep an eye on how you're holding the knife. You will very likely make a cut or two that has an angled edge you did not intend. Fear not, this happens to the best of us. This is where a practiced hand will really show its value.

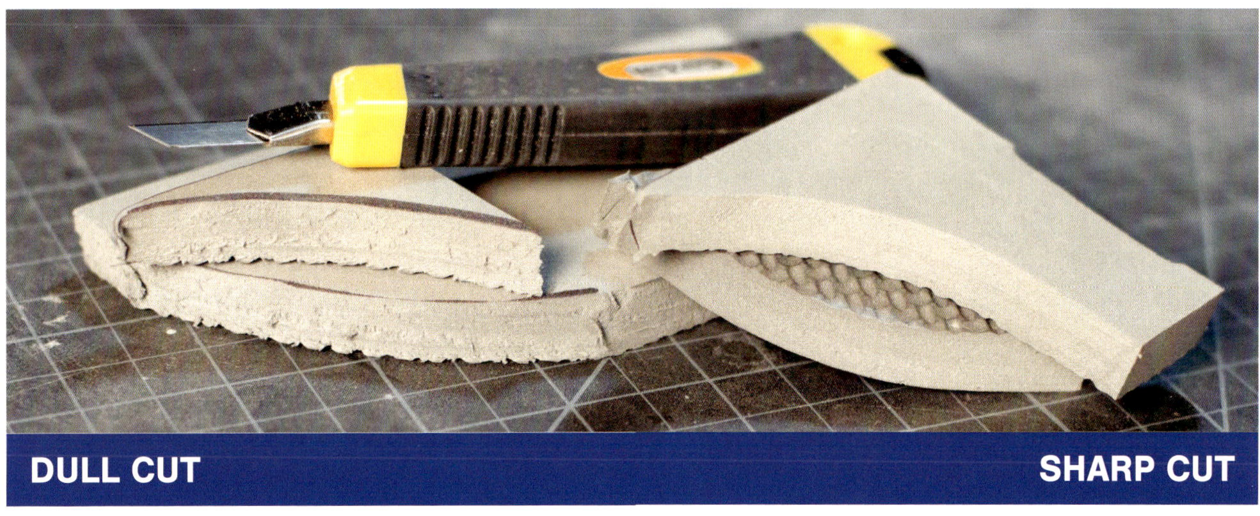

I cut out some foam! Yaaaaay! Now what?

With your very first foam armor piece cut out, it's time for a healthy dose of frustration. It's time to do some test forming and gluing. Start by heat forming your pieces to push them into a close approximation of their final form. Hit the foam with even heat from your heat gun to make it more malleable. Don't overdo the heat and don't leave the gun shooting in one spot too long. It's very easy to start melting your foam.

When the foam is good and hot, use your hands to bend, form, and stretch the piece. This will take a lot of practice. Fortunately the foam is very forgiving and can be reformed many times. Just be sure to wear protective gloves if the foam gets too hot to touch.

Wear a respirator and work in a ventilated area when heating foam!

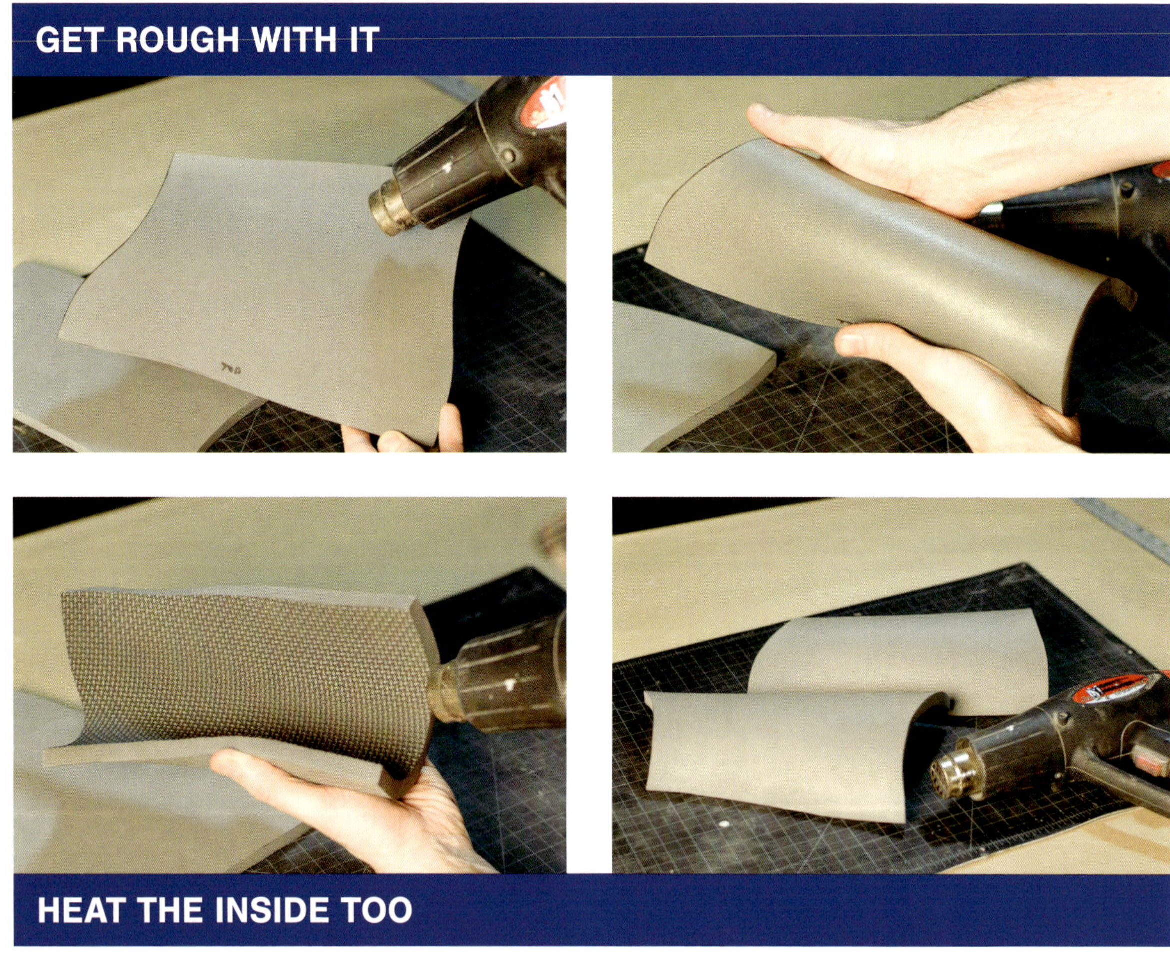

GET ROUGH WITH IT

HEAT THE INSIDE TOO

If you're using a cutting mat, don't let the heat gun warm it up too much. It will definitely warp the crap out of it.

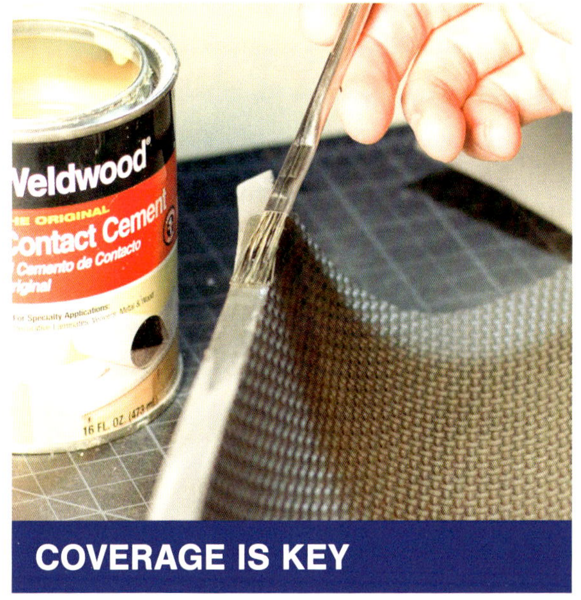

COVERAGE IS KEY

With your piece looking a little more like an actual armor bit, it's time to glue it to the next piece. Adhering seams together is best done with contact adhesive. Brush some of the cement onto each exposed edge in a nice, thin layer. Be sure to cover every bit of exposed edge. Any spots that you miss will create a small gap in the seam.

After 5 to 10 minutes, the adhesive should be ready to attach. Slowly touch two of the edges together at once side, taking care to line them up as closely as possible. As soon as the contact adhesive touches, it'll be bound for all eternity. No take-backsies. Working slowly, but firmly, press the two edges together until the whole seam is closed up. You may need to hold some areas together tightly for a few seconds to be sure the bond is firm.

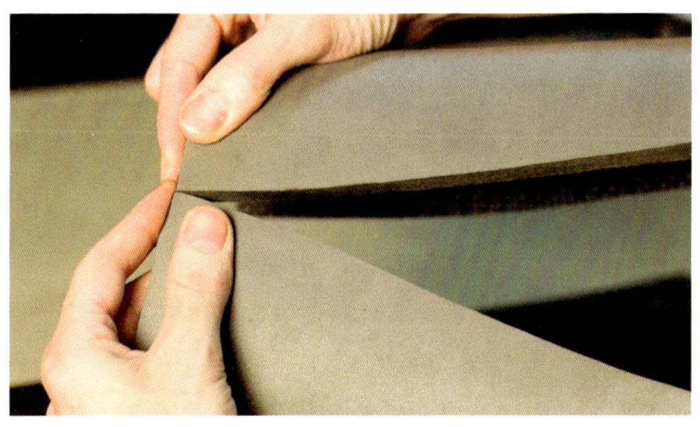

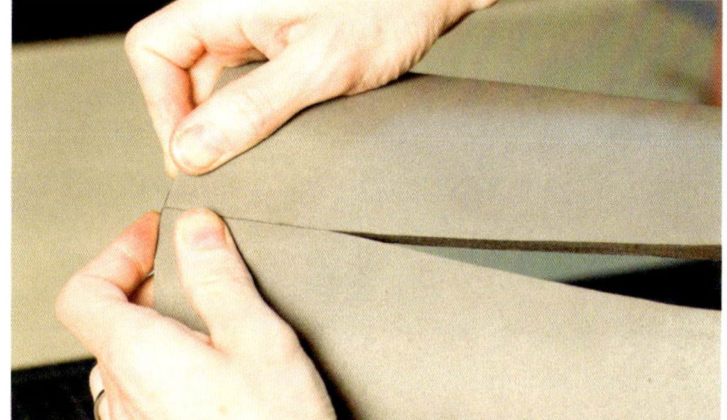

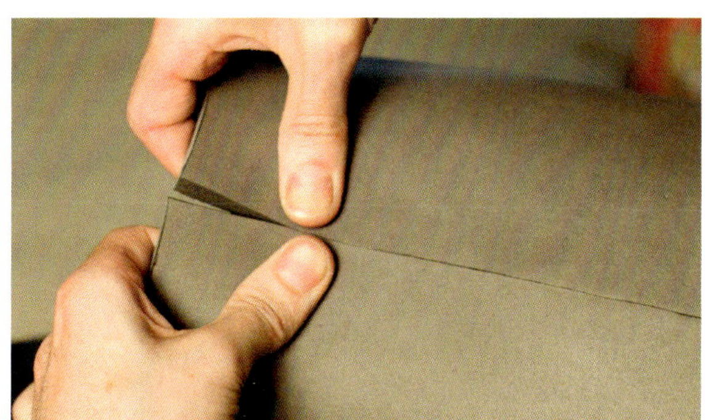

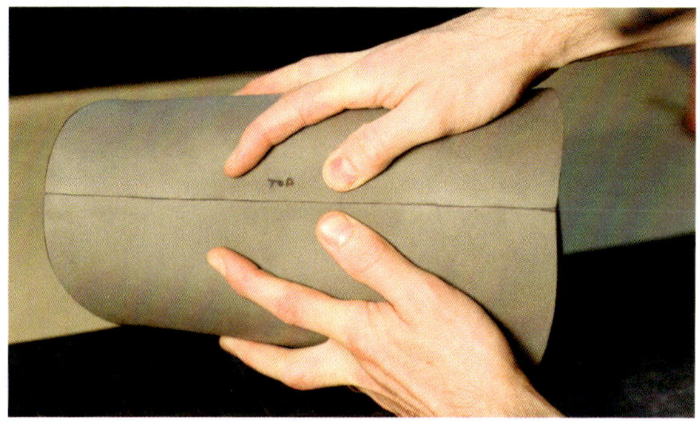

If you're putting together curved edges or complex curve seams, you may have to get a little rough with your foam. Also, hash marks on your template along the seam will help you keep the curved parts lined up as you press it together. Don't worry, it can take the abuse and it'll be trivial to heat form and fix the shape after the seam is completely bonded. Once your seams are done, you can heat form the piece some more to get it closer to the shape you desire.

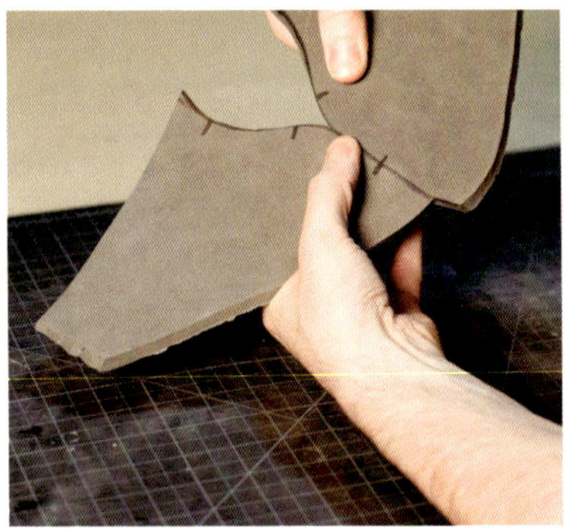

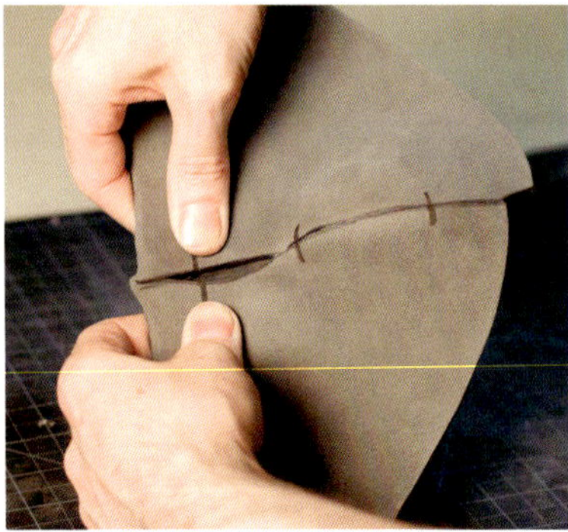

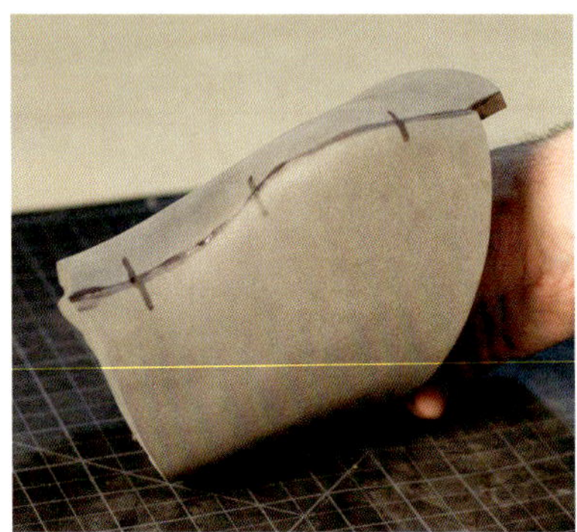

One of the questions that I get a lot about EVA foam is how one might best fill and finish unintentional gaps in between foam pieces along the seams. For those who work with rigid materials like wood, the answer is easy: use a filler resin, let it cure, and then sand it down until smooth. For a flexible foam, that just plain ain't an option. The best thing to do is to get the seams as perfect as possible from the get go. This is one of the reasons why contact cement is such a powerful method for attaching seams. If a small gap is completely unavoidable, a little bit of superglue can be employed to stick the offending edges back together. Having a cyanoacrylate accelerant spray on hand becomes almost necessary for this process. It takes a little bit of doing, but it works.

Also, you can plan your templates so that your seams will be covered with another layer of foam on top of it, completely obscuring any botched seams you might have! Eureka!

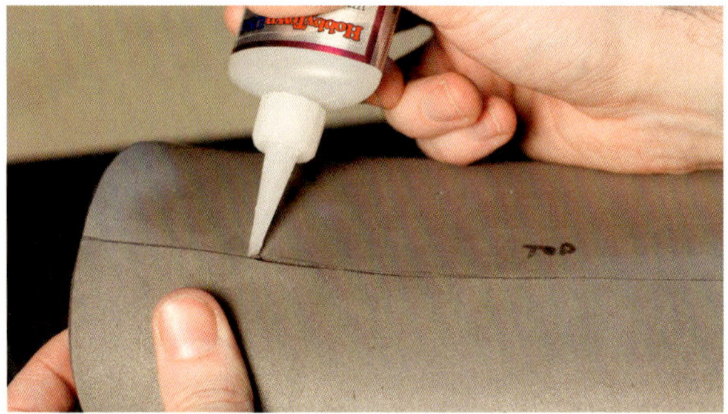

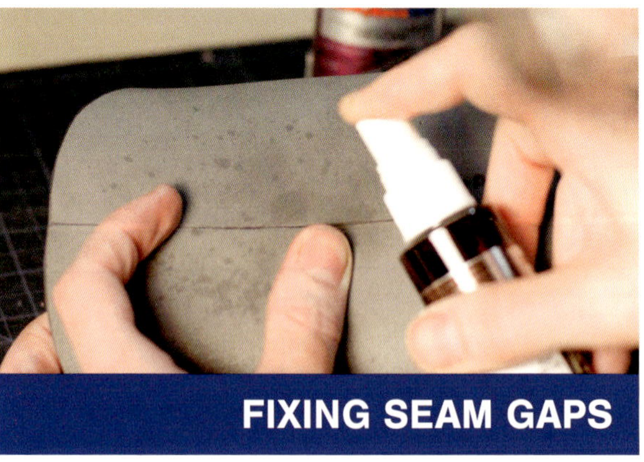

FIXING SEAM GAPS

Now you should have a piece that you can try on or at least hold up to your body to test the scale, shape, and form. If this is your first piece, it may very well be completely wrong. If the piece is too small, you're out of luck. Go back to the template, redraw it larger, cut out a new piece, and try again. If the piece is too big, you can cut away pieces to get it looking pretty good. Or you can cut apart your seam, trim away some of the offending material, contact cement the seam again and give it another test fitting.

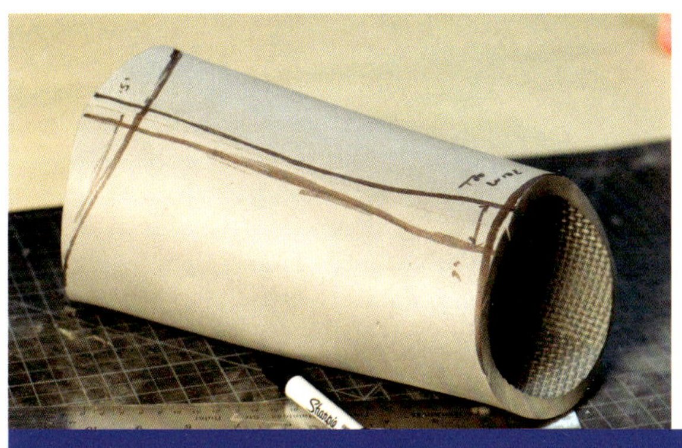

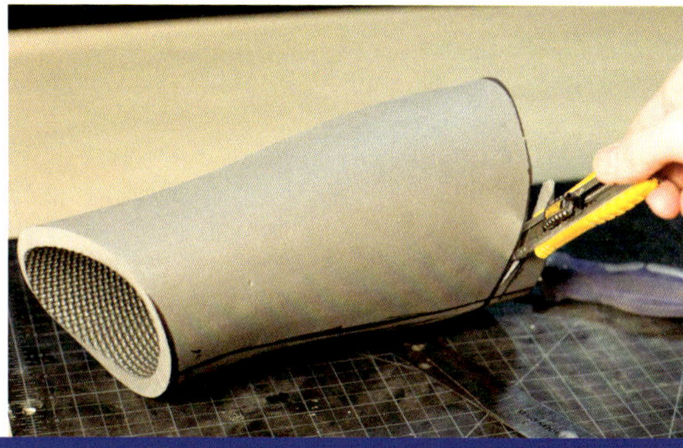

SIZING CHANGES

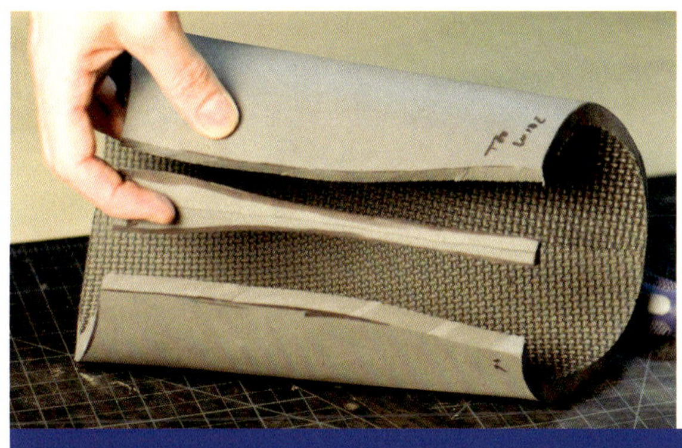

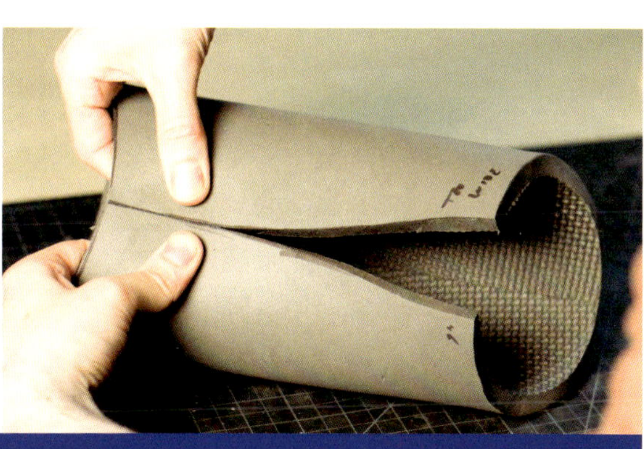

MODIFY & REGLUE

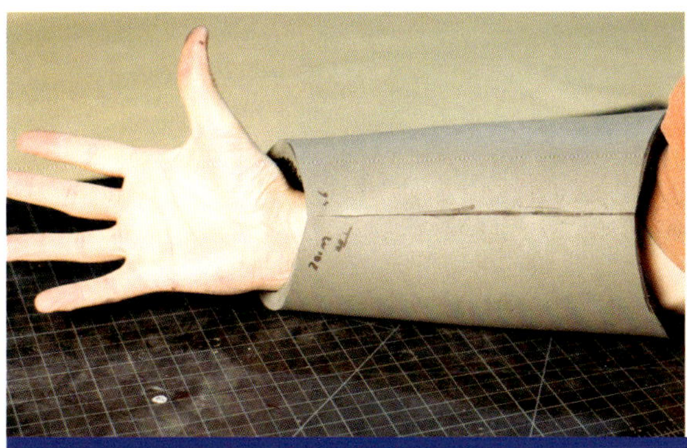

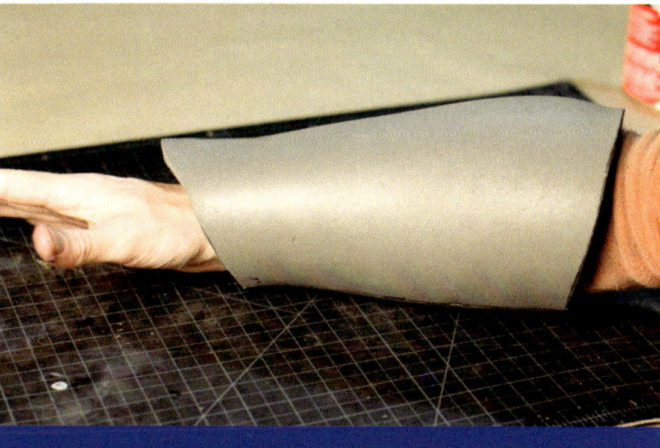

PERFECT FIT!

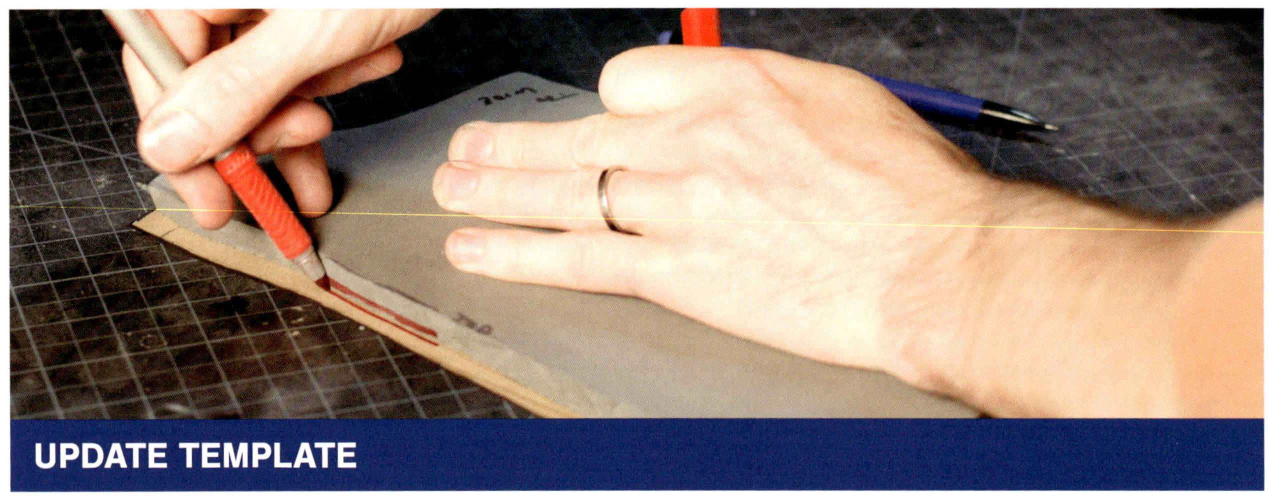

UPDATE TEMPLATE

If you're happy with your final piece, it pays to take the time to update any changes you made on your template paper. You may be able to just make some measurements and translate those changes to the template. On the other hand, if you're planning on making more than one of these pieces (like the other arm or the other side of the torso), you might want to just cut up that finished foam part and trace it on a fresh piece of masking paper. It's likely that your first piece is mangled from all the changes you made anyway. The second and third armor parts you make will look way nicer!

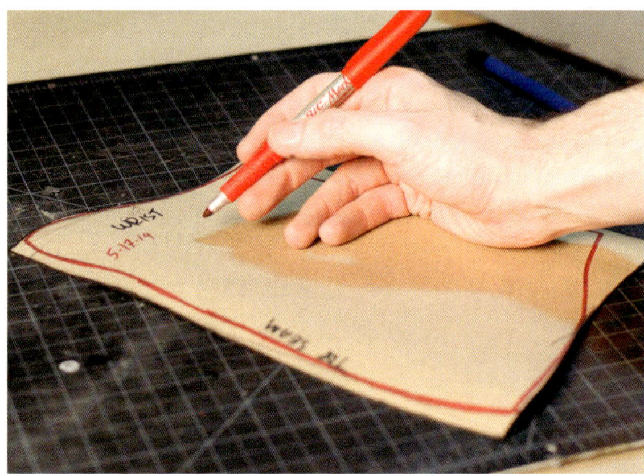

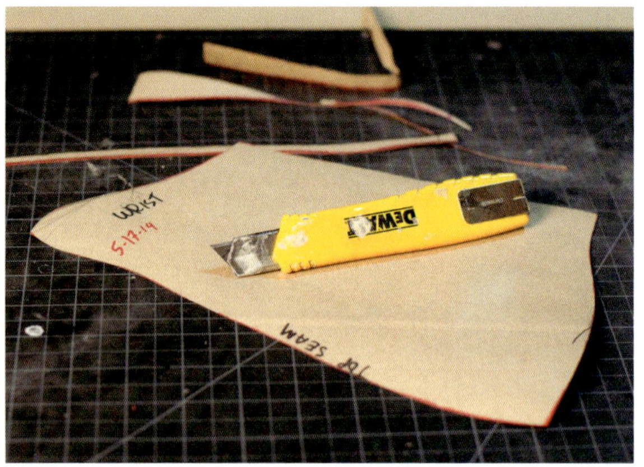

Armor Has Layers, Like an Onion

Utilizing multiple layers and thicknesses of EVA foam will add all kinds of detail and dimensions to your armor pieces. With half inch, 6mm, and 2mm varieties of floor mats and craft foam, the sky's your limit!

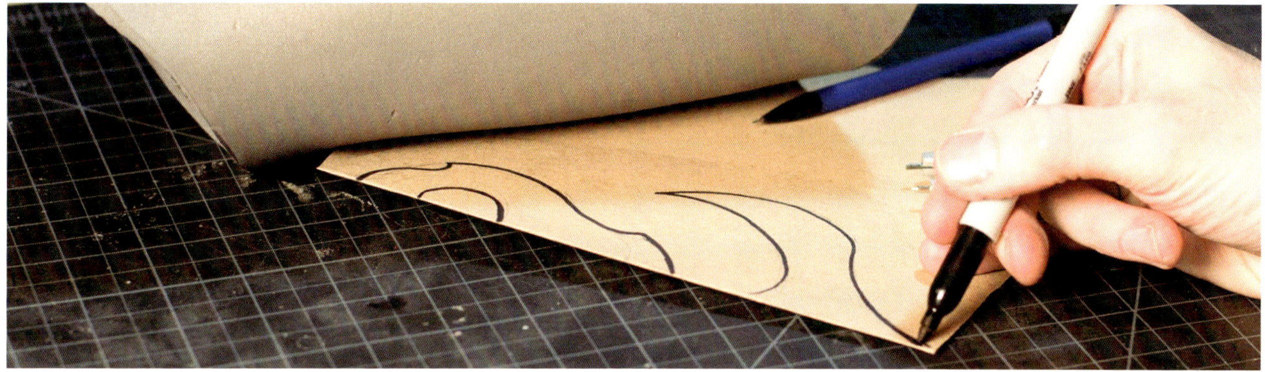

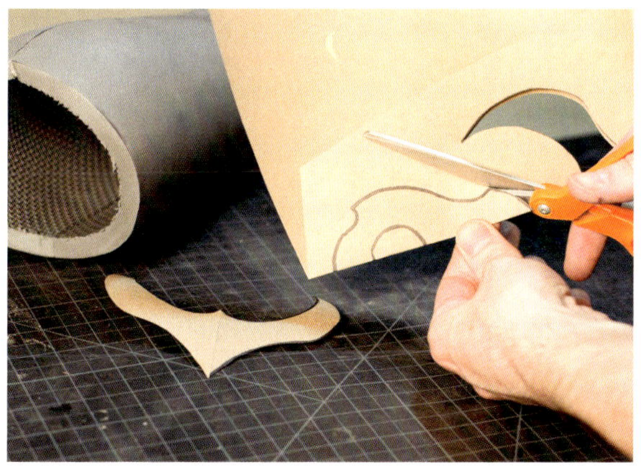

This is another place where making nice paper templates will benefit you in the long run. You can draw up some ideas, cut them out, and lay them down on your base parts to see how they look and modify them to fit properly. When you're happy with your templates, cut out your foam parts and prep them for adhesion. This is a great time to utilize some angled, beveled edges on some of the thinner edges. Any sort of rough cut marks here can be cleaned up with your rotary tool.

Also consider cutting any sort of relief textures (explained in a later section) into the surface of additional layers before gluing them down.

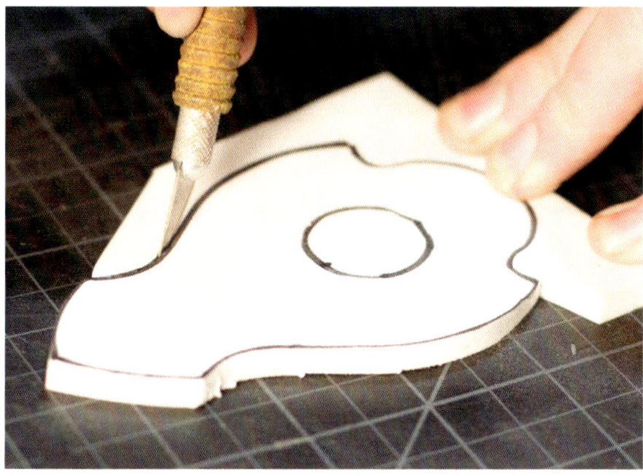

"Any sort of rough cut marks here can be cleaned up with your rotary tool."

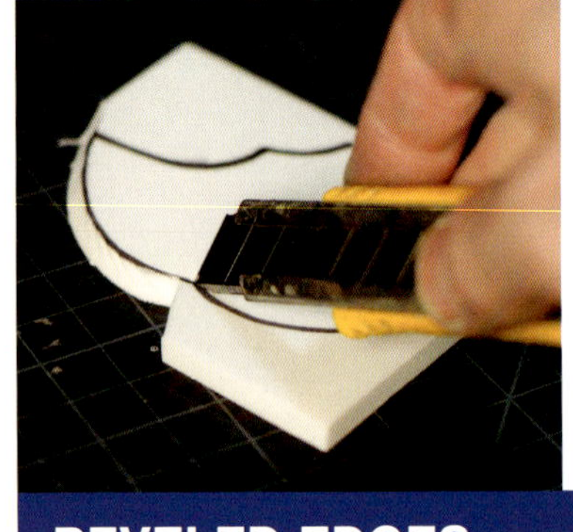

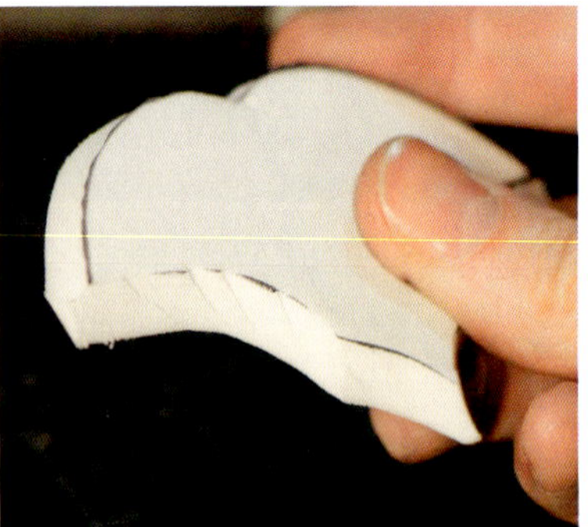

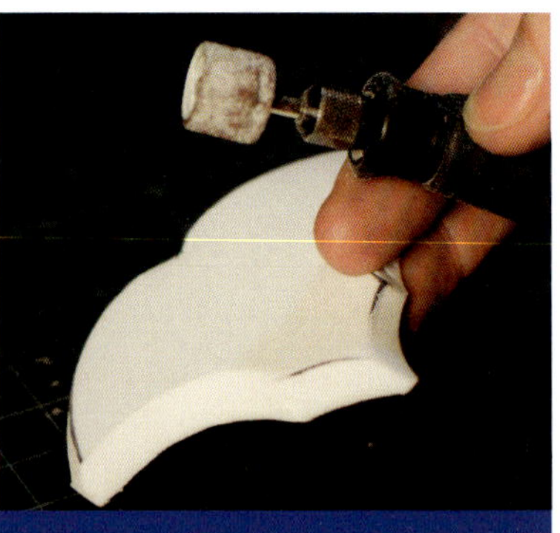

BEVELED EDGES

For gluing down large, flat pieces, contact cement is again our go-to goo. Lay down your piece onto the base form and trace it with a marker so you know where to brush your cement. The only thing you'll need to be wary of is if you're trying to stick a piece to a bit of floor mat that has the texture showing. You'll want to at least rough up the texture with some sandpaper or remove it entirely with your rotary tool and a sanding or grinding bit.

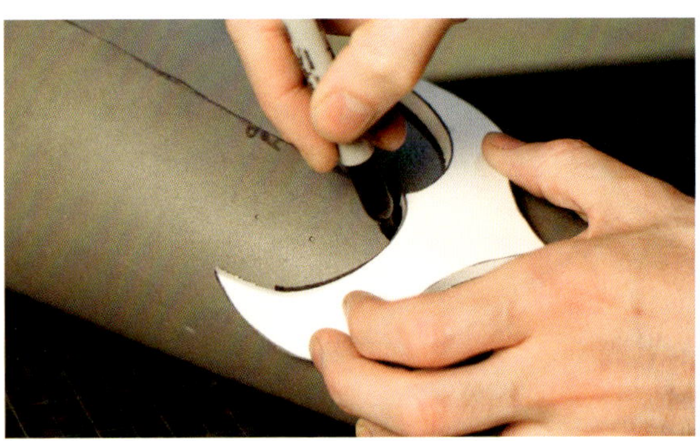

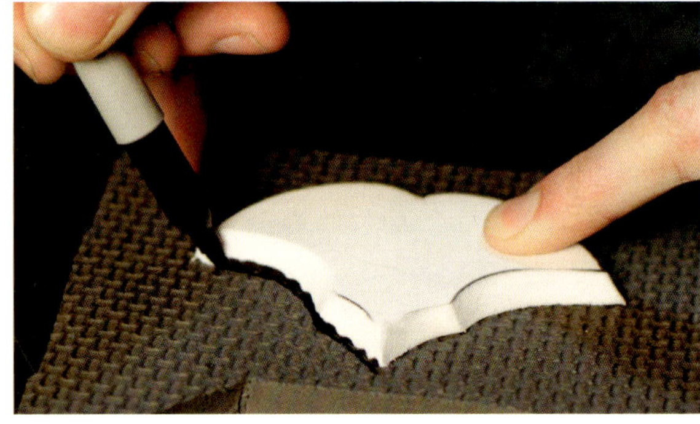

With your additional layers prepped, all that's left is applying contact cement to the adjoining faces, letting it dry for 10 minutes, and then pressing the new piece into place.

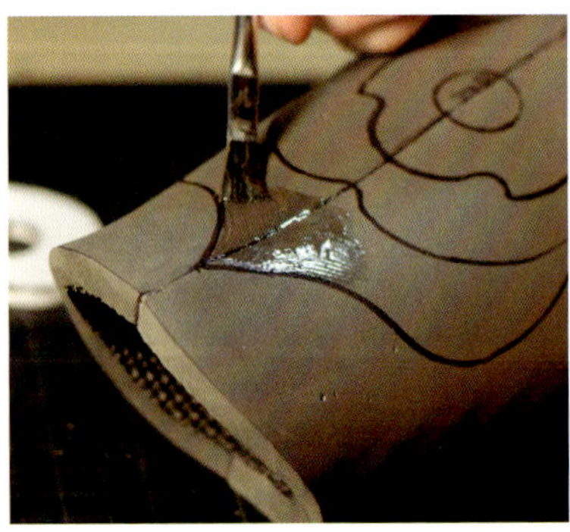

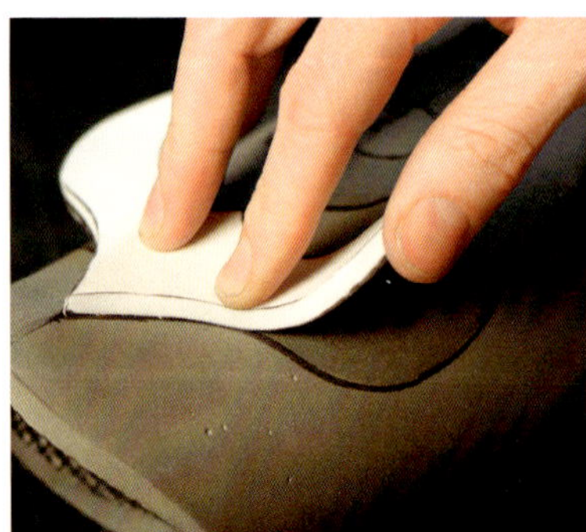

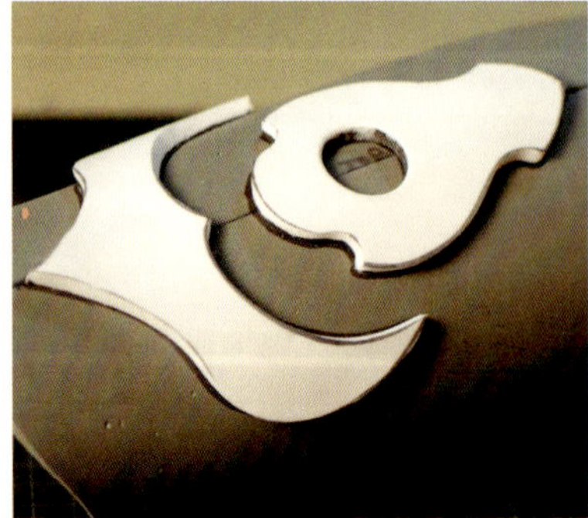

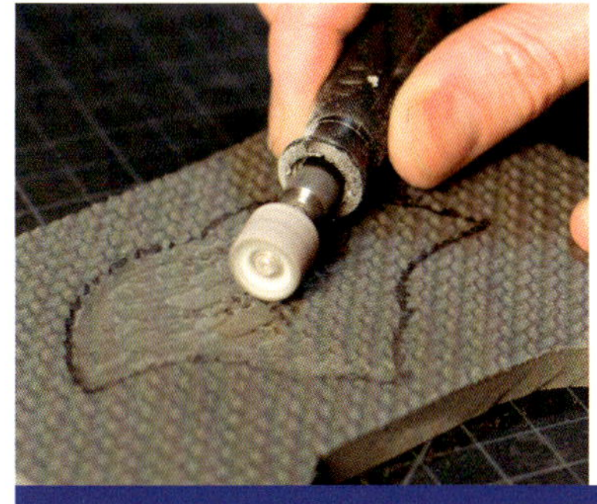

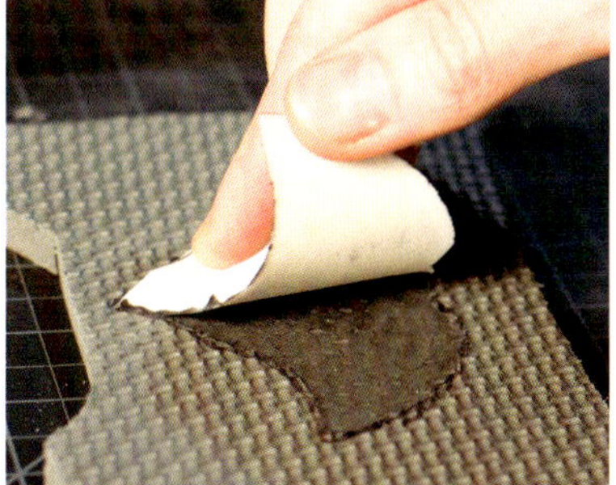

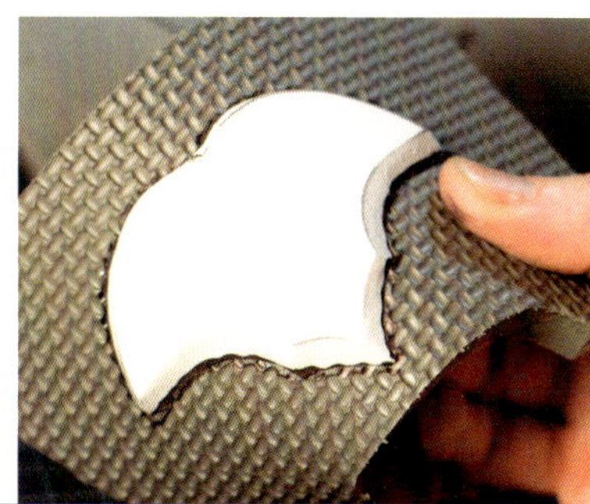

TEXTURE REMOVAL

You're not stuck to just big, flat pieces either. Consider cutting out thin straps that can be wrapped and shaped into detailed filigree patterns. For this to work properly, you'll want to draw out the design on your base form first. Then lay down a bead of superglue along the line in short segments and then press the strip of foam down along the line. You could definitely do this with contact cement too, but I've found that it's a bit more manageable for really thin pieces if you use superglue. This is a really great method for making intricate knotwork as well as adding raised bits to the edges of your armor.

Have fun with adding layers. There's a lot of room for some inventiveness and artistry at this point, especially if you're running with your own custom design. Definitely try out any new ideas you have on your growing pile of scrap EVA foam. Experiment with beveled edges, simulated rolled metal edges, curved edges, and multiple thicknesses. You'll be a super pro at this in no time!

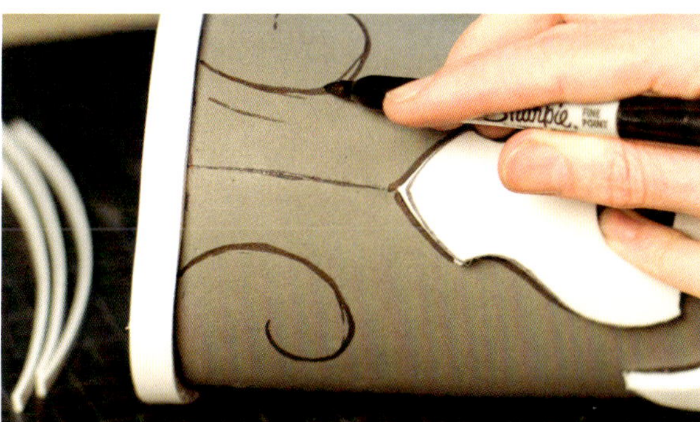

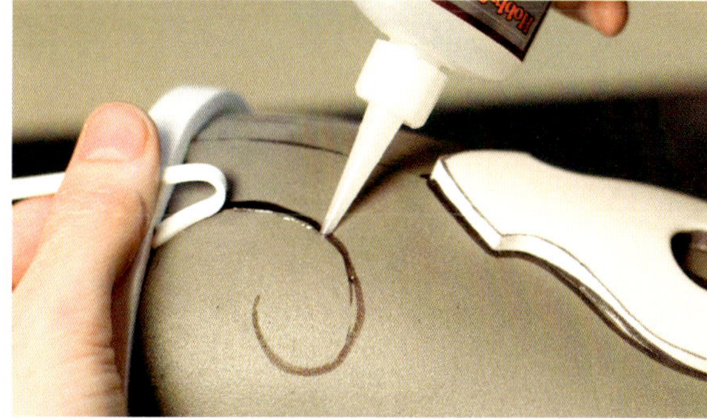

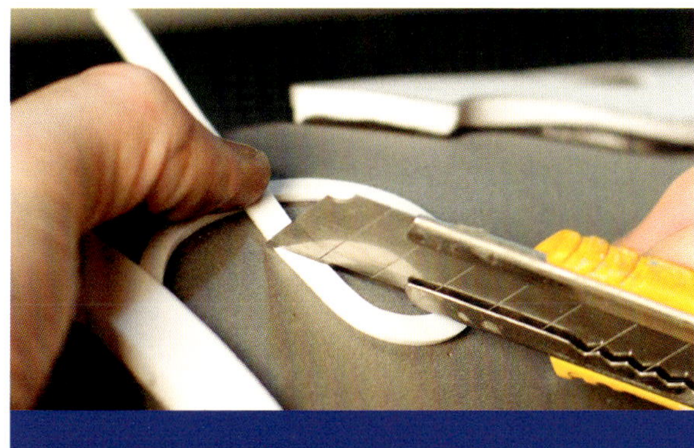

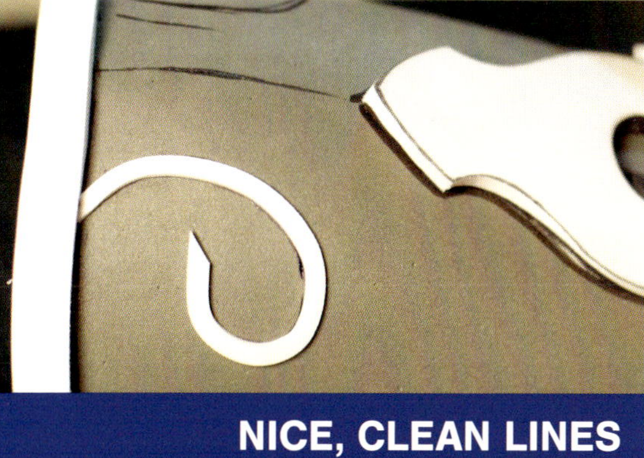

NICE, CLEAN LINES

What a Relief!

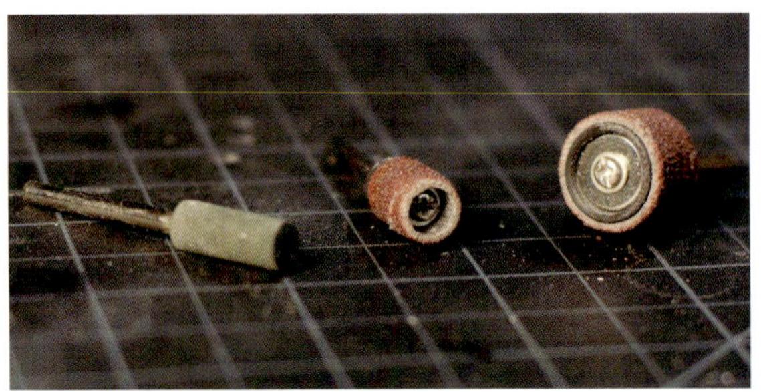

Up to this point, you've mostly been adding things to your basic forms. Now, why don't we play with some subtraction? You can get some incredibly detailed patterns in your foam armor by removing material.

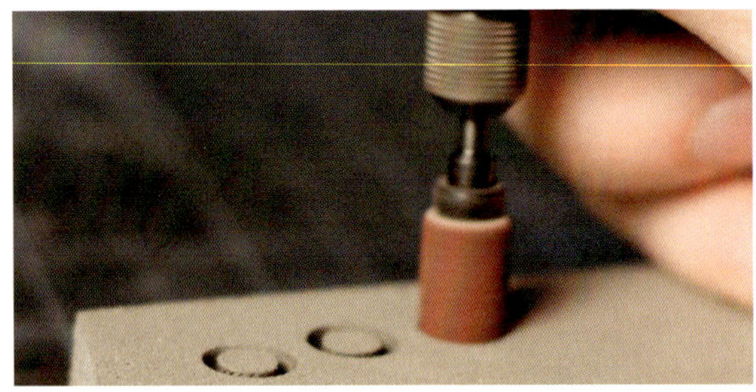

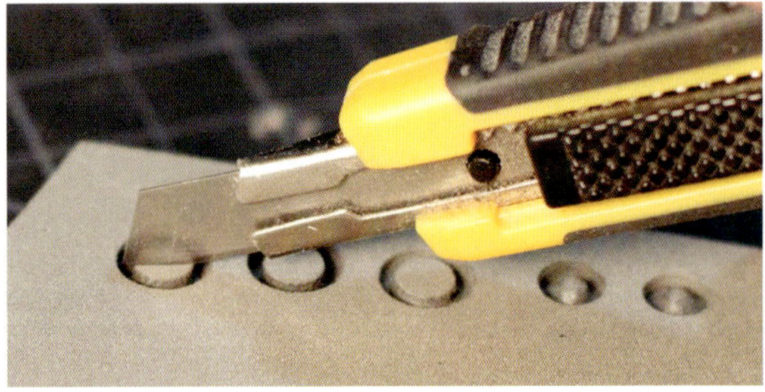

Many sets of armor, both real and fictional, are covered with screws, bolts, rivets, and other types of circular embellishments. One ridiculously simple way to achieve this look is to take the sanding drum in your rotary tool and spin it head first right down into the surface. This will cut a doughnut shaped circle into your armor. You can control the depth of the cut by sliding the sandpaper off the end of the bit a little. This effect can be achieved with grinding bits and different sized sanding drums as well. If you want it to look like a screw, use your hobby knife to cut one or two slits across the raised center of the circle and then hit it with your heat gun for a little bit. The slits will open up and you've got yourself a screw!

RIVETS & SCREWS

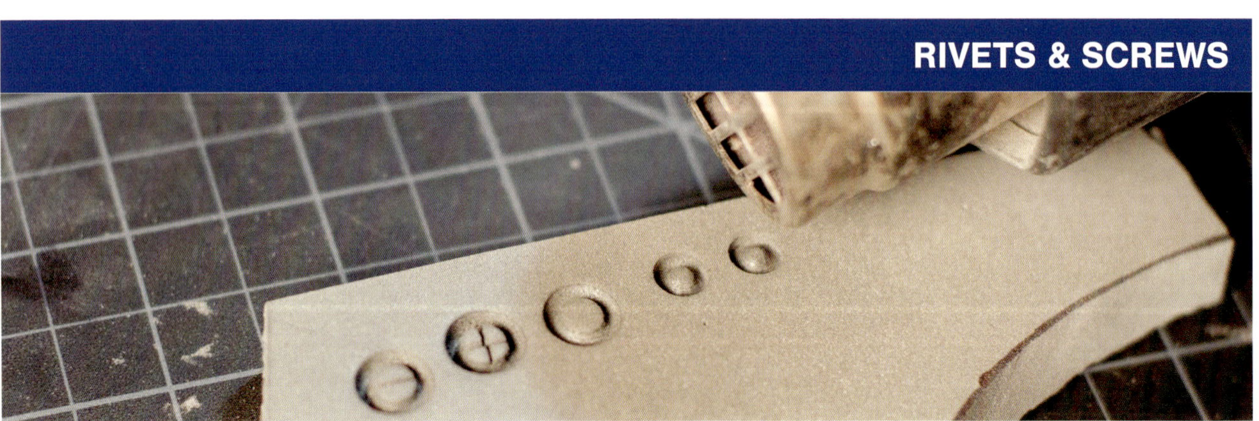

If you need a hole punched all of the way through a layer of foam, I've got you covered! Using either a metal or PVC tube in your desired diameter, use a file, sandpaper, or dremel to sharpen the edge of the tube opening. This new tool that you've invented can be pressed straight down into a piece of foam and, with a little twisting, will produce a perfect circular hole all the way through!

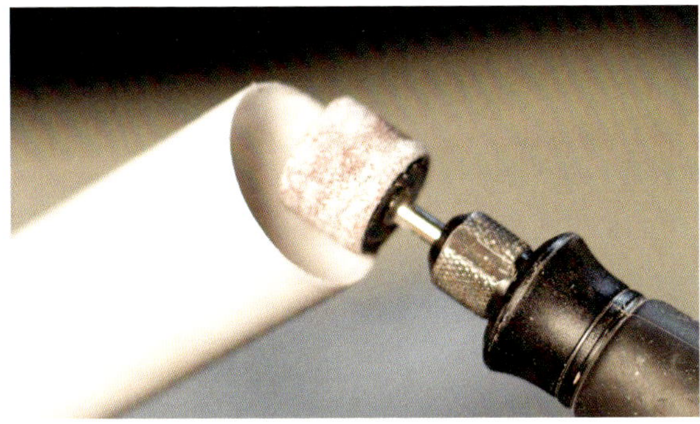

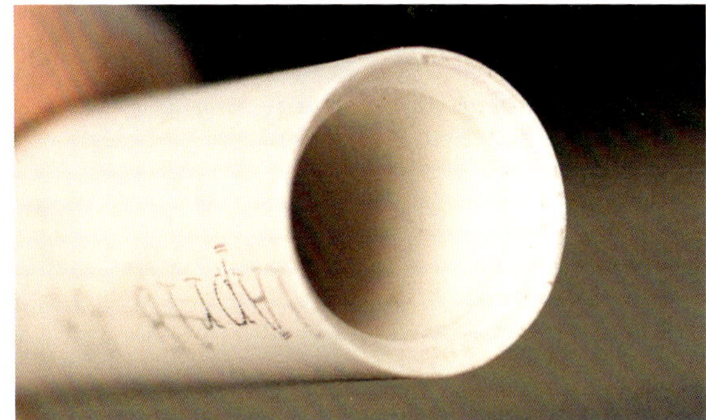

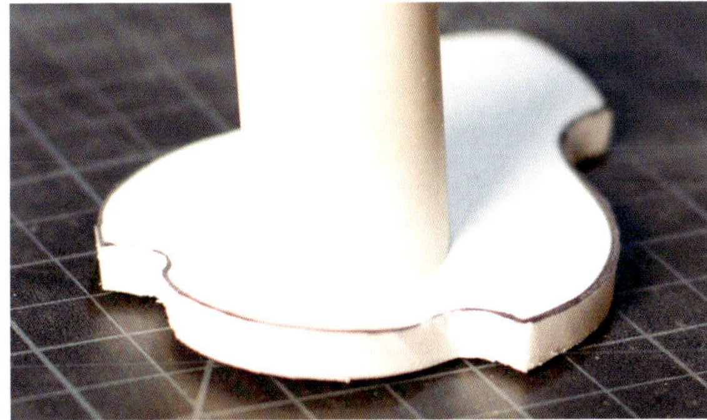

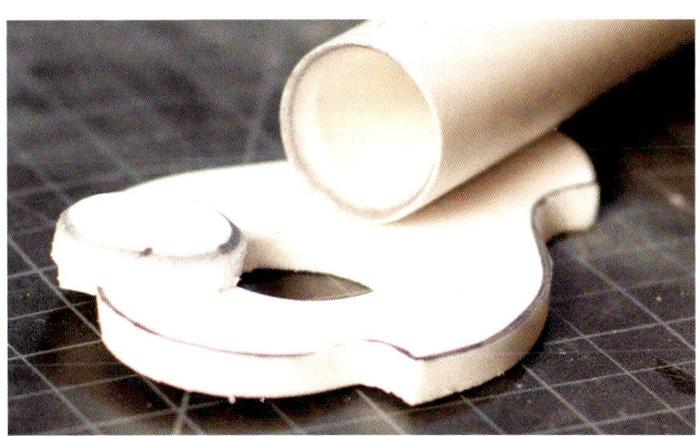

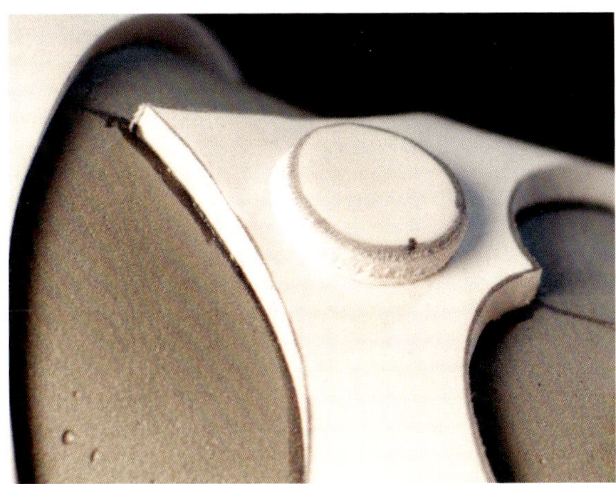

Be sure to keep the circle pieces that are punched out, those can be added on to another part of your armor elsewhere.

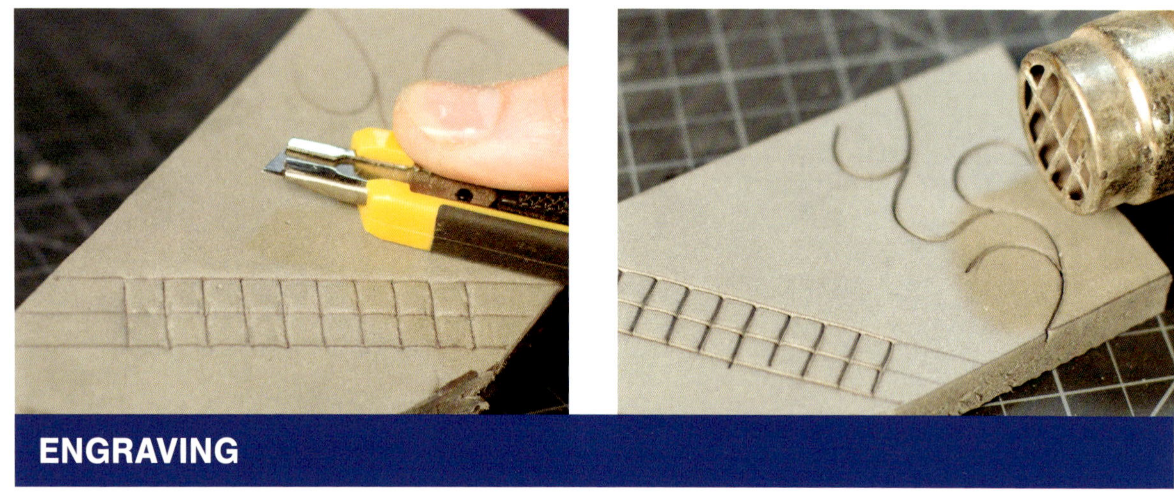

ENGRAVING

For super fine engraved details, you'll want to grab your hobby knife. First, draw your design onto the foam piece that you'll be cutting in to. Then it's cutting time! This is where I really like my ratcheting knife. I like to pull the blade into the handle until just the tip is peeking out. Using the blade tip, simply cut a shallow line along your design. Having just the blade tip sticking out will help you cut at a consistent depth.

Once your pattern has been completely cut, bust out your trusty heat gun and warm up the surface a bit. You'll see the shallow seams split apart, revealing your design as if by magic! You can do some amazingly detailed work with this method, so go nuts!

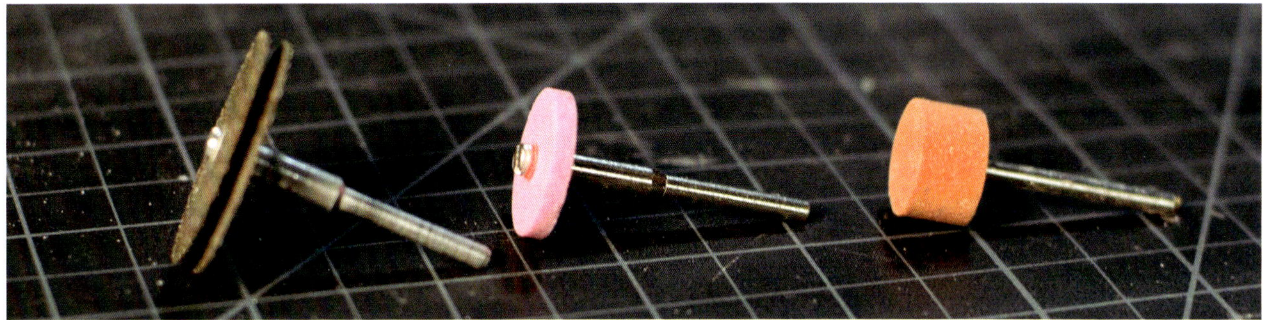

If you fancy thicker, machined looking lines, you'll want to use your rotary tool. Pick out a grinding bit that is as tall as you want your line to be thick. Again, draw your design lines onto the foam so you know where to cut. Then, hold your rotary tool parallel to the surface of the foam and, using the edge of the bit, cut a trench into the foam. Pull the tool towards you, following your design lines. If your lines are straight, you can actually use a ruler to keep the tool going in a smooth direction. Just run your finger across the edge of the straight, edge instead of the spinning bit. You can see how having that extended, flexible shaft for your rotary tool would be really fantastic here.

You can get pretty creative with your bits, too. For example, I tried layering different diameter cutting wheels together to be able to cut two parallel lines at once. Experiment with all of the bits you have to see what you can come up with.

This will definitely take some practice. By now you should have more scrap foam bits than you know what to do with, so draw some lines on them and get to practicing! You can get some pretty clean looking cuts with enough experience.

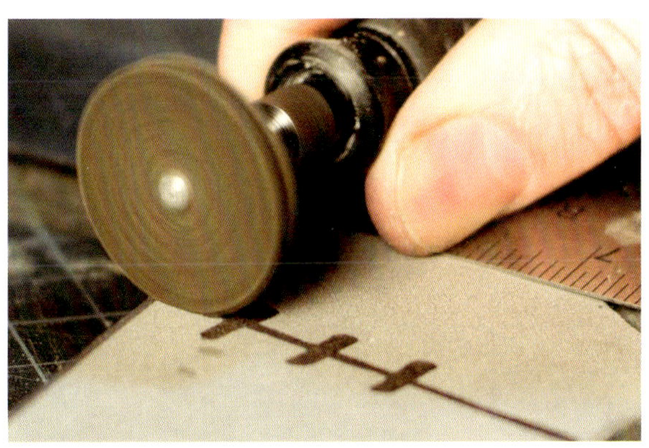

More than anything, how much you practice will determine how good your lines look. Foam is cheap, so don't skimp on the hours necessary to get a solid, consistent look to your detail lines!

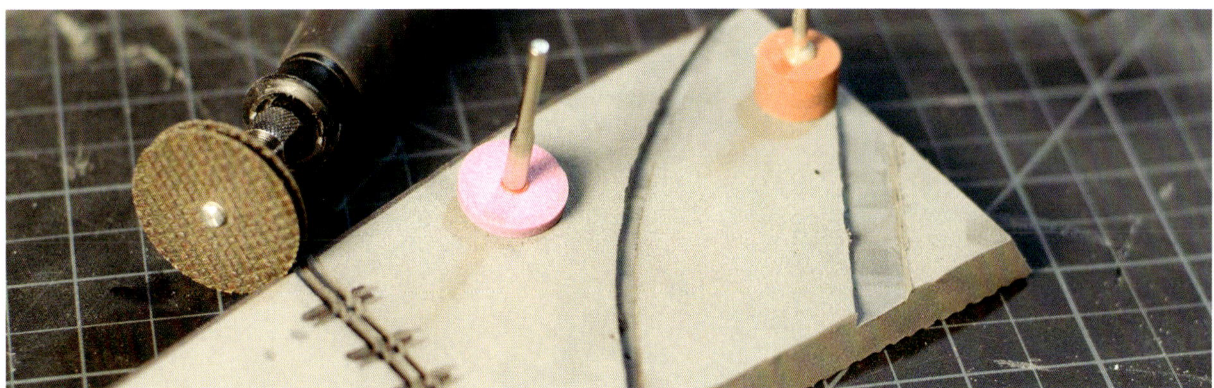

You like sculpting? Foam does that too!

Believe it or not, EVA foam also comes in bigger blocks of the stuff, not just in thin sheets. Foam yoga blocks. I kid you not. And, while they tend to be drastically overpriced, you could definitely use one of them to carve out some really neat forms.

If you don't want to spend a king's ransom on a yoga block that you're just going to cut up anyway, there's a cheaper alternative! You can contact cement a bunch of layers of your foam floor mats together to make a big old chunk of foam. The only hitch is the textured side of the floor mats. You could just use the 6mm craft foam and not worry about it, or you could sand off the texture on the floor mat completely. This is where owning a belt sander comes in handy. Just be sure you aren't breathing in all of that nasty foam dust. Respirators for the win!

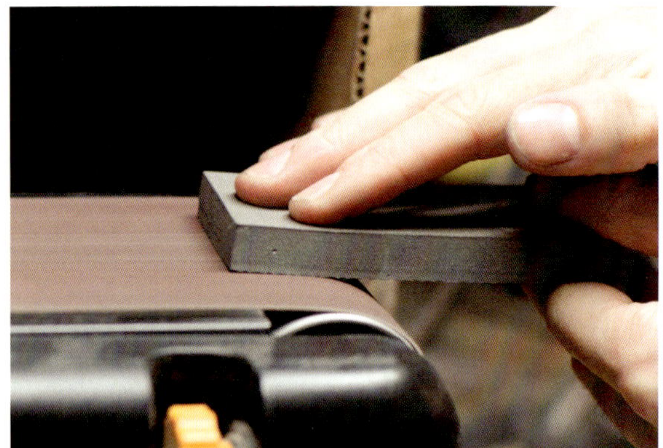

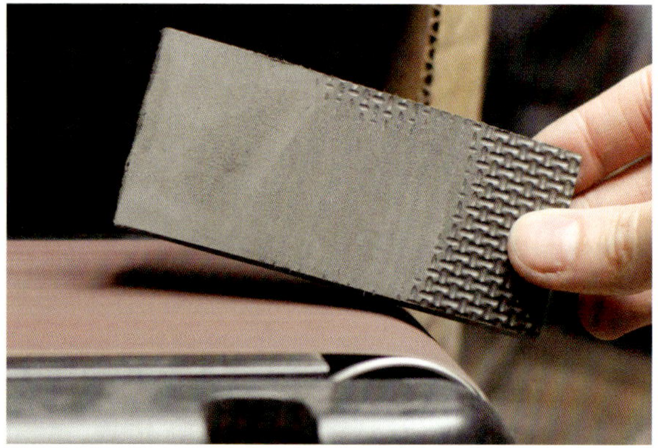

With your foam all prepped, brush the contact cement on all of the sides to be adhered. If you're good, you can stand them on edge and get both faces on a single piece at once. When the cement is ready, carefully squish your pieces together, forming a nice solid block of foam!

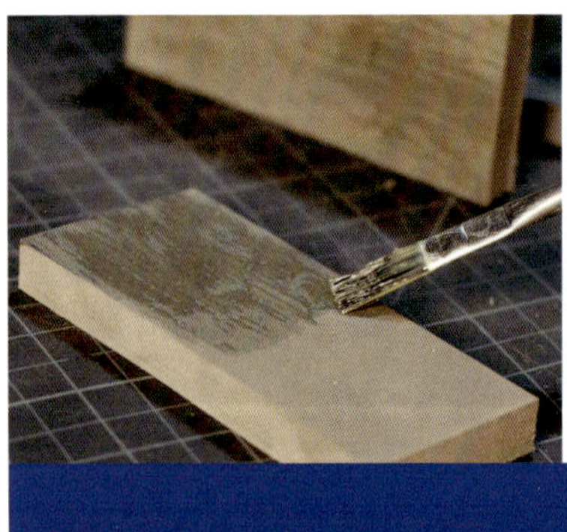

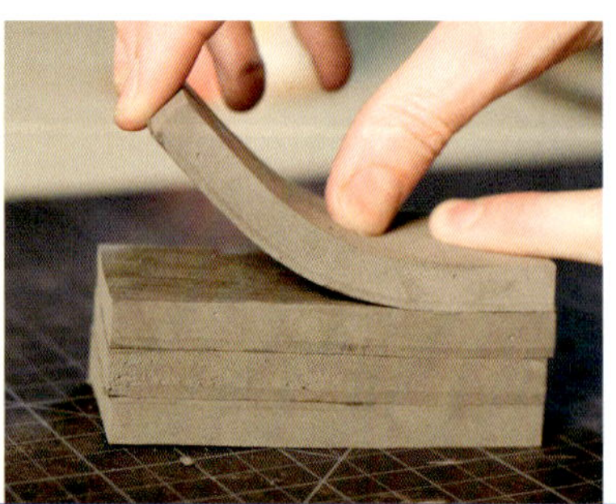

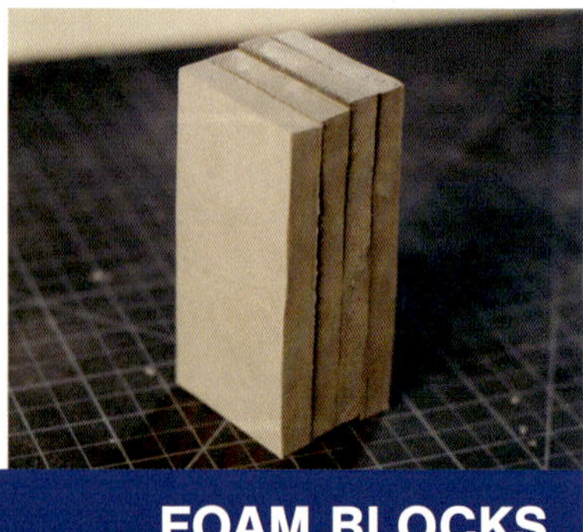

FOAM BLOCKS

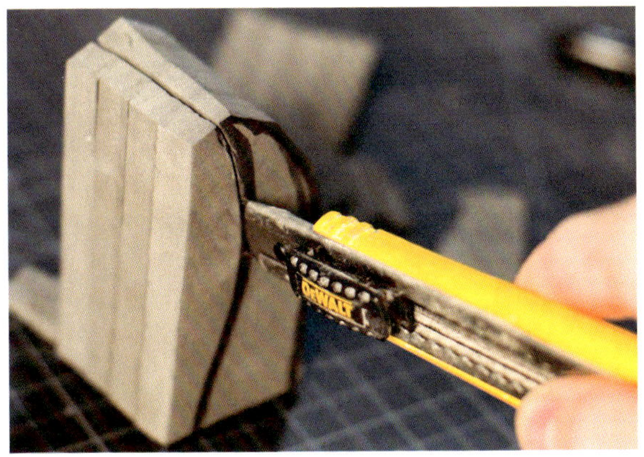

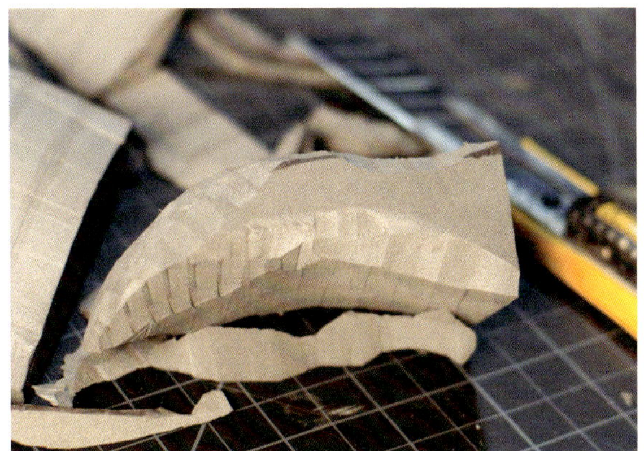

This block can be cut and carved to shape using your hobby knife. For more fine detail, use the sanding bit on your rotary tool. This method is really great for making lightweight (and safe) horns, teeth, and spikes for your armor. This type of technique is pretty limitless, so let your imagination be your guide!

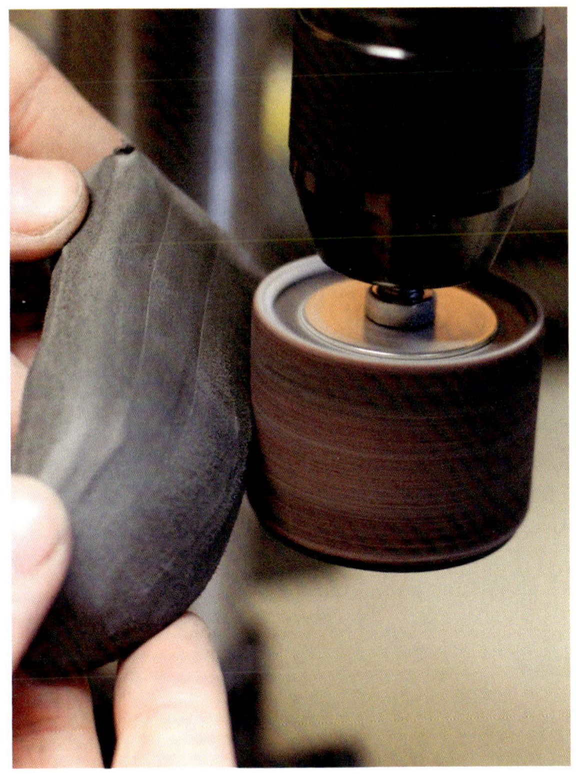

A large drum sanding bit in your drill press will make this kind of sculpting a dream.

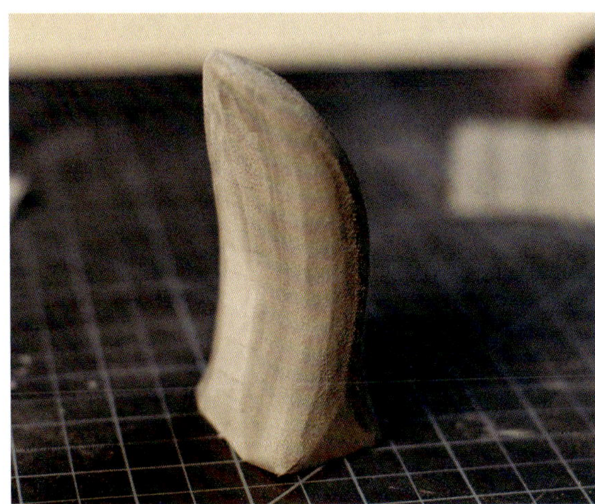

LET'S CLEAN UP THOSE EXPOSED EDGES

Once your pieces start to near completion, you may notice that the exposed edges of your armor still have that raw, ninety degree cut look to them. You may very well want this look, depending on the type of armor that you're making. If you prefer to clean up and round off those edges, you can totally do that.

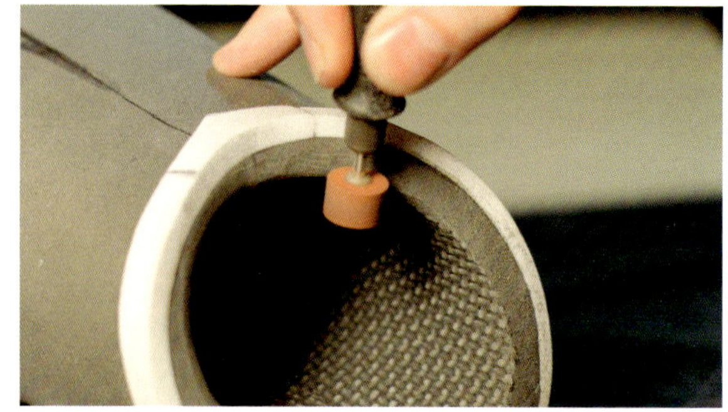

For this type of work it pays off big time to have a belt or drum sander. If you don't have either of those, the sanding bit on your rotary will do the trick, it will just take a lot longer. Run your edges along the spinning sandpaper to smooth out the sharp edges. Don't push too hard or else you can carve into the form a bunch. There is a certain finesse to this technique to get it just right. As always, practice on scraps first to get the hang of it. Once it is smoothed out to your liking, hit it with your heat gun to finish smoothing it out. With practice, you can create some really neat effects with this technique, especially if you combine it with multiple layers.

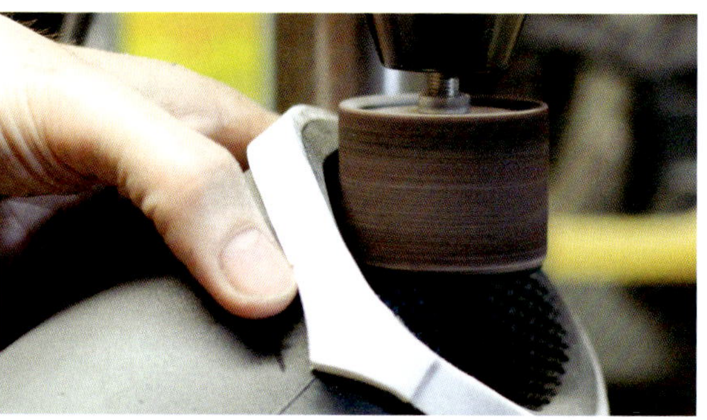

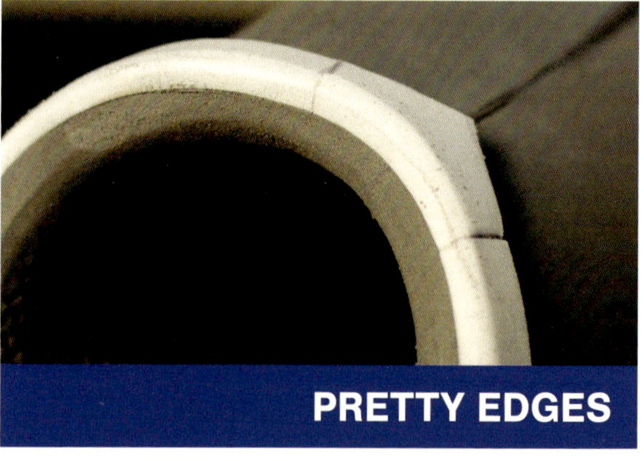

PRETTY EDGES

Let's try some more intricate techniques!

That's some damn fine looking armor you've got there! For most sets of costume armor, the above techniques will get you most of the way through the fabrication process. You probably want to do something super radical and fancy with whatever you're building though. With that in mind, here are some more techniques to help you bring your armor to the next level of comfort, functionality, and style!

THE SHOE ISSUE

There is no more underappreciated, yet vastly important part of your costume than the humble shoe. If one part needs to function properly for the duration of a convention day, it's the shoe. Durability is paramount and aesthetics usually need to be compromised in lieu of not murdering your feet.

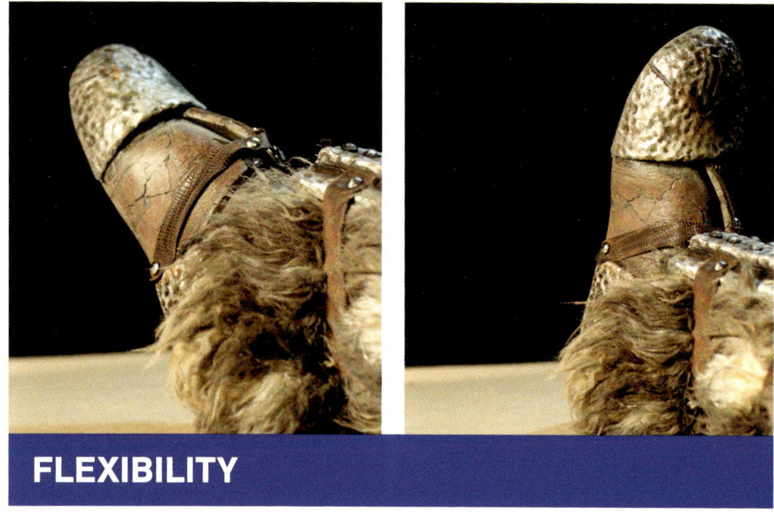

FLEXIBILITY

Every single step of your foot will bend your shoe, and the armor attached to it, at the ball of your foot. EVA foam will flex just fine, but the paint on it usually will not, and will crack off. If you can, try to add a seam or overlapping flex points across the top of your instep.

The same is true for your ankle. I like to keep my foot armor separate from my shin armor. If I need to, I'll make sure the two pieces overlap to give the appearance that they are attached, while retaining the full range of motion in your ankle.

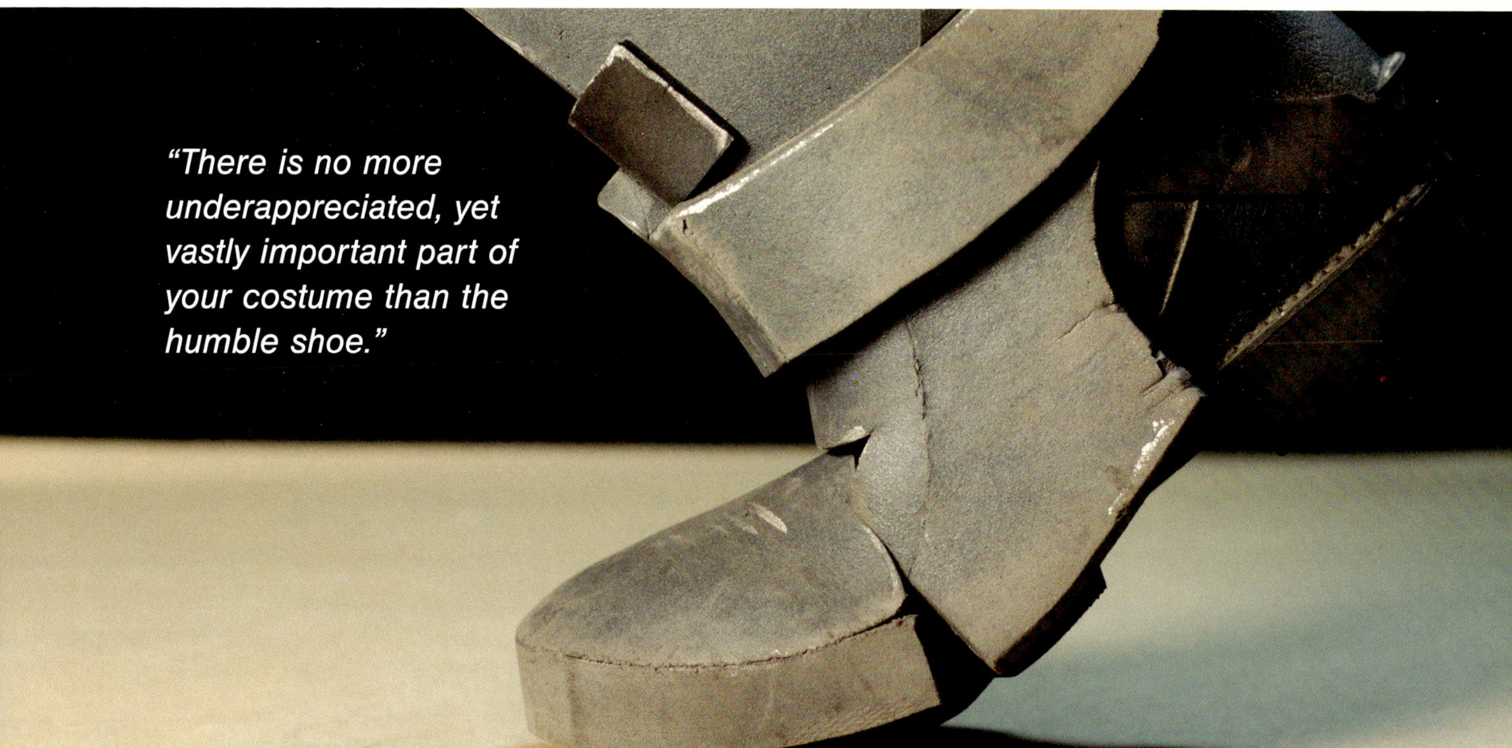

"There is no more underappreciated, yet vastly important part of your costume than the humble shoe."

No spot on your armor will require more trial and error than your foot armor, so be patient. Once you do have a pretty comfortable and functional foot piece, be sure to try it on a whole lot. Make sure it's easy to slip on and off without being so loose that it'll fall off if you make a quick step. If you can, wear the shoes for a day to get used to having the extra bulk on your feet. I'm sure the folks at work will understand if you show up wearing your greaves for a day!

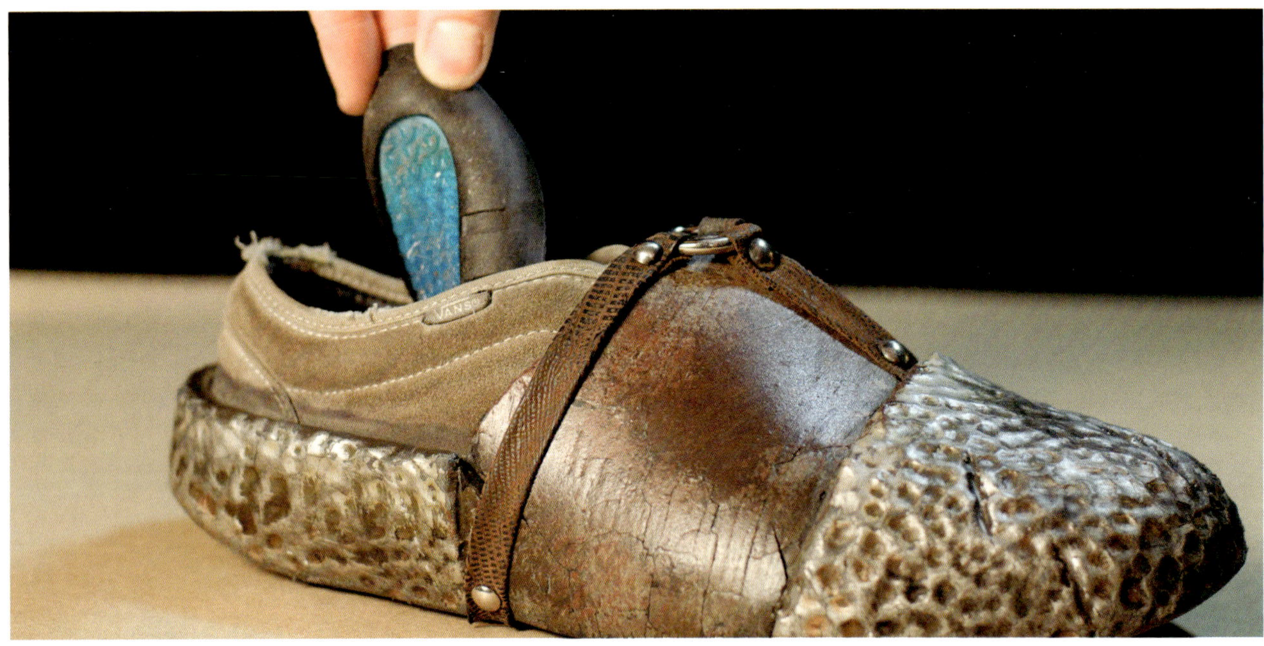

Finally, get your hands on some shoe insole inserts. Especially if you're wearing a brand new pair of shoes, you're going to be thankful for that extra layer of padding once you've put a dozen miles on them at a convention.

BOOBS NEED ARMOR TOO

Overlooking the fact that, realistically, breastplates with individually shaped boob cups actually provide a perfect channel for a spear to pierce the wearer's chest, lots of female armor designs have boob cups. Why? Cause it looks rad!

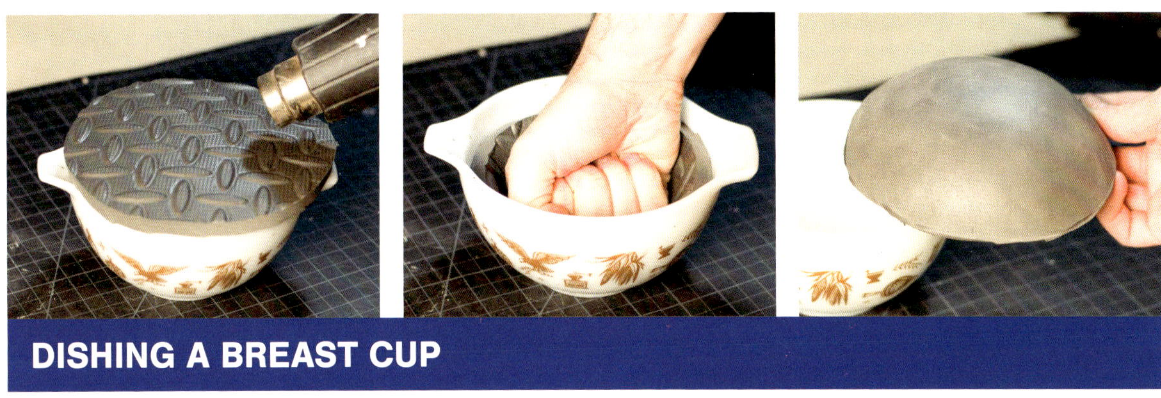

DISHING A BREAST CUP

If you're planning on adding well defined breast cups to your torso armor, I would recommend making the cups first and then designing the torso templates around them. The most important tool you'll need for this method is a sturdy bowl that is slightly larger than the breast size you'd like your armor to end up being. Then cut out a section of foam that is quite a bit larger than the opening of the bowl. Heat up your foam a whole lot with your heat gun and then push/punch it into the bowl. Be sure to face the texture inside or outside depending on which side you want to end up showing.

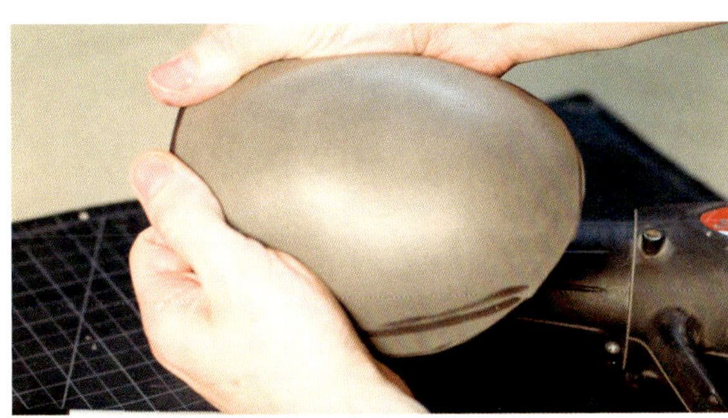

You'll end up with a nice looking dome shape that should be roughly the right shape. Now you can trim the edges to get it to fit exactly the way you like. You don't have to keep it perfectly spherical either. Most of the time a teardrop shape is preferred, so a combination of trimming, shaping, and heat forming by hand will get you to a good looking form. This will also be necessary to smooth out the flat bit that you may pick up from the bottom of your bowl.

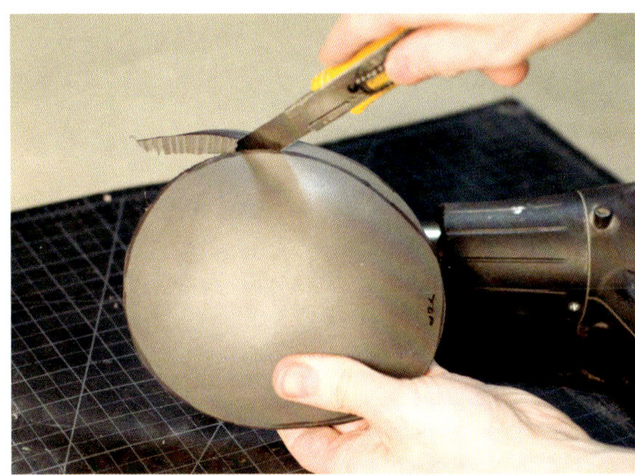

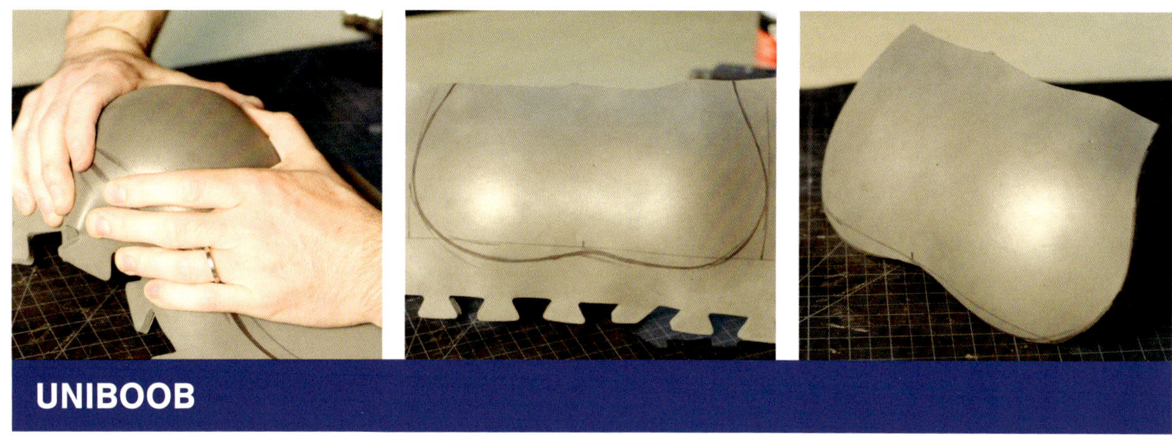

UNIBOOB

A similar technique can be employed if your armor features a "uniboob" design. The main difference is that you'll have to heat form the dome shapes on the outside of your bowl or in my case, a small medicine ball. You can probably form both half dome shapes from a single piece of foam, leaving plenty of extra foam at the edges that you can more accurately trim back while fitting the piece to your chest.

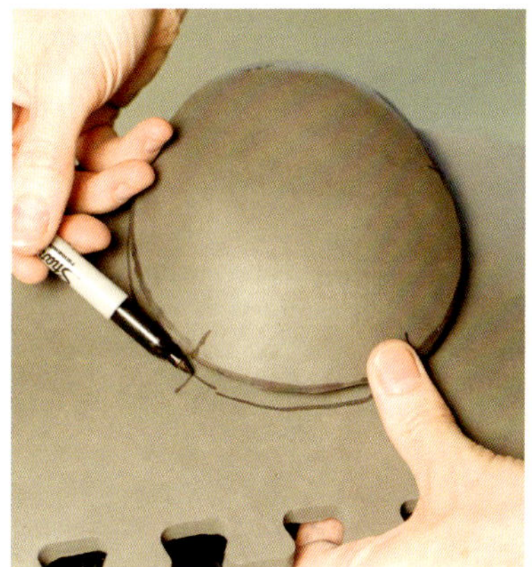

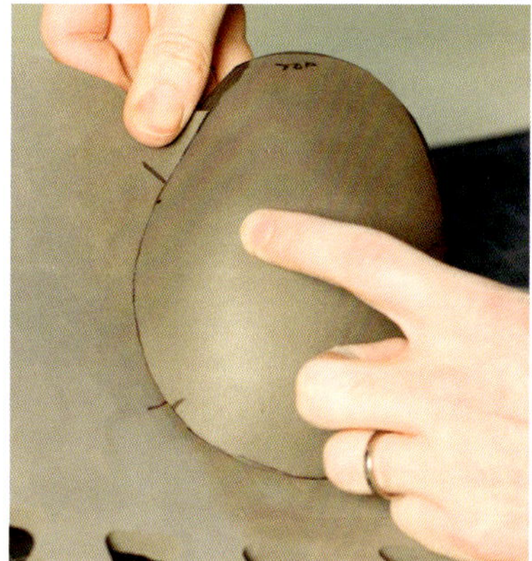

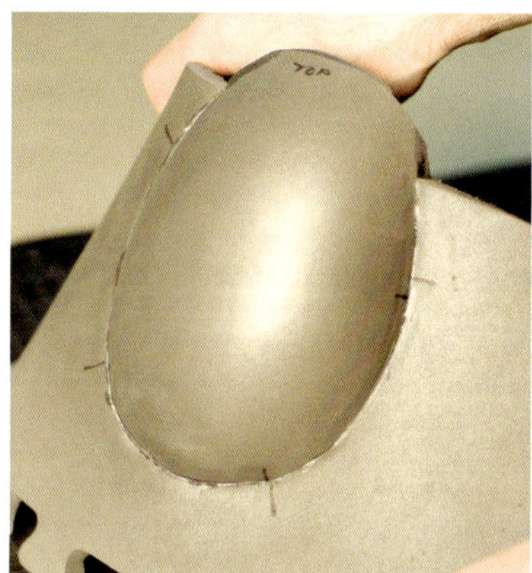

Leave plenty of extra room on your torso foam piece in the area where the cups will be placed. I would try to heat form the torso foam piece to your body just a little bit before adding the cups. Then you can trace the edges of the cups and cut away the torso foam to fit the cups right in. Use your fancy pants contact adhesive to stick them in place and you should be set!

THIS ARMOR HAS ME IN STITCHES!

If your foam armor is supposed to be simulating leather or cloth, you may want to incorporate some stitching to really sell the effect. This is the sort of detail that can add that head-turning special sauce to your pieces.

The type of string that you use depends on the look that you're going for. To ensure onlookers can see your stitching from afar, I recommend going with something that's thicker than you might think you would need. Most of the time this stitching will be completely decorative, so you don't need to worry too much about if it's strong enough, just that it looks cool.

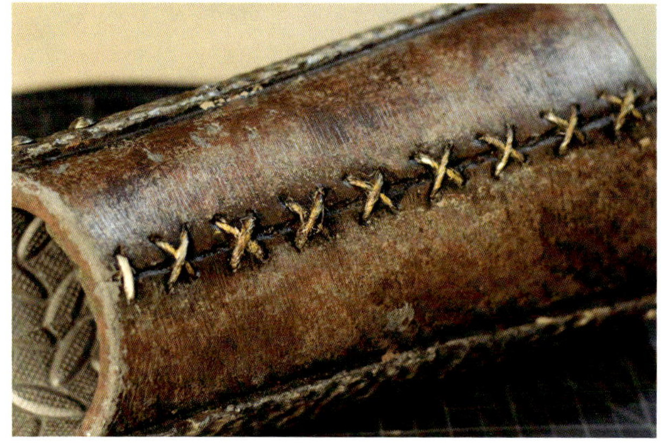

Leatherworking shops tend to have a fantastic variety of strings and thin leather straps that work great with foam. They also sell all manner of needles in various sizes. If you can't make it to a leather store, many craft stores have a small leatherworking section or a good variety of strings. You can even use cheap twine if need be.

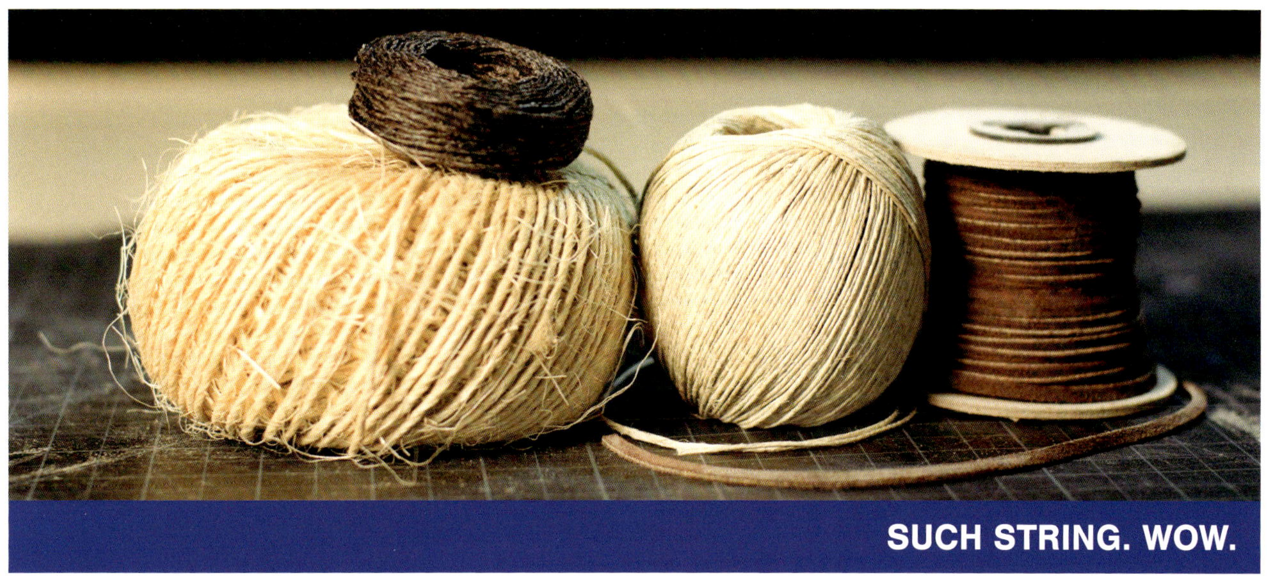

SUCH STRING. WOW.

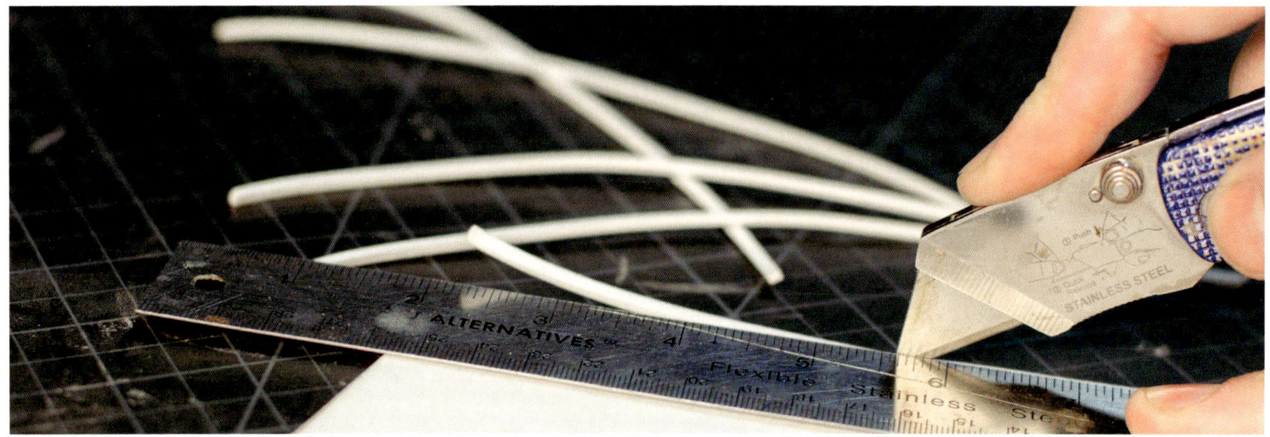

Another option is to cut your own thin straps or strings from your 2mm craft foam. You could even cut it out in a spiral pattern to get really long pieces. This won't be as durable as actual leather or string, but it's just gotta look good.

As far as the actual stitching technique, the sky's the limit. Just try to match whatever source material you're following. Since it doesn't need to be functional, just get it looking good and you're set. For cris crossing stitches, use two needles on either end of the same piece of string. This will save you all kinds of time!

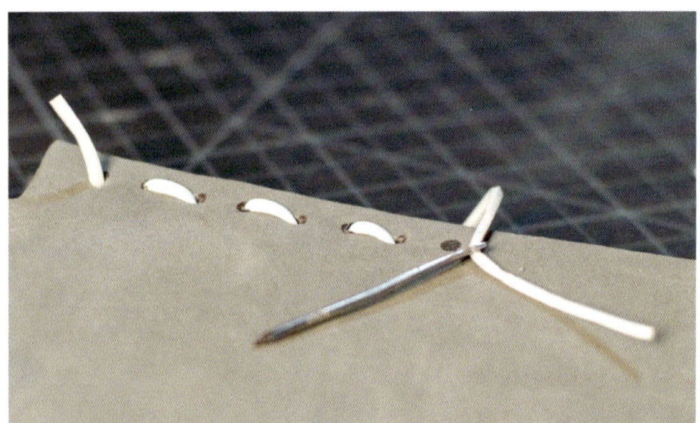

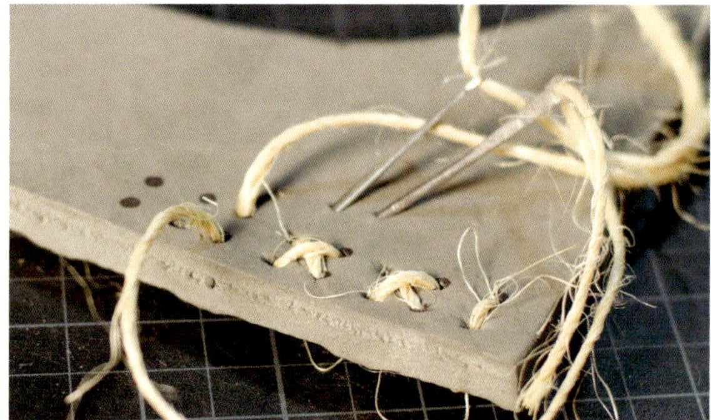

If you, like me, can't find a needle with an eye large enough to fit the string or straps you have, you can totally make some. Using a hammer and the flat part of a vice or anvil, hammer the head of a finishing nail nice and flat. Then, with a good drill bit and a drill press, drill as big a hole as possible through the flat part of the nail. Voila! Gigantic sewing needle! Make a couple of these while you're at it, they're extremely useful to have on hand.

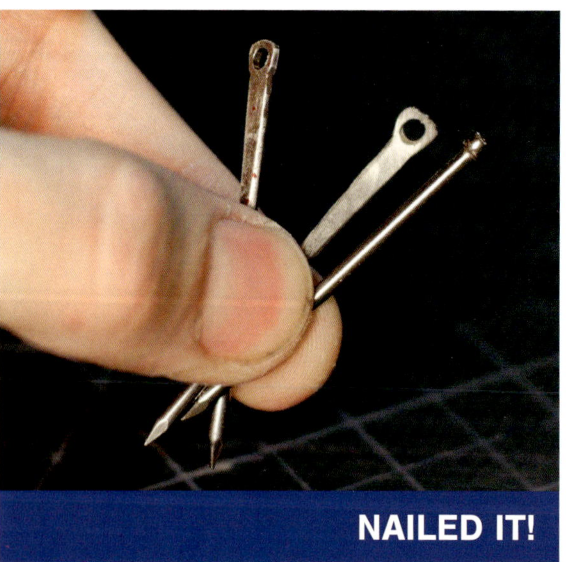

NAILED IT!

ARMOR TOO PRETTY? THERE'S A SOLUTION FOR THAT!

It's very likely that you'll want your armor to look world worn and beaten up. Your character has probably seen some combat and you want your foam to reflect that experience. Buckle up, cause this part is fun!

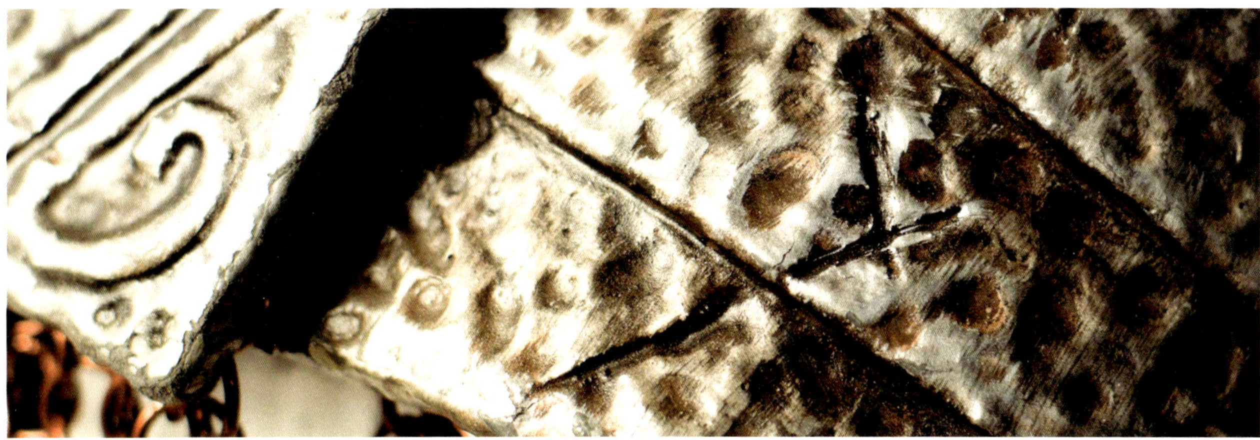

Consider the fictional history of your armor. What sort of weapons has it protected your hide from? Does your character have a scar that matches a damaged piece of armor? Did the attacks simply ding the armor or did it actually remove material? What kind of battle damage would make you look like a total badass? Once you've figured out where your damage is going to be, draw it out in marker on the armor surface.

Your first thought might be to actually attack your foam with real weapons. In some cases, this will work. Making quick knife slices and then hitting them with a heat gun will will make a nice "cut leather" effect. Mashing your foam with a real mace, on the other hand, won't actually dent it.

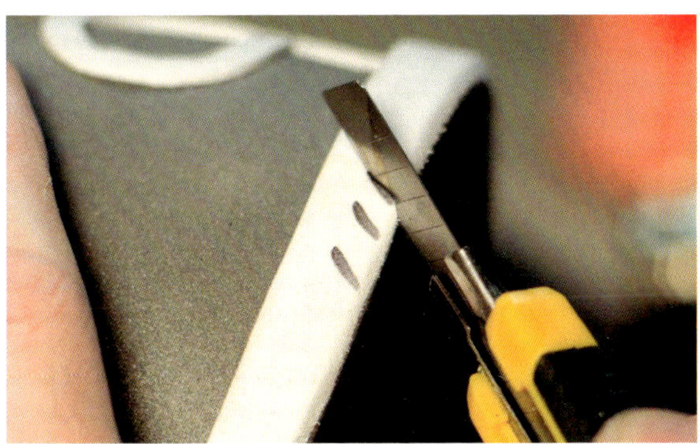

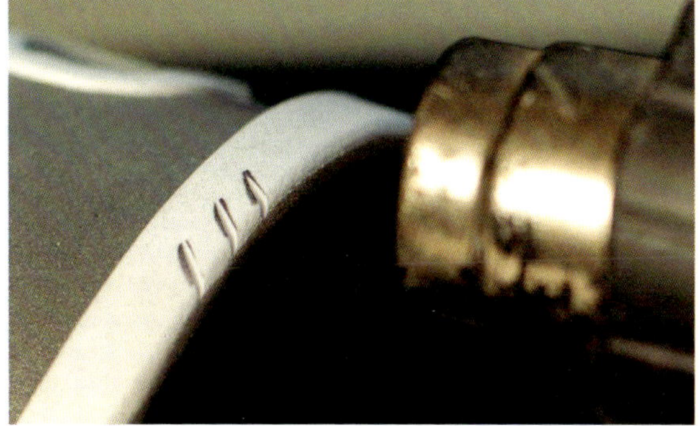

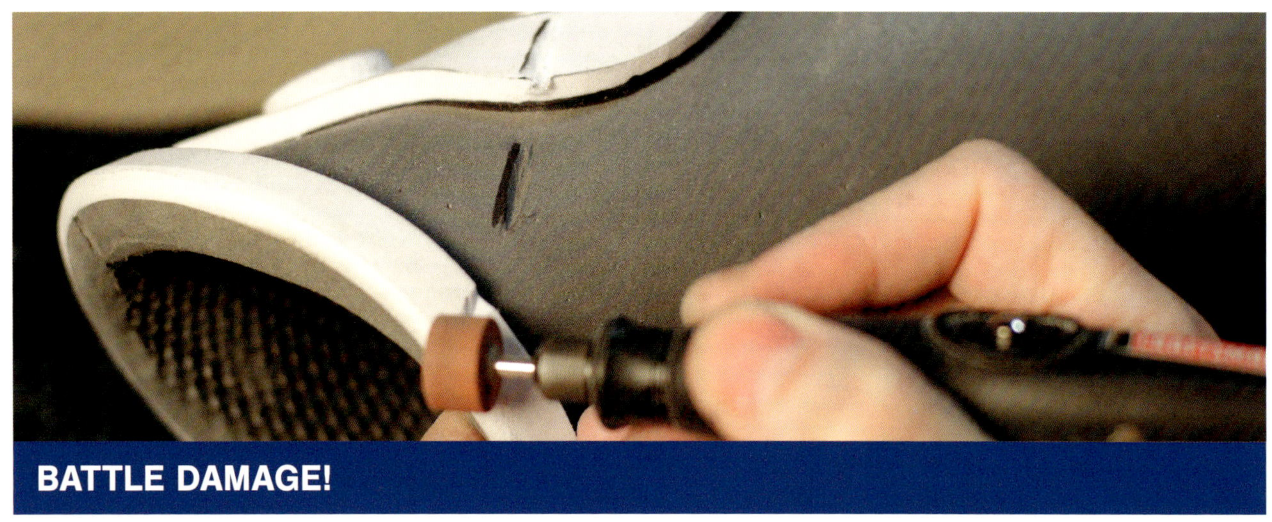

BATTLE DAMAGE!

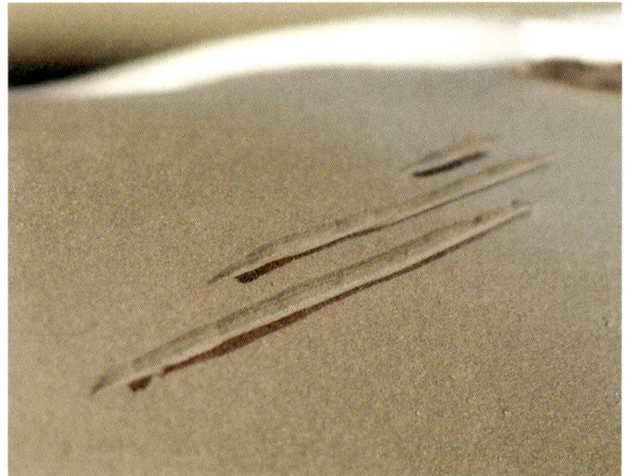

To get realistic looking dents and gouges, you'll actually have to remove foam material. For this, your rotary tool is your best friend. Using sanding and grinding bits of various sizes, as well as a steady, practiced hand, can yield some really nice looking battle damage effects. Practice these types of techniques on scrap foam a whole lot until you're happy with the results. Trying to replicate a haphazard damage effect on purpose isn't an easy task. Be patient and deliberate, always considering how this type of damage would have been caused in the real world.

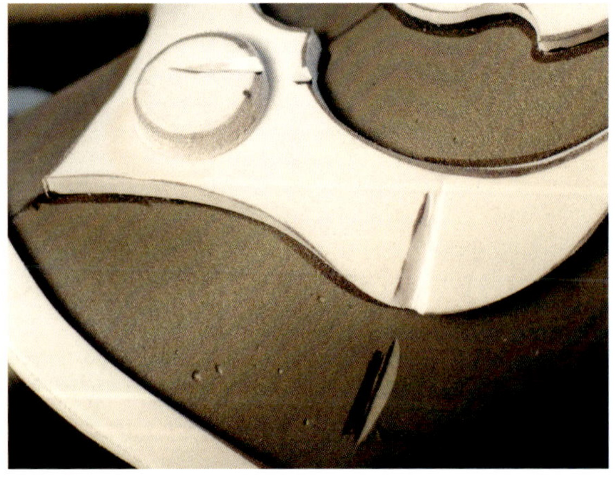

If you'd like to go totally bonkers, I've heard tale of crafters dragging their pieces behind their car on a gravel driveway to get that ultra realistic "been through hell" look. If you're looking for something fun to do on a weekend, give it a go! I assume no responsibility if you end up accidentally running over your armor.

Bone, Wood, and Scales. Oh My.

Most of the techniques discussed so far are for smoother, more manufactured armor pieces. What if your armor is supposed to be made from some kind of natural plant or animal part? How about bone and wood? You better believe we can do that with foam!

The most important thing you can do to achieve these types of textures is to study lots of reference material. Even better? Get your hands on the real thing. Fresh out of dragon scales? Study things like snapping turtle shells. Running low on skeleton parts? You can actually buy nice, clean animal bones on the internet!

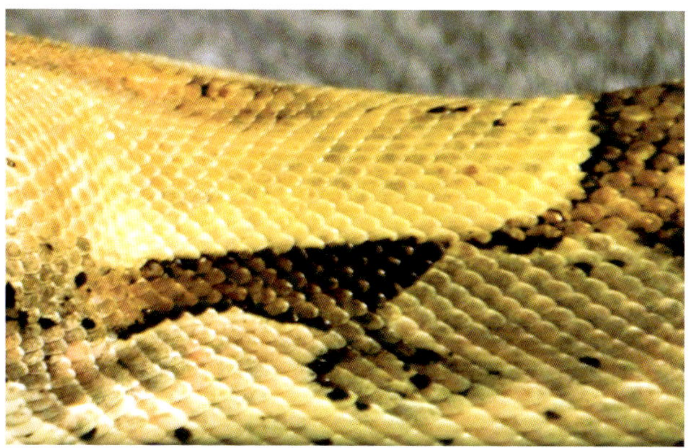

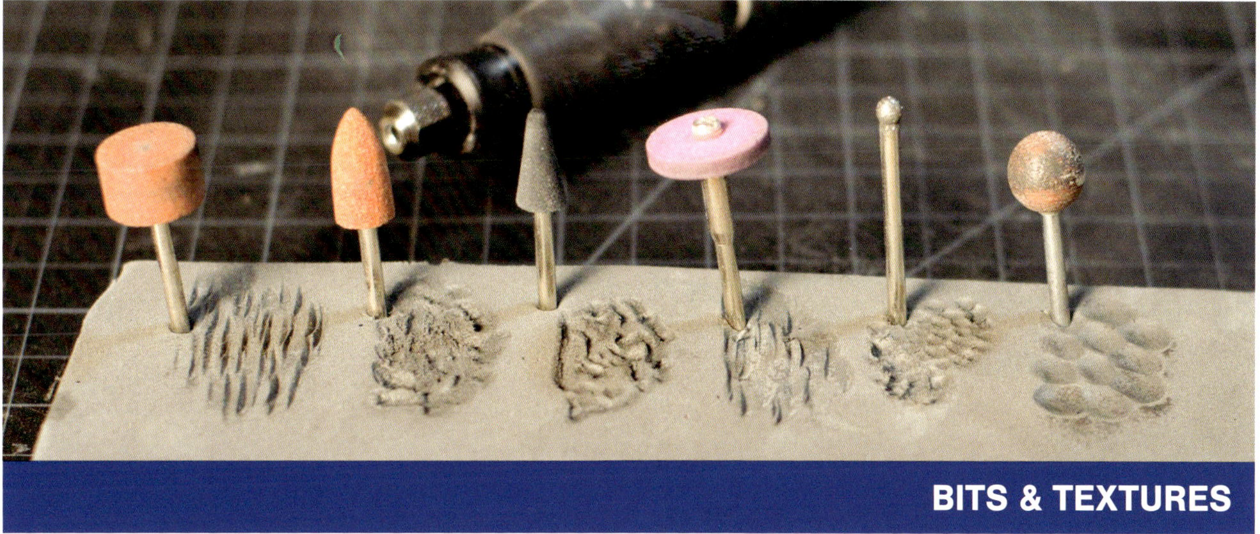

BITS & TEXTURES

There isn't going to be one perfect tool or technique to make something look exactly like the piece of wood you're trying to emulate. You're going to have to do a lot of experimenting to get in just right. Try playing with every bit your rotary tool came with to see what effect they achieve in your foam. This will likely kick up a lot of foam dust, so be sure to wear your respirator!

Get friendly with your hot knife and use it in conjunction with your rotary tool. Yes it's melting the foam. This will land you a very different surface texture than a sanding or grinding bit. It's up to you to decide if this texture works for your desired outcome.

That all being said, here are some things you can do with a rotary tool and various bits to get some neat textures.

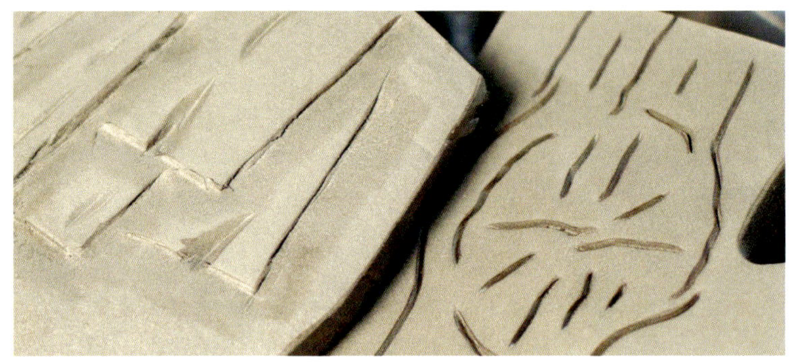

Use a small spherical bit to achieve a pitted look. This is great for armor that's meant to look like old, deteriorated bone. Use bits of various sizes and at various depths to add a nice, natural texture.

A larger spherical bit can be used to create a really nice looking hammered look. While not a "natural" type of texture, it's super fantastic if you want to recreate hammered metal armor.

Use the side and corner of a cylindrical grinding bit to cut long, tapered grooves into your armor bits. This can be useful for making things like dragon scales.

Combine these techniques with adding more layers of foam. You're essentially sculpting the foam, which can be both additive and subtractive. Sanding away parts of foam can blend one layer of foam into another, making them look like they came from the same piece of bone or wood!

Bear in mind that when you rip up the surface of your foam, the texture will change drastically when you hit it with a heat gun. This is a great technique for cleaning up your work.

Also experiment with adding this type of texture both before and after you've heat formed and assembled your armor pieces. It will depend very much on the size and shape of your design, so there is no hard and fast rule as to when you should add your textures.

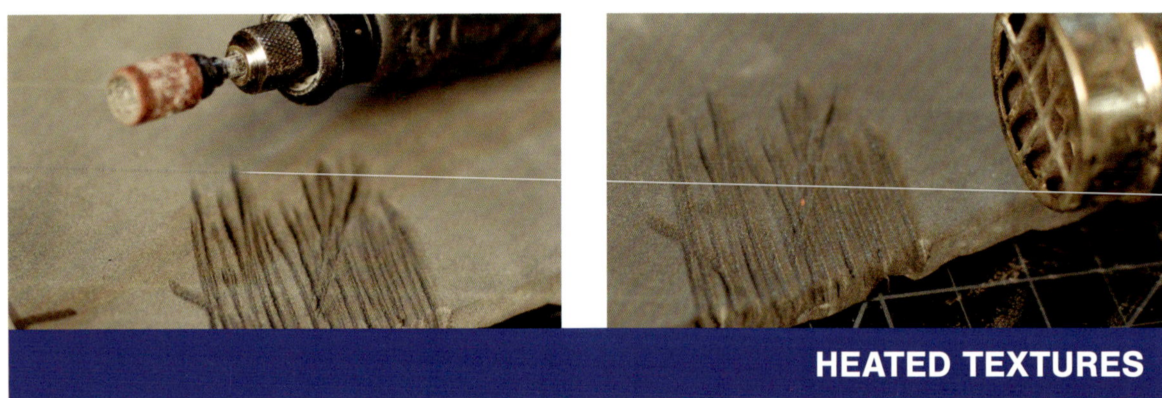

HEATED TEXTURES

Dragon Scales? Dragon Scales.

Or snake, alien, or basilisk scales. If you want to make overlapping creature scales, you've come to the right place! You will be adding them individually, which can be rather tedious, but the effect is worth the effort!

First decide how thick you want your scales to be. Generally, smaller scales will be thinner and can be cut from 2mm craft foam. If you're making just a few, large scales, you can go whole hog and make them from the thicker floor mats.

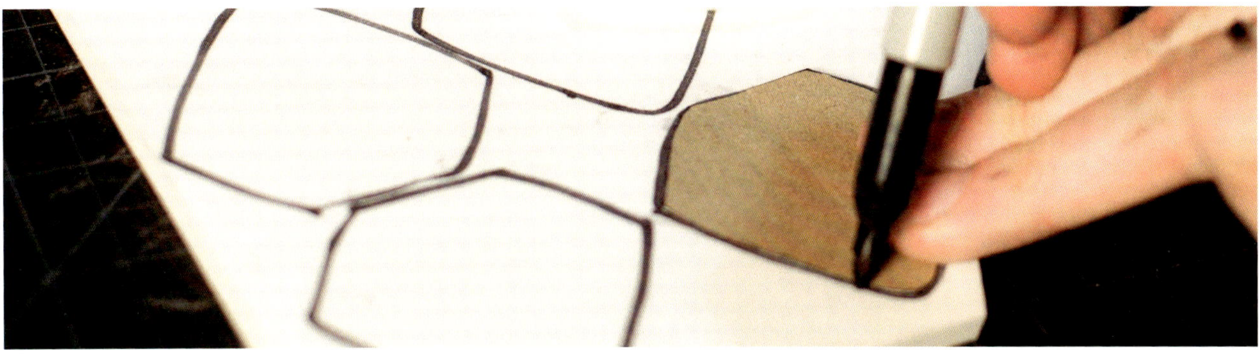

If the scales are all the same size and shape, make a sturdy template from masking paper or card stock. You'll be happy you did if you end up needing to make hundreds of them. Or you may consider making several templates that are all just slightly different. That way you can add a little bit of variety in the final texture. Then start tracing and cutting out your scales. Keep that blade nice and sharp and cut out more than you think you'll need. It doesn't hurt to have extra foam scales lying around your shop!

If you want to add any kind of texture to the scales, I would suggest you do so before assembling all of them onto your base armor form. Tedious? You bet it is. Looks fantastic? Heck yeah!

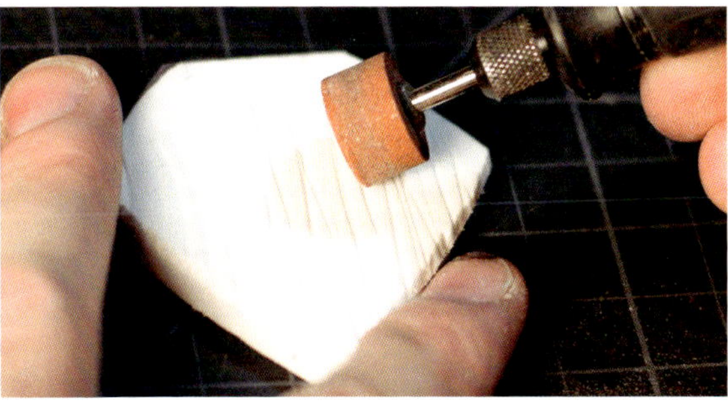

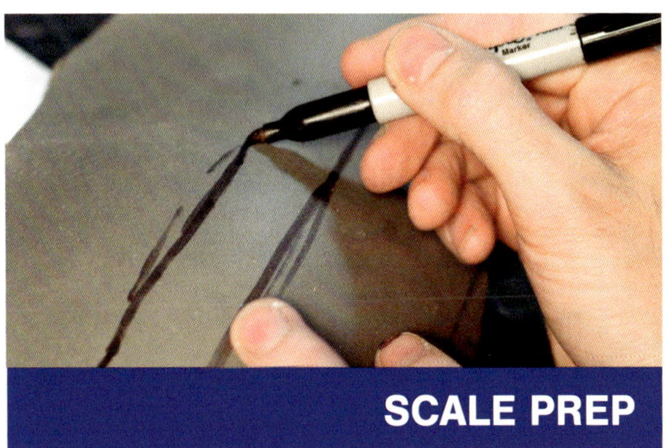

SCALE PREP

Before you start sticking the scales together on your armor, plan out where they're all going to go. Then draw horizontal lines along the base form. This is where you will be lining up the top edge of each scale. Also bear in mind that this top edge will will be overlapped by the scales above it. Make sure the lines are close enough together so that you won't see any gaps between each layer of scales.

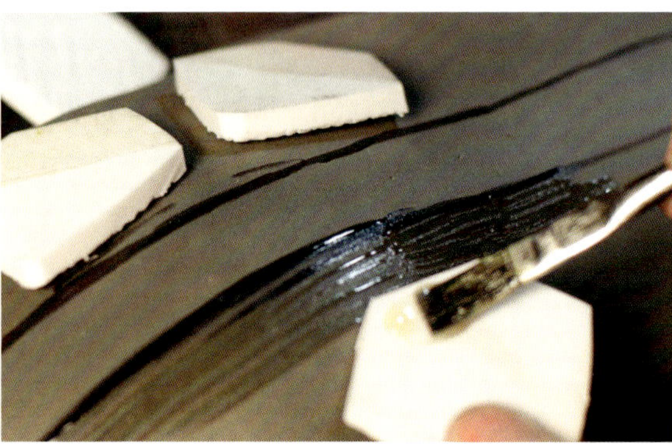

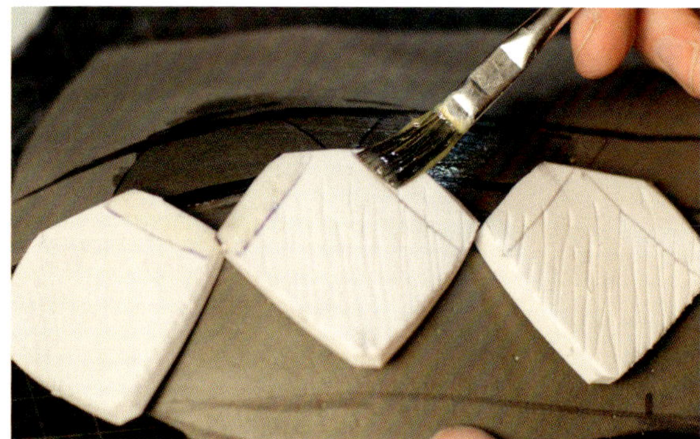

When you've got your roadmap o' scales all laid out, grab your contact adhesive. Starting with the bottom layer of scales, brush the glue below the first line along its entire length. Then brush a little bit of adhesive onto the backs of a whole bunch of scales. Give the cement a good ten minutes to set up and then start sticking on your scales. You can just press them right along the line you made, piece of cake!

The next layer is done exactly the same way, except that you'll be going over the layer below that you just finished. Stagger your scales so that the points from your current layer are between the gaps in the scales below.

This is the most basic form of overlapping scales, so feel free to experiment with the look you're trying to achieve. Also study real animals that have scales to see how they move, especially around their moving joints.

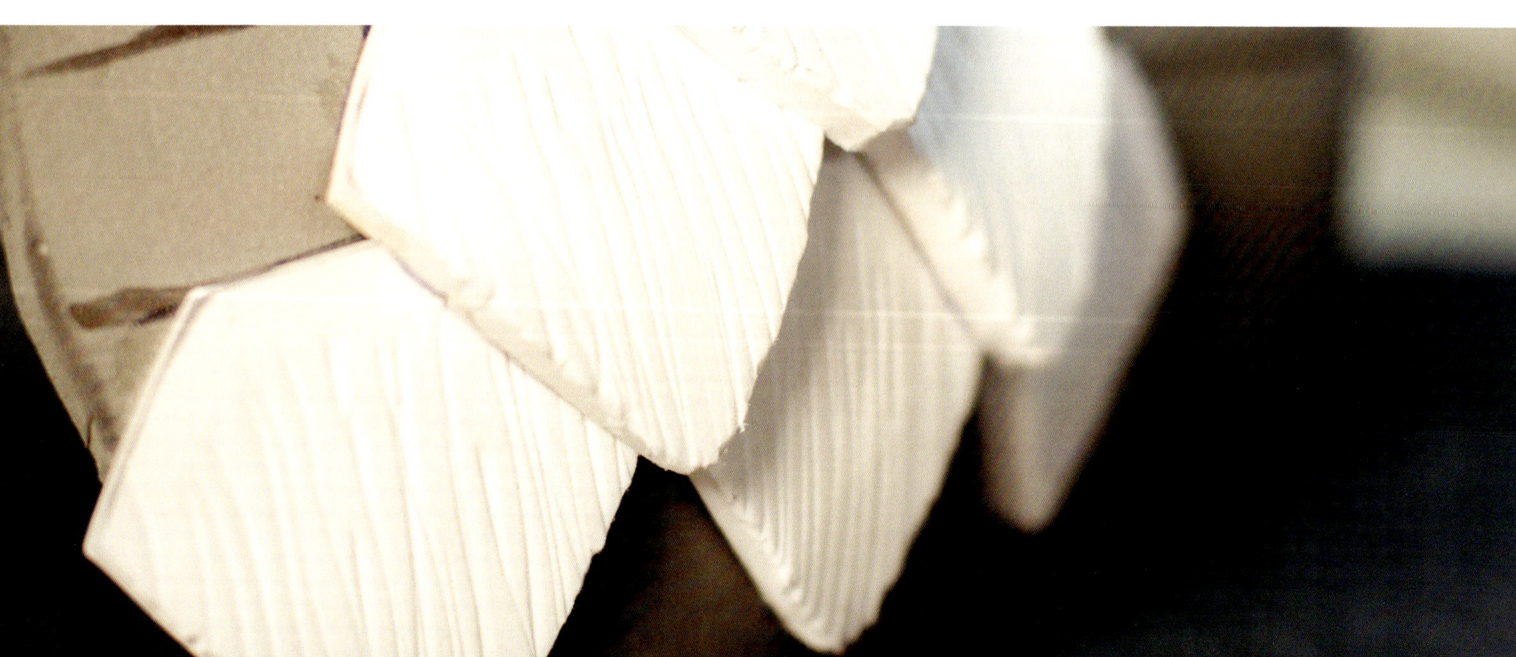

We can do segmented armor too!

Lobstered, segmented armor was a super popular type of real plate armor in human history. So, it's no surprise that it's made its way into so many fictional armor sets.

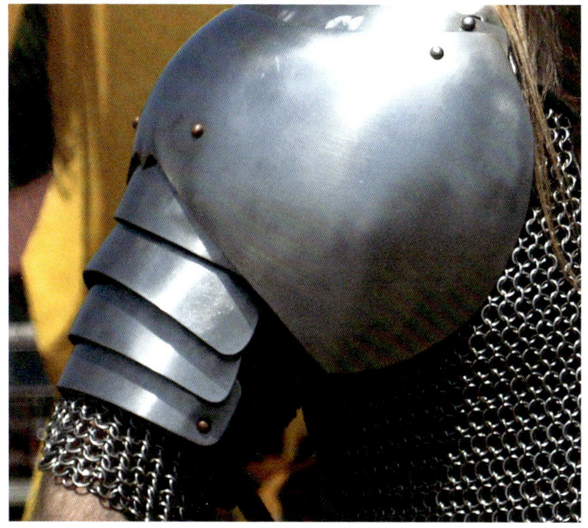

The same effect can be achieved with foam using various methods, including techniques that are very similar to the way real armor is made. The most important factor is going to be your planning and templates before you start attaching segments together. You'll be dealing with moving parts that can easily restrict your range of motion if done improperly, so some experimentation will be necessary to get it right.

Also consider that not every segment will need to move. Sometimes you'll just need some pieces to look like they're mobile segmented parts. In cases like this, just make sure you have plenty of foam to overlap the two segments and contact cement them together.

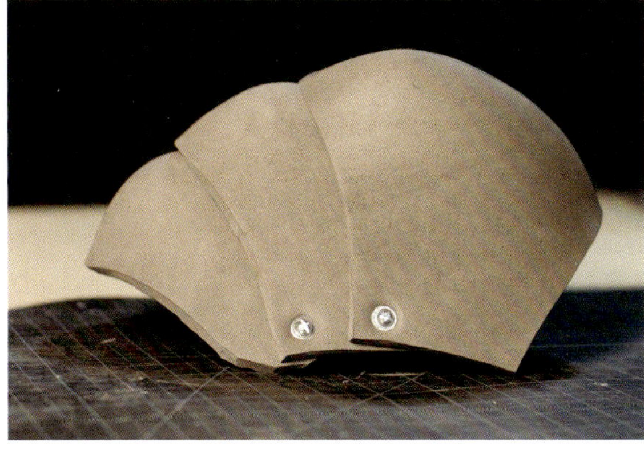

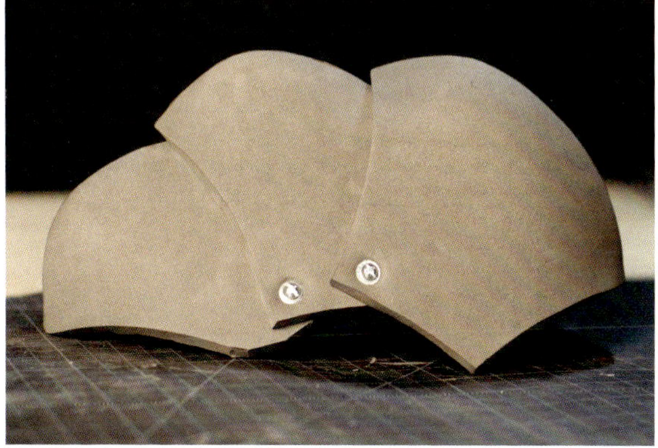

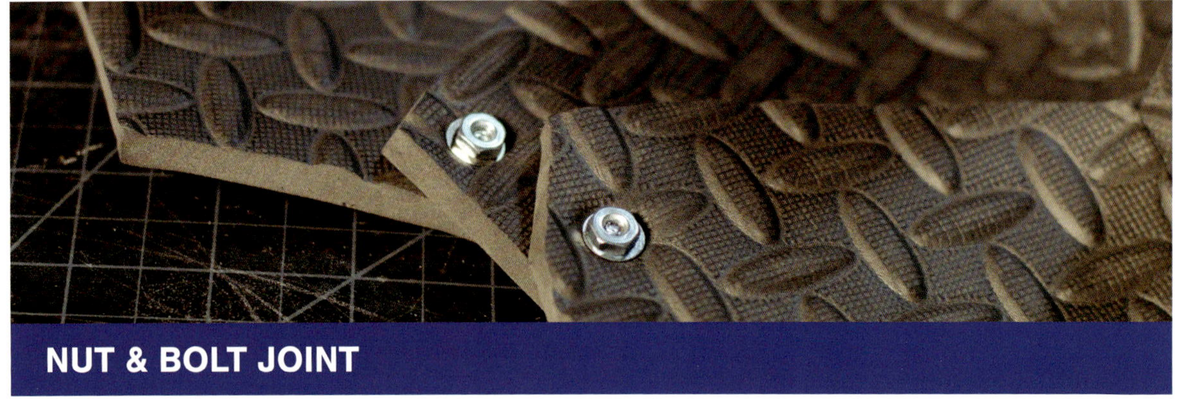

NUT & BOLT JOINT

Real segmented armor pieces are usually held together at riveted pivot points. This gives each segment a single axis to rotate around. This same mechanic can be achieved with foam using a number of fasteners. Placement of your pivot holes is pretty key, so be sure to study where real armorers put their pivots on each segment. You can punch these pivot holes using a small, sharpened tube (as discussed earlier), or drill them out with a dremel or power drill.

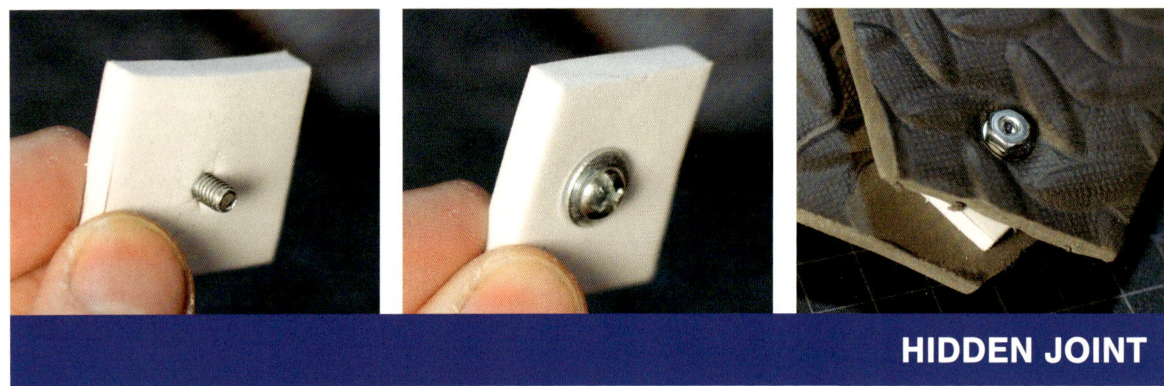

HIDDEN JOINT

Types of fasteners:

The good old fashioned nut, bolt, washer combo isn't very elegant, but it'll get the job done. This also a great solution if you have to make it through several layers of thick floor mats.

Chicago screws are really rad for attaching many types of materials, including foam! They can be picked up at many hardware and leatherworking stores. You can even get metal or plastic ones.

Doll joints are also really great, since they are designed to attach two things that rotate. They usually come in a set thickness though, so you may be limited to attaching just two thinner pieces of foam. You can get them at craft stores.

A couple of things to keep in mind. You may need to make your segmented armor from foam that's thinner than the floor mats, especially if you have many smaller segments that will be very close to one another. Fasteners like doll joints are perfect for this. Also, your fasteners don't necessarily need to be visible. You can cover them up with other layers of foam embellishment. Or you could attach one side of the joint to a piece of foam that's attached to the back side of the overlapping armor piece.

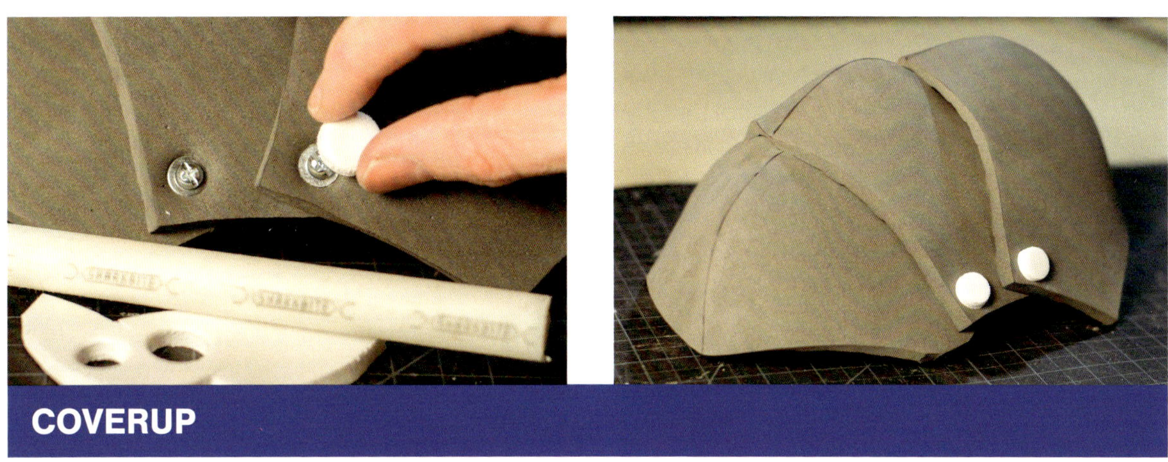

COVERUP

You may not want to use fasteners at all! You could simply attach your segments with elastic straps on the back! This is a really fantastic solution for elbows, since the outside of your sleeve will want to stretch as you flex your arm. This will be discussed in great detail in Part 3.

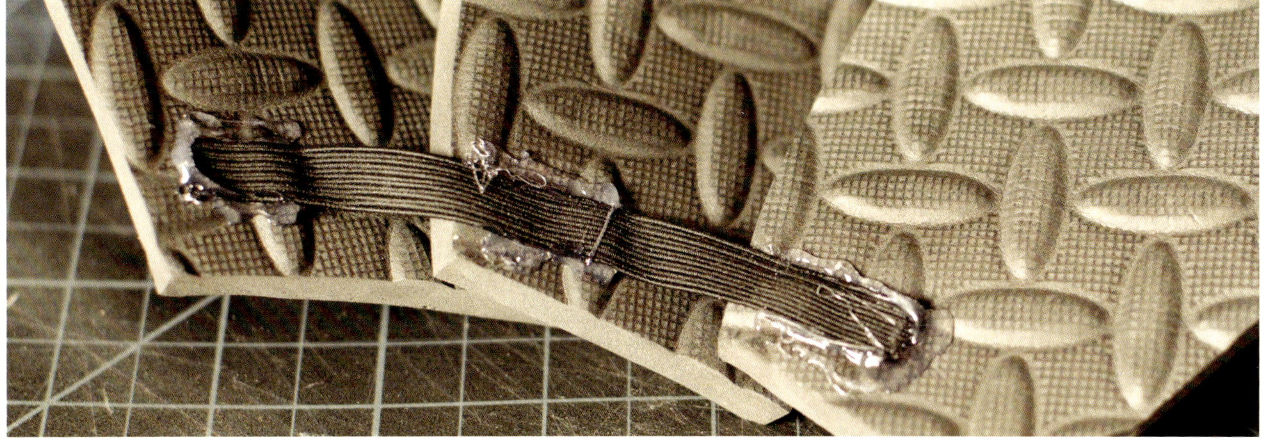

Magnets! Science!

Let's say you need a part of your armor to be able to come completely apart from the rest of it. Perhaps you have a visor that you'd like to be detachable, but would really like for it to stay in place properly while wearing it. Well then you'll want to get your paws on some neodymium magnets! Also known as "rare earth magnets," these little guys are absolutely perfect for temporarily attaching foam pieces together. You can usually find them at hobby stores in various sizes or order them online. I like the cylindrical ones.

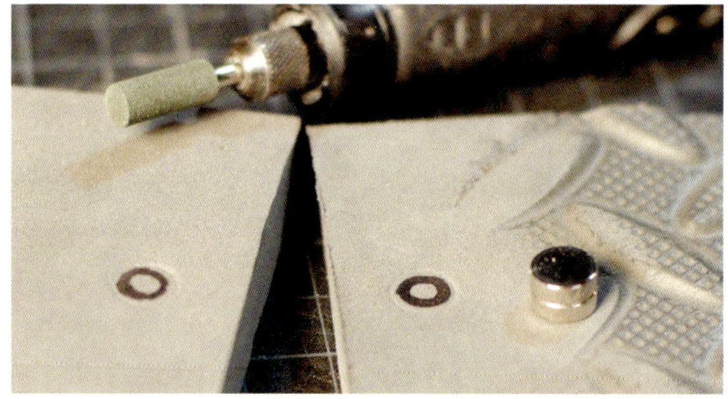

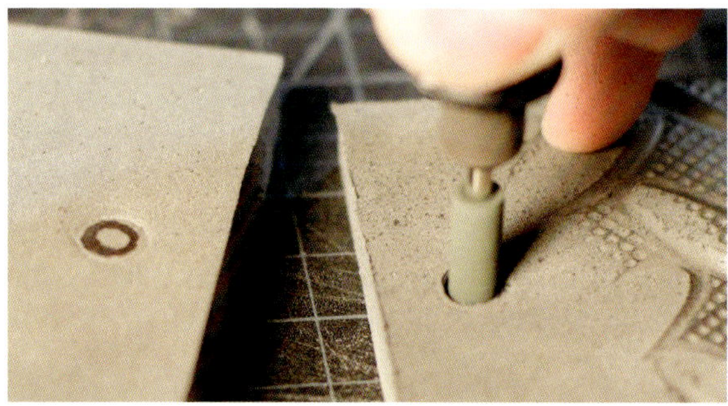

Neodymium magnets, also called "rare earth magnets."

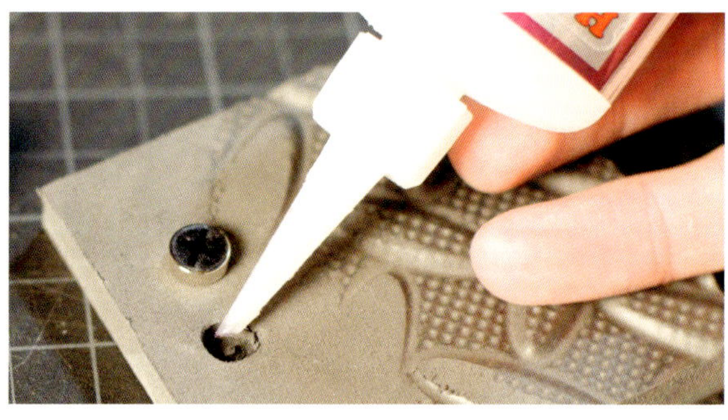

The most important consideration you need to make for the magnets is to confirm they're facing the correct direction. So long as you get that right, your foam pieces will snap together and stay together like magic with just a few small magnets!

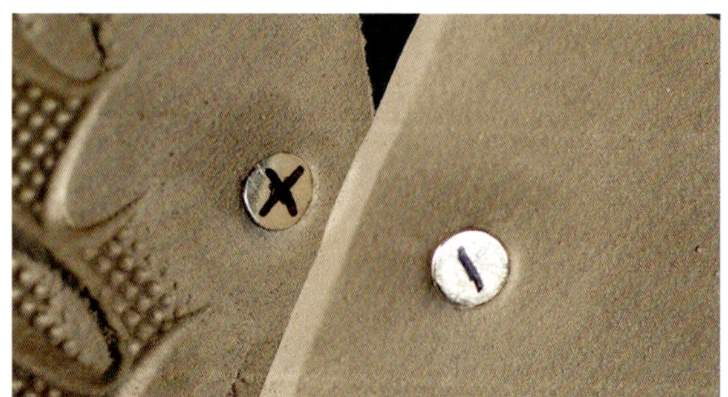

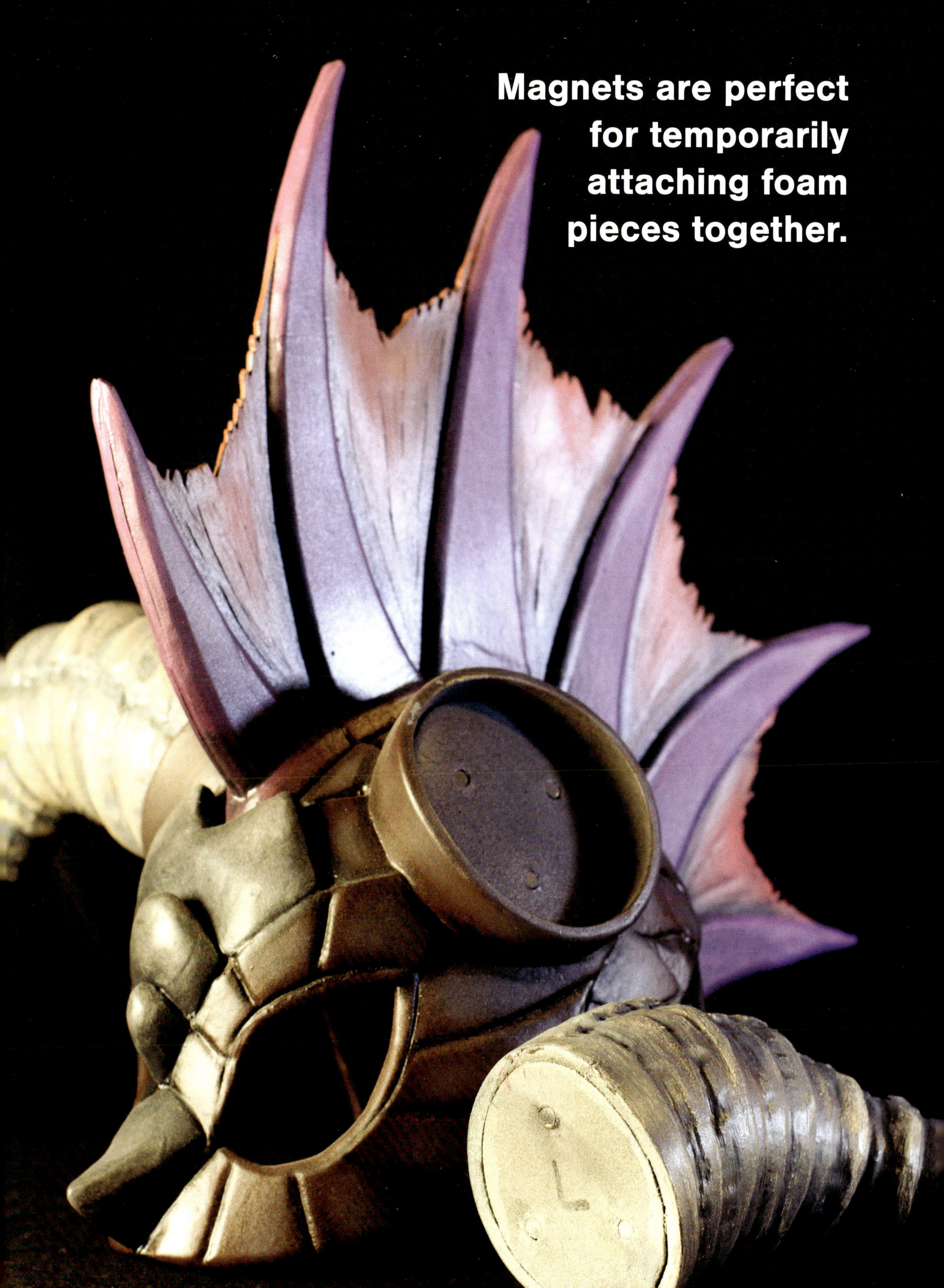

Magnets are perfect for temporarily attaching foam pieces together.

Part 2
Finishing & Painting

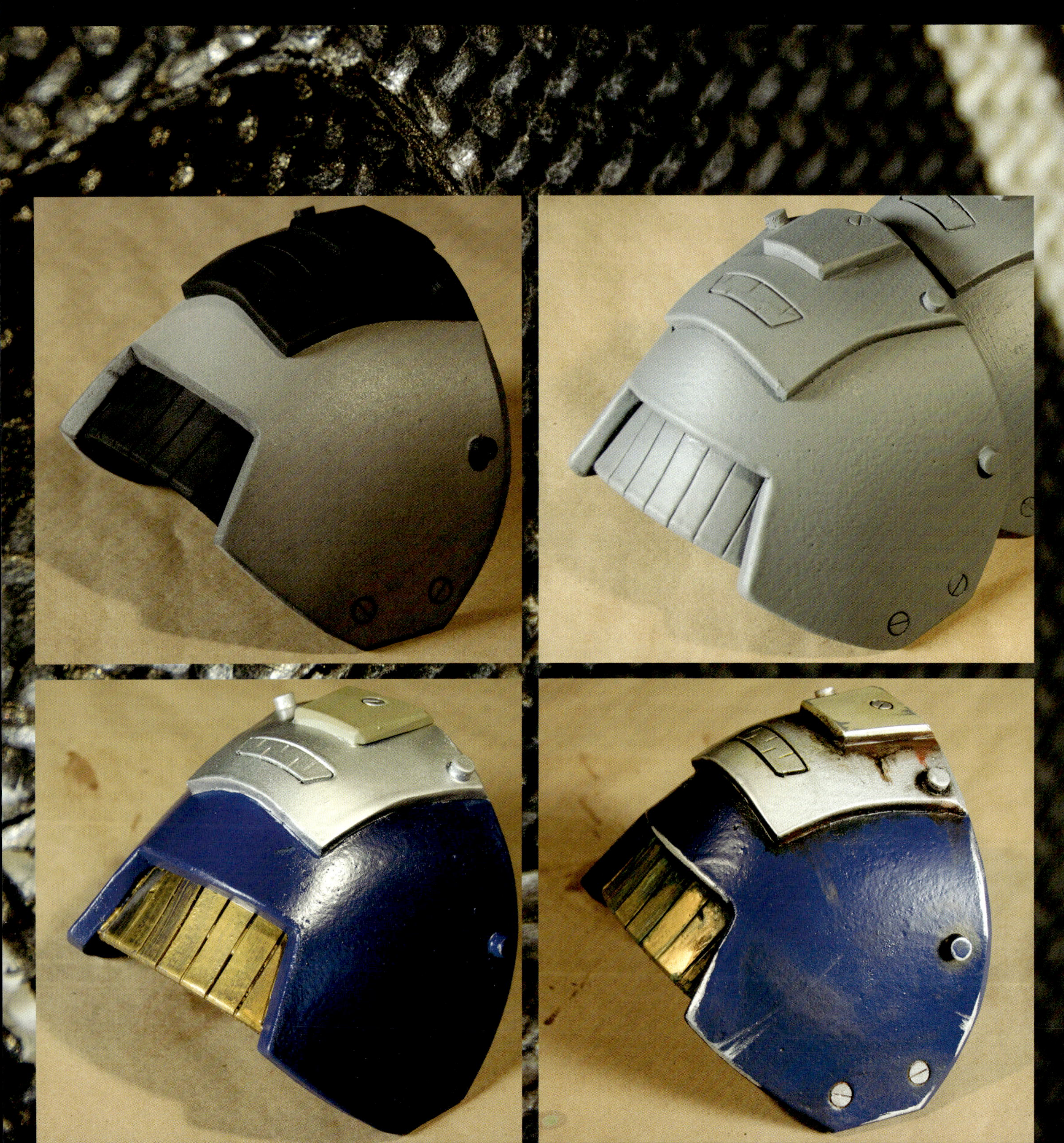

PAINTING SAFETY

Safety is always the foamsmith's number one concern. While you might not be cranking up the power tools for your paint job, you will be using some paints and chemicals that you desperately want to keep out of your lungs. Especially when using spray paints, an airbrush, aerosol sealers, and epoxy resins, work in a well ventilated area or even outside. A respirator is also a no-brainer.

Before you have fun, read the paint instruction and warning labels!

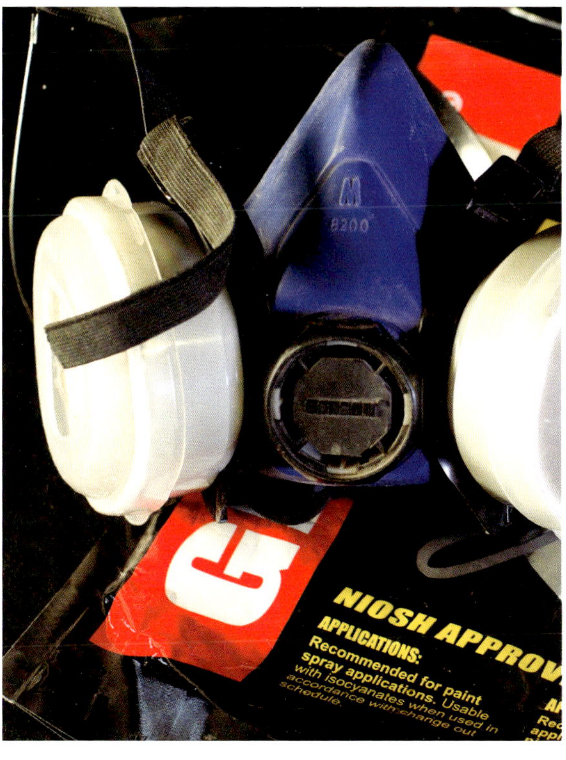

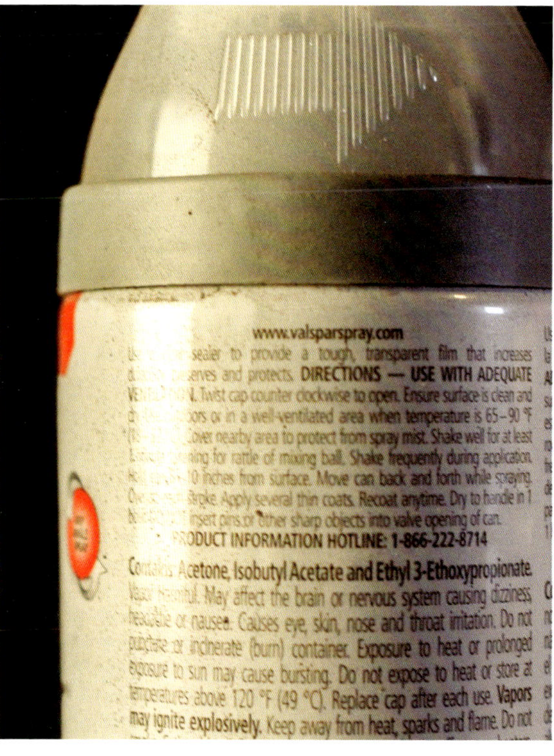

Tools of the Trade

Compared to the fabrication process, painting requires far fewer tools, but there are some that can't be skimped on.

Brushes are pretty necessary, but there's no need to break the bank. I keep a wide range of them on hand as well as a whole bunch of cheap, single use brushes for applying epoxies and other resins.

Masking tape is mandatory too. There are a lot of options available, but the blue painter's tape from the hardware store will get you most of the way there. Everyone has their favorite brand, so try a couple out and use whichever one works best for you.

An airbrush isn't 100% necessary, but I have one and I couldn't imagine my life without it. You'll also need a compressor, so if you're new to it, pick up a kit that includes everything you need to get started. Once you get good with the airbrush, start to consider upgrading to a really nice one.

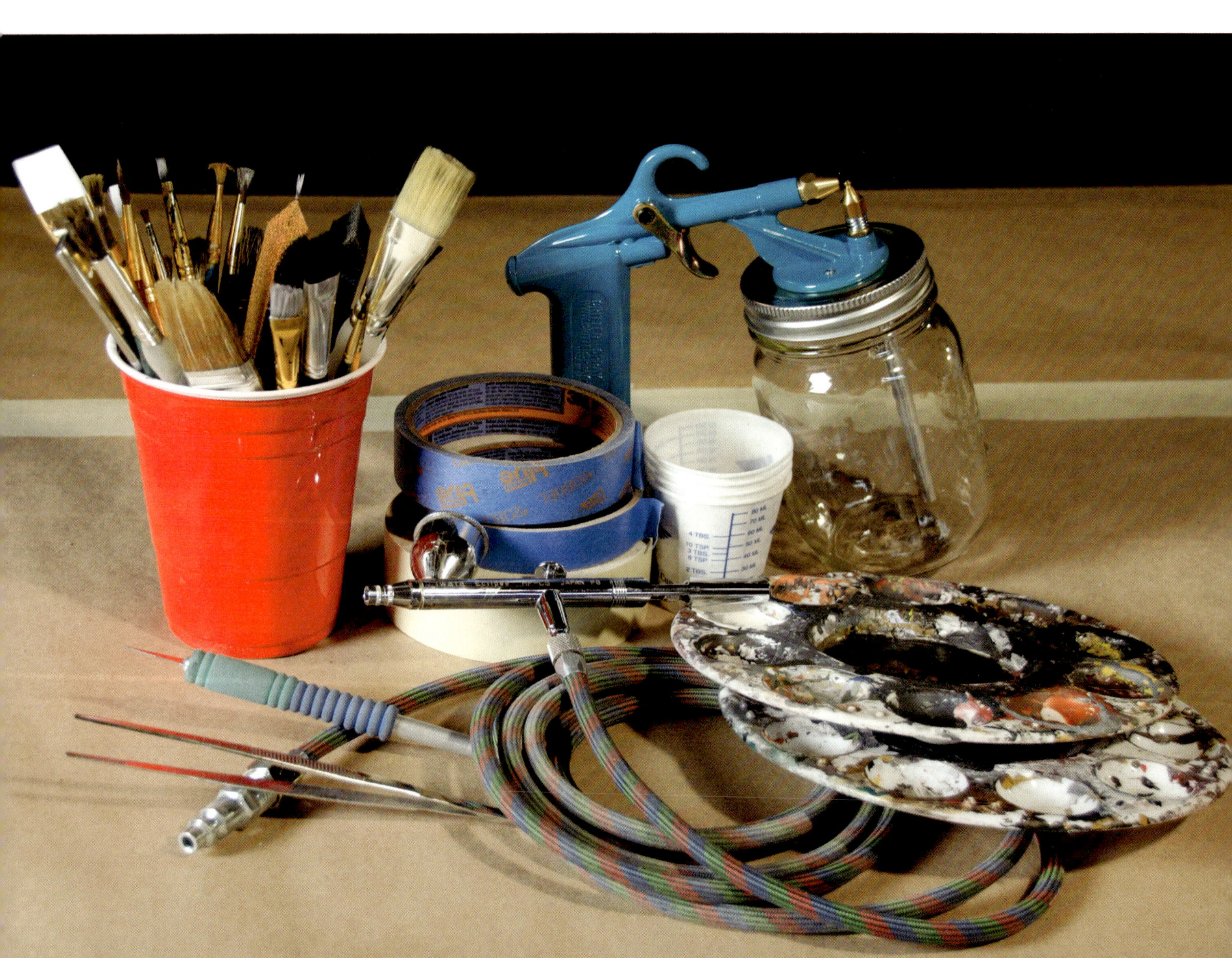

If you've got that compressor, you may also want to get a bigger spray gun, like the Critter. This is great for applying latex to seal your foam, if you're into that kind of thing.

Single use mixing cups are super handy, especially if you end up using epoxy sealers. I would advise against cheap party cups; epoxy likes to eat that type of plastic. I get my mixing cups from a local plastics store called Tap Plastics.

Paint pallets are kind of a no-brainer for mixing custom colors. They are available from any store that sells art supplies for a couple bucks. It's worth picking up a few of them.

A good X-Acto knife is really handy for trimming your masking tape. Also consider getting a pair of tweezers for pulling up the masking tape once you've painted over it.

Read the paint warning labels. Some paints are safe for your skin, but not all of them. Wear gloves to avoid paint-covered hands.

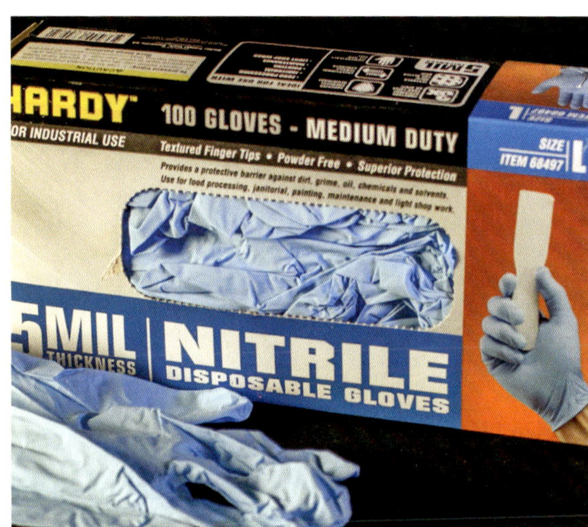

You've got all your supplies and your armor is all built, let's start slinging paint! WOOO! Not so fast, foamsmith! Have you considered sealing your foam? Well, you should.

To Seal or Not to Seal

You've built your super rad foam armor and it's looking really great! Of course you're going to want to jump right in and start painting some color on it right away so that it'll look all nice and finished. Before you go bonkers with a rattle can, consider if you want to do something to seal the foam. Why might you want to do that?

- Even the "flat" side of foam floor mats has a texture that you may find undesirable.
- Sealing foam will make it more durable.
- Different types of sealing methods can provide a better base for your paint for a more long lasting finish.

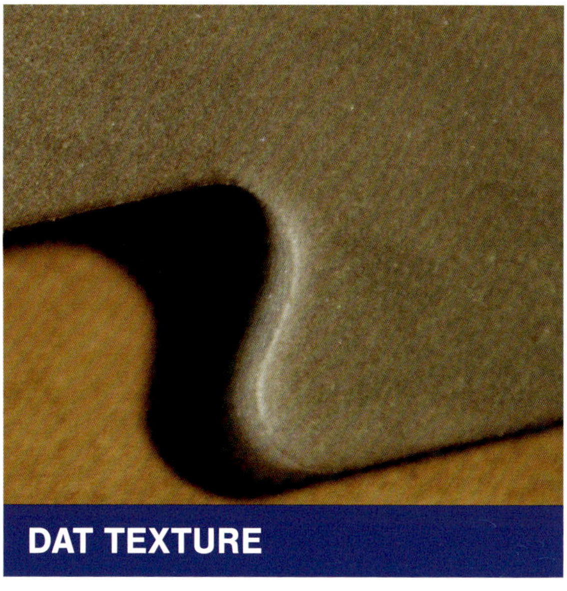

DAT TEXTURE

If none of these things concern you, go ahead and just start throwing paint right down on the raw foam. I did exactly that for my Mass Effect armor. Sure, the paint wore off in some spots, but I was OK with the gray or black foam color coming through. It actually made the armor look more weathered and world worn. As a general rule though, if you want your armor to look nice, new and pristine, you're going to want to seal it.

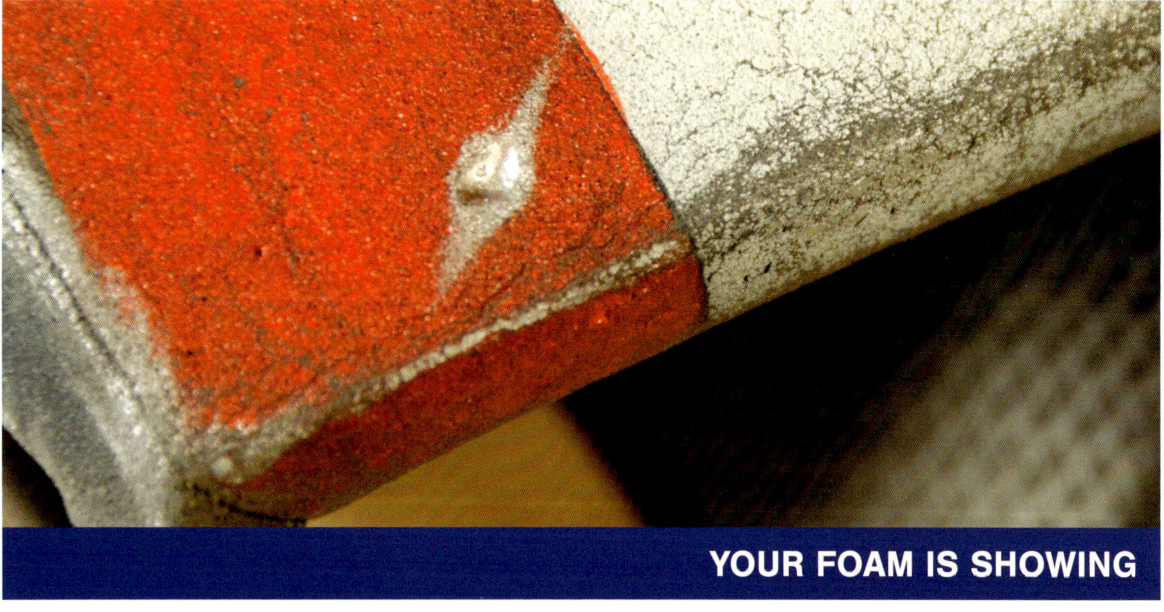

YOUR FOAM IS SHOWING

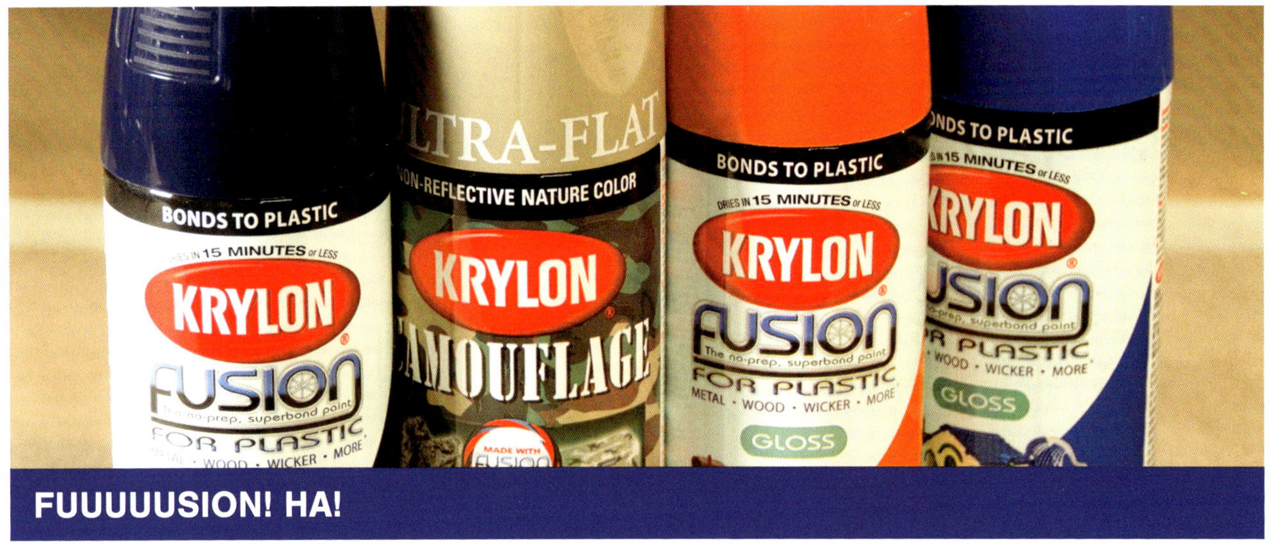

FUUUUUSION! HA!

Also, you may have thought ahead and made all of your armor from floor mats that are already the texture and base color you wanted for your armor! If so, you're way smarter than I am and I congratulate you on your foresight. Most of your base coloring is already done and you can skip ahead considerably.

I also really like Krylon Fusion spray paints for foam. They dry quickly and adhere very well to EVA foam. I will sometimes use these types of paints by themselves for an entire, unsealed foam build, especially if I'm short on time.

This prop gun was made entirely from EVA foam. I didn't seal it at all. Instead, I painted it entirely with Krylon Fusion. It dries fast and binds really well to the foam.

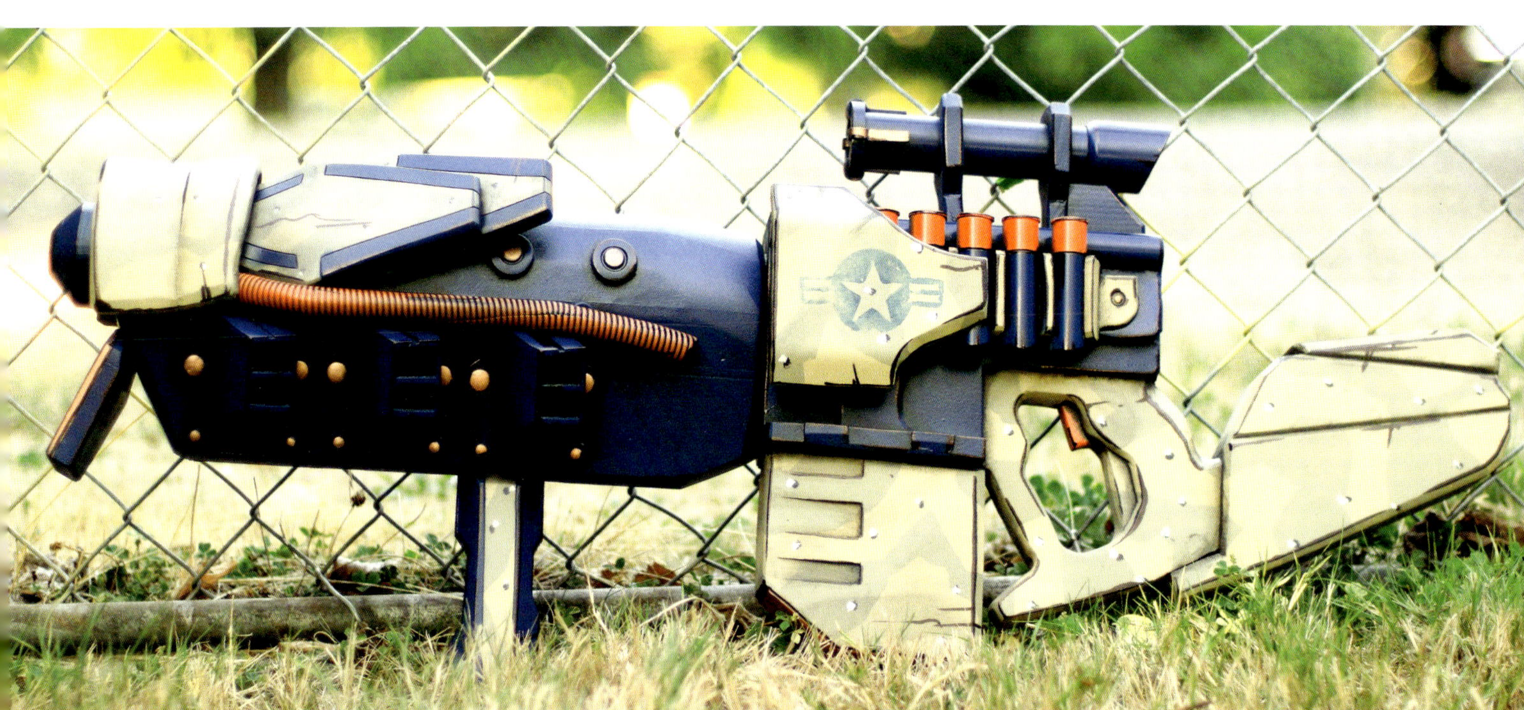

Sealing Your Foam Armor

Here are several methods for sealing your armor before painting it. As with most techniques, test these out on some scrap pieces before applying to the armor you've just spent a significant portion of your life building.

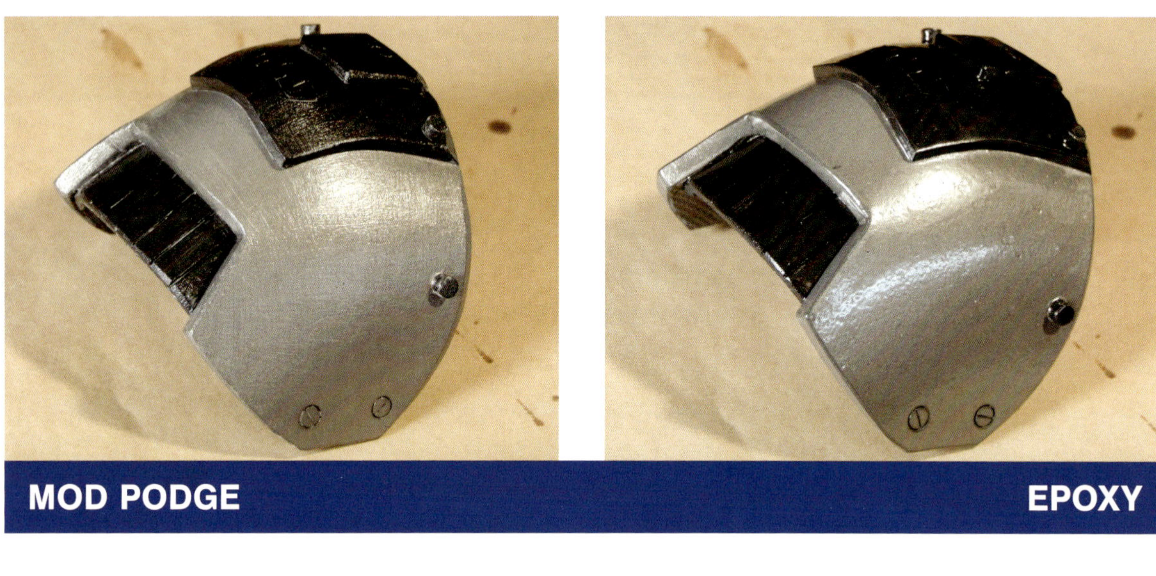

MOD PODGE

EPOXY

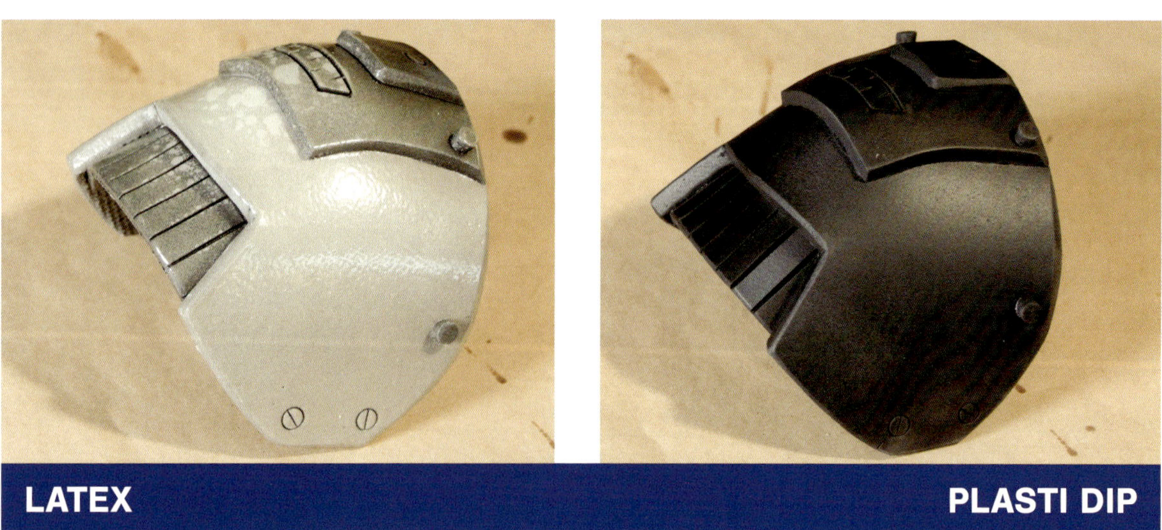

LATEX

PLASTI DIP

Preparing the Foam

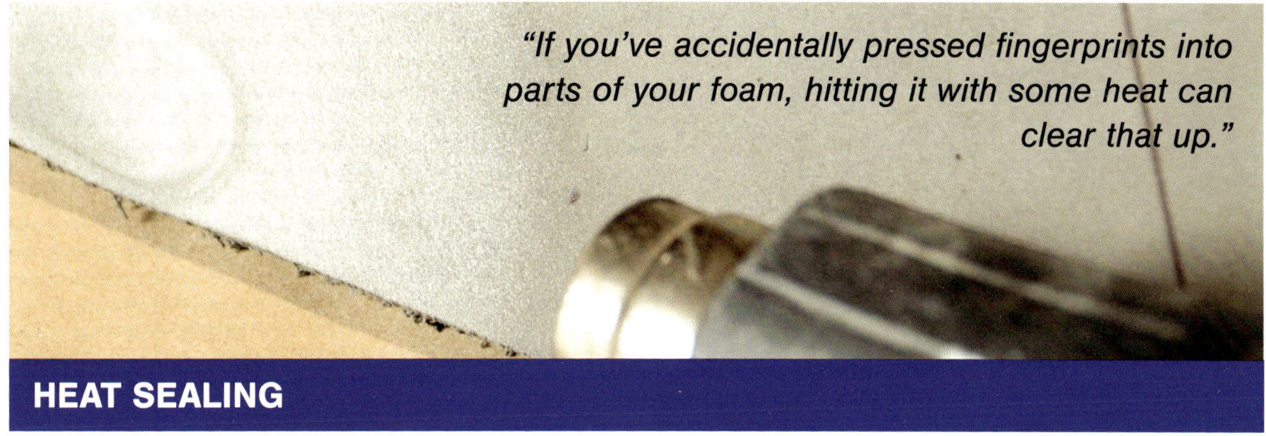

HEAT SEALING

If you've done any heat forming on your armor, chances are it's already been heat sealed. It's worth going over all of your armor with a heat gun anyway. It'll smooth up the texture a bit and help your foam take paint and other sealants better. Also, if you've accidentally pressed fingerprints into parts of your foam, hitting it with some heat can clear that up.

For sealing and painting, I like to hang up my armor pieces. Get your hands on some cheap, small clamps from the hardware store and feed a wire through one part of the handle so you can hang the clamp from a rack. Then, take a small scrap of foam and temporarily glue it to the back of your armor piece. This should be in an area that isn't getting finished. You'll rip this scrap piece off later. Now you can clamp on to the extra nub and hang your armor piece up for spray painting like a boss!

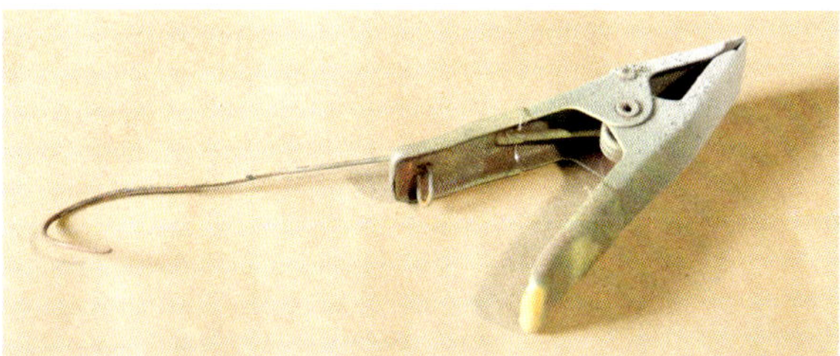

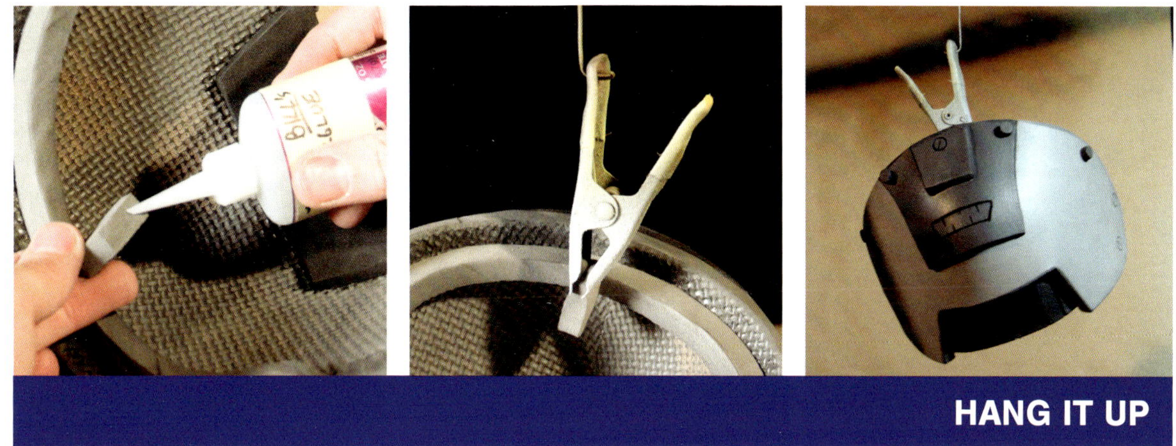

HANG IT UP

Plasti Dip

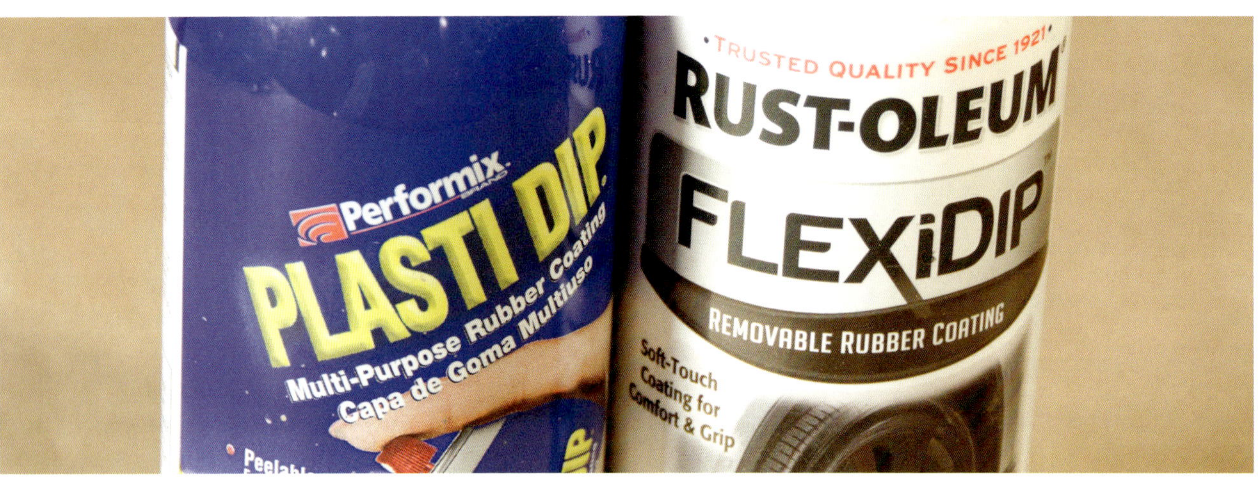

Originally, Plasti Dip was invented for adding rubberized grips to tools, but it turns out it's pretty good for sealing foam too. Many people prefer how easy it is to apply. You can find Plasti Dip at most hardware stores now. It comes in a rattle can in various colors. For just sealing something, I would go with a black finish compared to something like a bright orange. That way, if your paint chips, it will be much less noticeable.

You do NOT want to breathe this stuff in. If you can, spray it outside. Never forget to wear your respirator.

Apply the spray plastic in nice, even coats according to the directions on the can. Foam really likes to drink up Plasti Dip. You'll probably have to put a good three to six layers on to really get good coverage. Also don't spray a layer so thick that it starts to pool. Patience is a virtue.

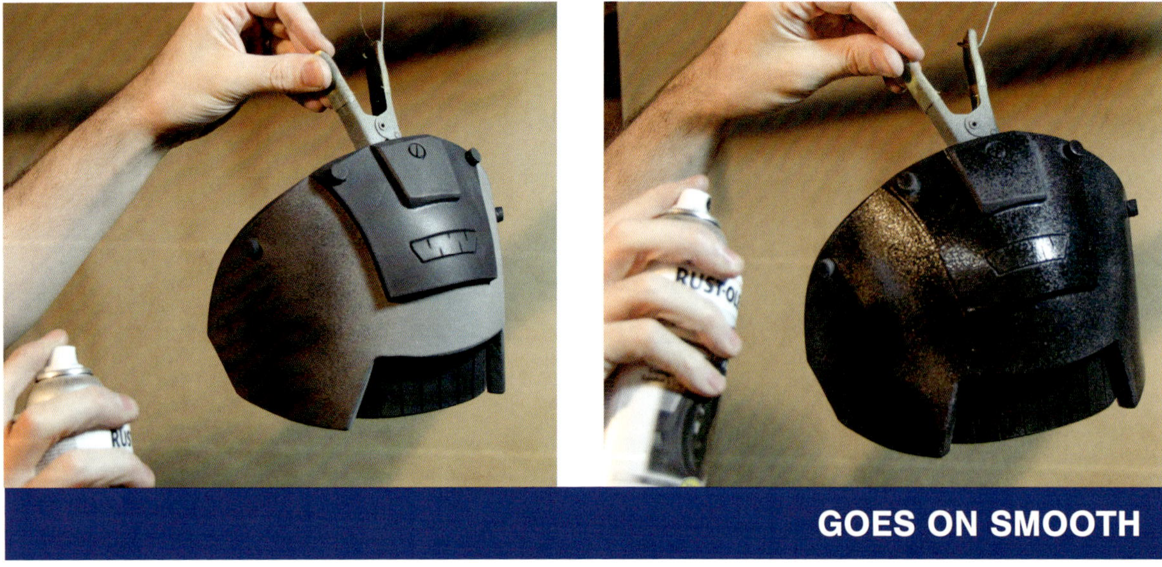

GOES ON SMOOTH

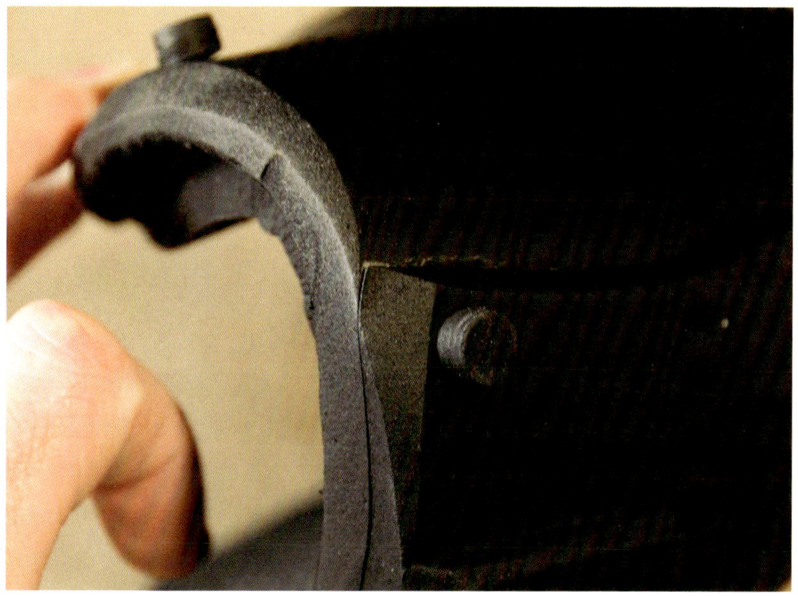

One nice thing about Plasti Dip is that it is pretty flexible. So long as your finish is equally flexible, you shouldn't end up with many cracks after wearing your armor for a while.

You can now get Plasti Dip in a wide range of colors, including clear and metallic varieties. This is amazing for both sealing your foam armor and putting down a metallic base coat of color.

Seal your Plasti Dip paints with clear Plasti Dip. It would be a shame to have a flexible coat crack due to a rigid clear coat.

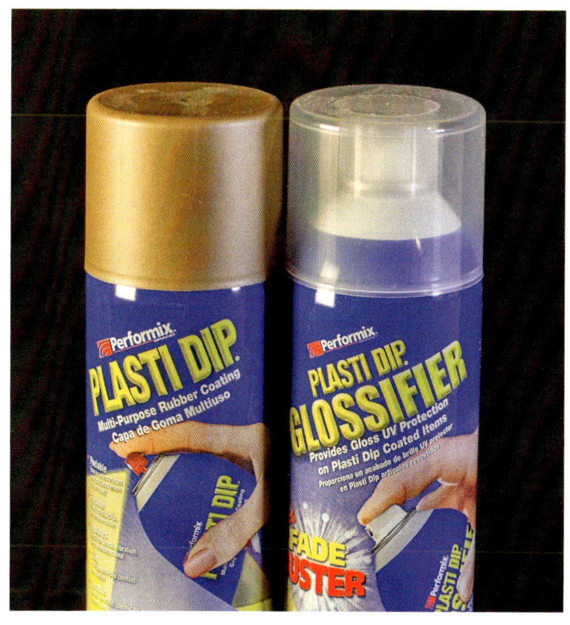

PVA GLUE/MOD PODGE/ELMER'S

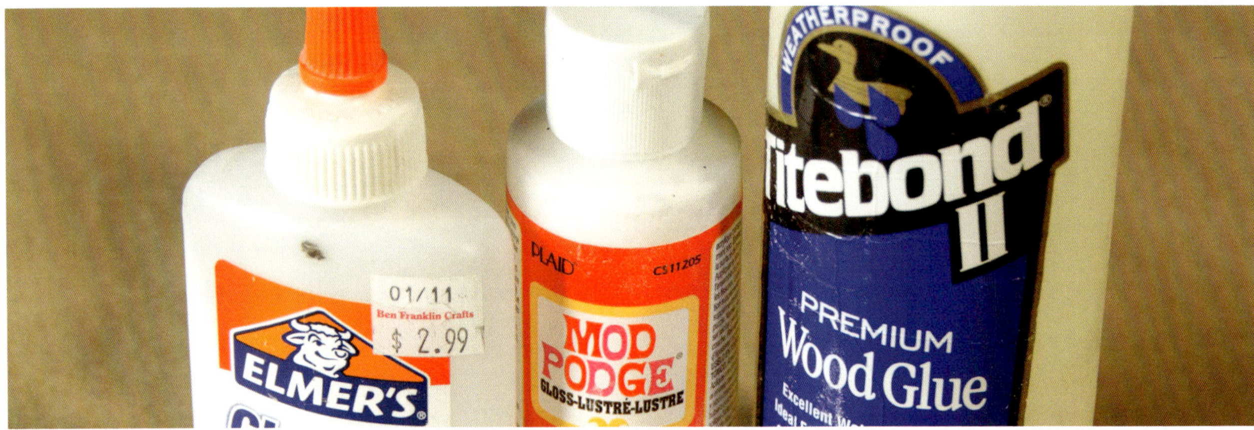

Another favorite finish is Mod Podge (or a number of other PVA glues). You can get it at most craft stores. It's a milky white goo with a fairly thick consistency. You'll need to brush it on, so be sure to pick up some cheap sponge brushes. Application couldn't be more straight forward. Simply brush your layers on in nice, consistent coats. I've found that three to five layers usually does the trick, depending on what finish you're going for. Be wary of low spots where the Mod Podge may pool. You could quickly fill in fine details that you worked so hard to achieve. Also, places where it pools will take longer to dry, so spread it out.

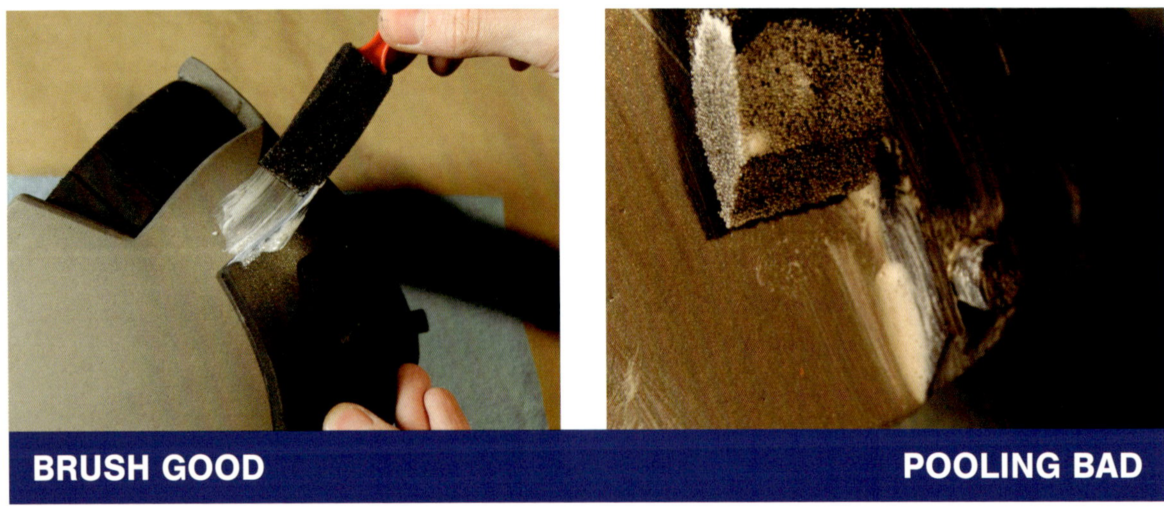

BRUSH GOOD **POOLING BAD**

Keep an eye on brush strokes. Since this stuff needs to be brushed on, stroke marks may be unavoidable. Consider adding layers in alternating directions to minimize this. This is where using sponge brushes helps a lot. You can also sand down any added brush texture once you've brushed on several layers and let it dry.

The number of layers you brush on is up to you, just be sure to let the previous layer dry before applying the next. I usually go with three to five layers to get a nice shell on my foam.

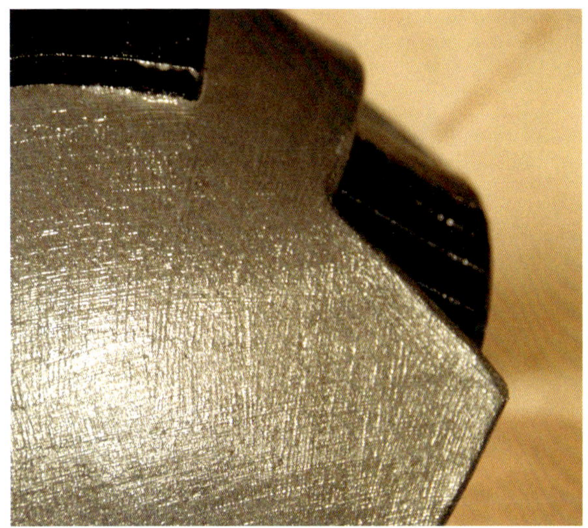

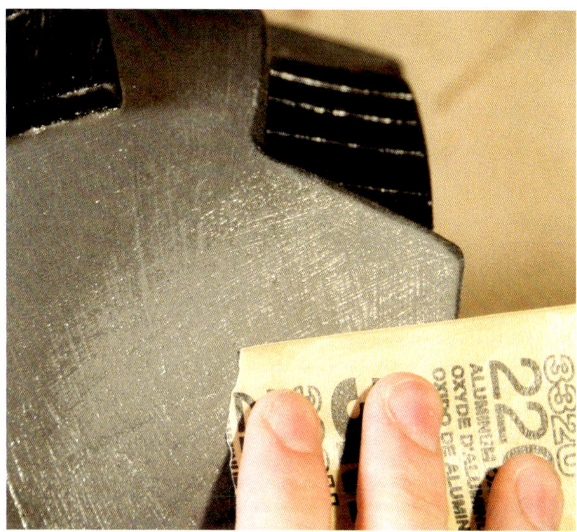

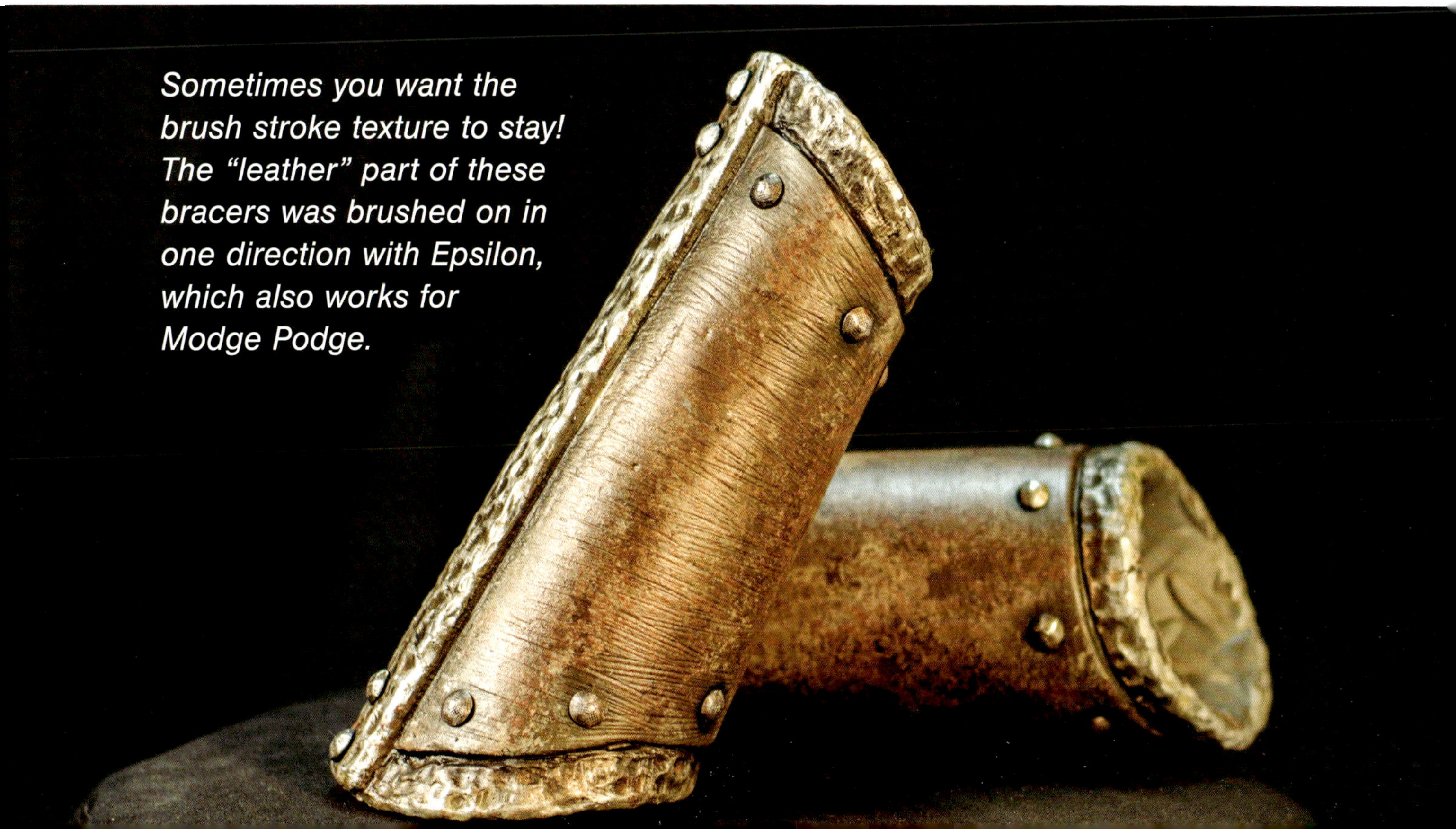

Sometimes you want the brush stroke texture to stay! The "leather" part of these bracers was brushed on in one direction with Epsilon, which also works for Modge Podge.

LATEX RUBBER

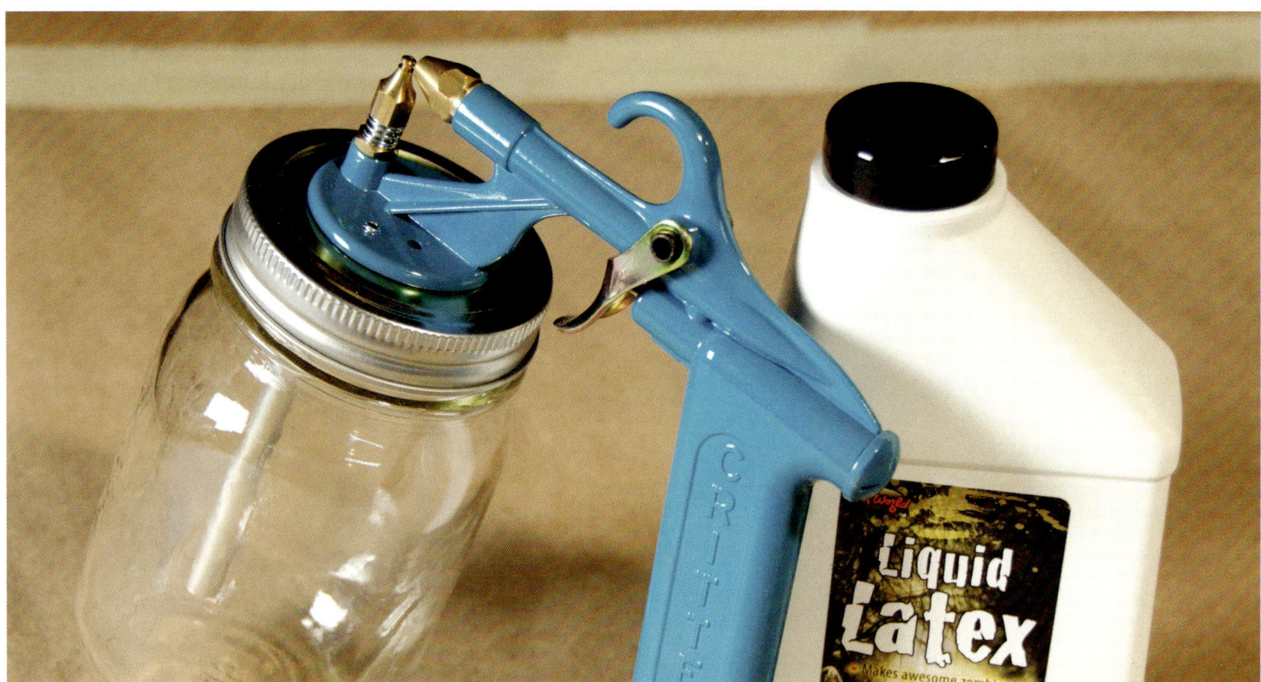

I have my pal Evil Ted Smith to thank for this amazing sealing technique (search for his helpful tutorials on YouTube). It may not be the cheapest method, but balloon latex rubber gives a consistent, durable base for your paint that simply cannot be beat. You will need to invest in an air compressor and a "Critter" sprayer, but those are really great tools to have on hand anyway, so spend the coin!

Once again, don't breathe this stuff in. Spraying outdoors or in a dedicated spray booth is a necessity, as well as a respirator.

Ted also likes to add a dye to the latex. Like the Plasti Dip, a black base coat is usually a good start for most base layers of color. He also likes to spray down a piece with a spray adhesive like Super 77 right before spraying on the latex to promote adhesion.

"Spray down a piece with an adhesive right before spraying on the latex to promote adhesion."

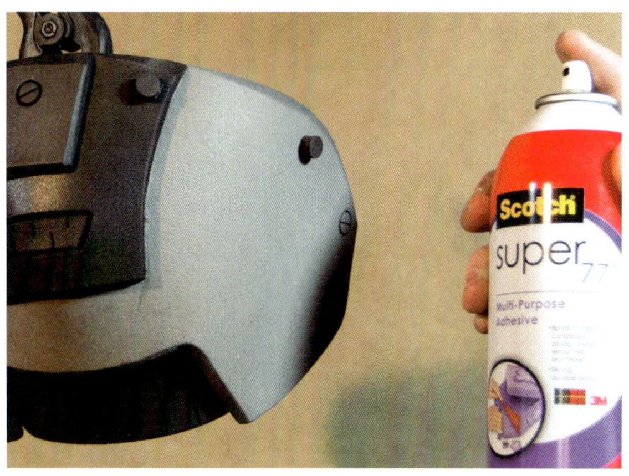

I didn't have any dye and I also couldn't get my hands on balloon latex in time. The latex in these photos is a bit glossier, white, and semi transparent. Your results may vary.

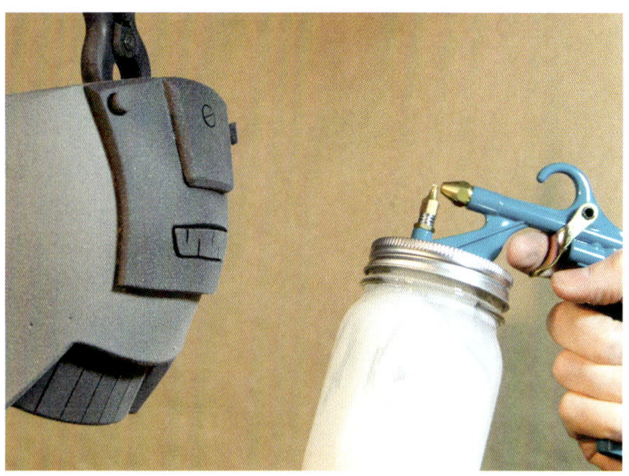

With your spray gun and latex ready to go, application is very similar to the PlastiDip. Just be sure not to spray so heavily that you get any pooling. If one spot looks a little light, just get it on the next pass. Also don't let the layer you just sprayed fully dry before applying the next one. Completely dry latex will not stick to a fresh layer of the stuff. When the current layer starts to lose its shine you can spray the next one on. Once you start spraying latex, you can't leave it until it's done, so make sure you set aside enough time in the day to get all the layers sprayed.

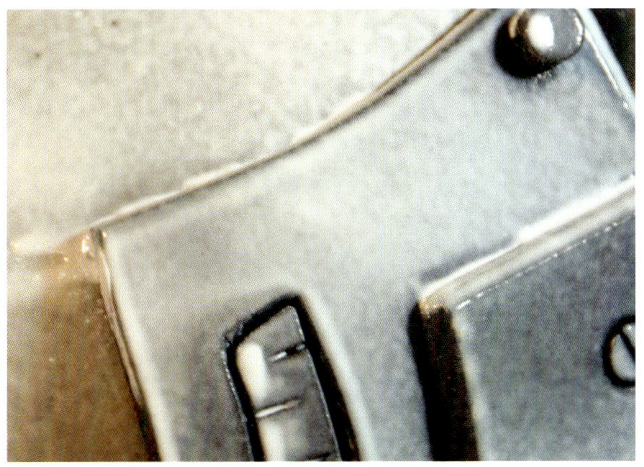

Here I've cleverly demonstrated what it looks like when you put on layers too thick. There is no way to fix that pooling. This is why it's vital to spray many, thin layers. You may end up doing six or seven layers. Practice on scraps first, especially if this is your first time trying this method.

Once you have several layers applied, let it dry overnight and you're ready to start adding color!

Epoxy Resin

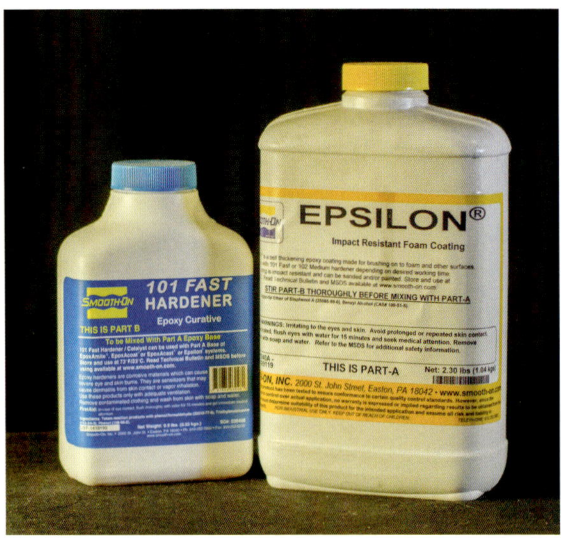

Another of my favorite sealing methods is an epoxy resin from Smooth-On called Epsilon. Again, not the cheapest method, but if you want a hard, sandable shell on your armor, this is the way to go. You can even get it in a trial sized container to save a little money. I've found that a little bit goes a long way.

Epsilon is a 2 part epoxy. It has a resin and a hardener and they need to be measured in a fairly exact ratio. For this, I recommend using your wife's digital kitchen scale (that's what I did anyway). When the parts are all measured out, mix them together with a popsicle stick and get to brushing it onto your armor. Some cheap, throwaway brushes are fantastic for this.

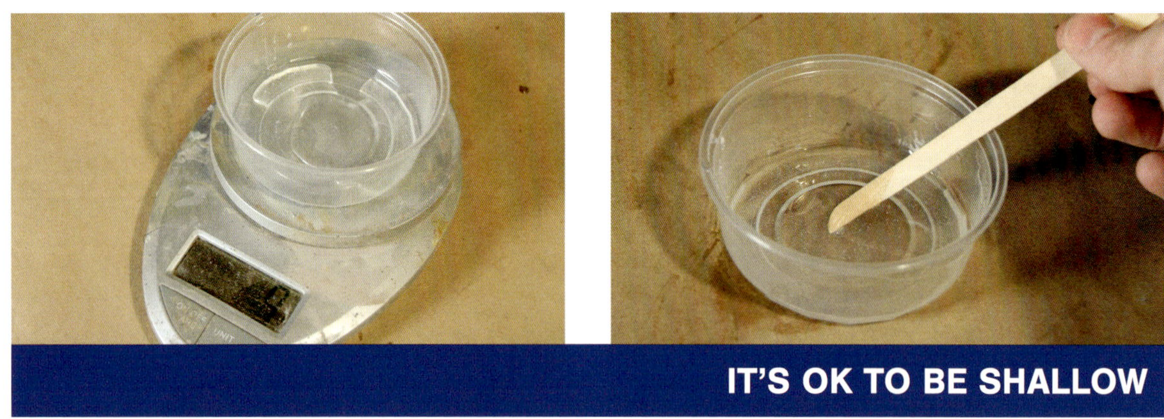

IT'S OK TO BE SHALLOW

Since epoxy resins are catalyzed, the chemical reaction likes to work faster in more concentrated volumes. For this reason, it's best to work in small batches in a wide, shallow container to avoid having a big batch of resin curing before you've brushed it on. If you run out of Epsilon before you finish covering a piece, you can always mix up another batch.

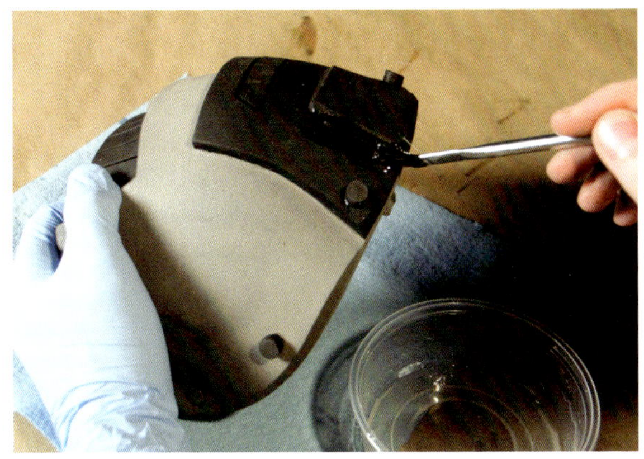

The reason Epsilon works so well to cover foam is because its specific viscosity keeps it tight to the surface. So long as you work in even, thin coats, it shouldn't pool very much.

If you've mixed it properly, Epsilon should have about a 5 minute (double check bottle for times) pot life. That means it shouldn't harden much until then, but when it does kick, you need to stop brushing. Smearing half cured epoxy around the surface of your armor will not yield pleasing results.

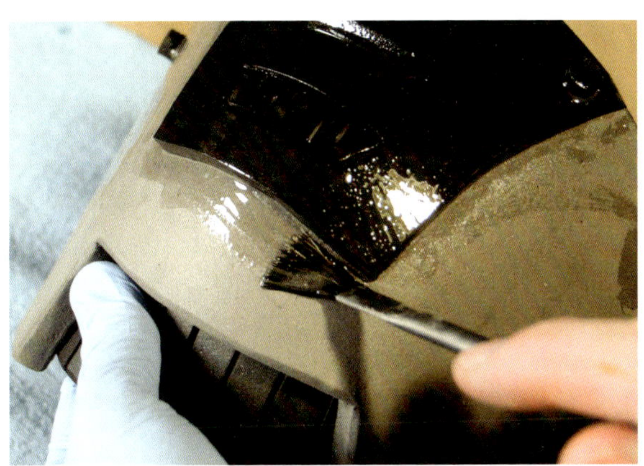

Add as many layers as you need to get the finish you desire, I prefer 2-3. You need to wait about an hour between brushing on new layers. Once your last layer is on, give it a good 8 hours to fully cure. If your finished surface is supposed to be nice and smooth, you may want to sand between layers to minimize any brush texture. When you've added all of your layers, be sure to sand the Epoxy down to the finish you want. You can get a super smooth surface with this sealing method.

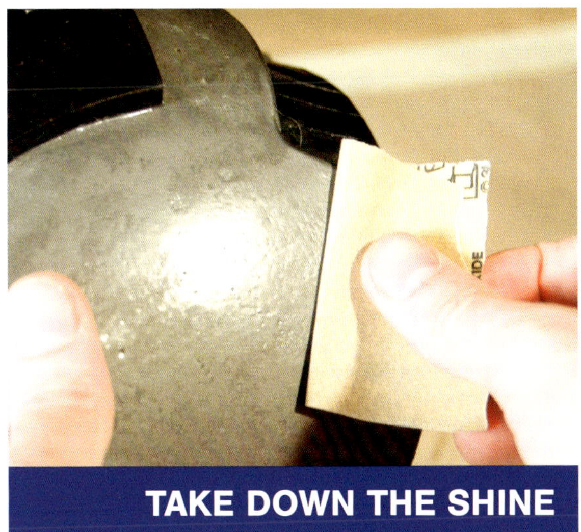

TAKE DOWN THE SHINE

Other Sealing Methods?

There are about as many methods for sealing foam as there are costume makers in Atlanta, so feel free to experiment. You may find one method works well for one type of armor and terrible for another. You may also find a combination of methods that works the best for you. Again, test out different methods on scrap pieces before committing to your full, finished armor.

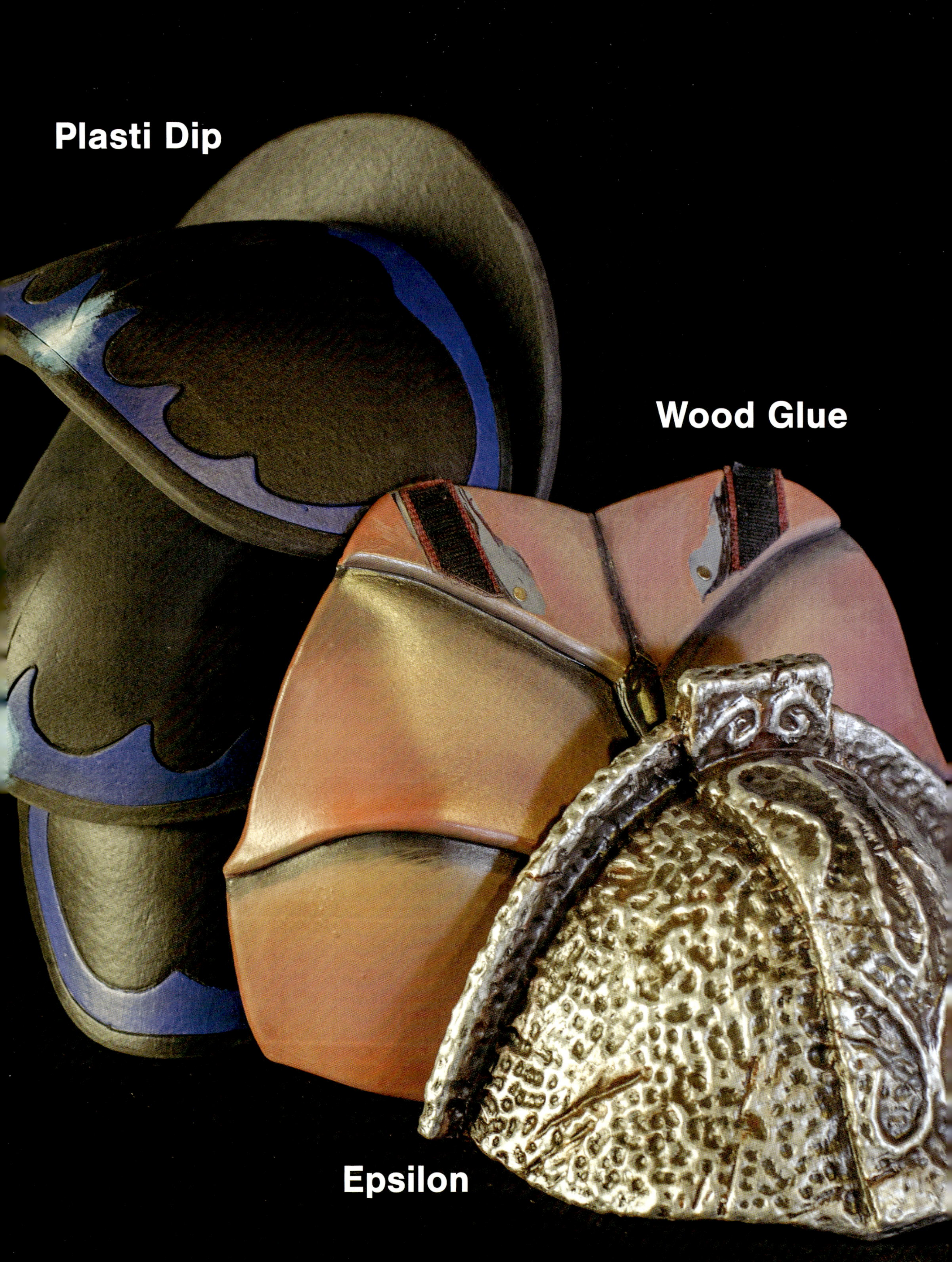
Plasti Dip
Wood Glue
Epsilon

That's Just Prime

You're armor is all sealed up and sanded to your liking? Well there's just one more step between you and paint. That's priming. Primer paint is used to create a nice, uniform canvas on your armor. It's designed to play well with just about every type of paint under the sun and will help your paint adhere to the surface.

If you want something really crazy durable, you can get some high-test automotive primer, but I've found that most rattle can primers from the hardware store work really well. Everyone has their favorite, but I prefer Rustoleum's Painter's Touch primer in the gray color.

Application couldn't be easier. In a well ventilated area, simply spray one or two even coats of primer onto your armor. You're just looking for coverage here, nothing fancy.

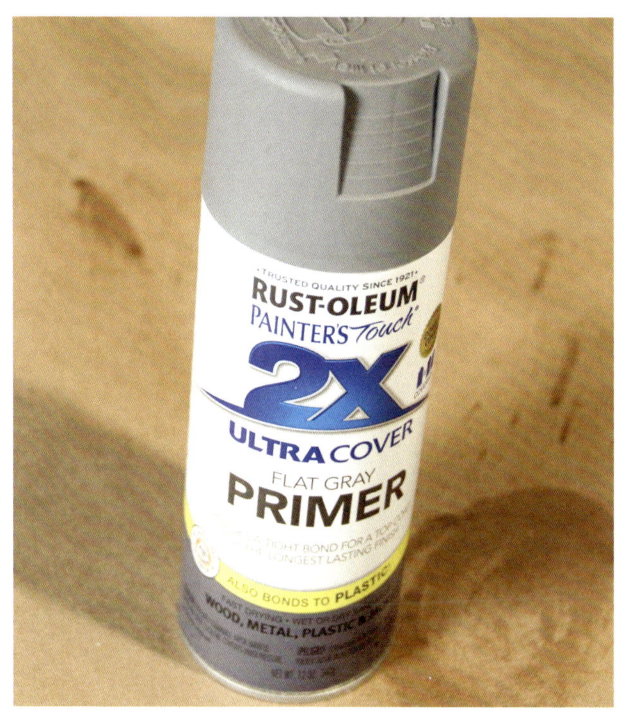

READY FOR PAINT

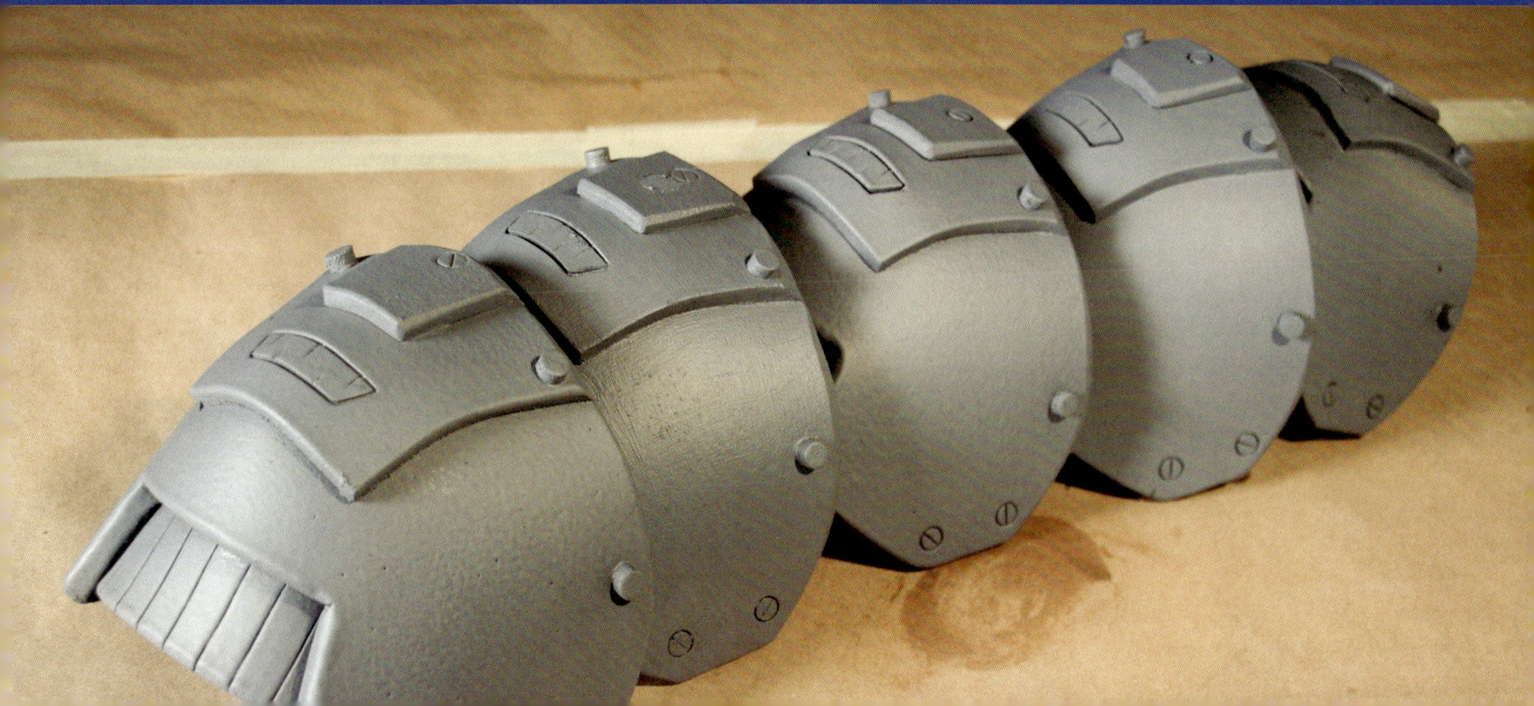

Let. It. Dry.

If the can says it should dry for 24 hours, listen to it. Especially if you're in a humid environment; it could take extra time for the primer to fully dry. You don't want your pretty layer of color paint to smear off because you rushed the primer.

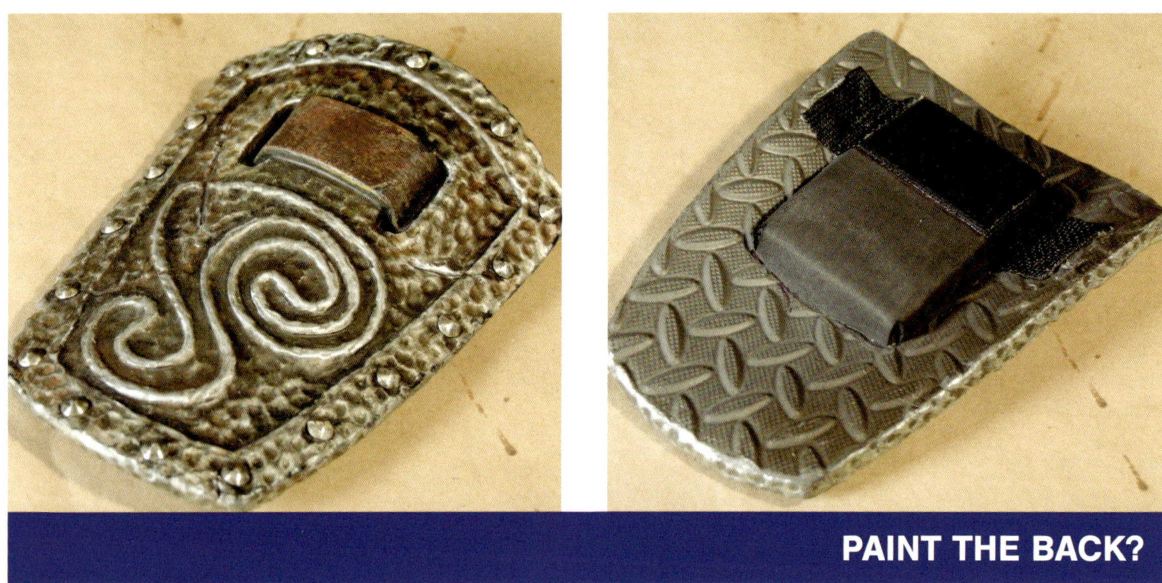

PAINT THE BACK?

If you won't see it when you're wearing it, don't paint it. You'll just be wasting time and materials on something that will probably rub off during regular use. Also don't worry about the floor mat texture on the underside if you aren't going to see it. If I'm concerned that it'll show, I just sand down near the edges and brush on a little paint around them to cover up anything that'll break the illusion that this isn't actual armor.

Spray Paint vs. Airbrush

Spray paint is one of the easiest ways to apply color to your armor. Just be sure you check on the can for what type of paint it is and how long you'll have to wait for it to dry. Some paints need days to fully dry.

An airbrush can be one of your most versatile finishing tools. You can use nearly any type of paint in an airbrush, just be aware that most of them will need to be thinned in some way before they can be sprayed.

I employ both methods of painting in nearly every project. Usually I will do most of my big swaths of color from a spray paint can. If I have tight details or a very specific mixed color or finish that I need to accomplish, I reach for my airbrush.

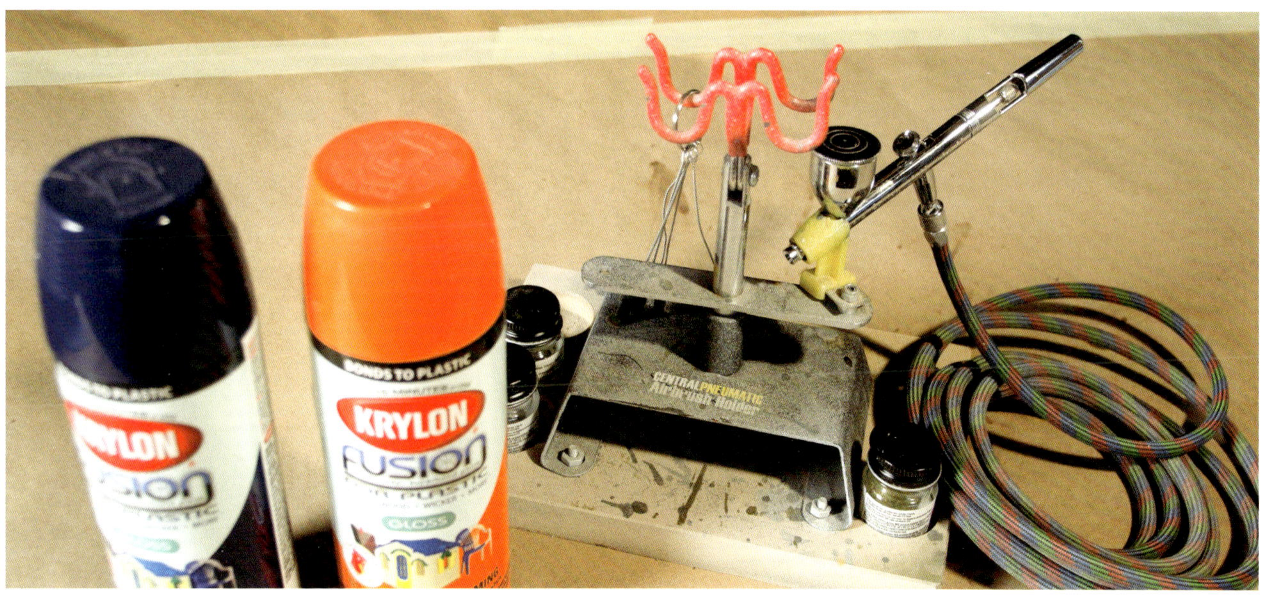

Types of Paint

So what type of paint should you use for the base layer of color on your armor? There are about as many types of paint as there are Deadpools at Dragon Con, so here's a rundown of some popular ones and application methods.

ACRYLIC

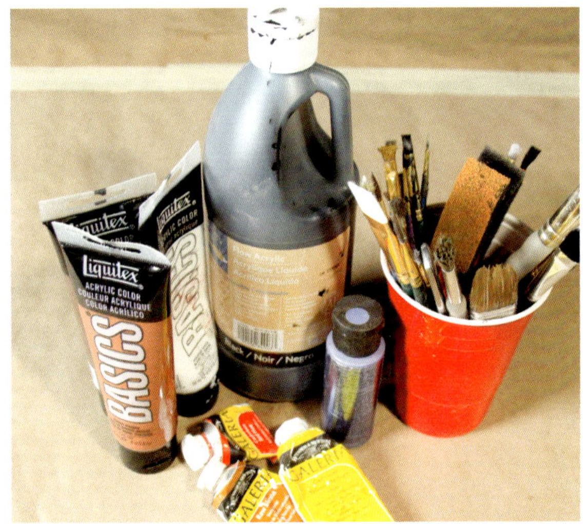

It's really hard to beat acrylic paint for most of your foam finishing needs. You can buy it in a myriad of colors from any art or craft store. Also look for some really neat colors in little bottles at hobby stores. It can be brushed or airbrushed with great ease. It mixes well and dries fast. Acrylic paint also remains fairly flexible compared to other types of paint. This should help prevent cracking in flexible areas of your armor.

You can also get some really cool additives to add texture to your acrylic paints. Some of them will even add a matte or glossy finish to your paint, depending on your desired outcome needs.

Also feel free to try out acrylic paints designed for leatherworking. There are a handful of brands out there and they work really well on foam!

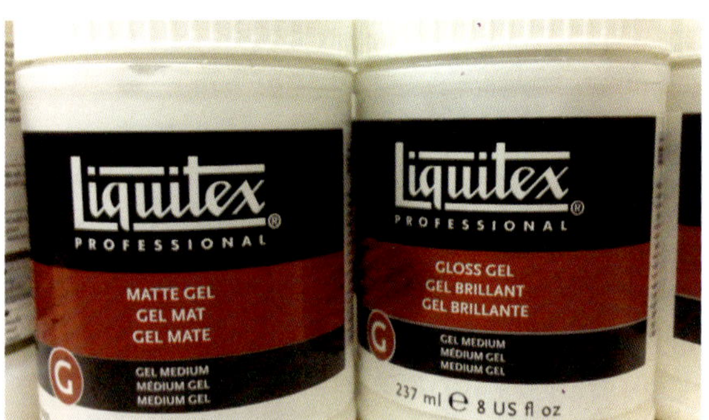

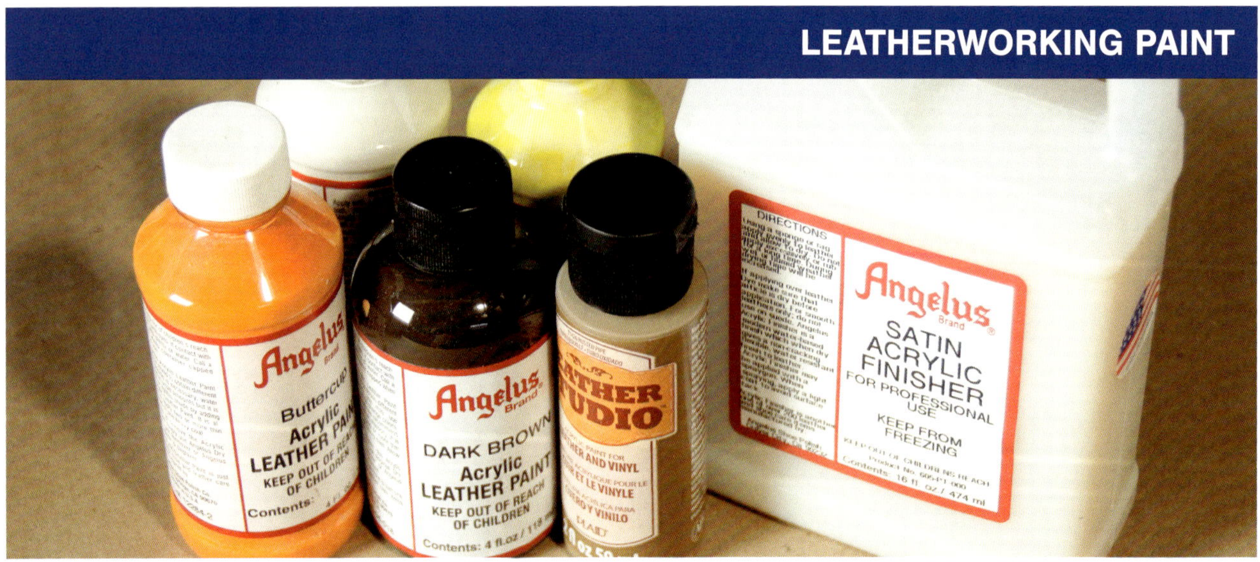

LEATHERWORKING PAINT

Enamel

Also easy to brush or airbrush, enamel paints can be extremely versatile and durable. They also come in some really wild and fantastic colors. Look for them at your favorite hobby store. Their major drawback is their drying time. Enamel paint can take up to a week to fully dry, so keep that in mind when planning your build schedule. These paints also dry to a fairly rigid shell. This means they are prone to cracking in flexible areas of your armor, but are otherwise quite durable.

I will usually only use enamel paints if there is a very specific color that I need and I've found it pre-mixed in a bottle. I will also only apply it to areas of armor that I am confident will not be bending or flexing.

Note that I painted my entire Mass Effect armor with enamel paints. It's clear to see that it has chipped off in many places.

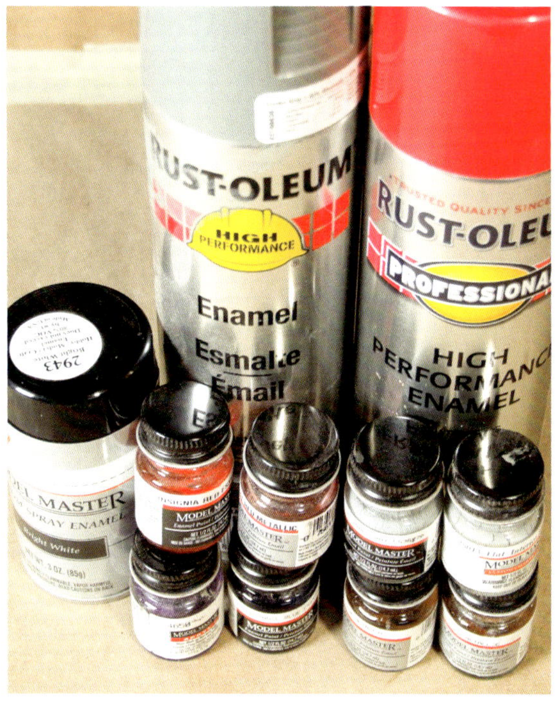

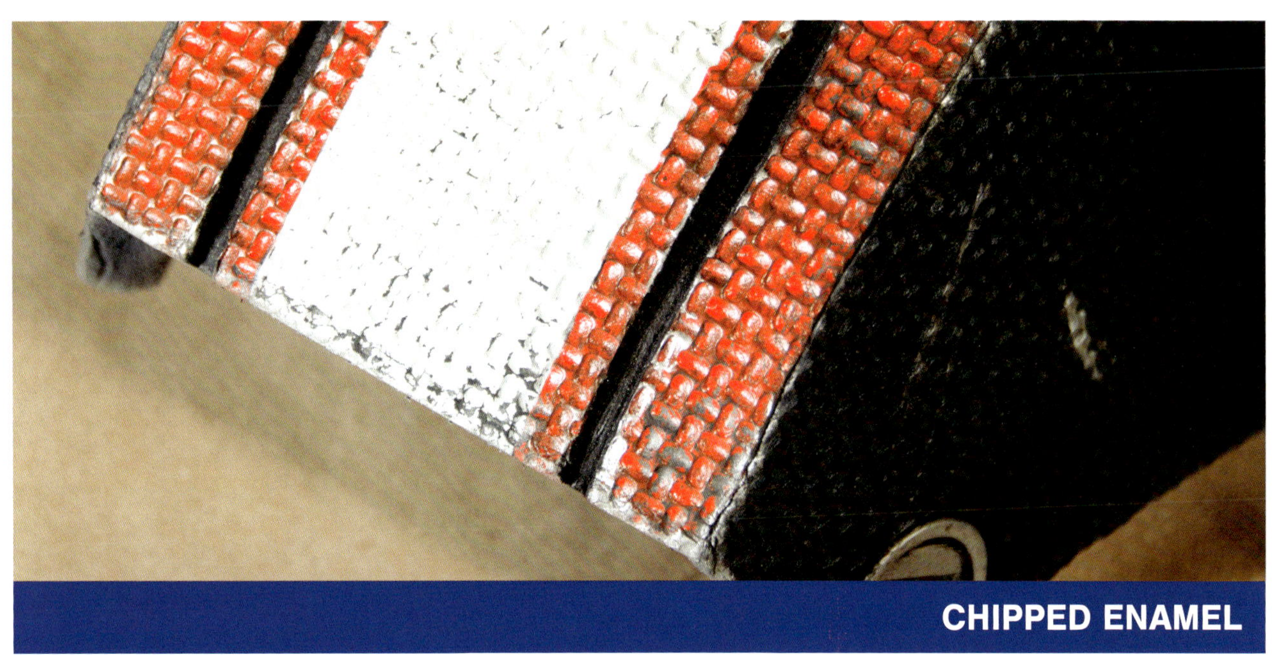

CHIPPED ENAMEL

Lacquer

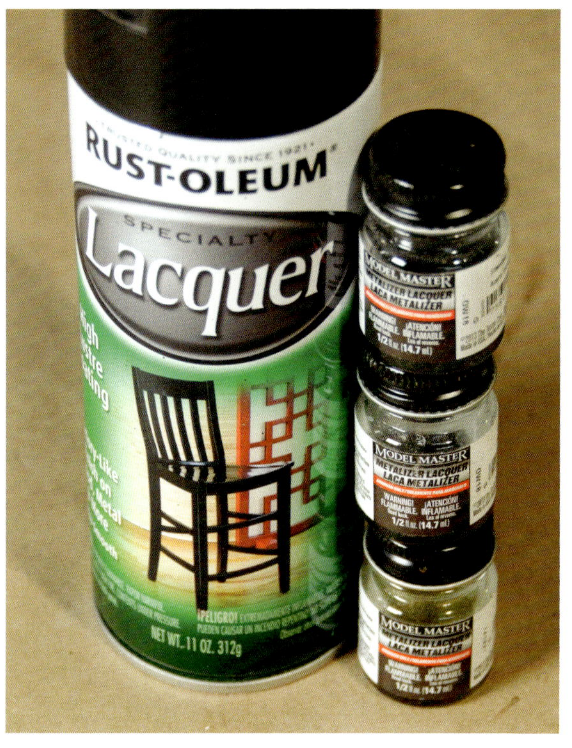

Lacquers dry super fast. If you need to paint something now and wear it in an hour, spraying some lacquer paint is really the only sure fire way to make that happen. I usually keep a rattle can of black lacquer around in the shop for these types of emergencies.

You can also get some really neat lacquer finishes. I am a huge fan of Testor's Buffable Metalizer Lacquer. You'll need an airbrush to apply it, but it doesn't need to be thinned. Simply spray on one good layer of paint, let it dry for ten minutes, then give it a buff with a cloth to bring out a nice, real metallic sheen. Be sure to grab the sealer that Testor's makes specifically for their metalizer line of lacquers. So far it's the only sealer that I've found that does a good job of maintaining the metallic shine after sealing.

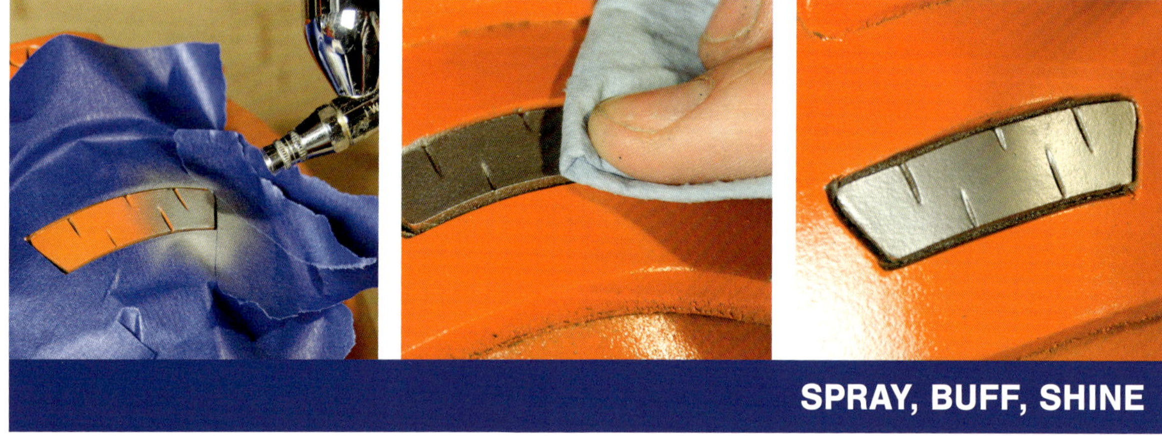

SPRAY, BUFF, SHINE

Oil Paints

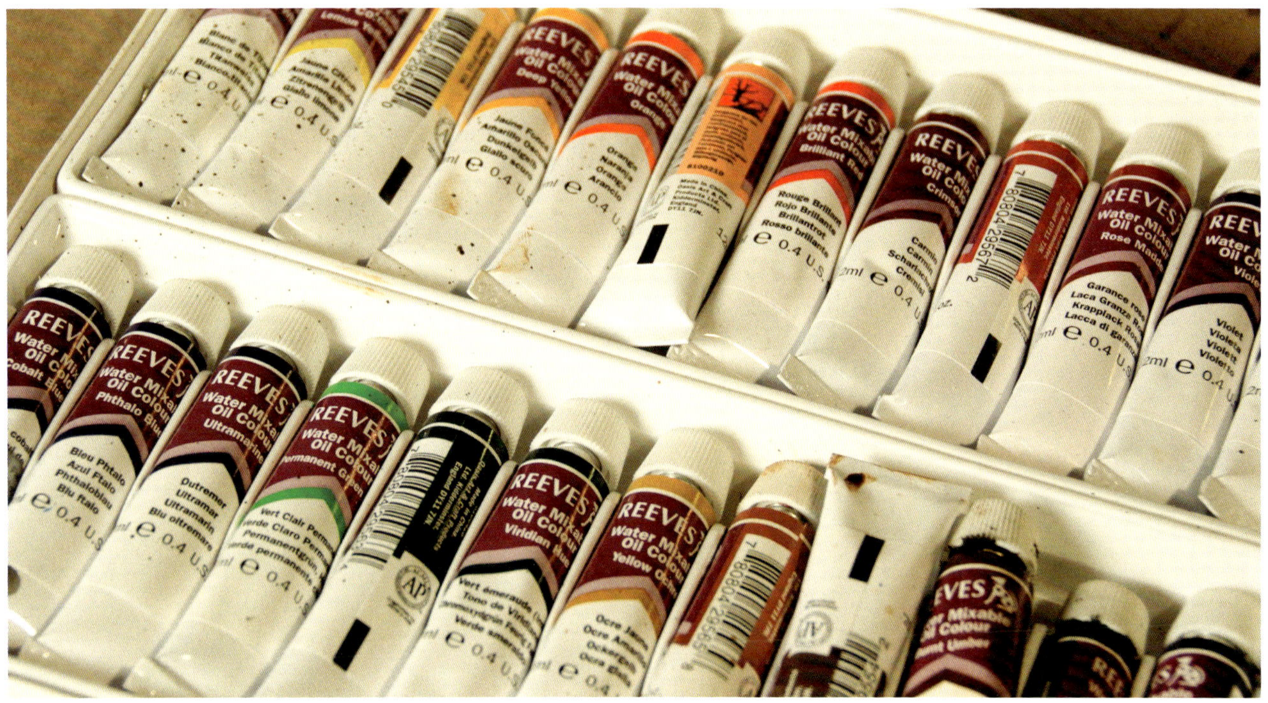

For the most part, oil paints are really terrible for painting any type of base color for your armor. However, it is really fantastic for adding a greasy, dirty finish when weathering mechanical looking parts. We'll talk more about that later.

Rub 'n Buff

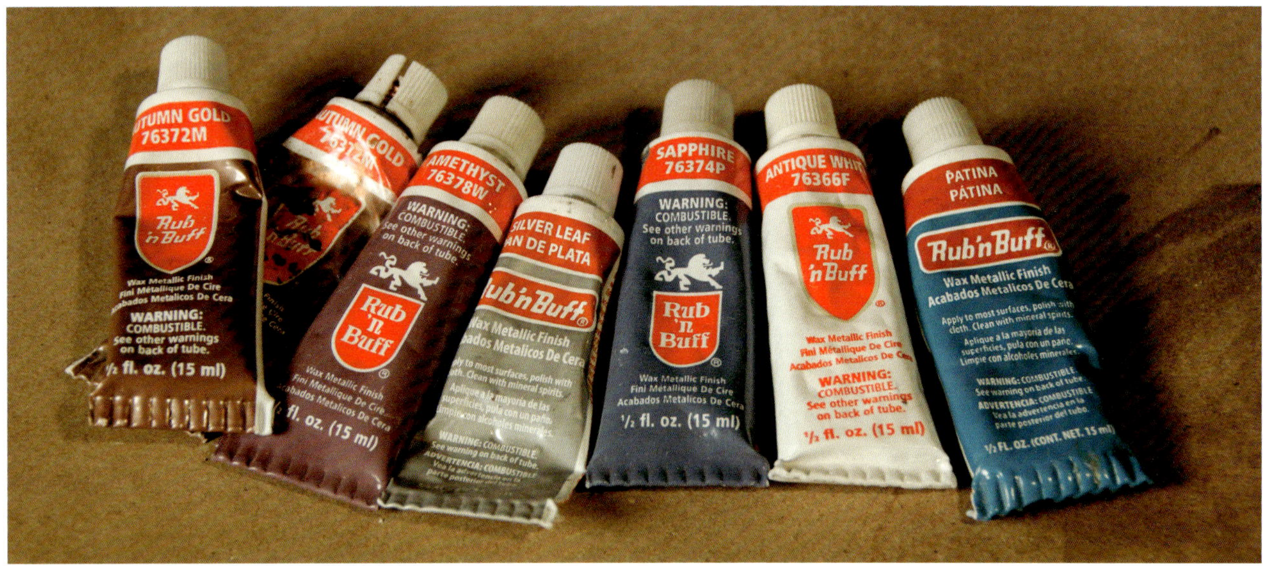

This is a wax based metallic paint, traditionally used for coloring ornate photo frames. It goes on pretty thick and leaves a very nice metallic sheen behind. I don't like to use it as a base color, but it's really great for adding metal scratches and highlighting edges when you're weathering your armor.

These tubes are small, but a little Rub 'n Buff goes a long way. Keep the cap tightly sealed or the tube will dry out.

Layering Paints

Some types of paints don't like to play well with others and will react in weird ways if applied over one another. This is another reason to try out all of your paints on scrap foam bits before going whole hog on the finished armor. This is one reason why I tend to stick with mostly acrylics when painting foam armor.

Once you've applied the base color on all of your armor pieces, it doesn't hurt to spray on a clear coat to "seal in" the color. This way you won't scratch off what you've already added and the new layers of paint will be less likely to pull up the layers below them. I usually keep a rattle can of both gloss and matte clear spray paint on hand for this very reason, depending on the finish I'm going for.

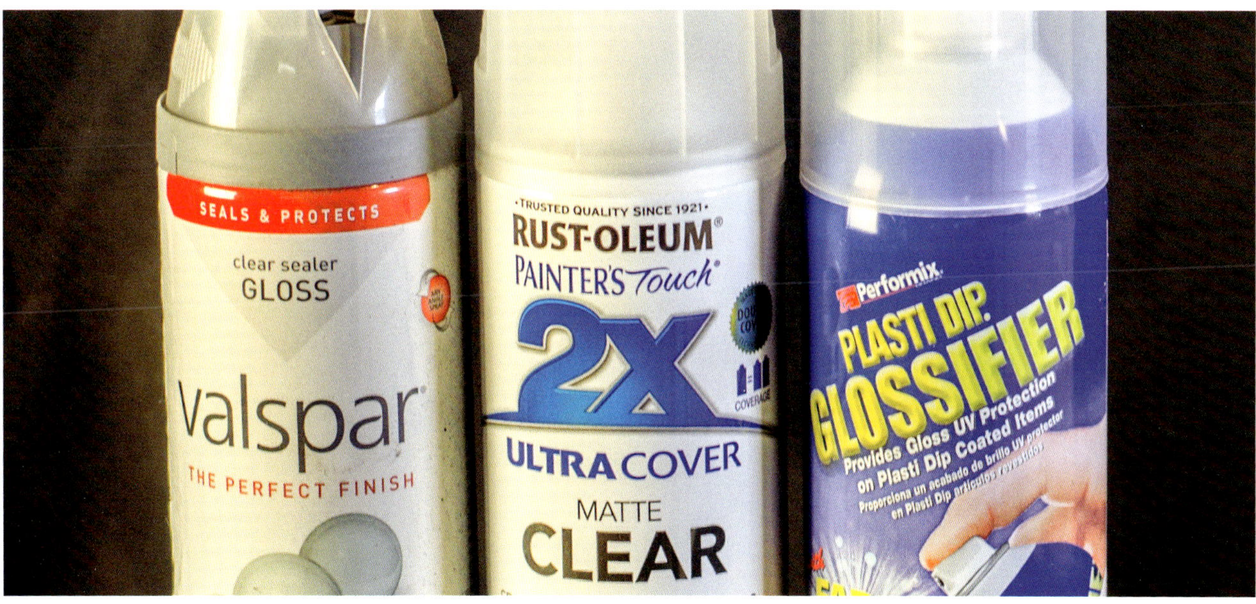

"I usually keep a rattle can of both gloss and matte clear spray paint on hand."

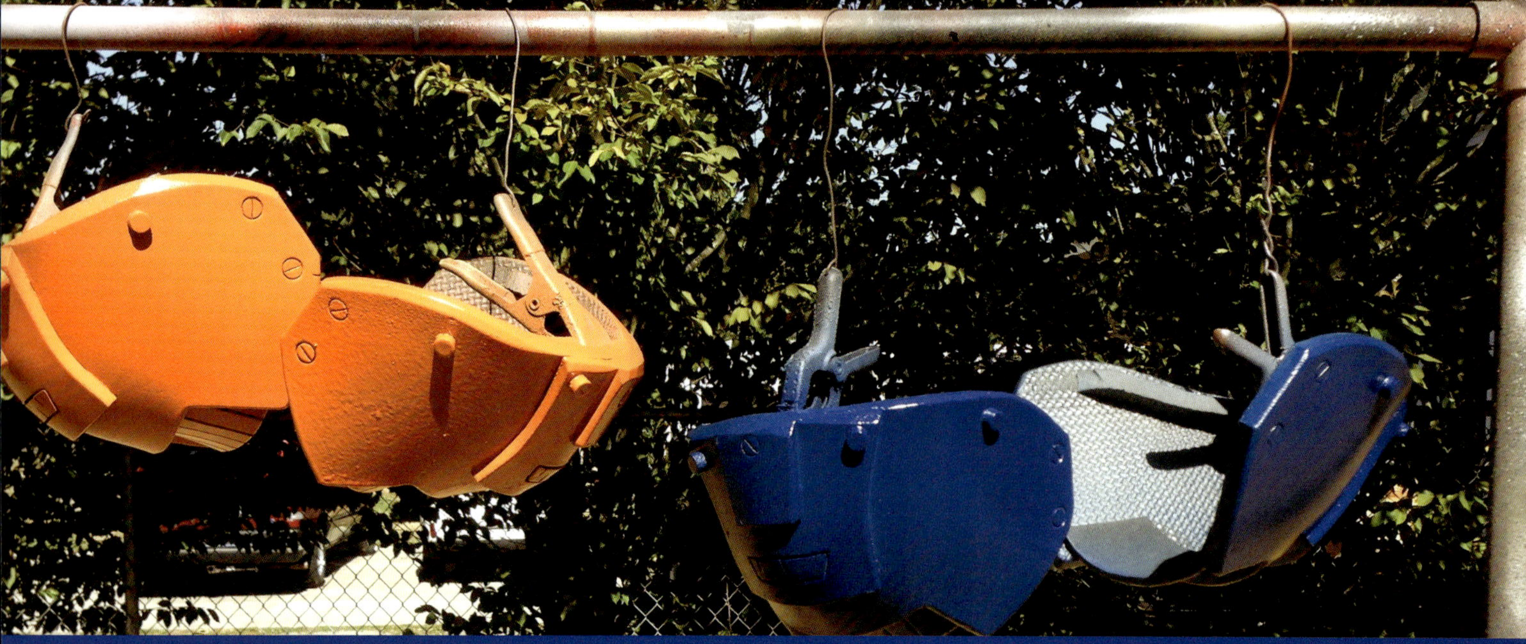

NICE RACK

Whatever the majority color is on your armor is usually what you'll want to use as the base coat. Also spraying on a lighter color first, if you're going to mask and paint on a darker color later, is very handy as darker colors cover lighter ones easier.

I prefer to spray on my base coat, rather than brushing. You can definitely brush it on if you like, but the smooth application from a rattle can or airbrush is really hard to beat. For spraying, a hanging rack made from PVC pipes is recommended.

Add enough base coat color to cover the primer. It's best to add several light coats than one massive one. Definitely let this coat dry all the way before adding anything on top of it. If time permits, hit it with a clear coat to protect all that wonderful color.

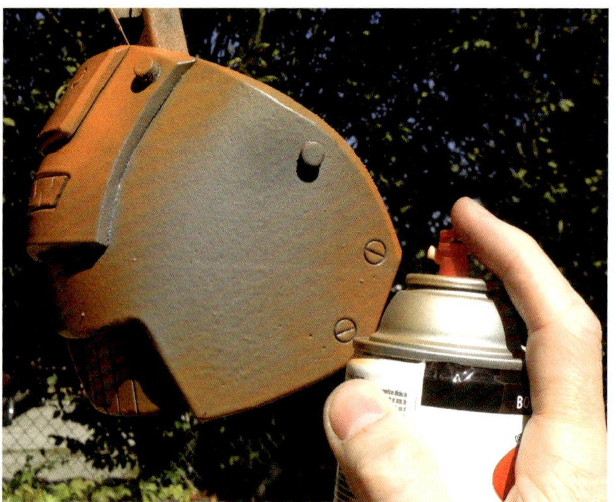

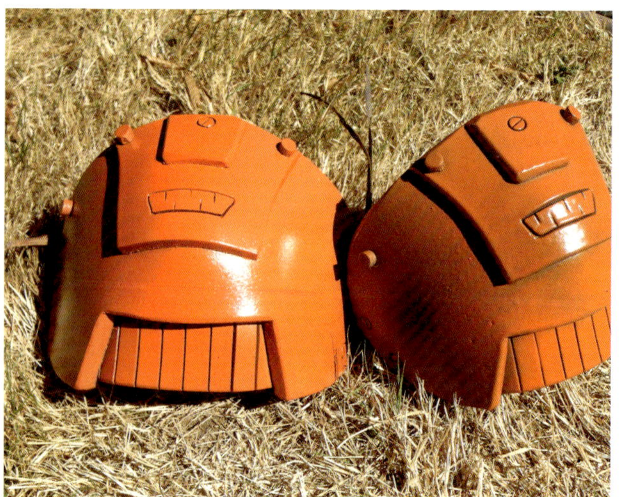

Masking

If your armor has more than one color of finish on it, you'll have to do some masking and layering. A good rule of thumb is to start with your lightest color as the base coat and spray or brush darker colors over the lighter ones since they will cover easier. You usually don't need to mask your first layer of paint. Just apply it to the primed layer willy nilly, making sure to keep the layers nice and consistent without any pooling. How many layers will you need? So long as you get enough coverage, you may only need one or two layers.

If you are going to spray on a different color, you will need to do some masking. This is where springing for the really nice painter's masking tape will really pay off. Oh yeah, remember how I said you need to wait for your primer to dry? This is doubly true for any layer of paint you plan on putting masking tape on. Usually letting it dry over night will be enough, but if it's a slow drying paint, you may find the tape lifting paint when you peel it off. This may or may not be the end of the world.

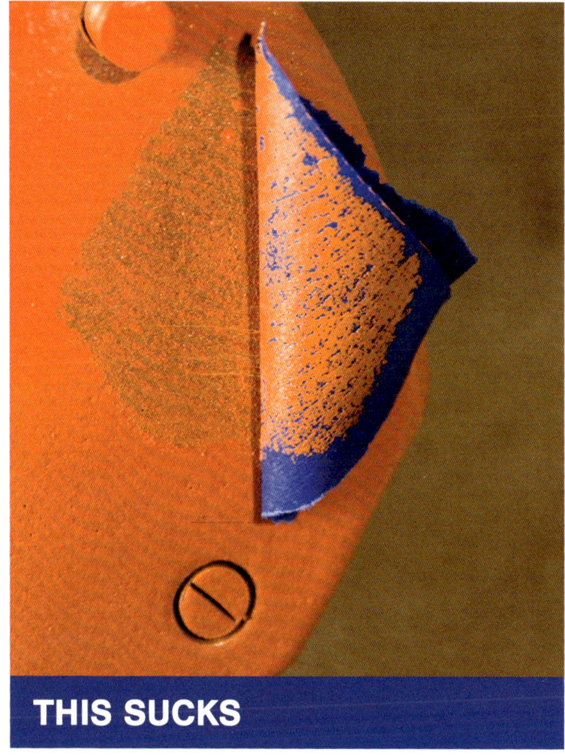

THIS SUCKS

If you do pull some some paint with your masking tape, you can re-paint over the affected area, or just roll with it and call it "battle damage" later on when you're weathering your armor.

Do you have to mask? Nope! You can go in with a brush and hand detail the remaining colors on your armor. The downside is that you could get brush strokes in the finish and it's kind of a pain to do fine detail. Sometimes if you have just one tiny part that needs a specific color, brushing is simply the quickest, best method.

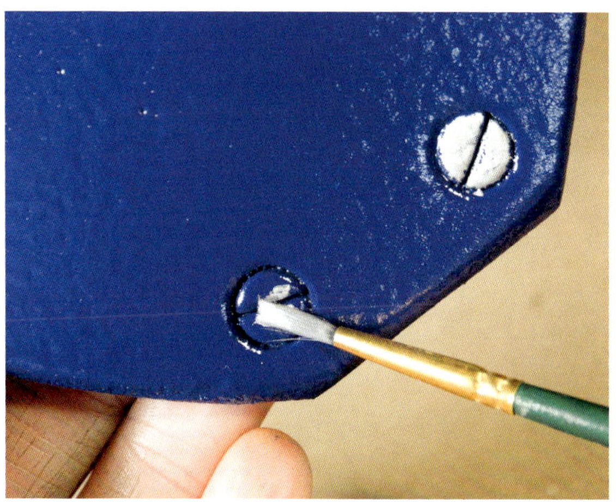

Masking can be a very tedious process, but being able to spray on the new layer of color will provide a very nice, even coat of color on those areas. Mask off the areas that you want to remain the base color with your tape, using your X-Acto knife to trim the tape to the specific shapes you need.

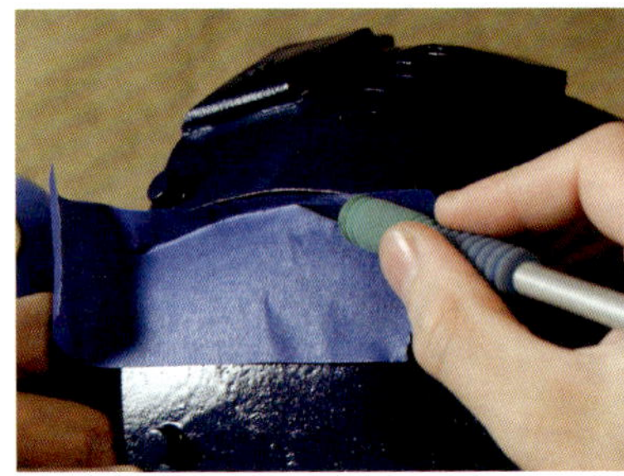
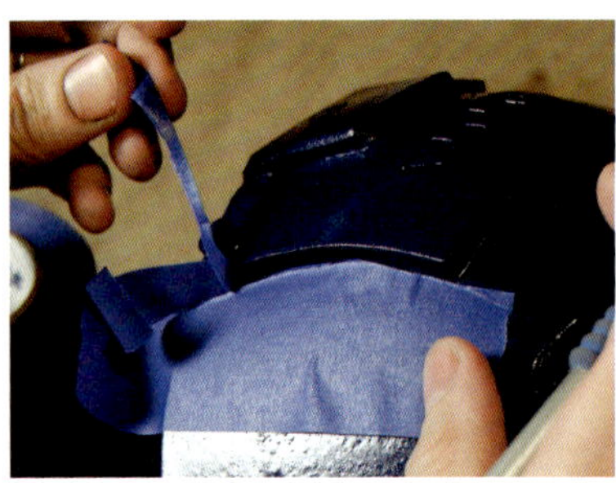
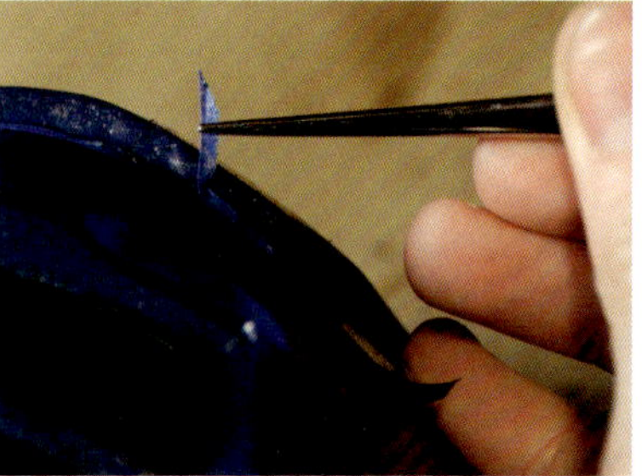

Remember that the edge of the tape is the only part that needs to be pressed tight to the surface. There's no need to press down tons of tape all over your armor. You can use newspaper to cover up large areas. This is way cheaper, quicker, and safer than gift wrapping the entire thing in tape. Once your parts are all masked off, you can spray on the next color to your heart's content!

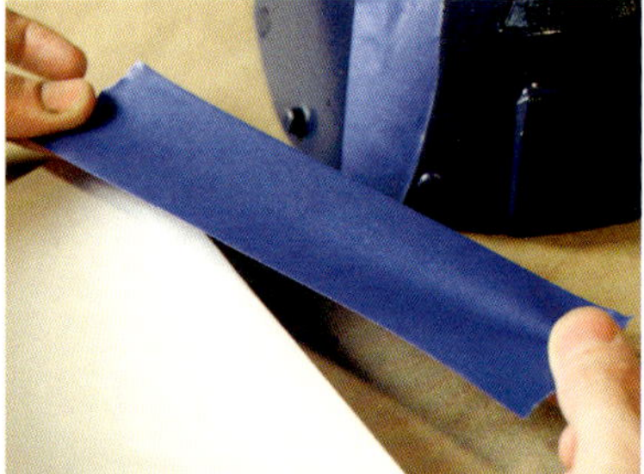
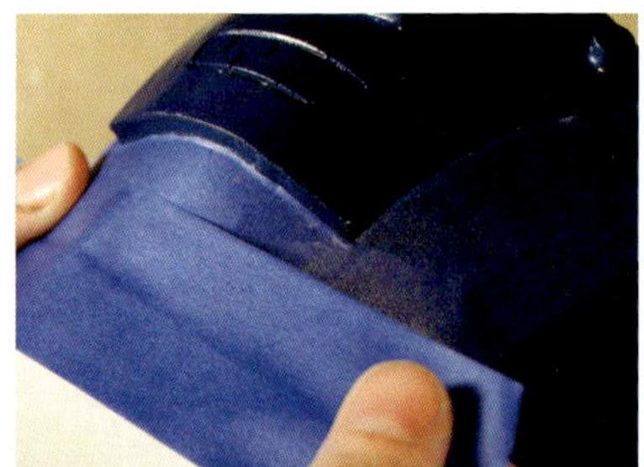
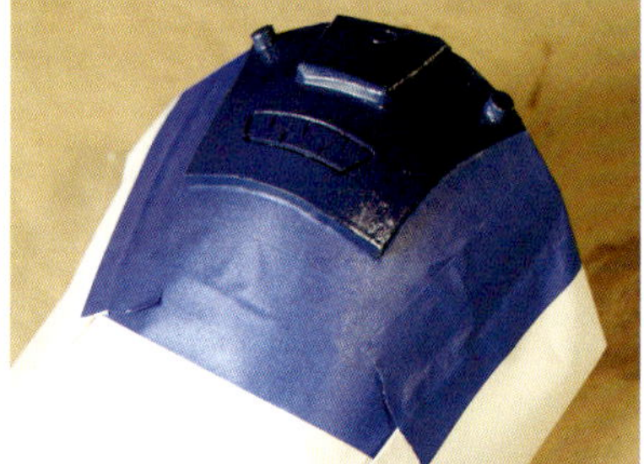

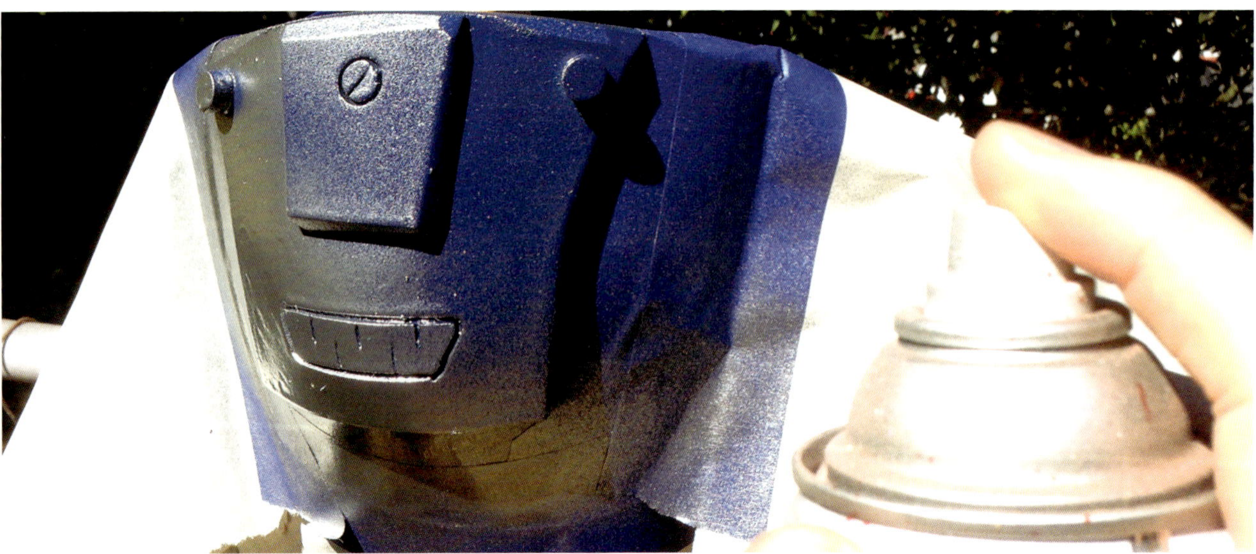

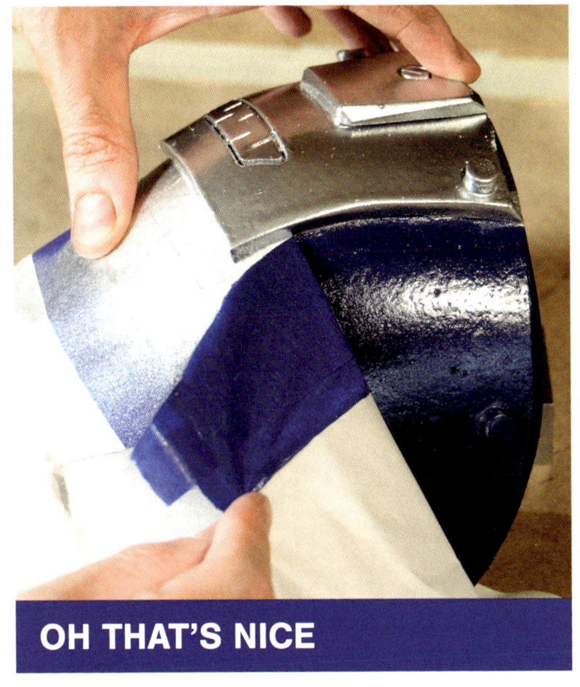
OH THAT'S NICE

Again, just add enough layers for coverage and then let it dry. Once it is dry, carefully peel off your masking tape. Don't go crazy here. Even if you've let the base coat dry and were very careful with the masking, the tape can still pull up some paint if you aren't patient.

If your pieces require even more colors, repeat the masking process for each additional layer. It can help to spray a clear coat between each layer and let it fully dry before throwing more masking tape down on your armor. This process could take days or weeks, so patience is truly a virtue for the foamsmith.

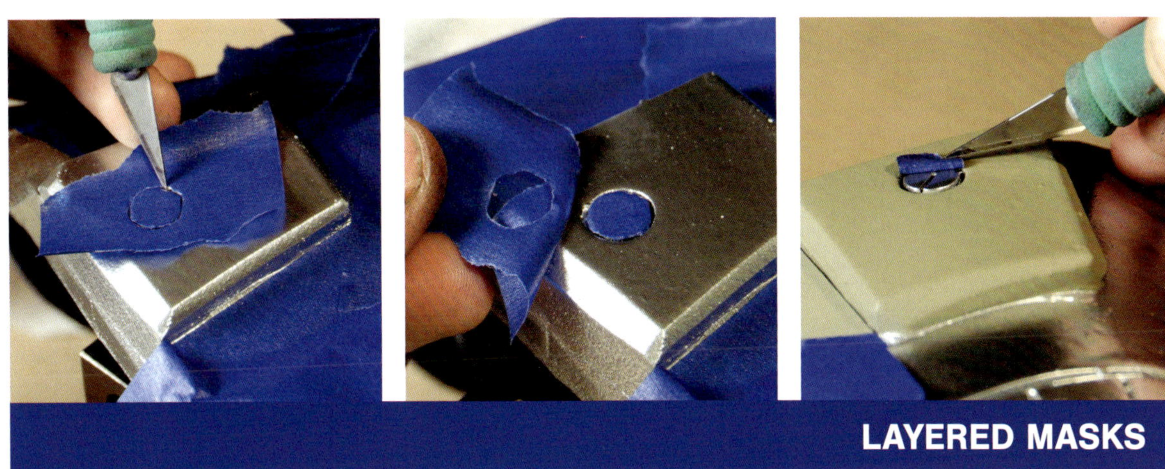
LAYERED MASKS

STENCILS

Especially if you're making some sci-fi armor, you may find yourself in need of some detailed stencils for your armor. Things like logos and text are best done by masking off a part of the armor with your own home-made stencil.

The easiest way to make these are by using an X-Acto to cut them out from a wide piece of masking tape. I like to draw the design out on paper, or with a vector application first, then tape it over a piece of masking tape and cut through the paper to the tape below.

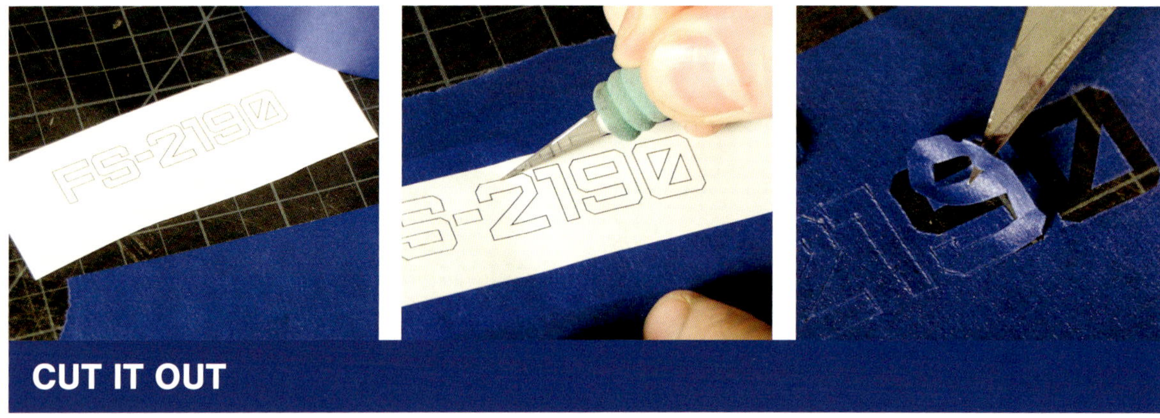

CUT IT OUT

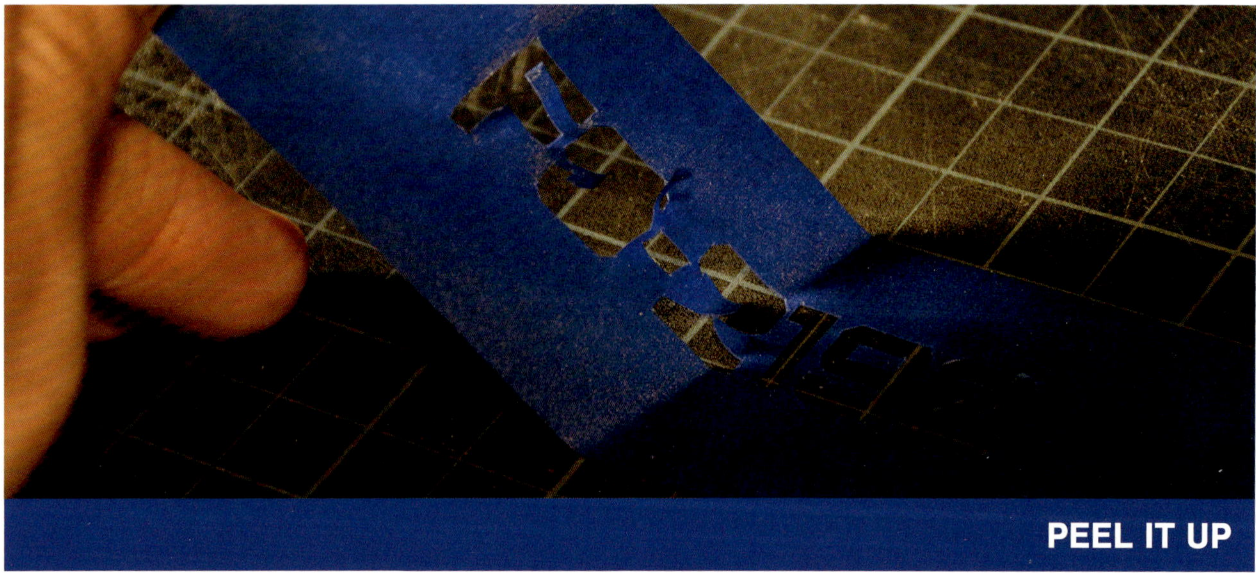

PEEL IT UP

You can then peel the tape stencil off your cutting surface and place it on your armor. You may have some floating pieces that need to be placed individually, especially if you're stenciling some text. The tip of an X-Acto or tweezers are rather handy for this process.

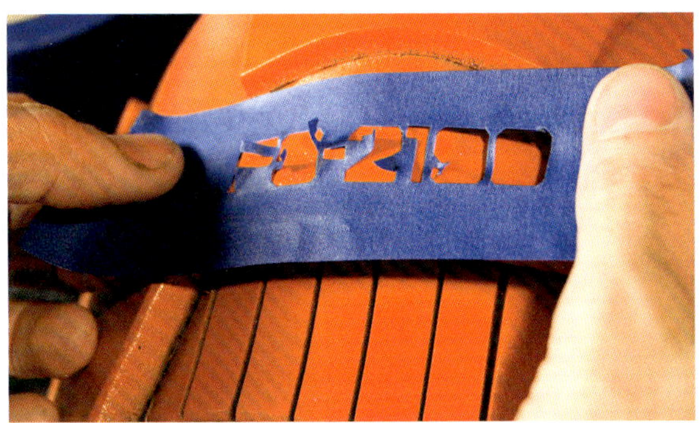

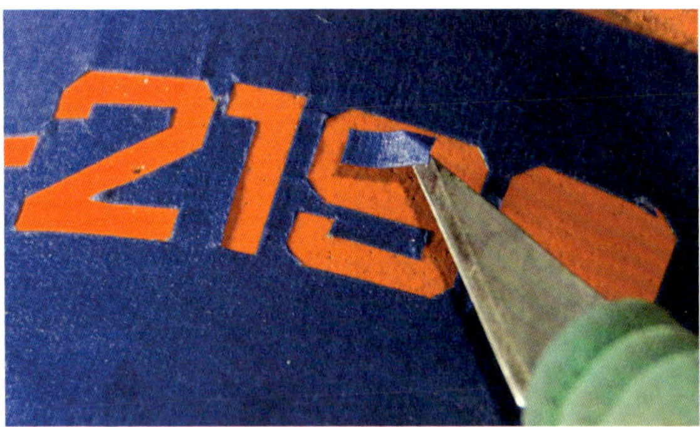

Once your stencil is placed, you can spray or brush the color on. If you're brushing, I recommend using a "dabbing" motion instead of swiping the brush across the surface. It is possible to force paint under the edges of the tape stencil if you aren't careful. Once your paint is laid down, you can carefully peel the stencil off.

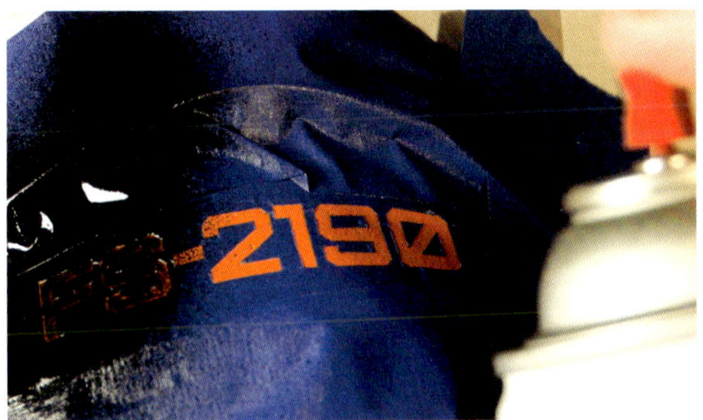

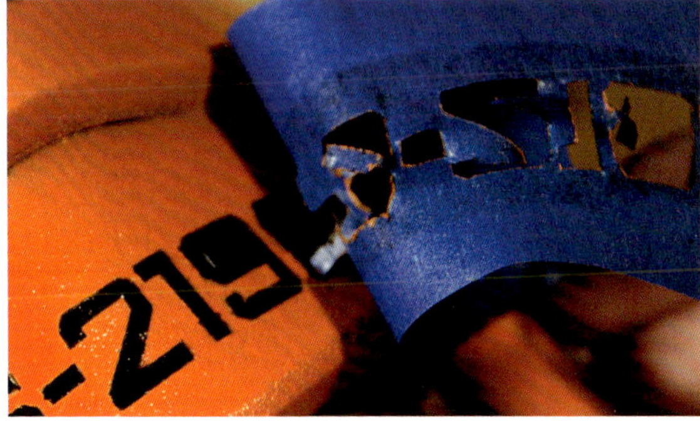

Not happy with the brushed look? An airbrush provides the foamsmith with a massive advantage for applying stencil paint in nice, even layers.

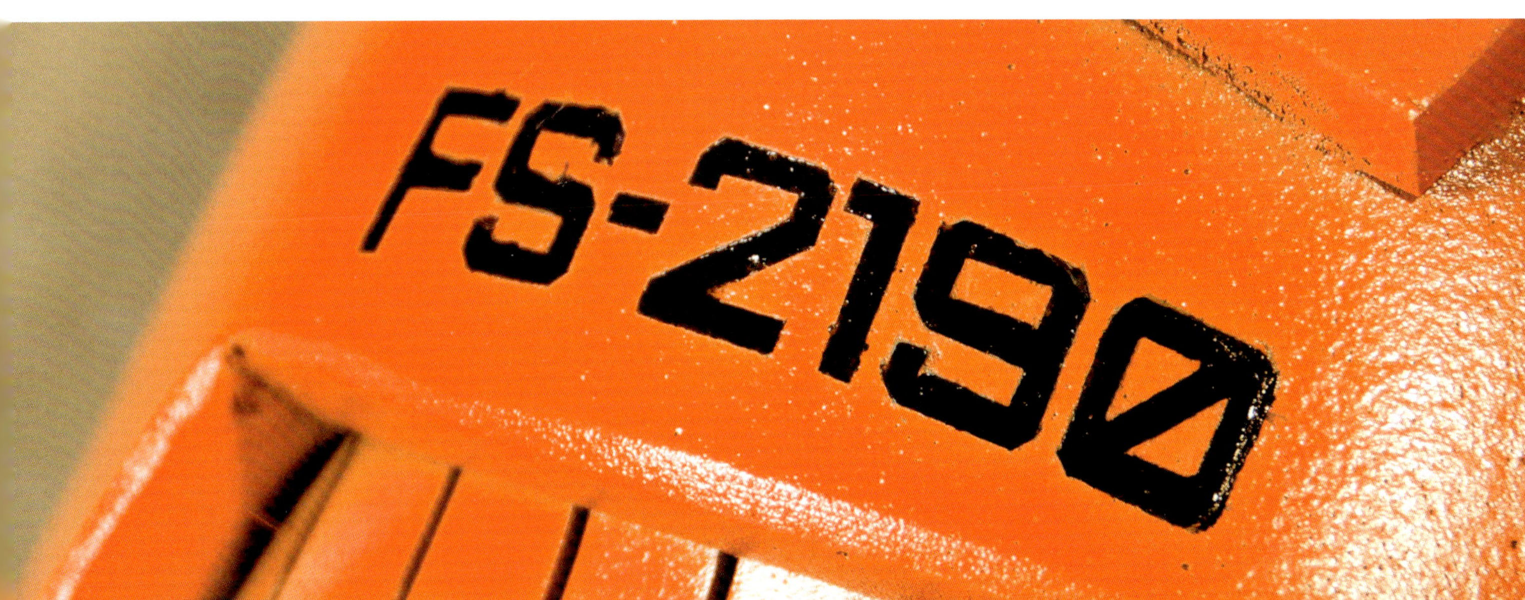

WEATHERING 101

At this point, if your armor is supposed to be really fresh and clean, you can call your paint job done! Spray it with your final layer of clear coat and cry happy cosplay tears!

However… you're probably going to want to add at least a little bit of weathering to sell a realistic finish. Heck, you may even go hog wild and make it look like your armor has been through countless battles and only barely survived! It's time… for weathering.

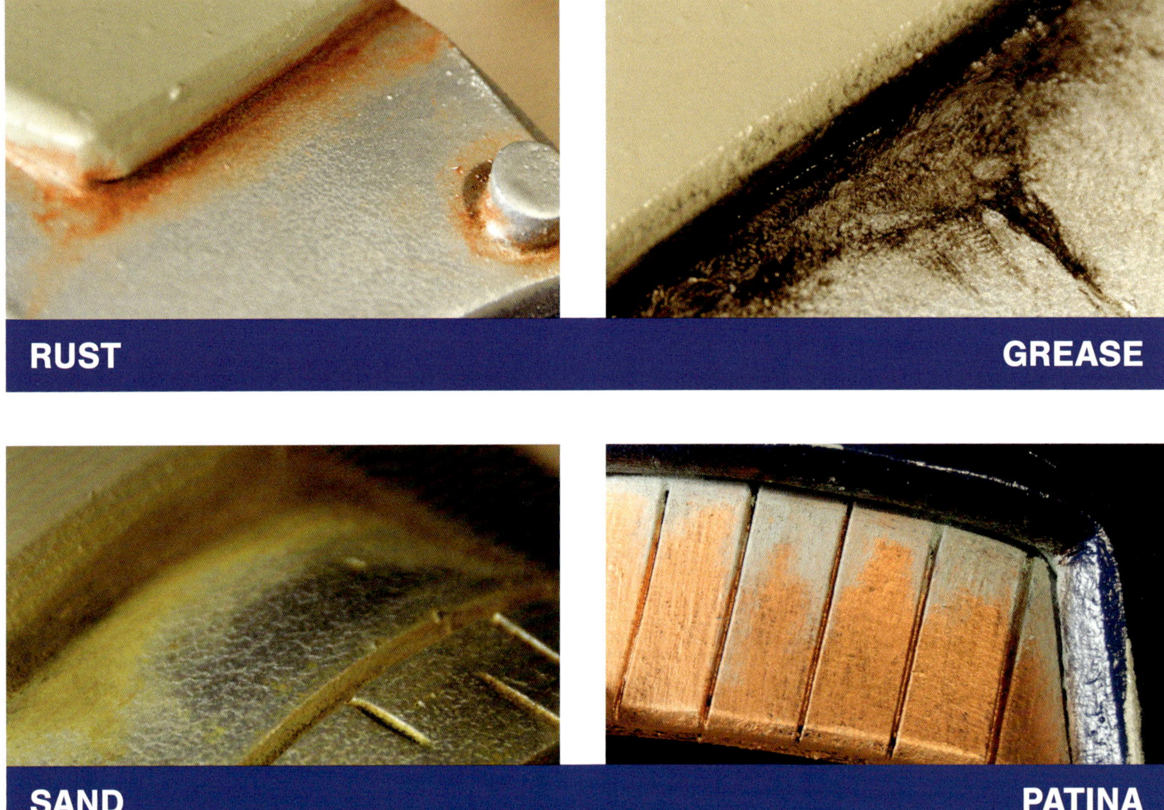

If your armor has been out in the world for a while, the deep details, scratches, and cracks are going to pick up some nastiness. Before you go smearing paint all over your freshly painted armor, take a moment to ponder what type of life it's had. The environment your armor lived in will decide what color the grime will be. If it was a desert, your dust accumulation will be lighter in color. Dirt and grease? Go with darker browns. Is it made of metal that can rust? Get some burnt sienna to simulate oxidation. If the metal is brass or copper, the rust will patina as a nice, green color.

For metal armor effects, think about layering oxidized metal with other types of grime accumulation. Maybe your armor was in a swamp for a few years and both rusted and grew some moss.

Don't be afraid to throw some reds, blues, and greens into the mix. A dash of color can help break up an otherwise bland paint job. Who knows, maybe that's some demon's blood that got all over your vambraces.

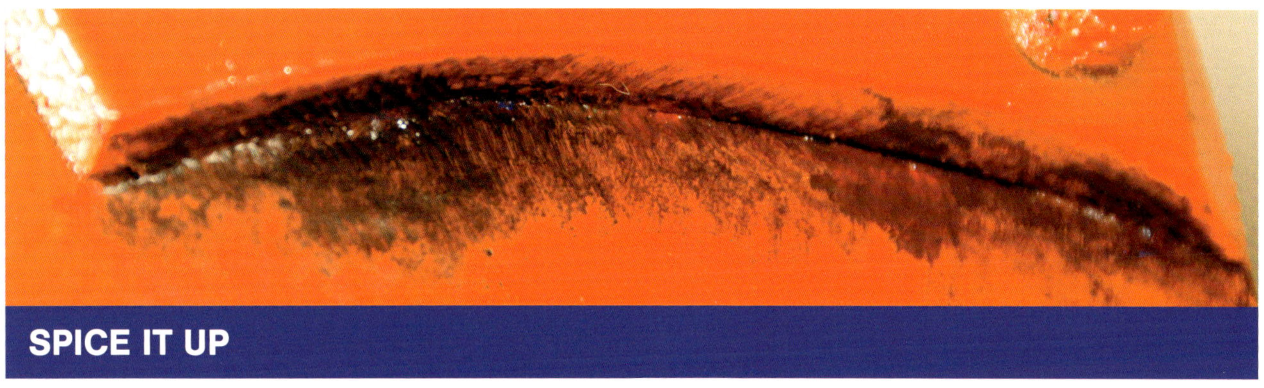

SPICE IT UP

The easiest method for adding grime to your foam armor is with acrylic paints. I like to lightly mix up my colors in my paint palette and then just smear it into the deep crevices of the armor. It's OK if the paint isn't mixed well; your grime shouldn't be one homogenous color. Work the paint into a small area of the armor and then, before it dries, wipe most of it off with a paper towel.

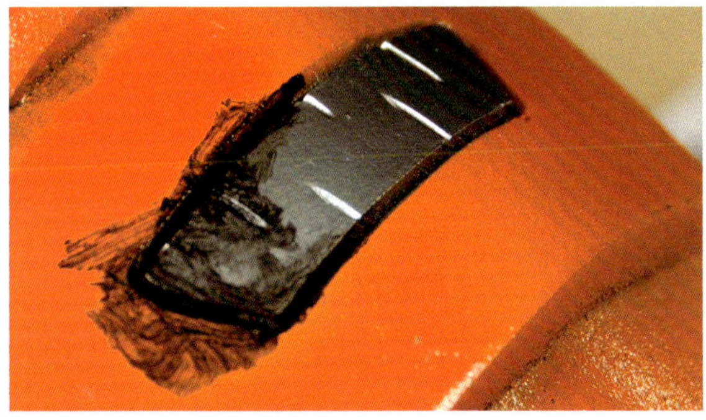

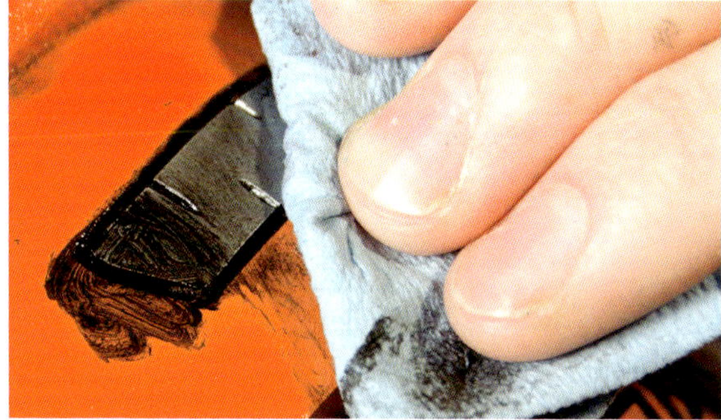

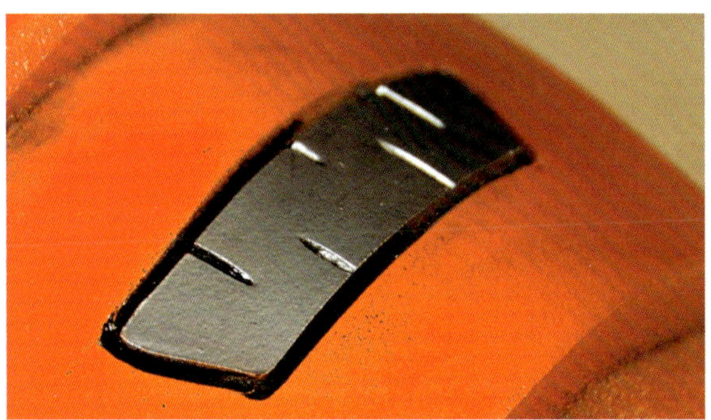

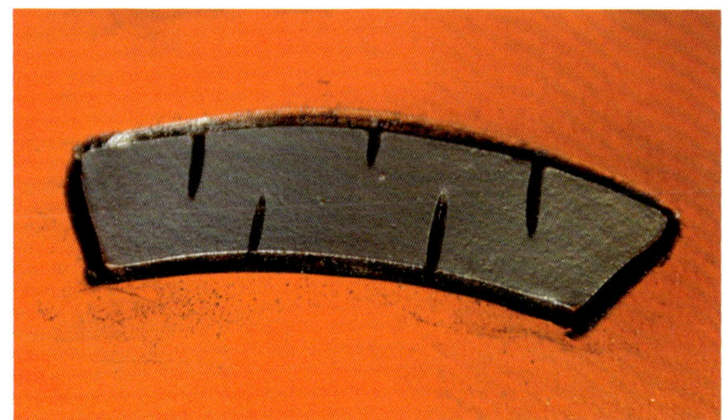

Some people like to use oil based paints for their weathering. They can be really handy for simulating greasy grime in armor parts that are supposed to be mechanical.

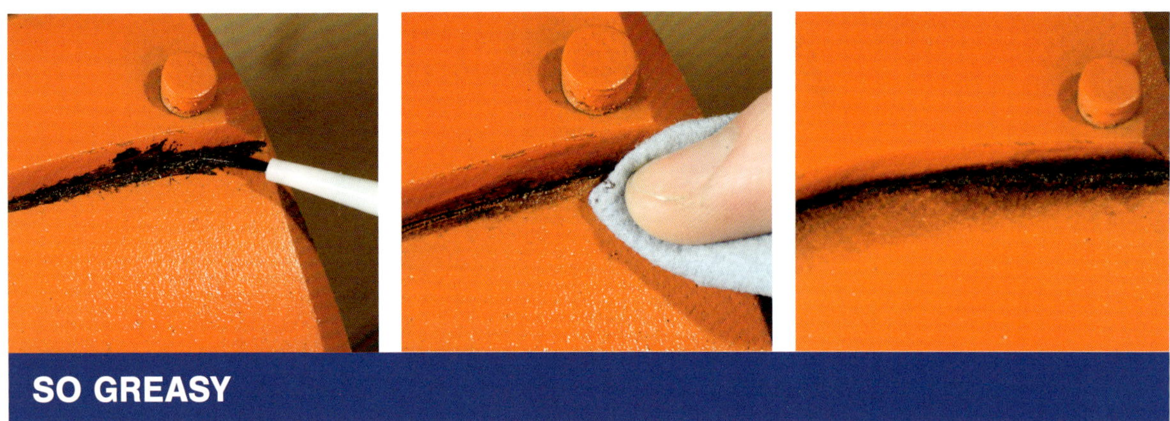

SO GREASY

The idea here is that your armor got really dirty and then you tried to clean it off, but didn't do a great job of it. The paint you leave behind will make the deeper parts of the area more pronounced and add a very nice layer of realism and contrast.

Continue this process in small patches all over your armor until it is sufficiently dirty. I prefer to do a couple of passes, with sprayed on clear coats between them, to get some very nice layers of grime in different colors. Don't rush here. You want the grime to look like it's taken a long time to get there.

Add some purples to your burnt sienna rust weathering. Grime is never just one solid color. Any variety you add will help sell the illusion that this is a real, world worn item.

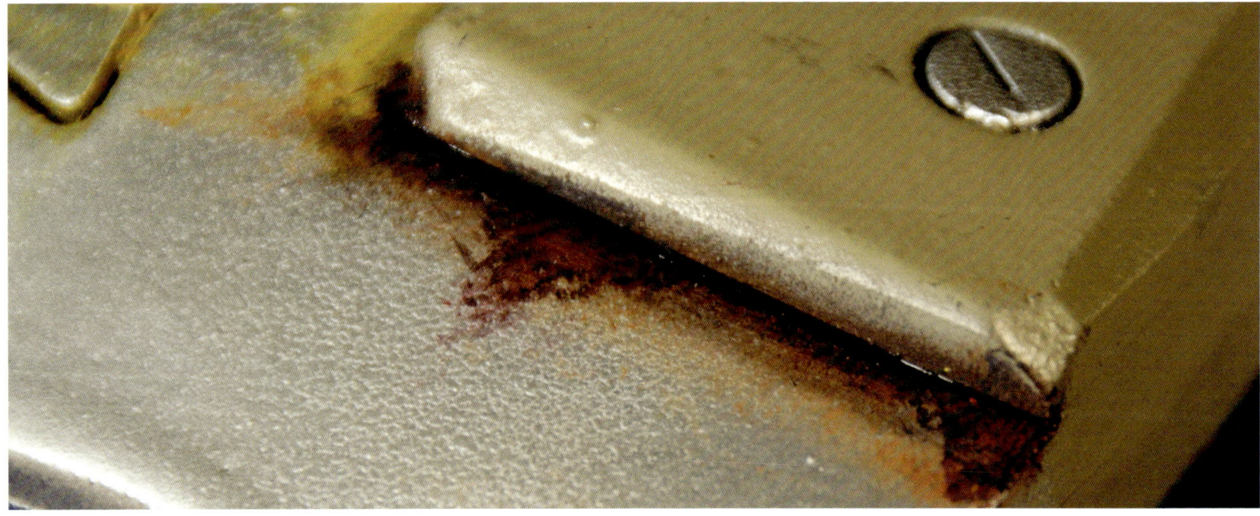

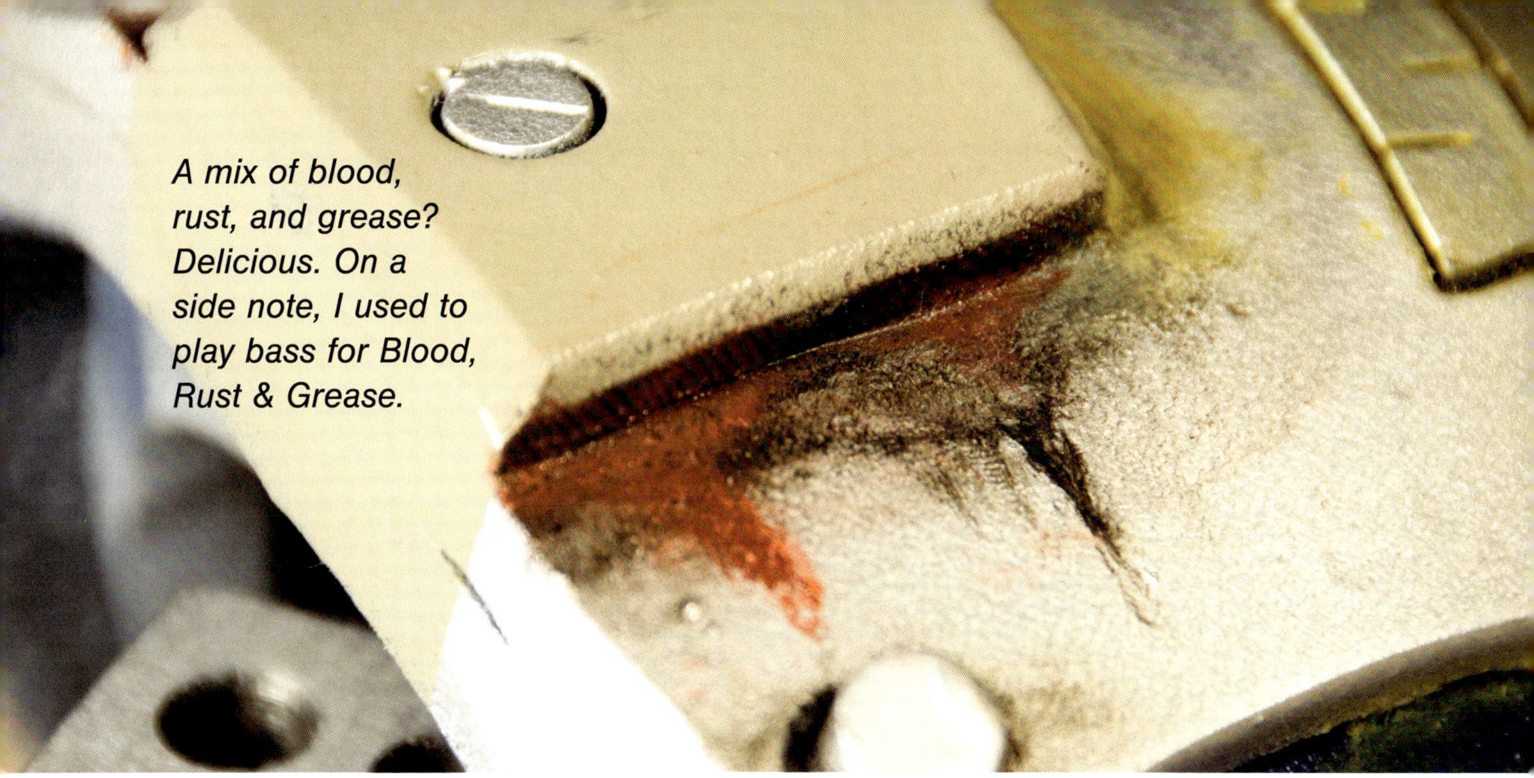

A mix of blood, rust, and grease? Delicious. On a side note, I used to play bass for Blood, Rust & Grease.

Another favorite technique of mine is the use of weathering powders. These are commonly found in hobby stores. Think of this stuff like dirty makeup for your armor. I like to ditch the applicator it comes with and use my own small, stiff bristled brush for application.

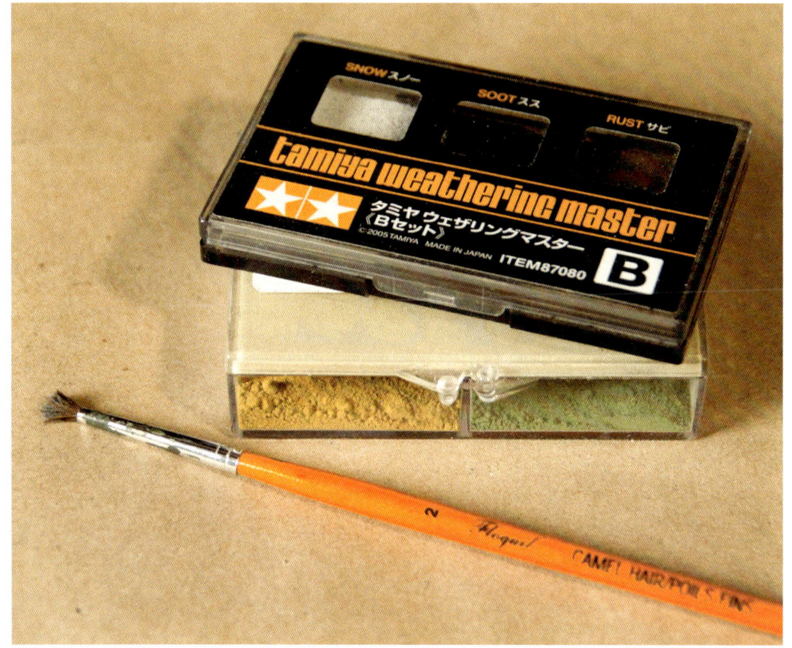

Weathering powders are a lot more subtle than acrylic paints, but can still create some pretty dramatic results. They go on light, so you can do a couple of passes to add up the effect. I really like them for simulating smoke or soot damage. Unlike acrylics, they can't be wiped away once they've been applied. This makes them less ideal for filling in thin gaps.

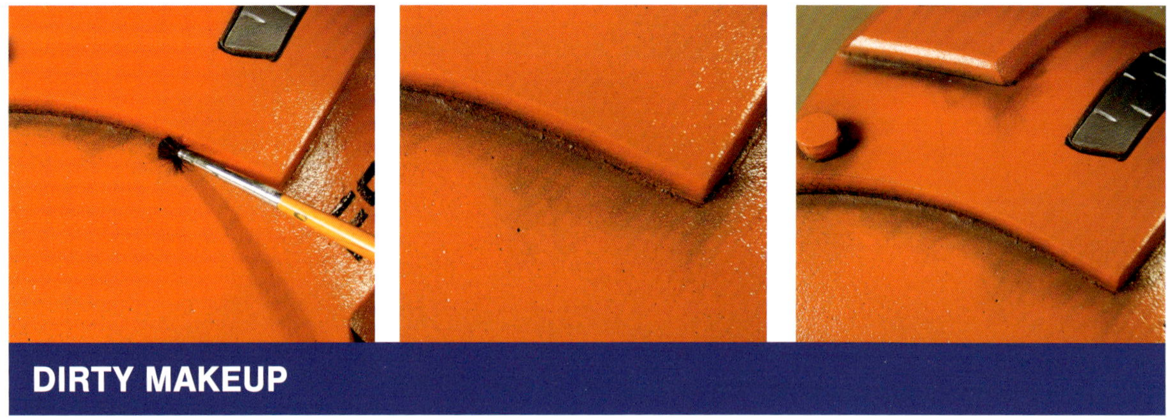

DIRTY MAKEUP

I will often use a combination of weathering powder and acrylics to achieve my desired results. Just about every set of armor is a mixed media project!

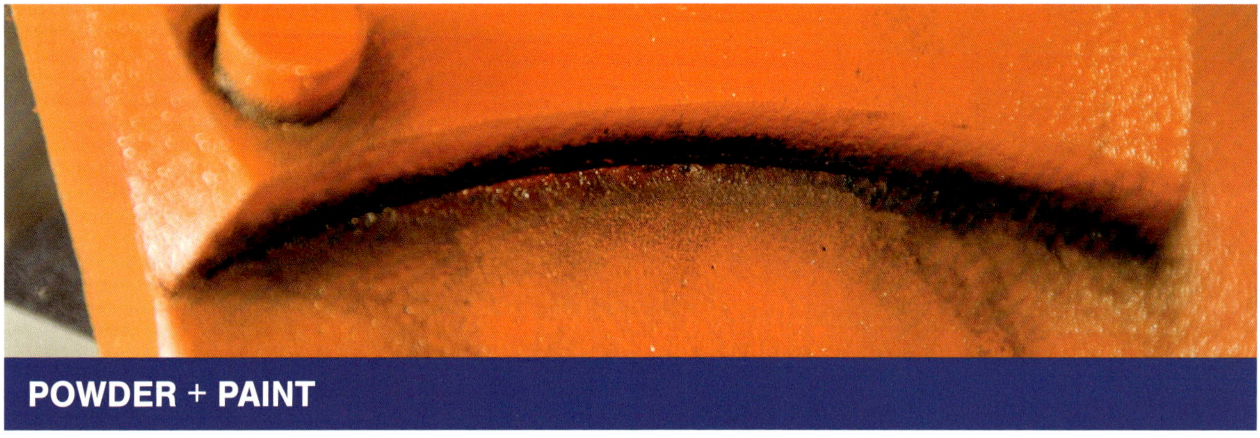

POWDER + PAINT

Also, try scuffing up any flat areas that picked up a lot of the grime paint with some fine steel wool. So long as the layers below are dried and protected with some clear coat, you should be able to scratch up just the newest paint layer and add a bit more depth.

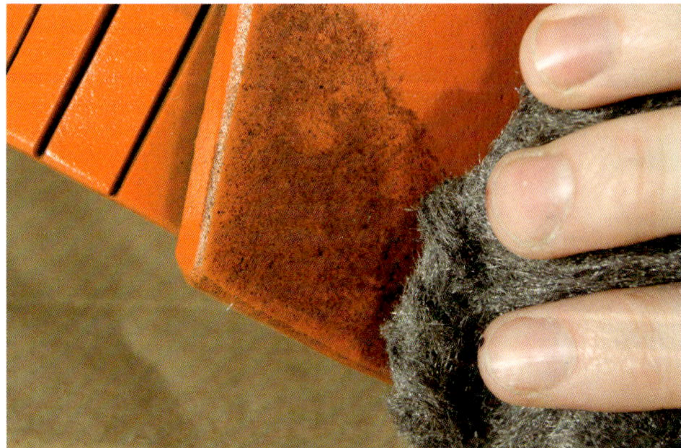

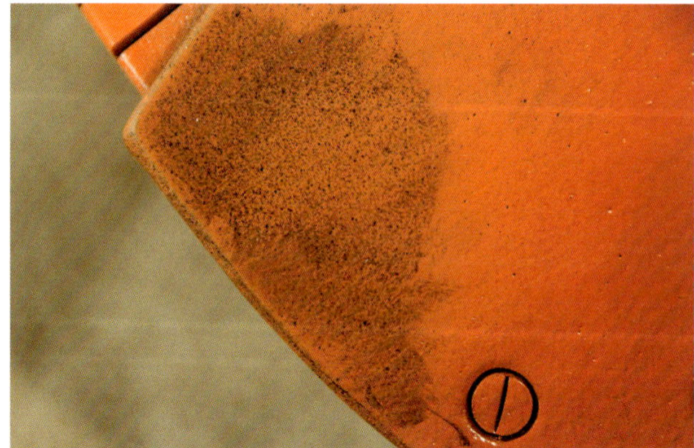

Your old-looking armor isn't only going to accumulate new, gross material; it's going to lose some material too! Especially if you want it to look like it's been handled a lot, chipped paint and worn edges will really sell the fiction.

I usually do a quick pass on a bunch of the high edges with a metallic pen, Sharpie, or silver Rub 'n Buff. This is, of course, if the "exposed" material underneath is some kind of metal. It could be wood, gold, or plastic. Try to think about the areas on your armor that would be prone to scratching or rubbing against other pieces of the armor. Even if your armor is supposed to look like unpainted metal, highlighting the edges with a slightly different metallic paint can change the specularity and yield some pleasing contrasty results.

My personal favorite method is to apply Rub 'n Buff with a Q-Tip. Use a light touch. A little bit goes a long way and it's easy to overdo it.

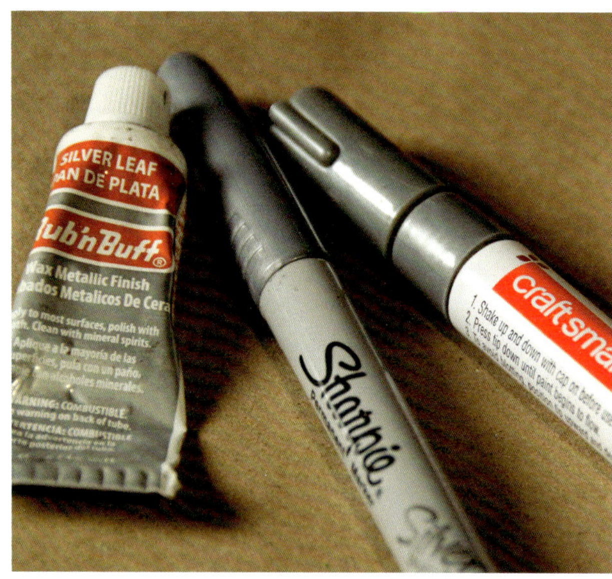

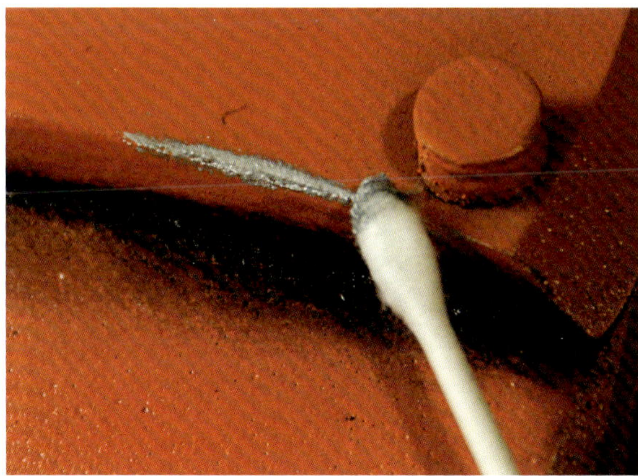

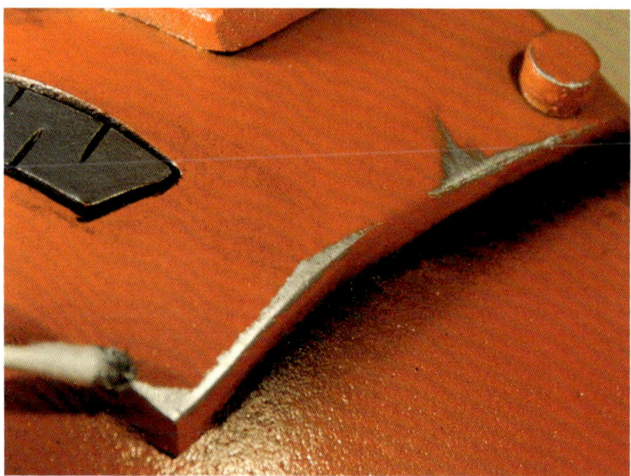

This is definitely a technique that you will have to hone over time. Less is usually more and it's easy to over-do it. Start by doing one light pass on a whole piece of armor and then step back to see how it looks. You can always add more. If you really get in there with a fine brush or a paint pen, you can even simulate chipped paint.

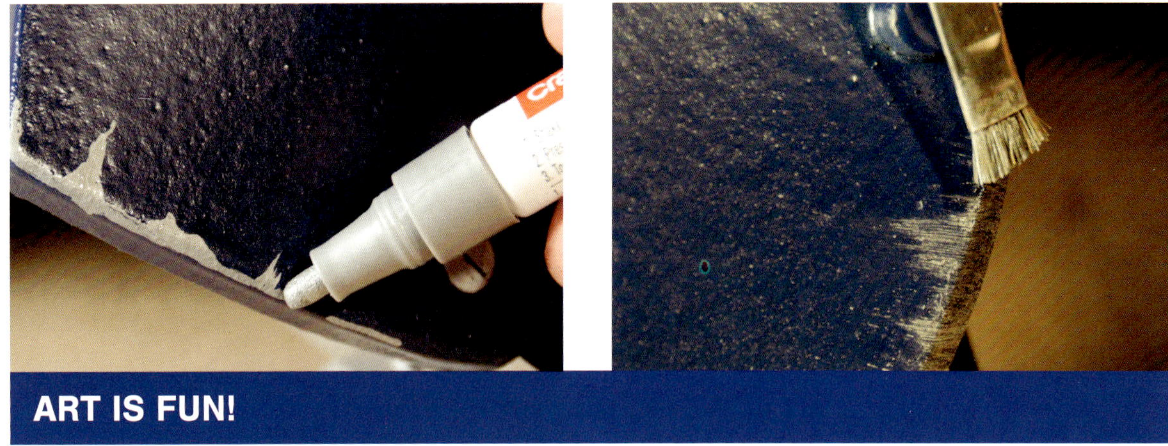

ART IS FUN!

If you want some areas to look extra scratched, give drybrushing a go. Essentially, you get the stiffest brush you own, apply just a little paint to the tip of the bristles, wipe most of it off on a paper towel, and then graze the armor piece with paint a little at a time. I like to do this in layers, adding a little bit each time. Again, practice and patience are your friend.

I try to combine painted edges and drybrushing together in a subtle manner. This type of layering, combined with your grimy low spots, will add a ton of depth, contrast, and believability to your foam armor set!

SO DIRTY, SO SEXY

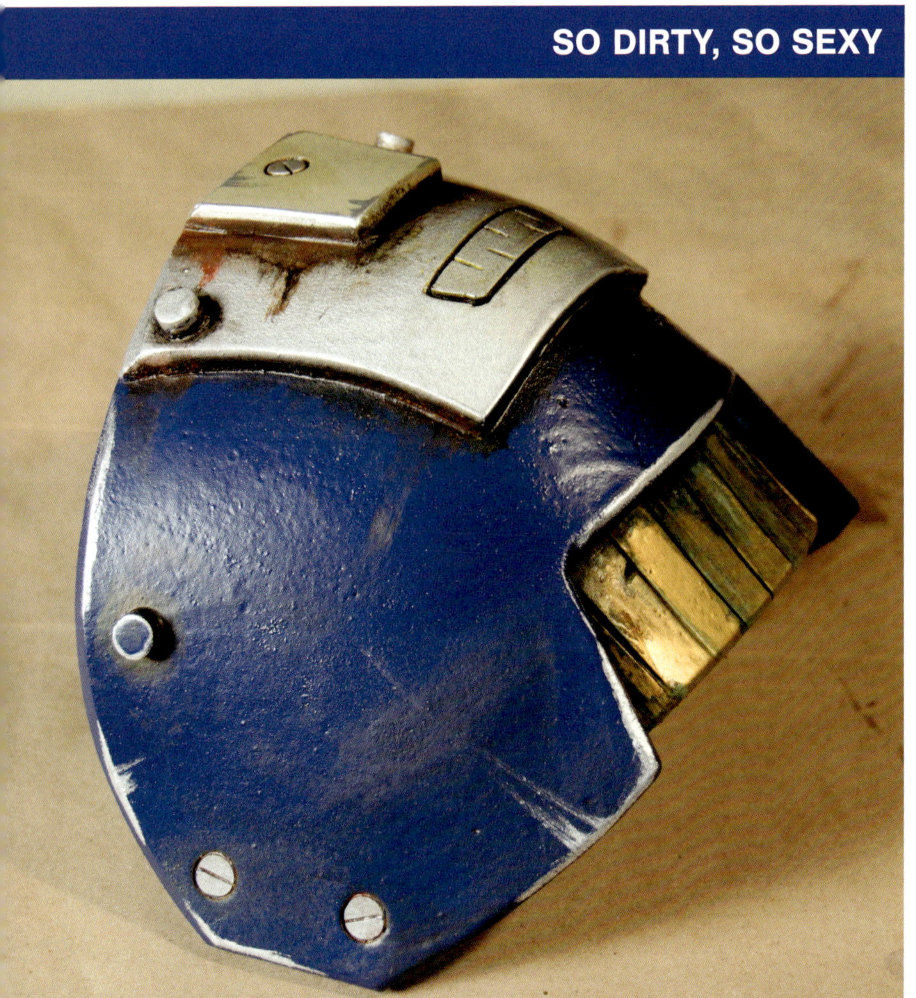

Once you're happy with your weathering job, clear coat the whole thing! I usually end up using a spray paint can of matte clear, though your results will vary depending on the project. A couple of layers of clear will protect the weathering paint, especially on the raised areas that will receive some real world wear and tear.

HIDING YOUR CRIMES

Sometimes accidents are completely unavoidable. If your armor piece is supposed to look pristine, you may have to rebuild a part that caught some extra love from your Dremel. If your armor is supposed to look damaged a bit, you can "hide your crimes" by weathering that damaged bit so that it looks like it was supposed to happen that way! As far as anyone else knows, you wanted that to happen.

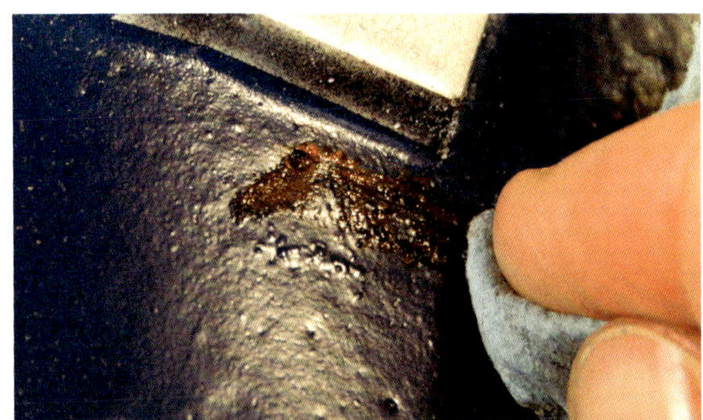

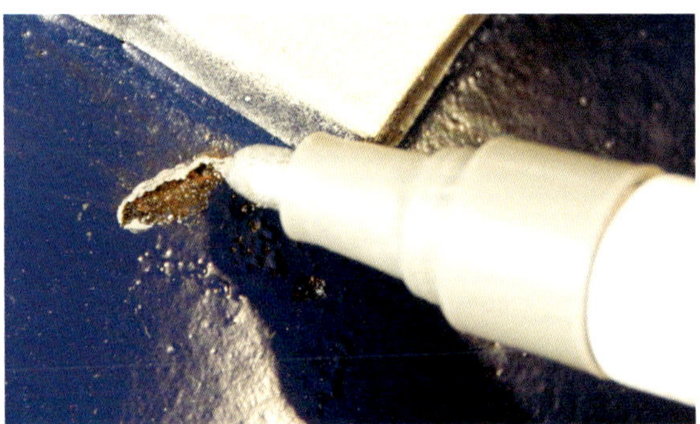

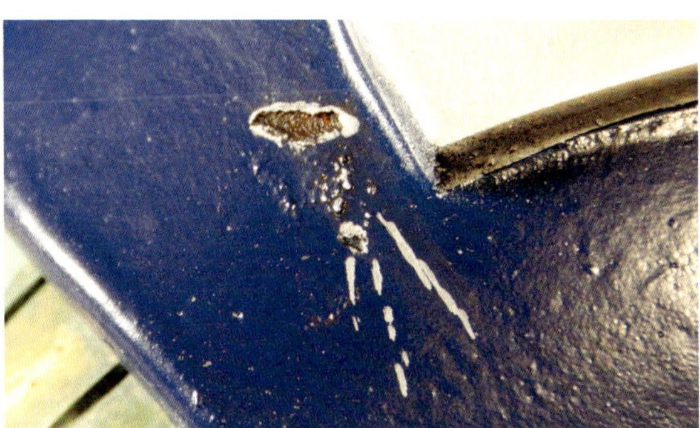

Hey, foamsmith. Your armor is painted, bravo! Depending on your project, you may be all done and ready to start strapping it on your fine self (covered in Part 3). Just for fun and giggles, here are some more techniques you can try when painting your armor.

Fun Techniques

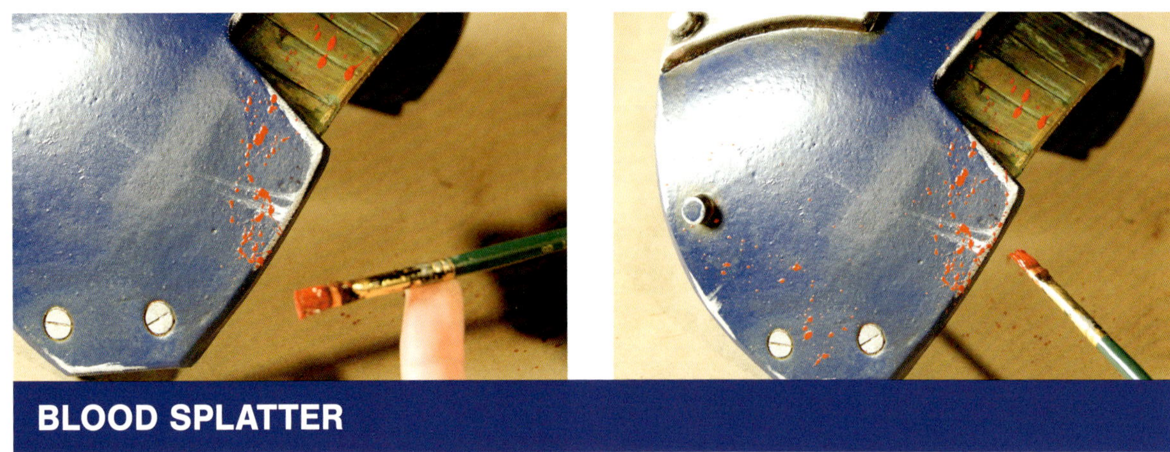

BLOOD SPLATTER

Going for that "I just curb stomped an alien and the jerk got his blood all over my new space armor" look? Try splattering some acrylic paint on to your armor pieces. Mix up the appropriately colored "blood" and then whip a fully loaded brush toward your armor as if it were coming off the tip of a mighty greatsword. I highly recommend practicing on a scrap to hone your technique.

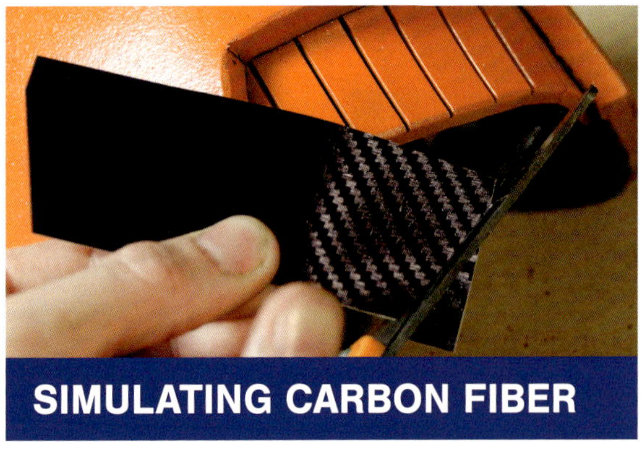

SIMULATING CARBON FIBER

All the coolest, hippest space marines have armor made of carbon fiber. Or so I've heard. You can actually get large vinyl stickers that have a carbon fiber texture on them. So if you're good with stickers, get a big sheet, cut it up, and start applying it to your foam armor.

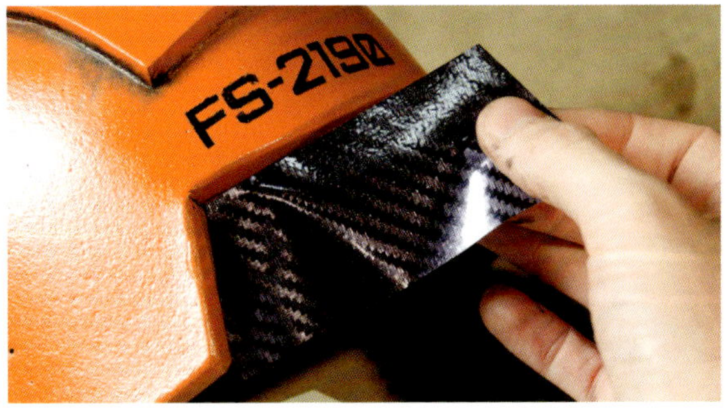

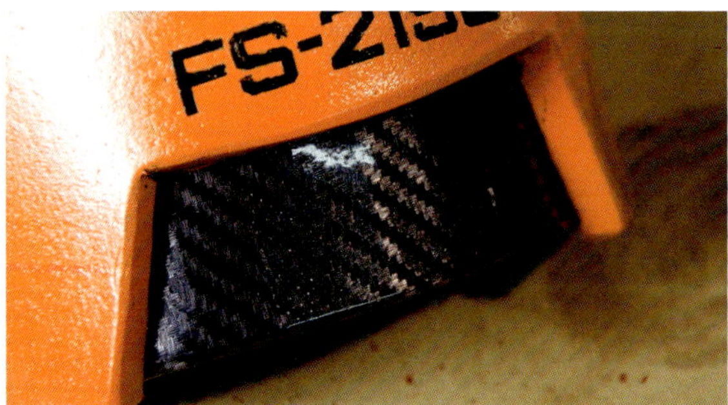

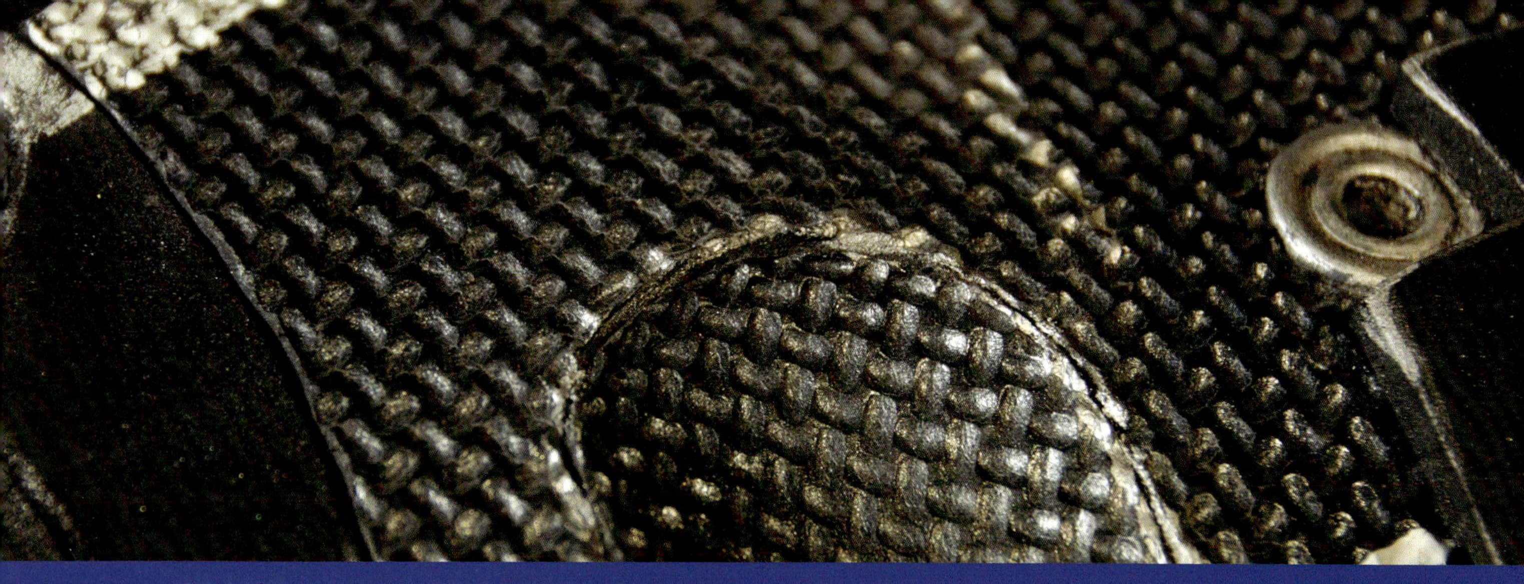

SPACE AGE MATERIALS!

I prefer to use the textured side of the floor mats to achieve a similar look. For this technique, you'll want to consider the direction of the pattern way back when you built the armor. It can be a bit tricky to get it to line up the way you want, but it'll look really nice.

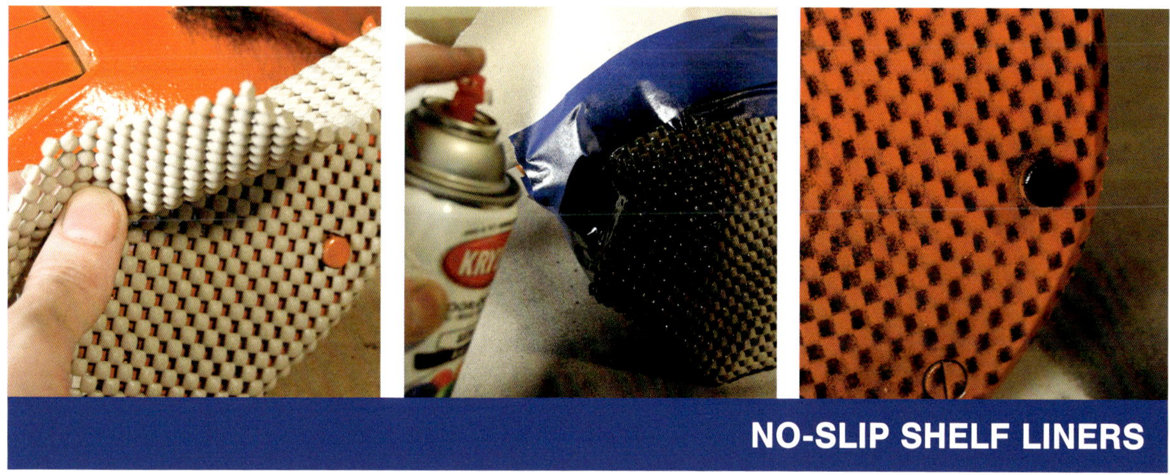

NO-SLIP SHELF LINERS

For a really quick faux fiber finish on your smooth armor pieces, get your hands on some of those no-slip shelf liners. Use them as a stencil and spray the second color over it to get a cool grid pattern on your armor!

Just because your armor is made of foam doesn't mean we can't make it rust. There are several brands of metallic paint that come with oxidising solutions that make them rust! One of my favorites is called Sophisticated Finishes. These paints are usually a system that include a paint, an oxidiser, and a clear coat. Be sure to purchase all of the necessary parts of the system. Read the directions on the bottles for specific details on the application methods.

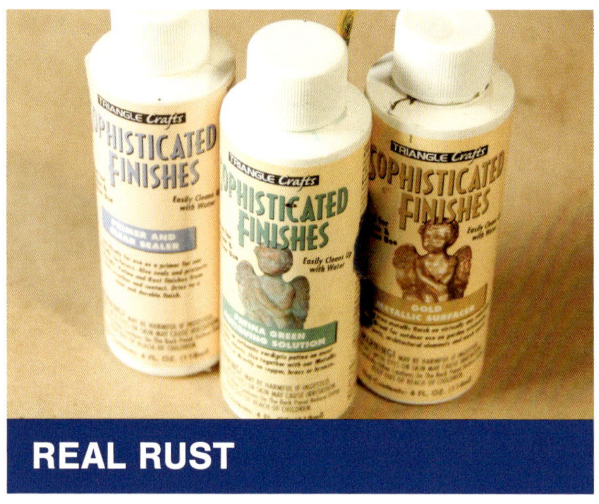

REAL RUST

Start off by painting your primed armor pieces with the colored metallic paint. Then, before it's had a chance to fully dry, dab on some of the oxidising solution in any areas that you want to rust. I try to get it in areas that would likely accumulate moisture. Or, go buck nutty and cover your entire piece. Maybe your bronze armor has been at the bottom of the ocean for a couple months.

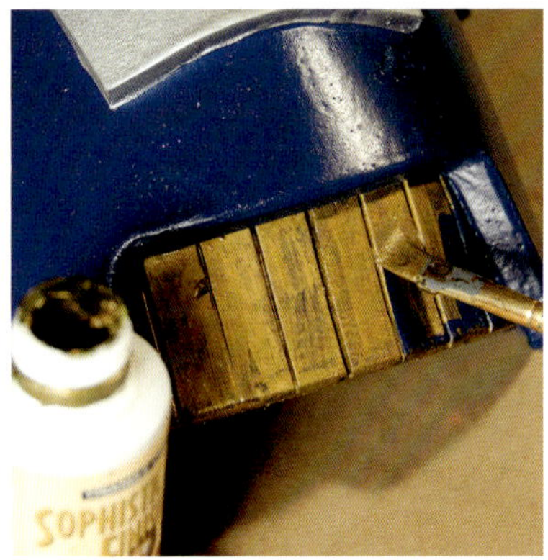

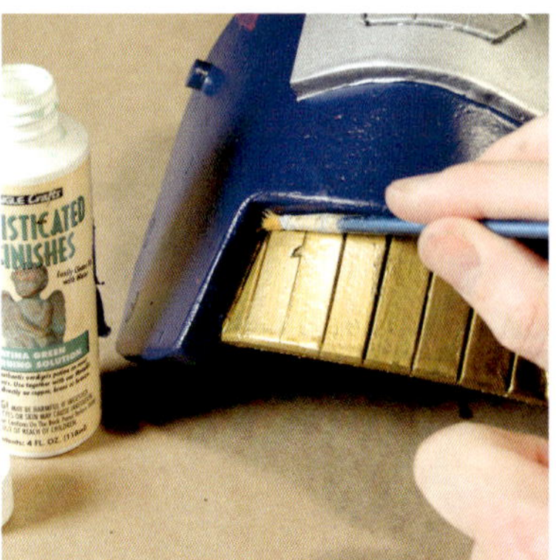

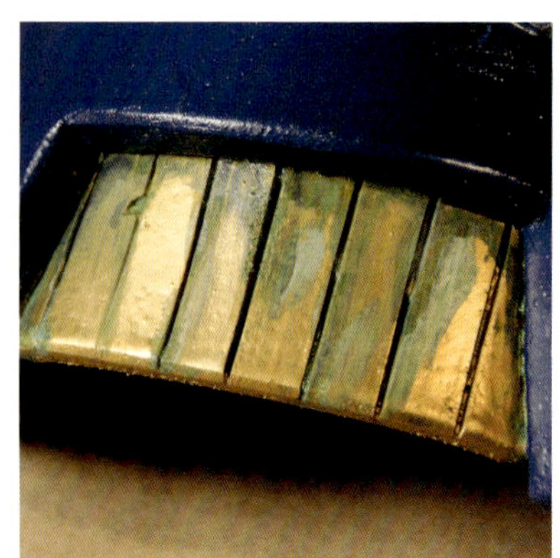

Don't put real rust oxidizers in your metal airbrush...oops.

You may be tempted to put the antiquing solution in your airbrush to apply it to your armor in a creative manner. This will indeed work, but you will quickly learn, as I did, that the oxidizer will rust your airbrush parts. Live and learn, eh? For a similar effect, put some of the oxidizer in a small, plastic spray bottle.

Once the chemical reaction has finished and the paint is fully dry, clear coat your armor and continue weathering your pieces. I like to combine this rusting technique with some good dirt and grime layering to really sell the look of a weather beaten piece.

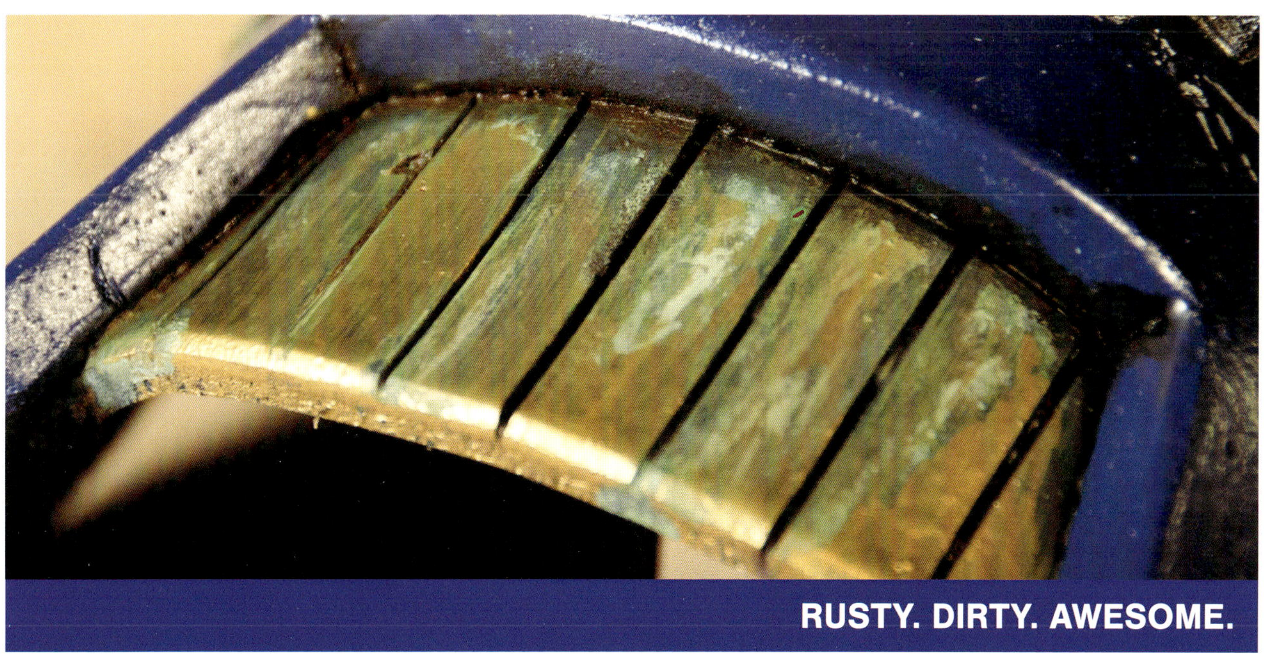

RUSTY. DIRTY. AWESOME.

If you want your armor to look like the paint is chipping off, exposing the material underneath, why not actually do that? This technique requires quite a bit more planning, but it's totally worth it!

Start by base coating your armor with the color you would imagine the armor is made of. For example, tactical armor that's made of metal, but has been painted, would be base coated with a metallic paint first.

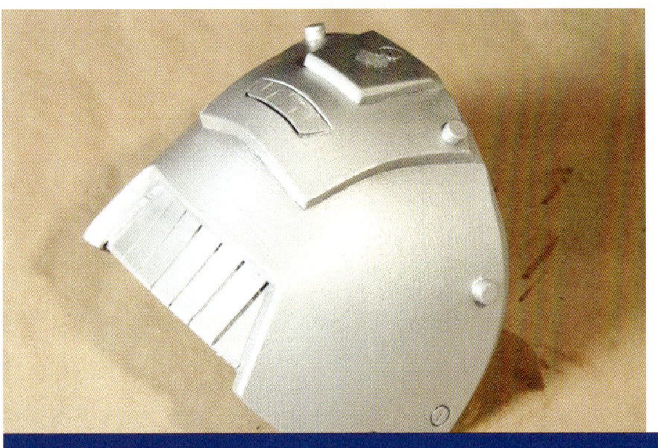

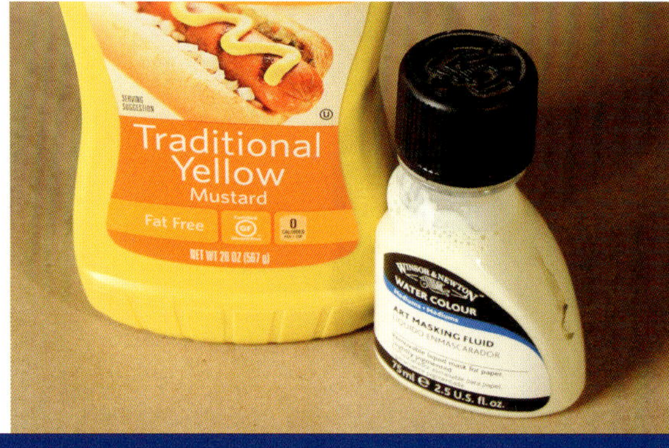

CHIPPED PAINT

Mask off small areas where you want to make it look like paint has chipped off. There are a wide variety of masking materials available. Some people like to use mustard. I like to use a latex masking fluid, available at art stores.

Apply your masking to edges and areas where you want it to look like paint has chipped off and exposed the material beneath. This can be done with a brush or toothpick, depending on how fine you want the detail to be. If your masking material requires some drying time, let it do so.

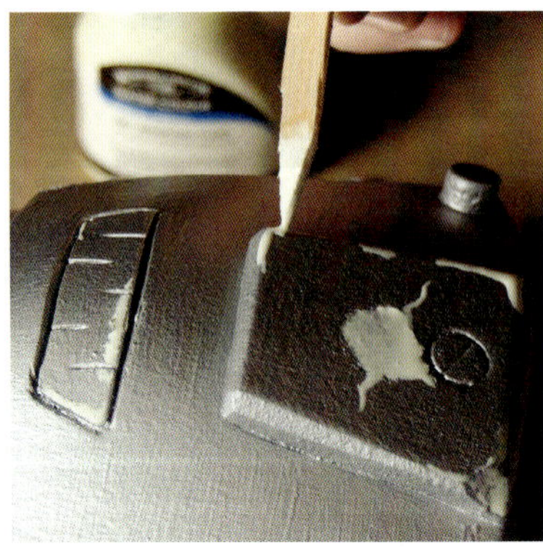

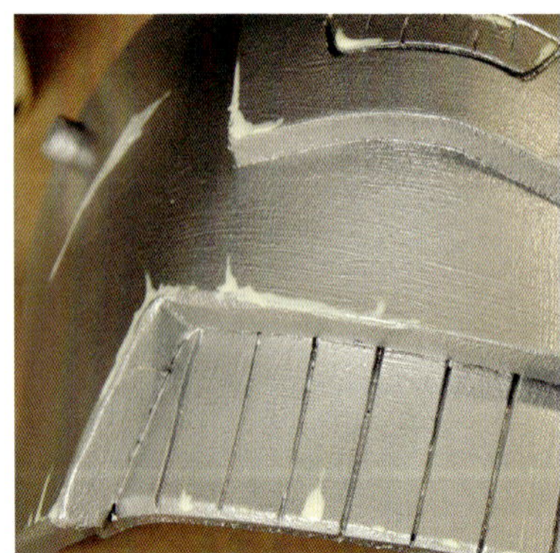

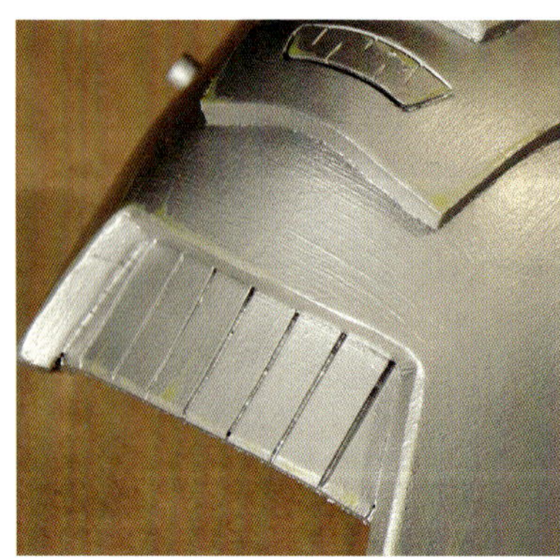

When you're happy with your "chipped" areas, paint over your armor with the color you want most of it to look like. For example, a blue paint covering a piece of metal armor. This paint will cover all of your base coat. It will look like you've simply covered the entire first layer of paint, but those areas that you masked are hiding a pleasant surprise.

If you want your chipped paint to be really deep, apply several coats of paint over the base coat. The more layers, the deeper the chips will be.

Once your outer layer of paint has dried, wipe, scratch, or peel off your masking material to reveal the base coat below! This is a lot of fun and super satisfying, especially if your chips are deep. It's hard to beat that level of texture and detail.

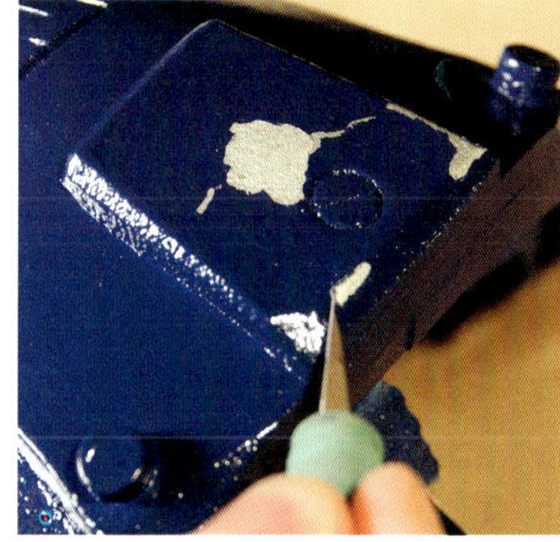

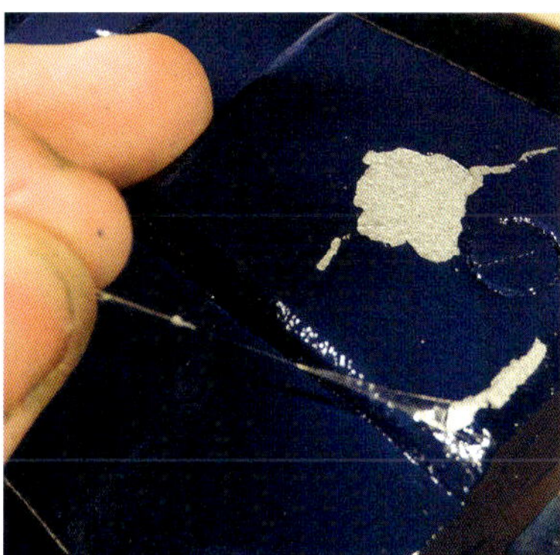

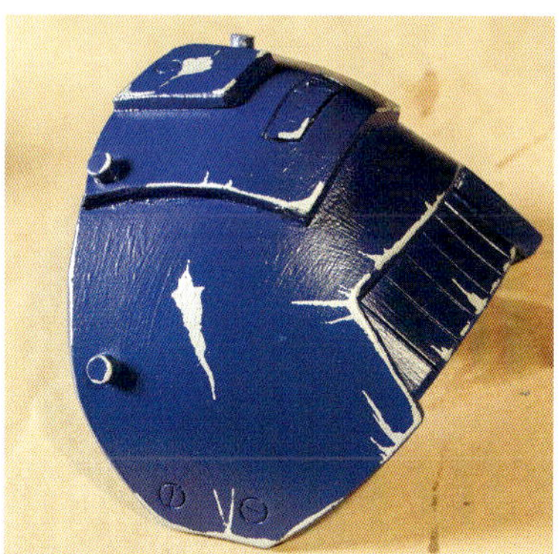

Want to take it to the next level? Add some rust color and weathering to these deep chips to look like your armor took that damage years ago and has picked up grime since then.

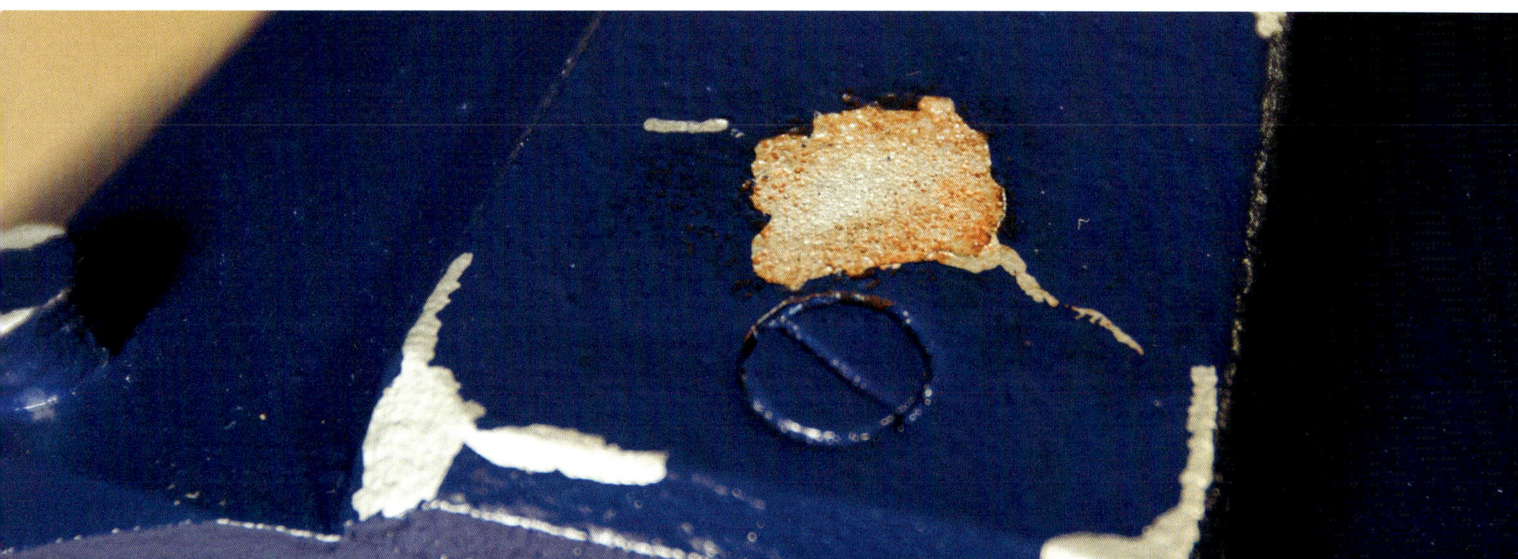

Part 3
Undersuits, Straps, & Lights

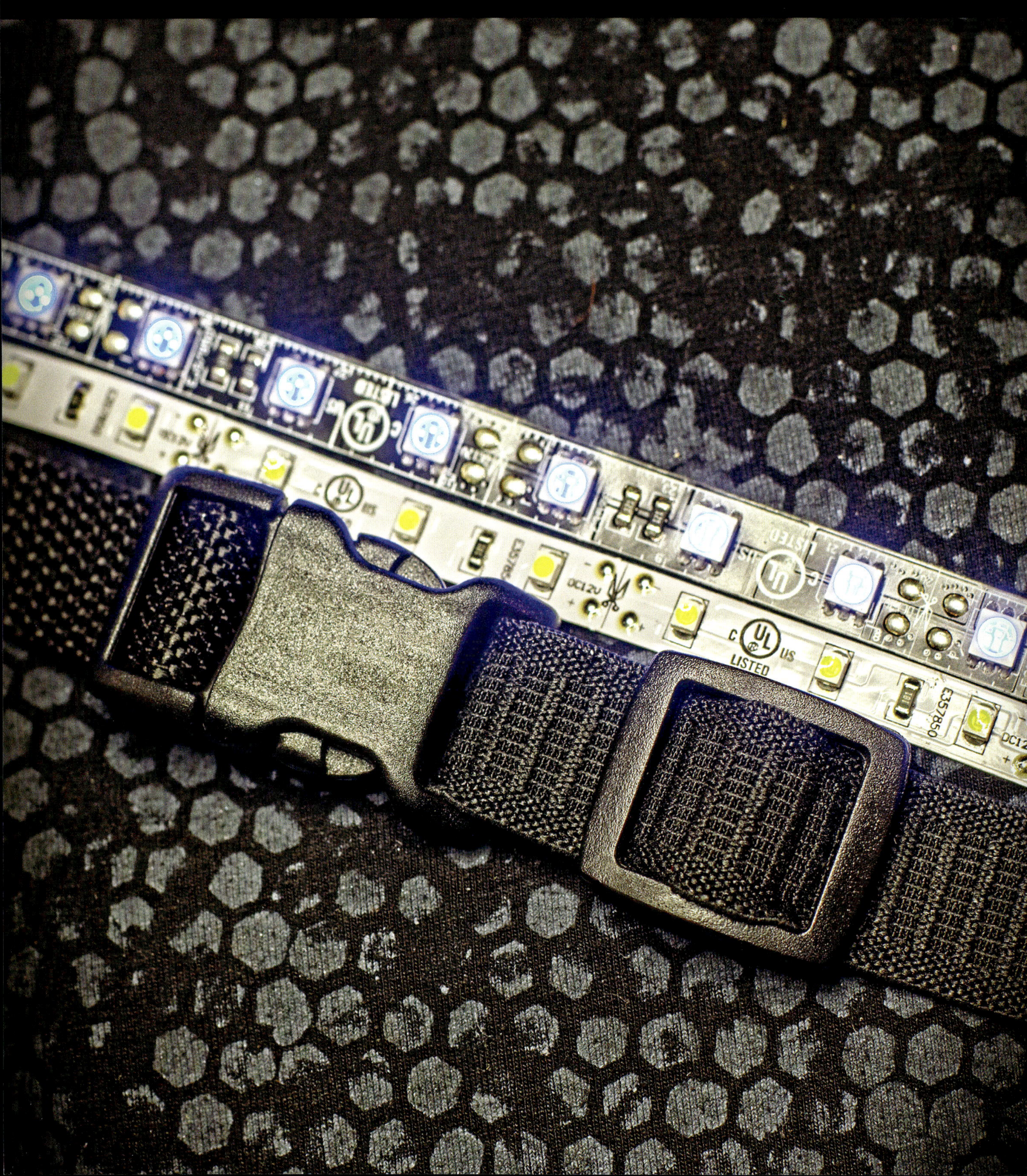

Safety

Safety is always the foamsmith's number one concern. Sewing machines can bite, hot glue guns can burn, contact cement is pretty toxic, and electricity is a fickle mistress. Always read the safety warnings on all of your materials and tools before beginning to work. Work in a well lit area. Wear a respirator whenever working with noxious fumes.

Have fun, but be safe. I want to see my fellow foamsmiths around for a very long time!

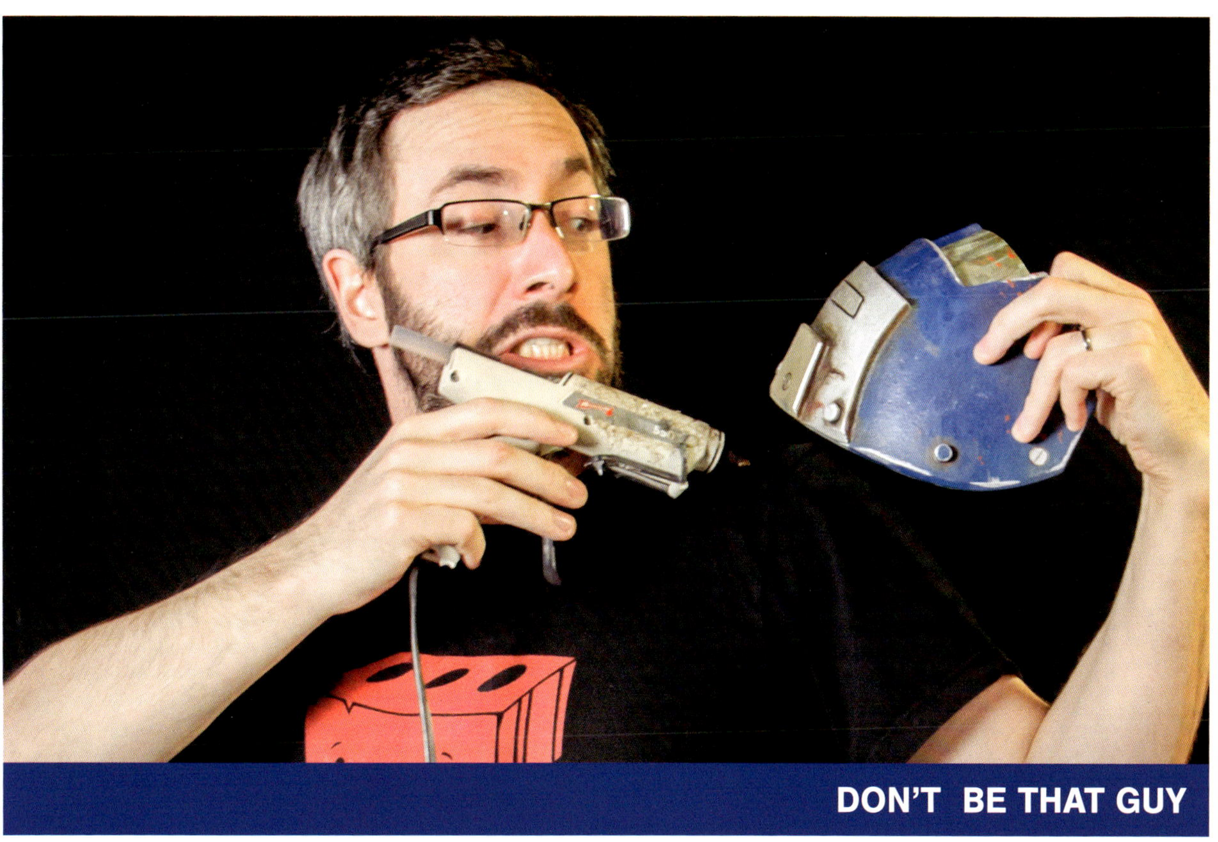

DON'T BE THAT GUY

The Functional Finishing Touches on Your Armor

So you've built a super amazing set of foam armor. You've sealed it, painted it, and weathered it. It looks incredible! There's just one problem. It's lying on the floor and no matter how much you rub it against the carpet, it won't stick to your body with static electricity. You're going to have to figure out some way to attach it to your person in a manner that is sturdy, yet not permanent.

Also, unless your armor set requires only a birthday suit underneath, you'll probably want to do something about your bits of body that show through the negative space between armor pieces.

To top it off, your costume might require some pieces to have glowing effects that add that special bit of magical flair! And you thought you were done. Think again, foamsmith! It's time to get to work and put those final, functional pieces together that will complete your armor and showcase all of your hard work!

You're not alone in this endeavor. Part 3 has everything you need to know to not only make your armor fit like a glove, but also make it look like you just strode off the battlefield in a blaze of victory. Let's dig in!

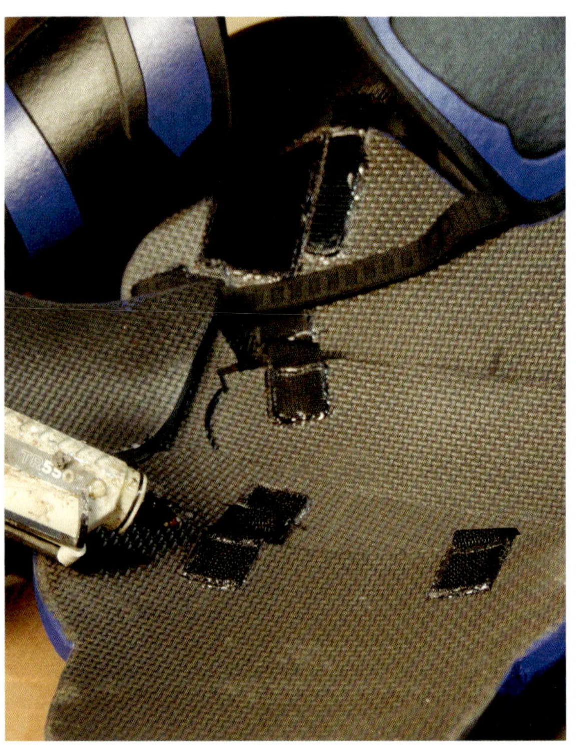

UNDERSUITS

What you wear under your armor can be just as important as the armor itself. A standard, solid color garment will get the job done, but why stop there? Simply adding a texture to the garment can break up the negative space between armor pieces in a way that really adds to the final look of your costume. If you take that a couple of steps further you can have an undersuit that sets off the armor in a glorious way that will leave onlookers wondering in astonishment as to how you pulled it off!

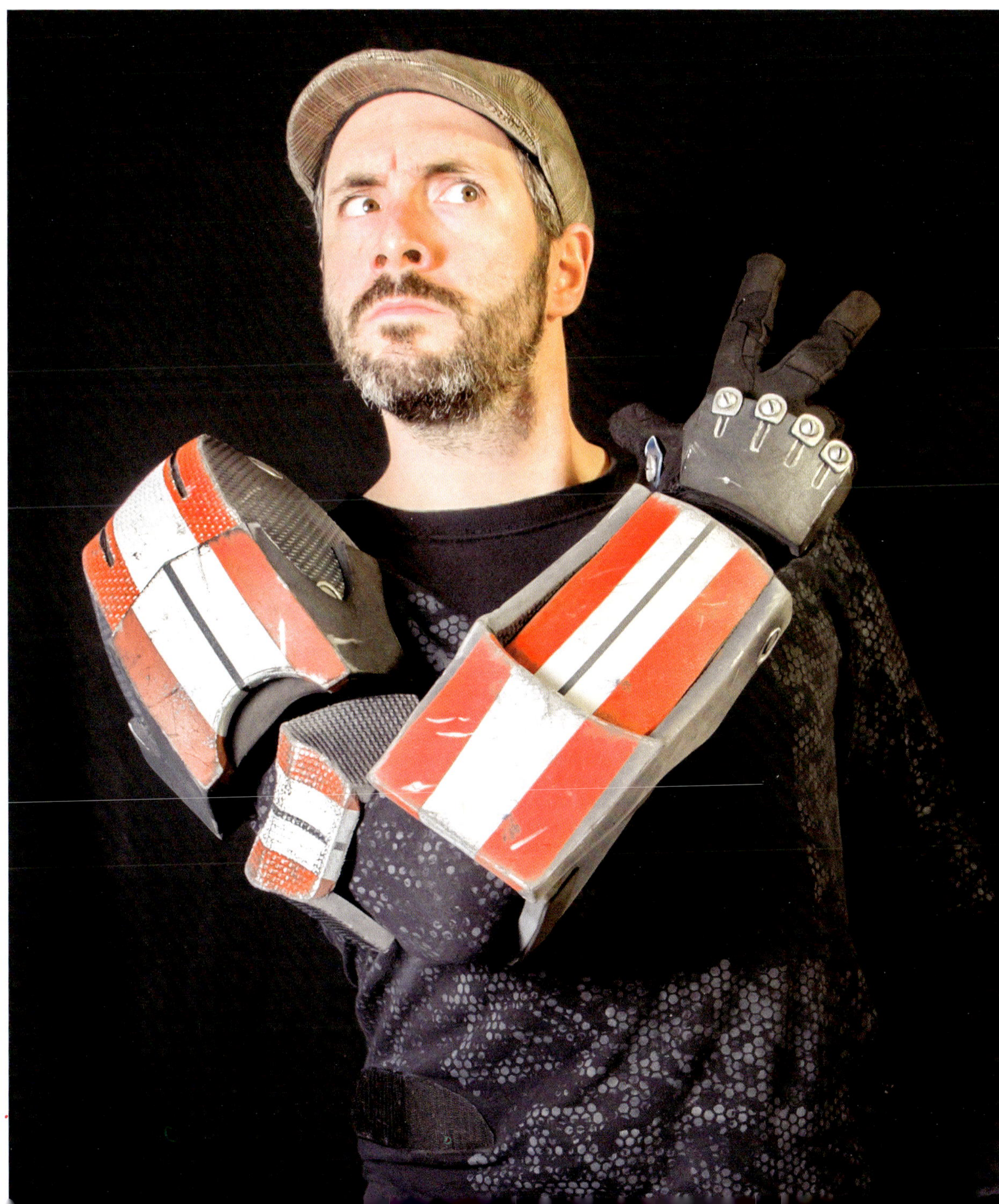

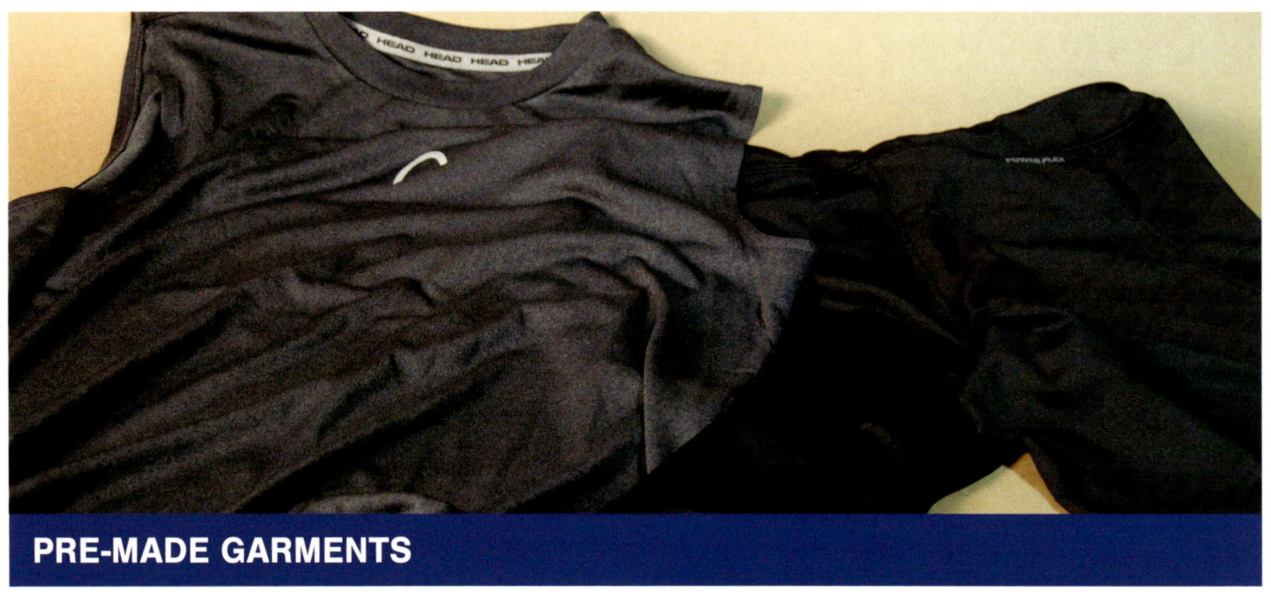

PRE-MADE GARMENTS

If your undersuit is fairly simple, I highly recommend buying something pre-made. This is a fantastic solution for your futuristic looking space armor. You can go a long way with a pair of tight exercise pants and an athletic, long sleeve shirt. Similarly, garments for dancers can be surprisingly useful underneath your armor. For the most part, these types of clothing are form fitting and will rest well under your armor.

If it's necessary that your undersuit not have a seam at the waist, you can purchase a full body Zentai suit. They come in a variety of colors and styles, including some that cover your entire head! They are made from a durable, stretchy material that responds well to being painted and modified.

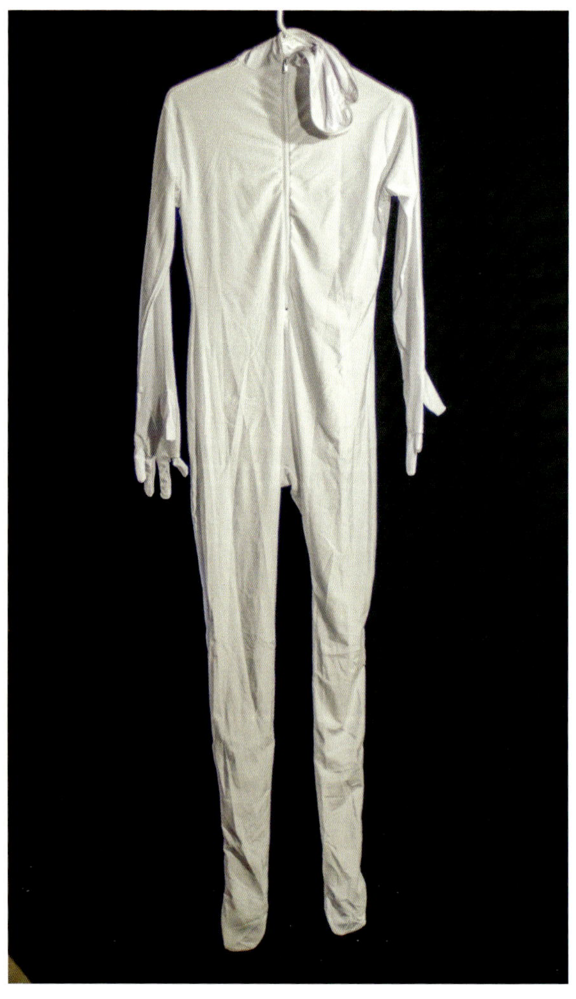

You may also luck out and find already made garments that look exactly like what you might need. If your armor is something from a fantasy setting, look for artisans who make period clothing for renaissance faires. I have a handful of clothing that I've used for pirate costumes that would also look pretty good under some plate maile. Or you may discover that perfect piece at a second hand store, depending on how long you're willing to shop around!

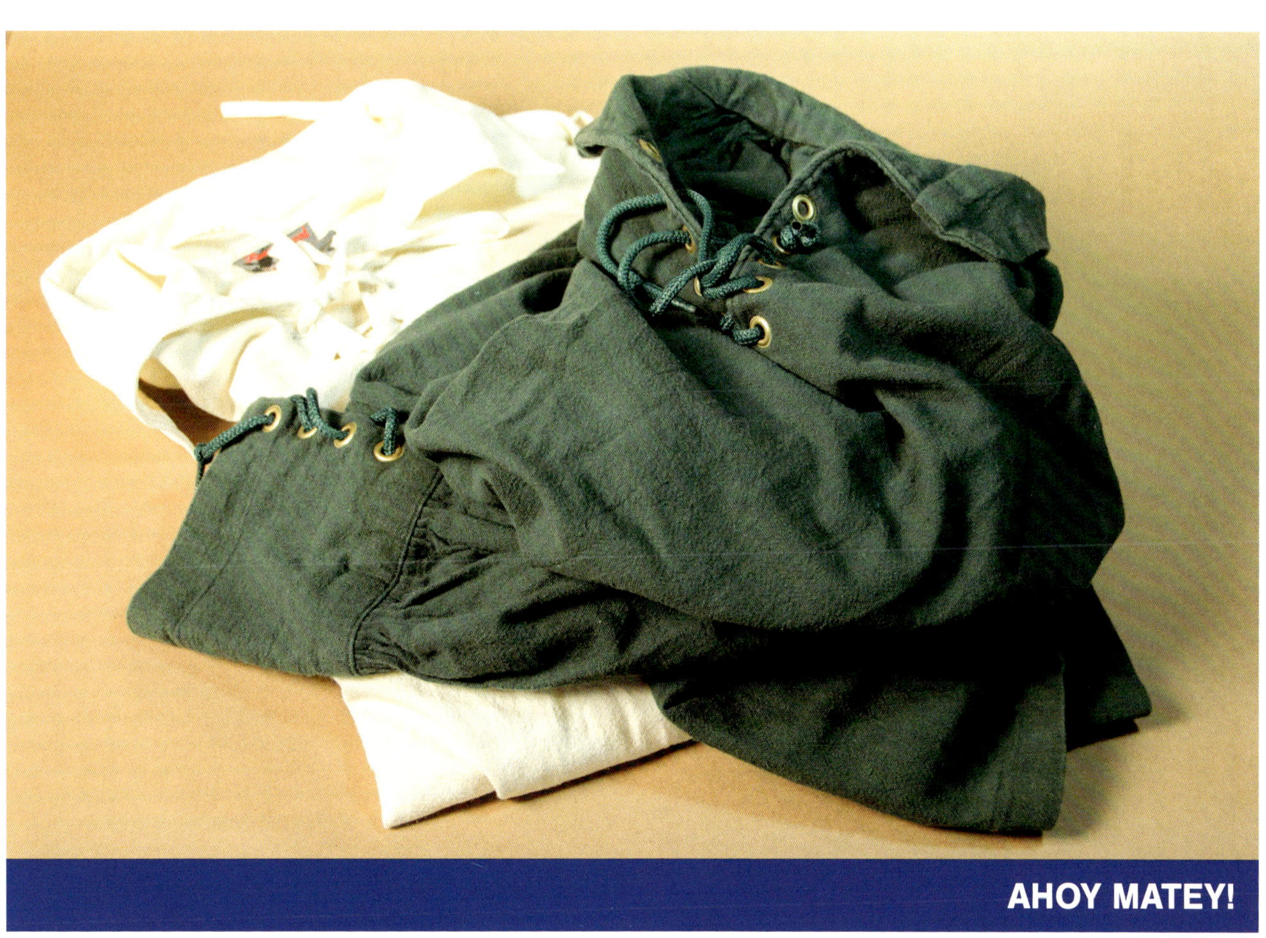

AHOY MATEY!

PATTERNS

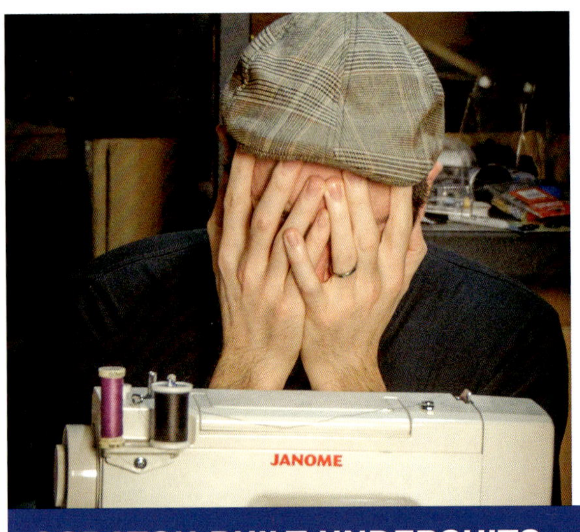

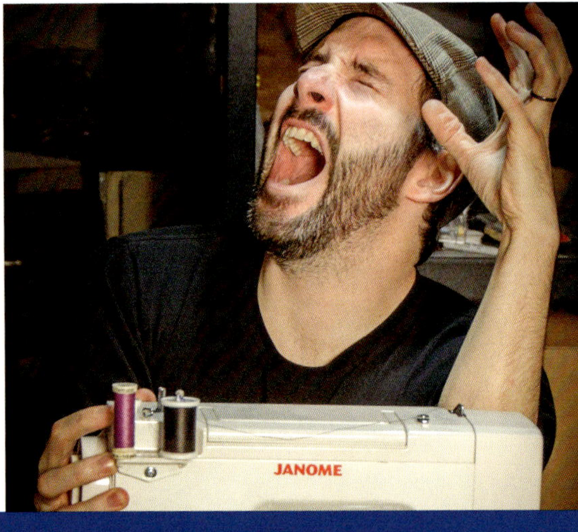

SCRATCH BUILT UNDERSUITS

Sometimes, getting that picture perfect undersuit can only be achieved by making a garment completely from the ground up. Hold onto your butts, foamsmith, this is going to require some sewing. I'll be honest, sewing is my own personal Achilles heel. Even if you're in the same boat as I am, this doesn't have to stop you in your tracks. Here are some tips to getting a leg up on sewing your own perfect undersuit.

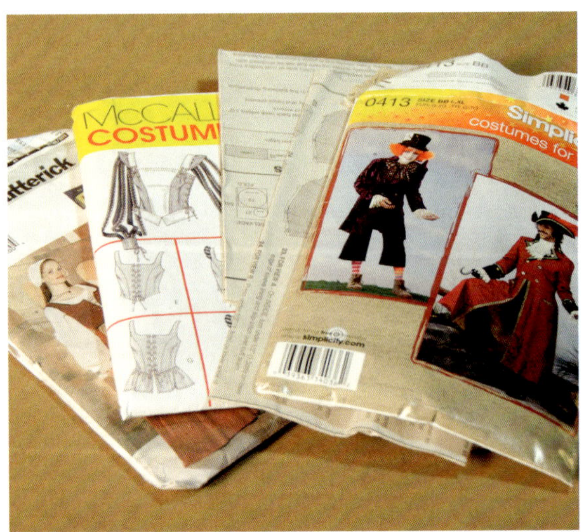

Your first impulse might be to run out and buy a pattern that perfectly matches the look you're trying to achieve. This is a good impulse. There are many companies that sell thousands of garment patterns that will help you get to your goals as soon as possible. Most serious costumers have vast collections of patterns, especially ones that make good undersuits, since they will be reused many times over.

McCall's
Simplicity
Vogue Patterns
Butterick

In your second hand store travels, you may stumble on a garment that is the perfect size and fit for you, but the cloth, texture, or color is all wrong. Fear not! Buy it anyway, carefully rip apart the seams, and then cut it up to make your own pattern! Consider transferring this pattern onto some sturdy pattern paper so that it can be used for more than one project!

Most sewing machines come with a seam ripper tool. Even the pros know sewing takes (lots) of practice!

OLD HOODIE, NEW PATTERN

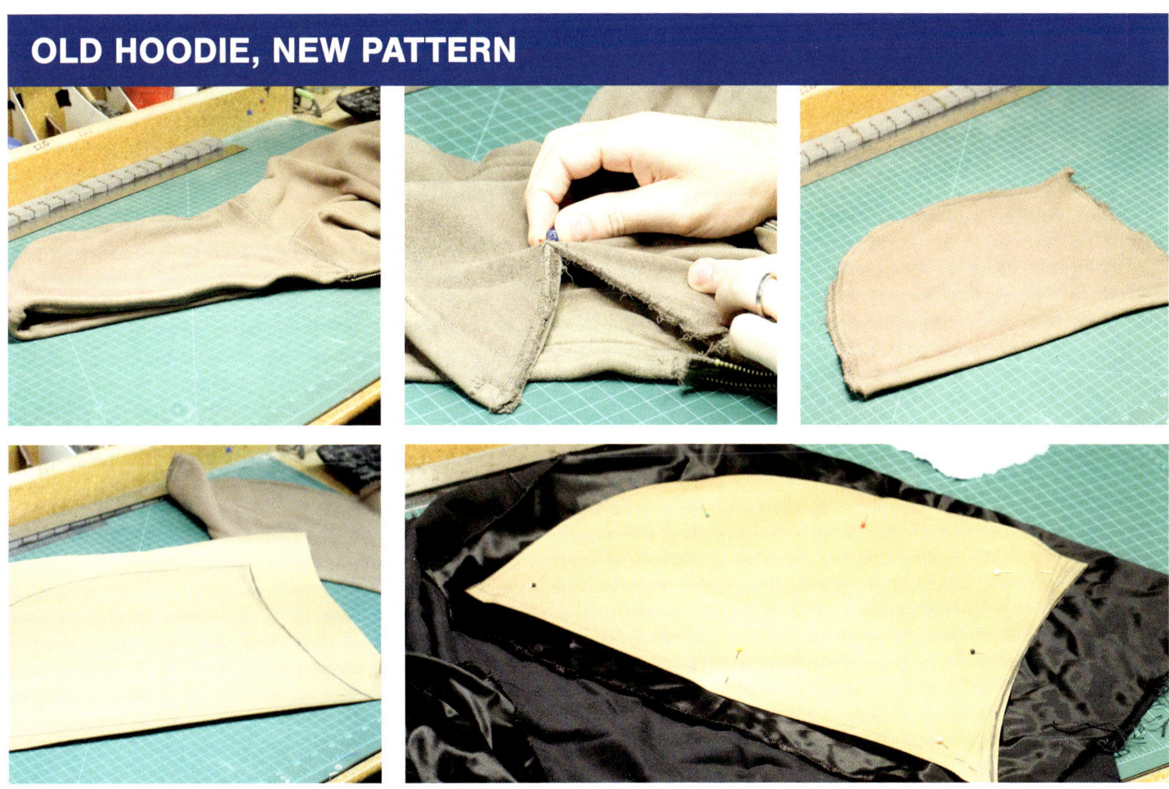

What if you just can't find that perfect pattern or pre-made garment for your form fitting undersuit? This is especially tricky for torso patterns. Fortunately, you can make a duct tape pattern of your body parts! You'll need a friend to help you out with this one.

Start by wrapping your body part in plastic wrap. This is to keep the tape from sticking to your skin. If you're wrapping your torso, you can wear a t-shirt instead. This t-shirt will be destroyed in the process, so don't use your awesome, vintage TMNT shirt.

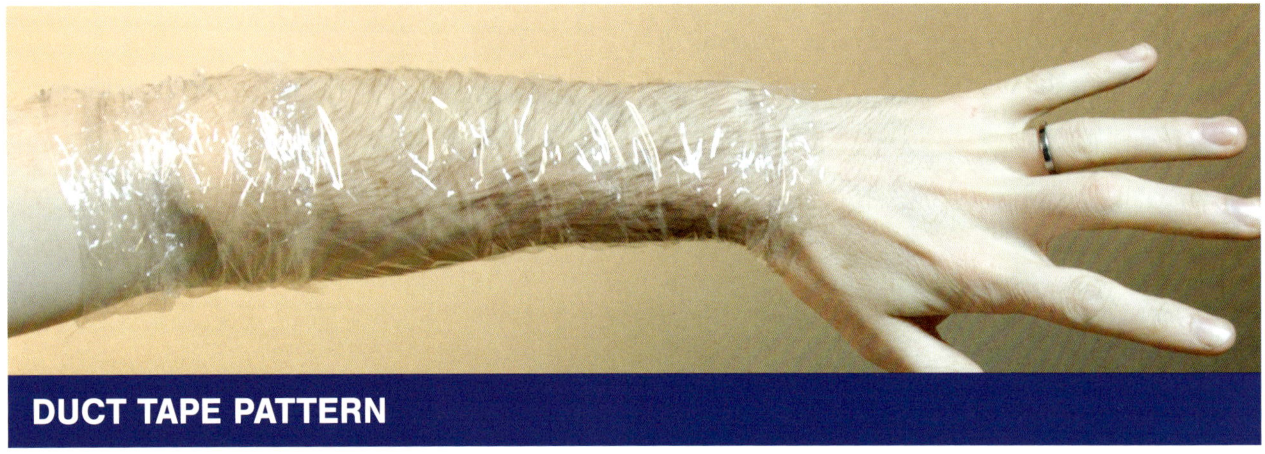

DUCT TAPE PATTERN

When you're prepared, have your friend lay strips of duct tape all over the area that you want to pattern. Be sure to have them overlap the tape so that each piece adheres to the piece below. As the model, you'll want to be as still as possible to help your friend. Don't mess with them. When you're a duct tape mummy, they will have an amazing amount of power over your fate, so keeping them happy is a priority.

When enough tape has been added to cover the pattern area, have your friend draw on the seam lines. These may be as simple as seams down your sides and shoulders, or they may be more complicated to accommodate different areas of color, fabrics, and texture.

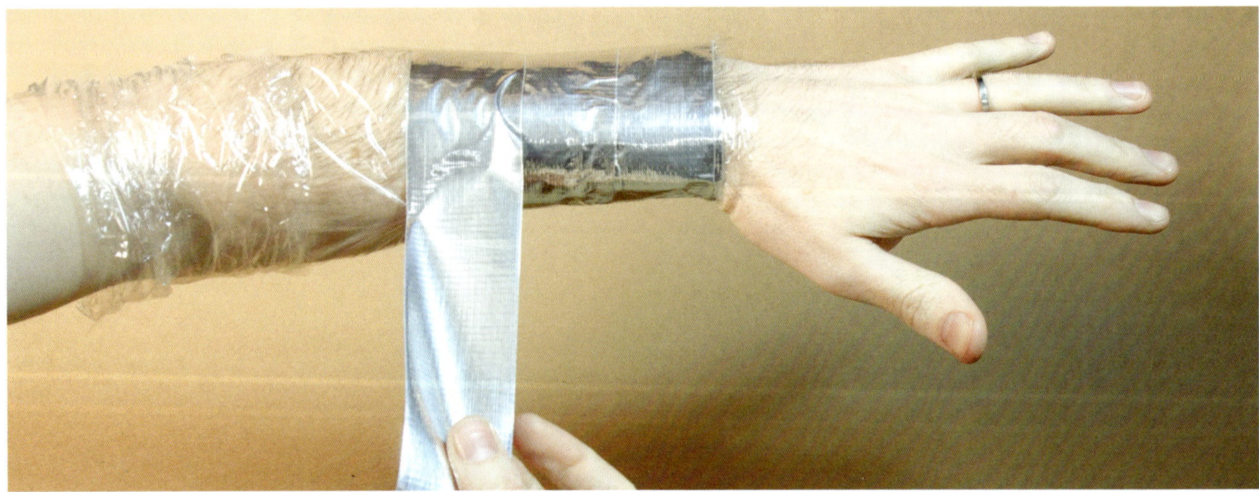

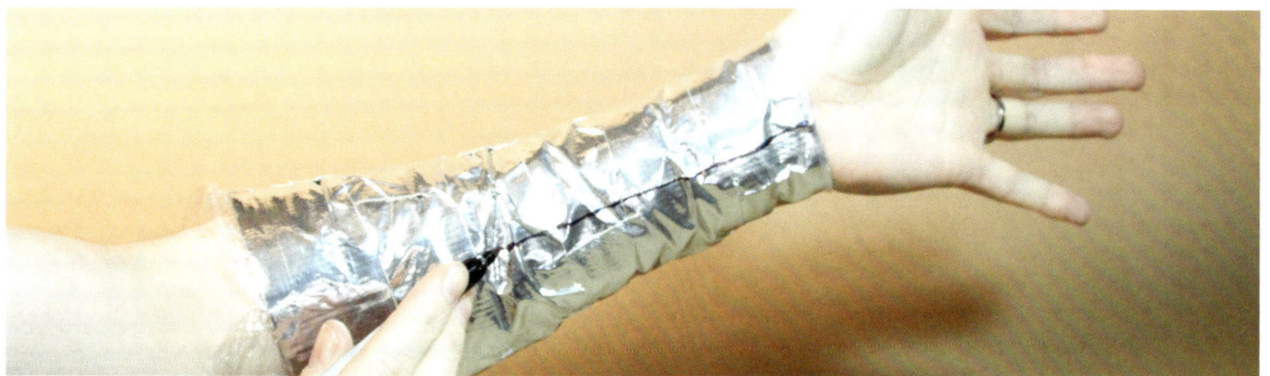

With the seams laid out, it's time to have your friend cut you free from your sticky tomb. I highly recommend getting your hands on some surgical scissors for this. They are designed for cutting clothing off of patients, so the bottom blade is rounded to protect the skin. If you don't have a pair, use normal, sharp scissors and pray that your friend has a steady hand.

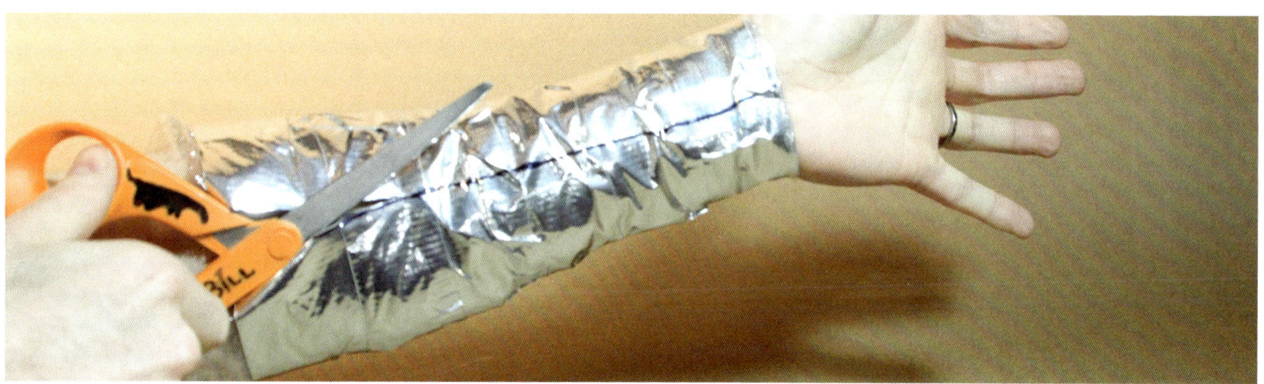

With the tape removed from your body, you can lay it down on some pattern paper, trace it out, and start using it to create your undersuit! You may have to add darts in any areas that require more shapely form *ahem* breasts *ahem*. You'll also want to add some offset to the outside of each piece for your seam allowances.

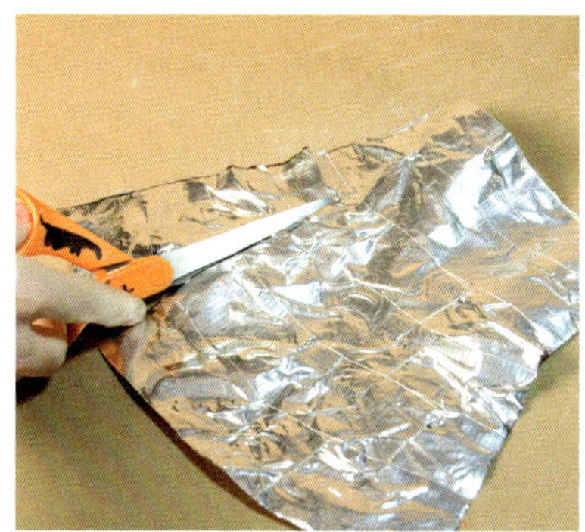

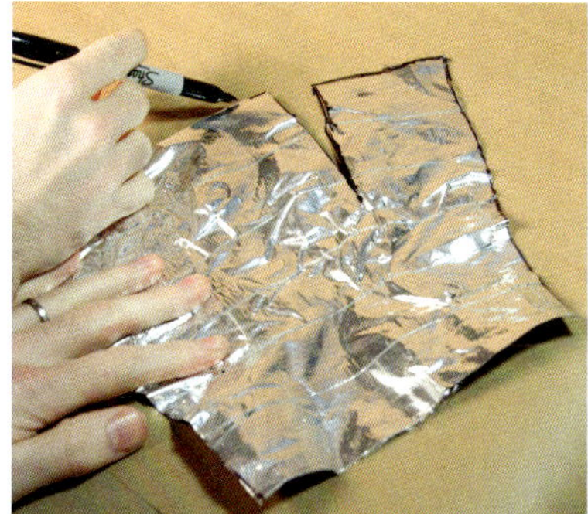

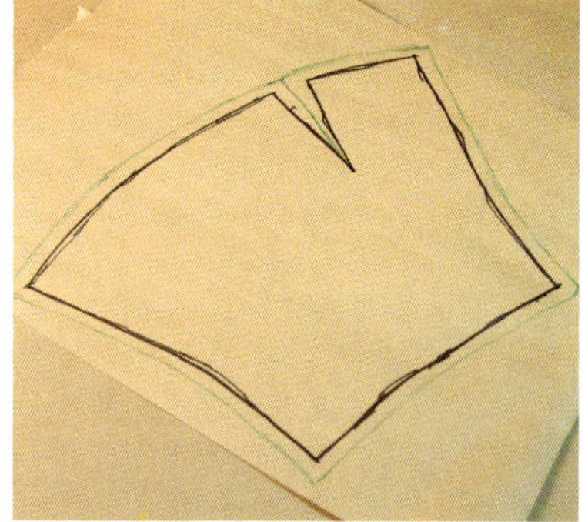

Fabric & Sewing

You have your pattern, sure, but what type of cloth are you going to use to make your undersuit? Most form fitting suits will need to stretch in all directions, so four way stretch cloth is going to be your best bet. If you're having trouble picking it out, talk to the nice people at the fabric store. They can guide you through their stock to find what will work best. They can also help you pick out what type of thread and what type of stitching will work best with your fabric selection.

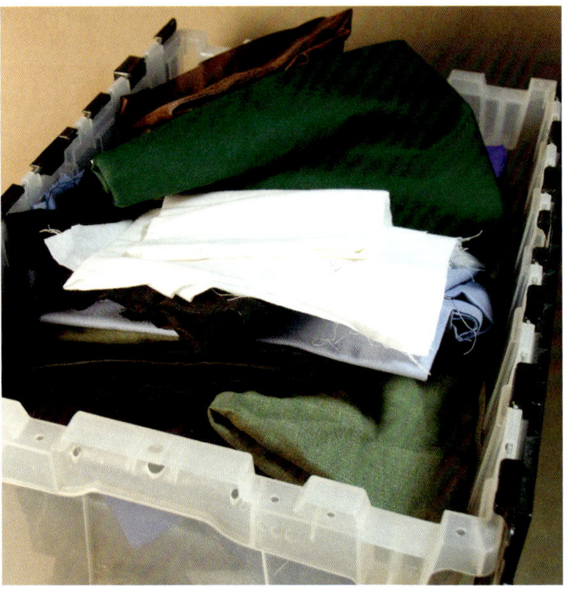

For the nuts and bolts of actually sewing your stretchy undersuit, you're going to have to do some learning. Many craft or fabric stores offer classes that will help beginner tailors get their feet wet with a sewing machine. Want to get started right now? YouTube has a myriad of free videos available to get the beginner tailor up and running in no time flat, so dive in and get started!

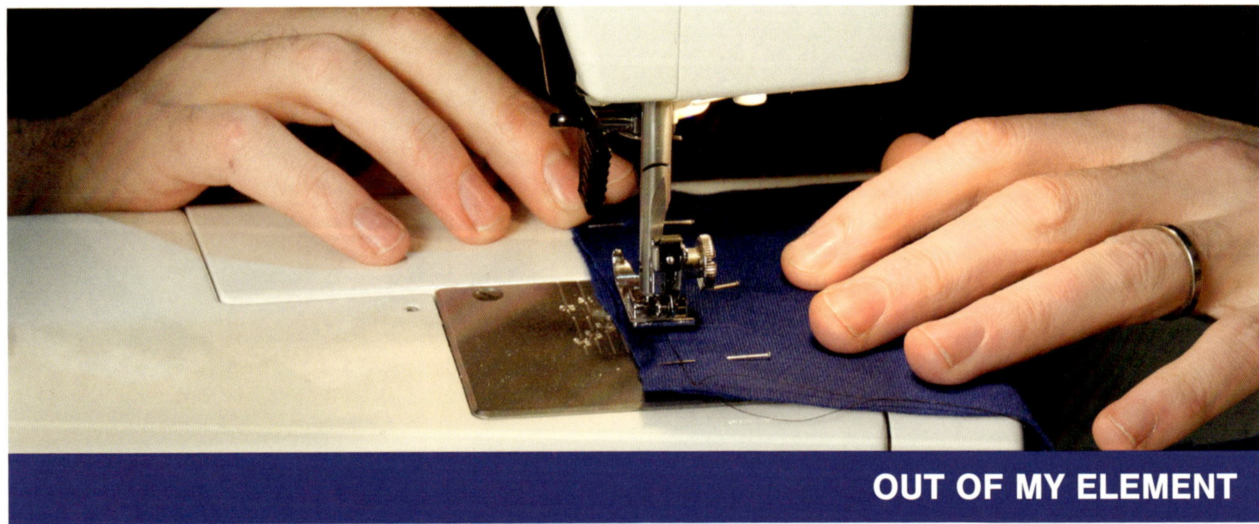

Made to Order Undersuits

Nowadays it is possible to get a completely ready made, custom undersuit. They aren't cheap, but if you're willing to spend the coin, you can order a die sublimated suit in any pattern or design. You can usually get them printed at a cloth company as a pattern and then sew it up yourself!

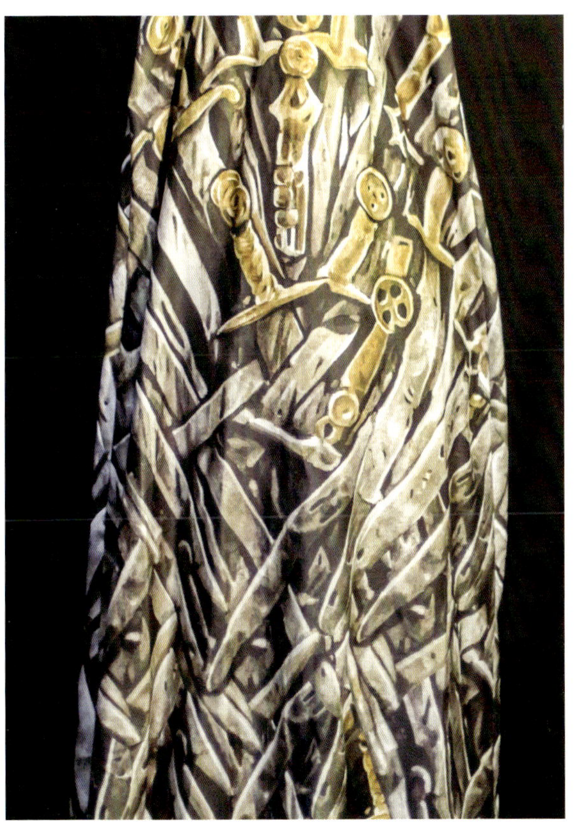

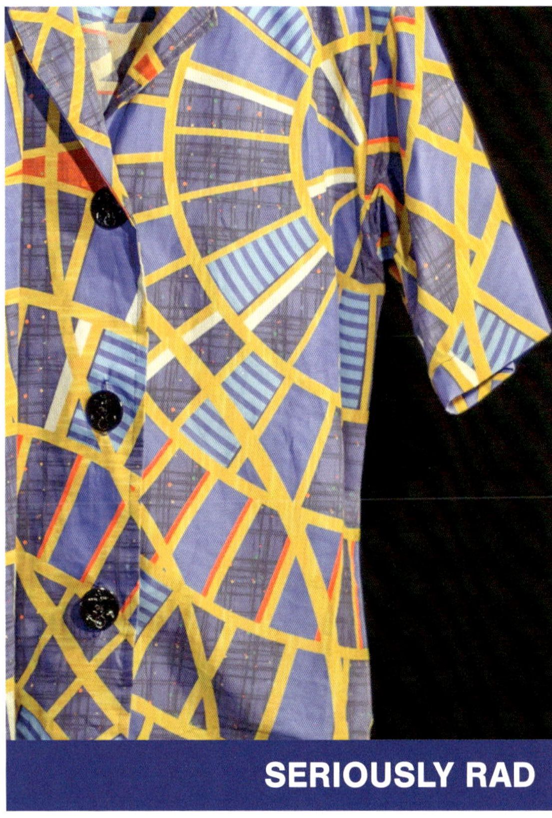

SERIOUSLY RAD

Texture: The Spice of Undersuits

Whether you've bought your undersuit or sewed it from scratch, adding a texture to your undersuit can push the final look of your armor from "ok" to "awesomesauce!" This is commonly done with fabric paints, available at your local craft stores.

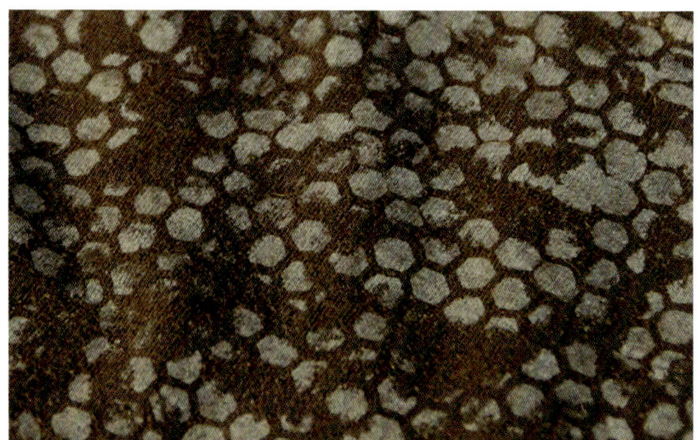

The quickest way to make a repeating texture on your suit is to use a stencil. You may luck out and find the perfect stencil at a craft or airbrush supply store. In which case, I recommend you just buy it. The time saving will be a massive boon to your mental well being later down the road.

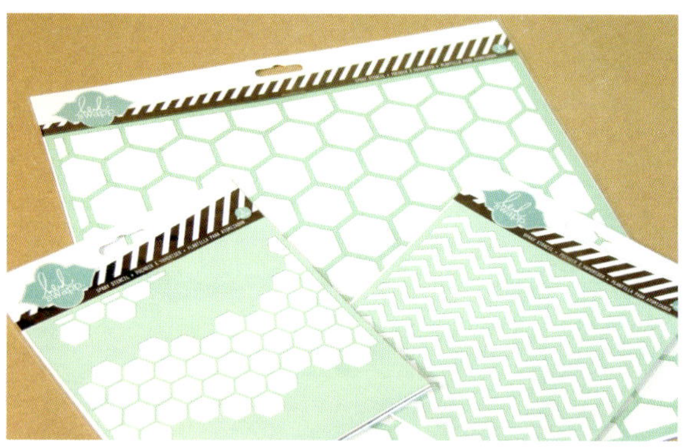

Oftentimes, the perfect stencil simply does not exist. In which case, you're going to have to make your own. Craft stores do sell blank stencil materials. This is usually a translucent piece of thin plastic. They cut fairly easily using an X-Acto knife and are waterproof, so paint won't break them down. Start by designing your texture pattern on a piece of paper using pencil. Consider that this will be a repeating pattern, so make it easy to overlay one impression of this stencil with one right next to it. Once the pattern is finalized, trace it in black marker to make it easier to see.

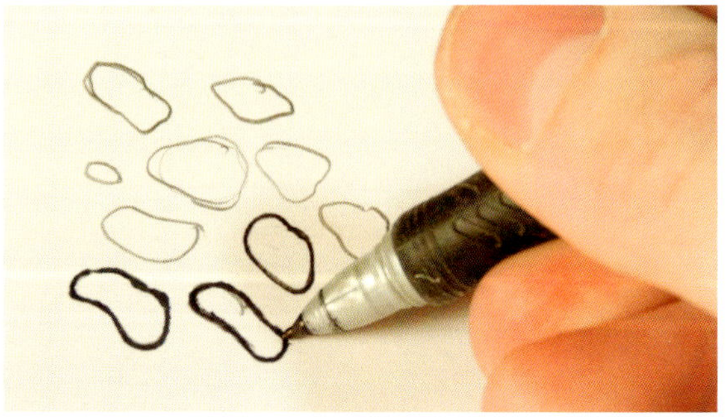

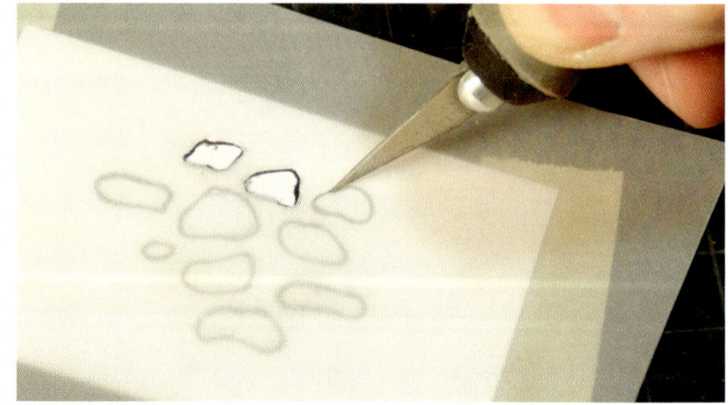

Once your pattern is laid out, tape it to the back of your stencil material so that you can see the pattern through the plastic. Now you can use your X-Acto to cut out the pattern. This may take some time, but you'll be happy to have this stencil when you need to cover an entire garment with a repeating pattern!

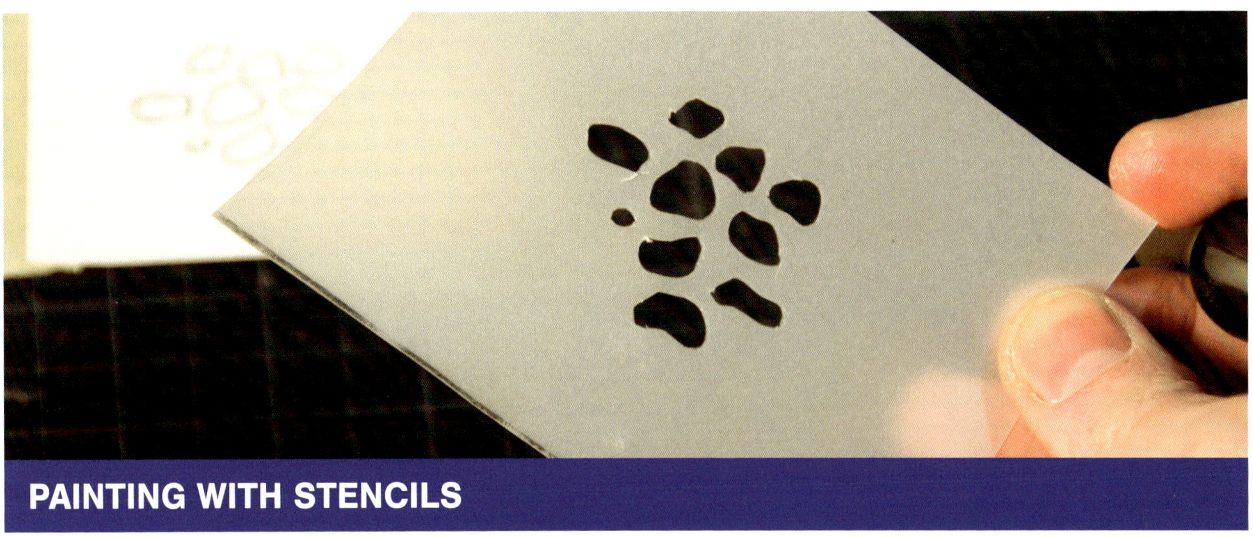

PAINTING WITH STENCILS

Armed with your super rad stencil, you're prepared to paint that texture onto your garment. Your first impulse may be to spray paint color right on to it. If you've purchased an airbrush stencil, you may be able to pull this off. Those stencils are usually made from metal and are heavy enough to not pull off the material from the force of the air. Thin, plastic stencils, on the other hand, have a tendency to lift when blown on, ruining the clean edges you're trying to achieve.

Instead of spraying, you can dab your paint on with a brush. Craft stores sell brushes made exactly for this purpose. Look for them near their stencils. Using a fabric paint, dab your paint on using the stencil in nice, even layers. Take care not to apply too much paint all at once. This can gum up the stencil and seep under the edges, again ruining the clean texture look you're going for.

"Thin, plastic stencils have a tendency to lift when blown on, ruining the clean edges."

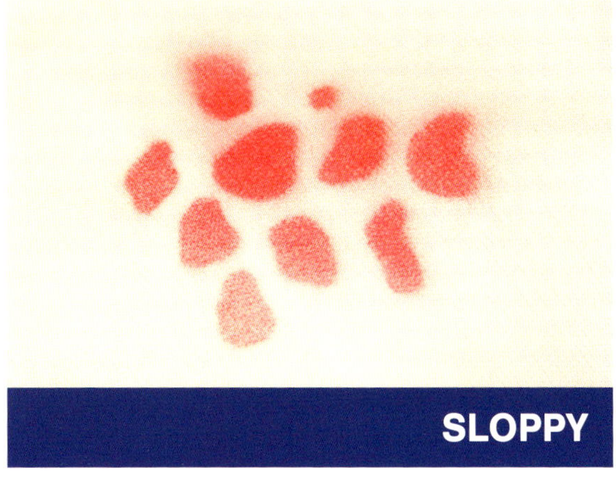

SLOPPY

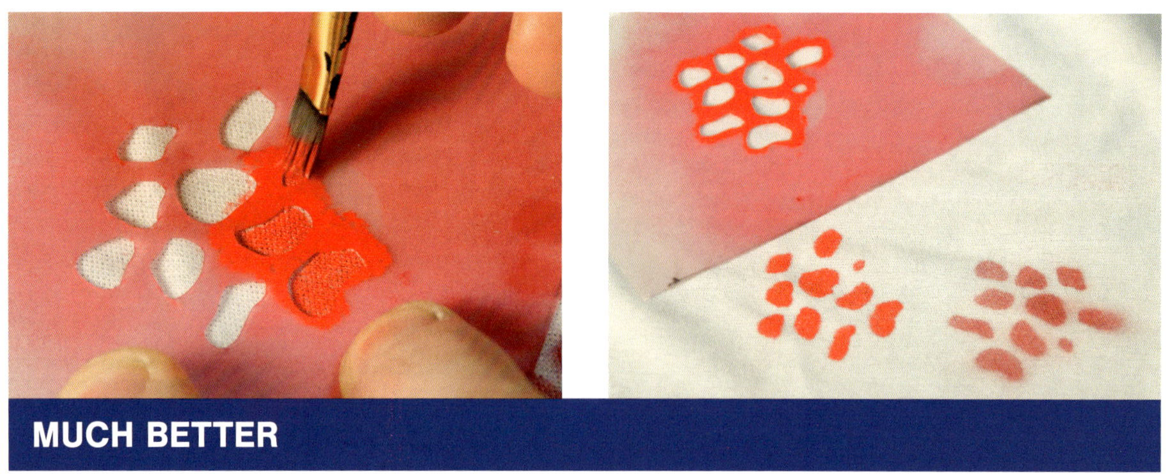

MUCH BETTER

If you're looking for a less than clean finished look, consider not going for total coverage with your stencil. You have the option to make it look kind of splotchy, revealing a worn looking texture when the stencil is removed. Also consider using multiple colors to add a bit of visual variety to the finished look.

You will need to overlap the stencil many times to cover your entire garment. While fabric paint dries fairly quickly, laying the stencil over paint that is still wet can be a bit of a problem. Keeping a heat gun or hair dryer on hand to quickly set the paint can help expedite this process.

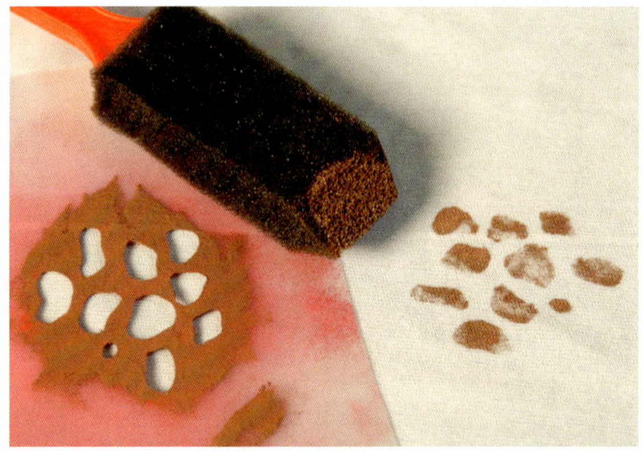

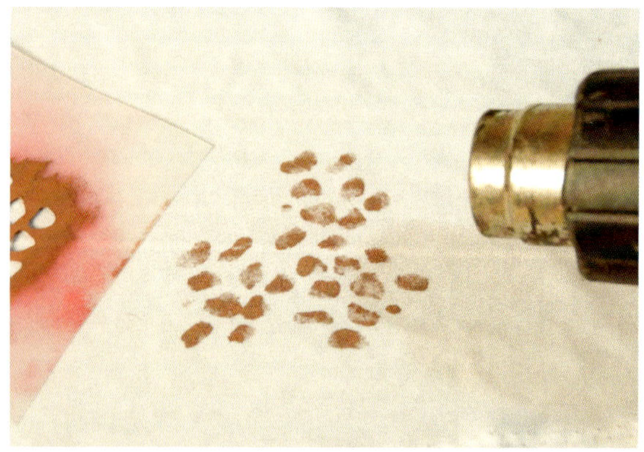

DRAWING ON MORE DETAIL

Some of your undersuit may have details other than the texture that you'll want to apply. Some of this detail may be included in the original garment, or you may opt to add it later, simply by drawing it on. Fabric markers are amazing for this type of work. I've also found that drawing on darker fabric works better with more robust paint pens. Be sure to test your markers on fabric scraps or an unseen area of your garment before trying to cover a vital area.

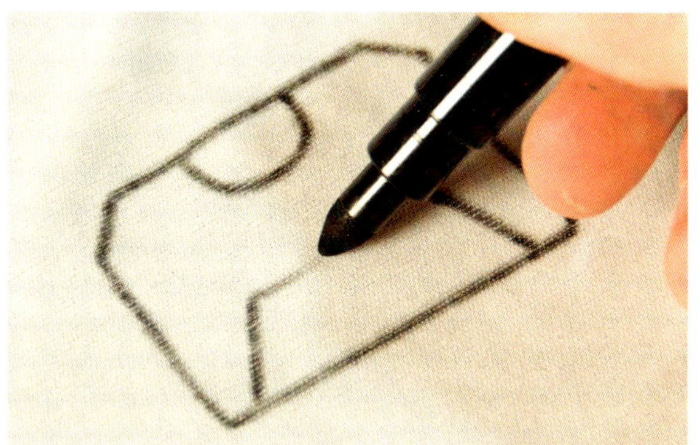

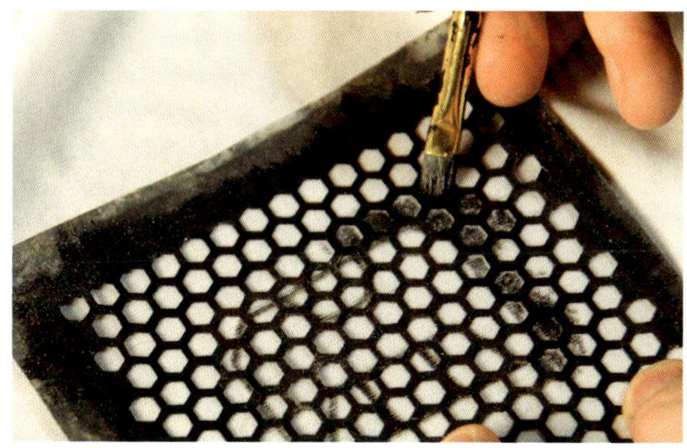

This technique is fabulous for adding detail to areas on an undersuit that will do a lot of flexing like the armpits, elbow pits, and knee pits. Generally, all of your pits.

This method can be overlapped with your texture stencil paint for some really stunning results. In fact, it may pay to draw any detail lines on prior to stenciling. This way you can lay the stencil over a drawn on detail and stencil paint around it, getting a very clean, finished look.

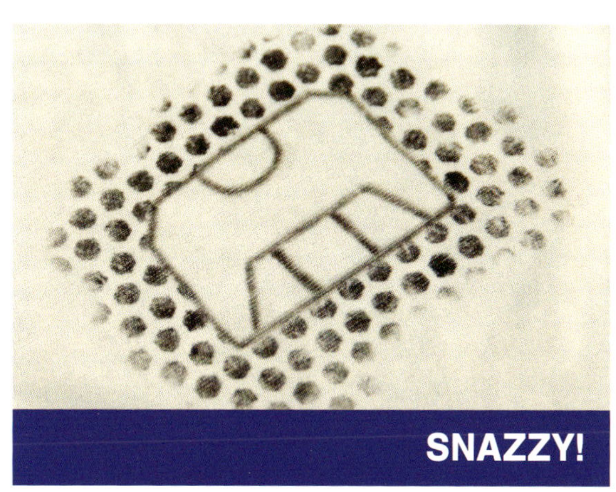

SNAZZY!

ZIPPERS

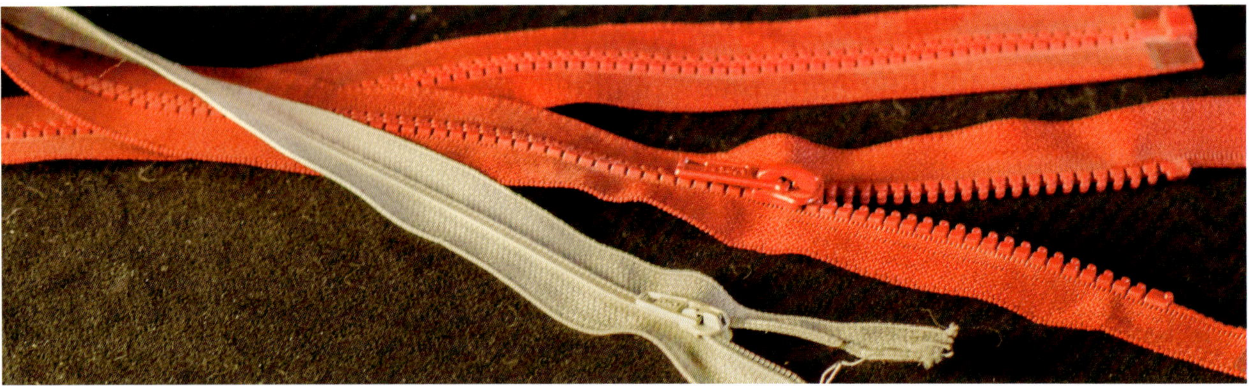

If your garment doesn't have a built in zipper handy, you may need to add one yourself. The back tends to be the best place to put one, but that may vary based on your armor. In general, look for the largest area of your torso that is covered by foam armor and add the zipper there. Keep in mind that you may need to add more than one zipper.

If you've purchased a Zentai suit for your armor, you'll find that it comes with its own zipper that goes right up your spine. This can be incredibly handy, provided that it's covered by back armor or some kind of a cape. I recommend adding a length of string to the zipper so that you can get it on and off by yourself, much like a wetsuit.

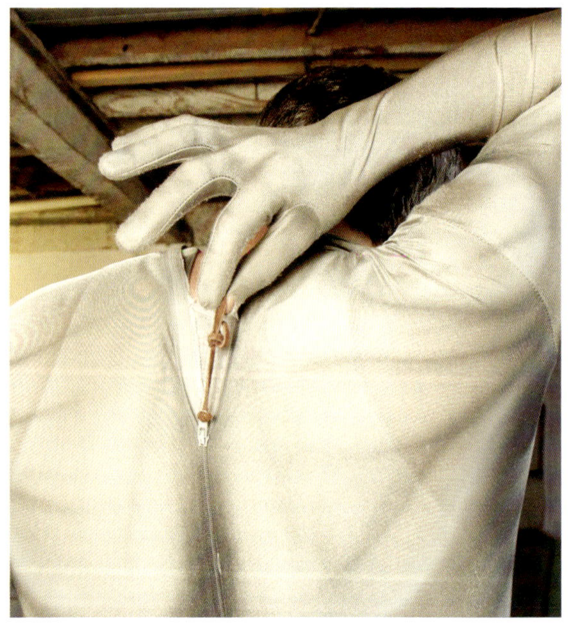

Personal Hygiene Considerations

One major downside of wearing a full body, back zipper Zentai suit covered in armor is the functional problem of using the restroom. For us gentlemen, adding a bit of a slit in the "crotch region" of your undersuit can solve 50% of your bathroom emergencies. For lady folk and the other 50% of restroom usage issues, you're going to really appreciate being able to get that back zipper down by yourself when the time comes. You might even create a horizontal slit along the back of the suit that buttons, zips, or Velcros closed when not in use. Your own personal experimentation at home prior to suiting up at DragonCon will go a long way to solve this issue before it's an actual life or death disaster.

You can also split your full body suit into a top and bottom (or, just use athletic shirt and pants). This may eliminate the need for a back zipper and will be a life saver come potty time. If you need the shirt and pants to line up perfectly at your waist, you can add velcro or snaps to the edges so that they seal you in while you're armored up, looking your best!

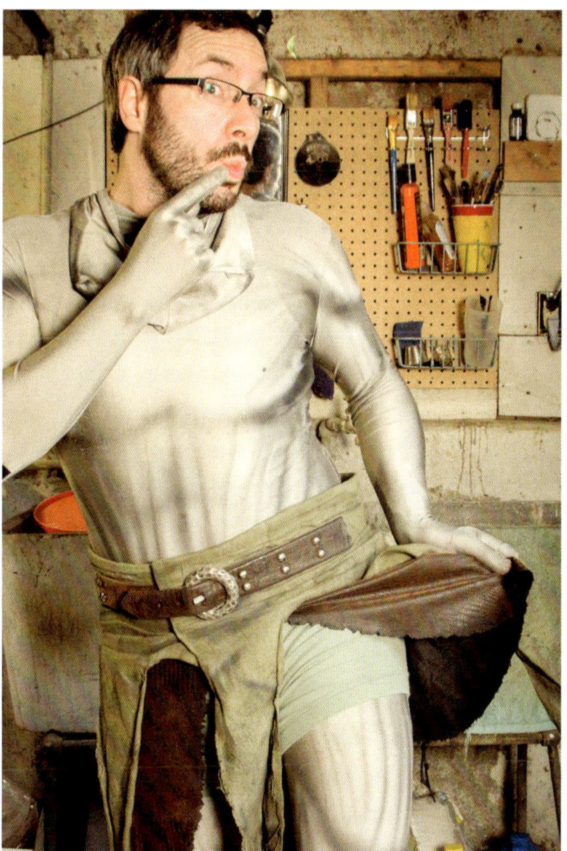

Also consider wearing something over your body suit to keep your "revealed" private areas a little bit more obscured. Your armor may have a codpiece or loin cloth, but these could become slightly airborne in one of your more spirited cosplay moments. Instead of revealing a bare body suit underneath, you might want to show off your Ancient Nord Briefs instead!

It's photos like this that keep me from running for public office.

While we're on the subject of our nether regions, let's have a chat, gentlemen. If you're wearing a skin tight undersuit, everyone else around you will appreciate any effort you make to keep your bait and tackle reigned in. The most effective method I've found is to wear a "dance belt," used by stage performers. It's like an athletic supporter, but it's designed to turn a wild bulge into a more visually pleasing lump. Other options are to double up on tight undergarments, like boxer briefs. I like to do this with the addition of a pair of constricting bicycle shorts.

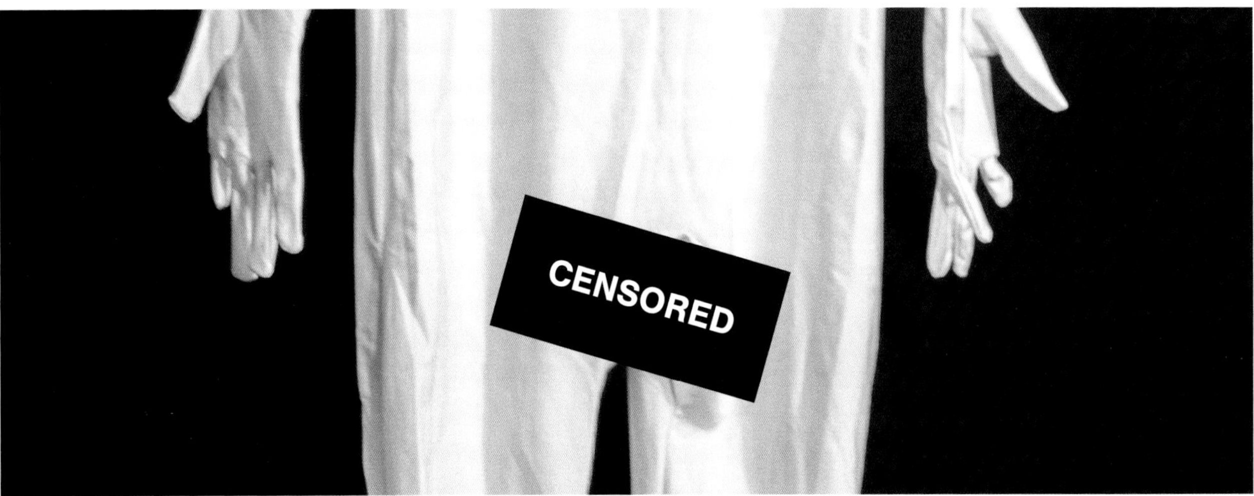

I'm not being prude here. Being able to clearly see the outline of your twig and berries is very distracting to the onlooker. You don't want to spend months working on costume armor only to find people's gaze drifting away from your hard work and down to your bits and pieces.

Thanks for listening, lads. I'm glad we had this talk.

Bare Skin, or Is It?

Have you ever wonder how figure skaters can stand to be out on the ice wearing next to nothing? Spoiler: They wear flesh colored cloth over their arms and legs to maintain their pretty appearance, but keep themselves from succumbing to hypothermia mid triple-lutz.

We can utilize this same concept to "show a little skin" while minimizing the instances of wardrobe malfunctions. It's also handy when cosplaying in Canada during the winter. Flesh tones can be sewn into the appropriate areas of your undersuit to give the impression that skin is showing. In fact, you may start with a flesh colored Zentai suit and just wear more undersuit garments over that.

This can also be utilized to show skin that isn't human flesh colored. If you're going as an undead ghoul, start with a Zentai suit that's gray and paint it to look like undead muscle and sinew. If you have a model who is willing to wear the suit while you are painting it, I recommend utilizing them. This combined with some legit airbrush skills can yield some impressive results.

The full body Zentai suit I mentioned earlier comes in several "nude" colors. So, so sexy.

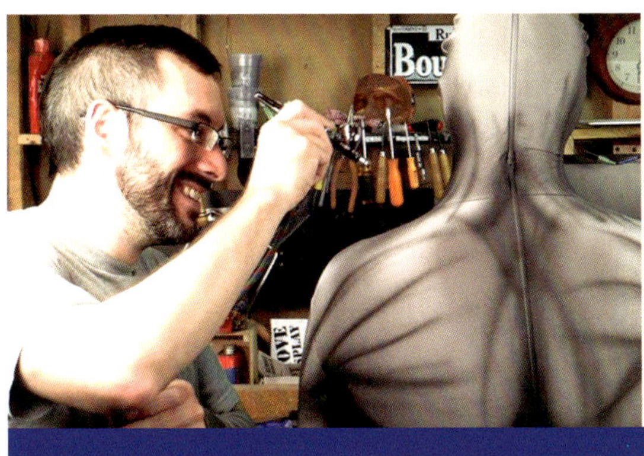

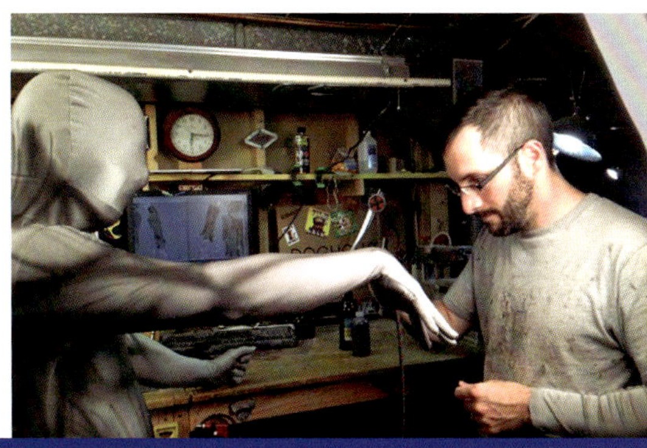

FAUX UNDEAD SKIN

Also consider a costume with a full body alien skin color. So long as you have a way to obscure where the neck connects to the body, you could use body paint to color your face and a colored Zentai suit to color the rest of your exposed "skin". Not only will this be warmer and less revealing, it'll be much easier and quicker to remove than painting your whole body every time you want to wear that costume!

My wife's Mystique costume was prime for using a colored undersuit in place of body paint on her arms and legs. The shirt covered up where her neck skin attached to the rest of her body, so she painted her face blue and just wore the same color blue as an undersuit. She's a pretty clever (and beautiful) lady!

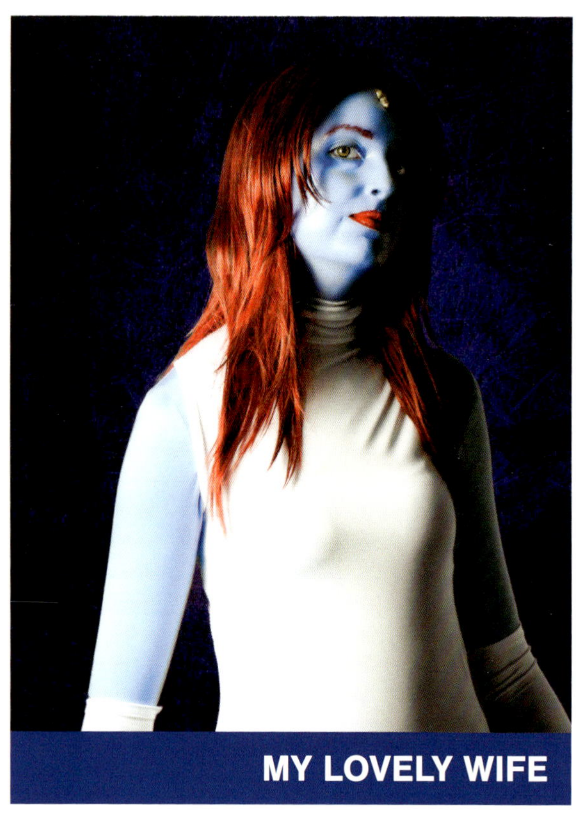

MY LOVELY WIFE

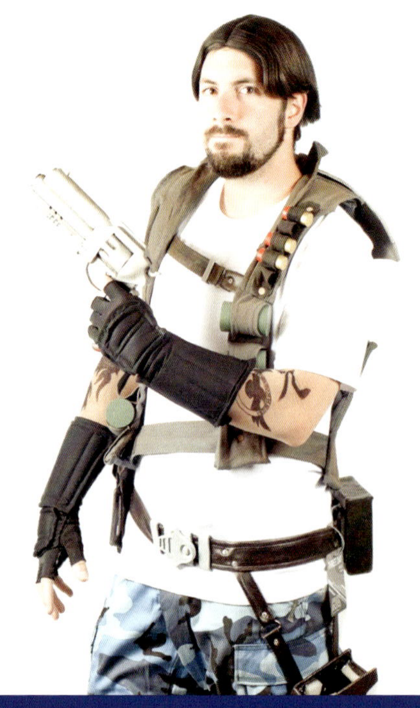

STOCKING TATTOO

If your character has a wicked rad tattoo, your body suit provides an excellent opportunity to show it off without actually getting yourself inked. A "bare" body suit area can be tattooed up with a fabric marker or paint. A similar effect can be achieved with a pair of stockings. This way, if you only want to cover one part of your body, you can get a stocking that matches your natural skin color and draw the tattoo right onto that!

Yes I know my wig is pretty terrible.
I spray painted it.
I didn't know any better.
We all started somewhere and I started with spray painted wigs.

ATTACHING ARMOR TO CLOTH

Provided your body suit isn't going to stretch too much, you may be able to attach some of your armor pieces directly to your undersuit! This is really fantastic for smaller pieces that tend to "float" around a bit, like elbows and knees. You can even use this method along with strapping to make parts of your armor partially detachable to facilitate sitting down or using the restroom.

One method for making armor pieces removable from your undersuit is to use snaps. These handy gizmos can be found in a range of sizes and styles at your local fabric and craft stores. Some of them are simply sewn on and others use a small tool and hammer to attach them. Whichever style you prefer, you should attach the snaps to small pieces of non-stretchy cloth or nylon webbing before sewing it to your undersuit or hot gluing it to your armor.

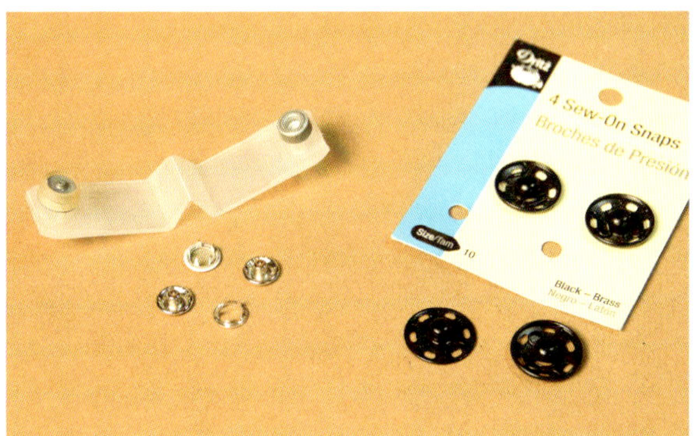

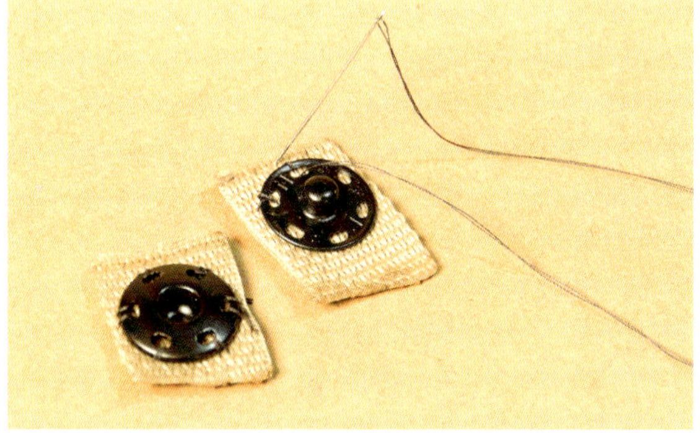

One side of the snap will be attached to your undersuit in the appropriate area. The opposite side of the snap gets attached to your armor piece and the two can be snapped on and off at your convenience! You may want to add more than one set of snaps for some armor pieces to keep them from rotating.

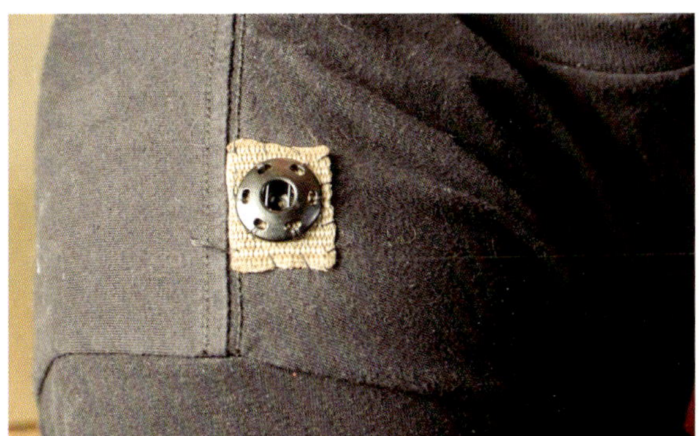

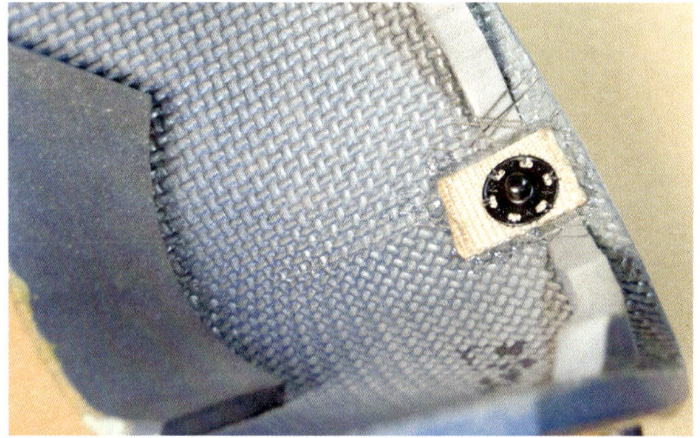

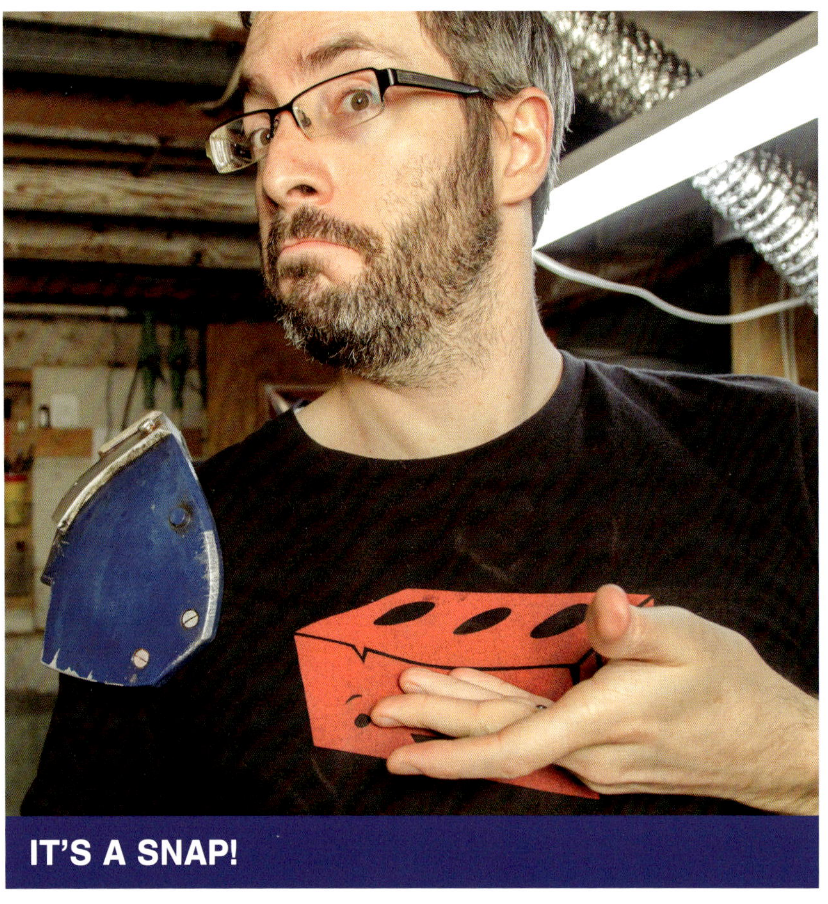

IT'S A SNAP!

Velcro is another viable way to attach small armor pieces to your armor. Similar to the snaps, Velcro has two different sides. I highly recommend putting the less abrasive side on your undersuit and the more abrasive side on the armor. This will keep the undersuit from sticking to itself and pulling the cloth when not being worn.

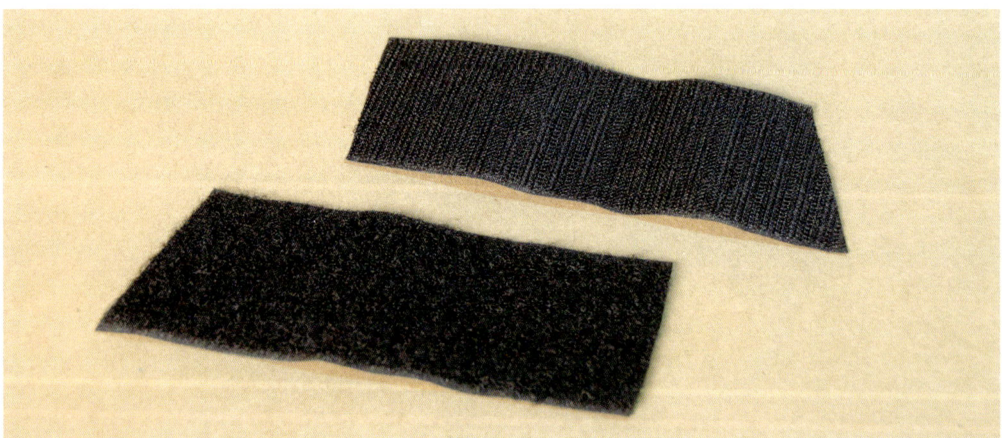

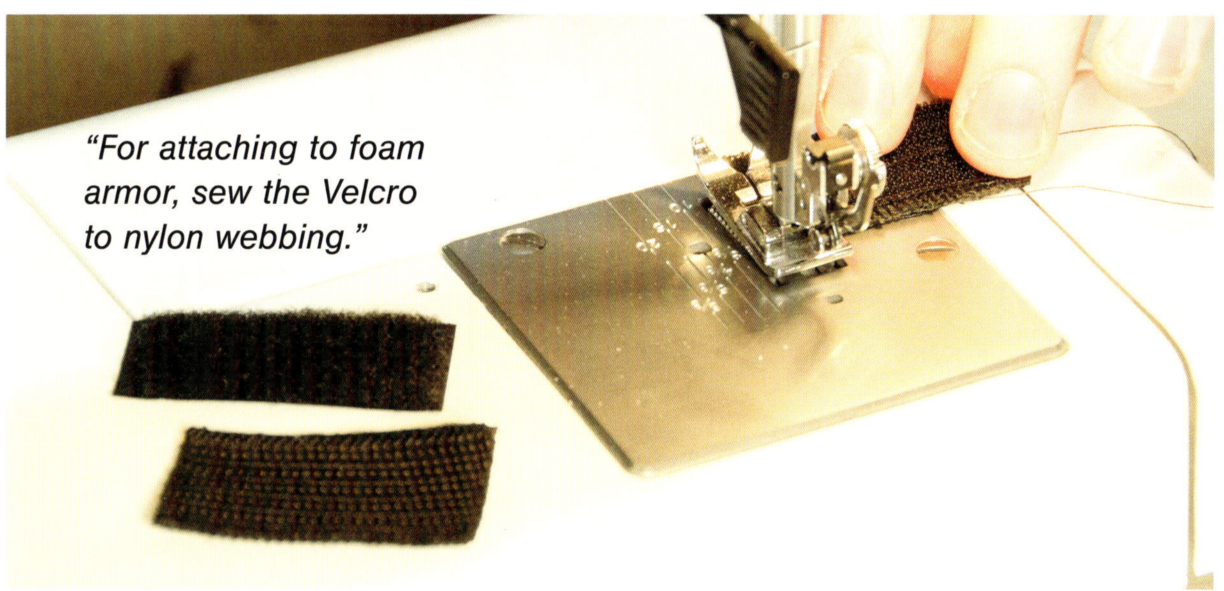

Velcro doesn't like to be glued, so you'll want to do a bit of sewing to attach it to your body suit. The good news is that you can cover a large area with Velcro fairly easily to keep a good sized chunk of armor in place.

For attaching the velcro to your foam armor, you'll want to sew it to a piece of non stretchy cloth or nylon webbing first before hot gluing it to the foam.

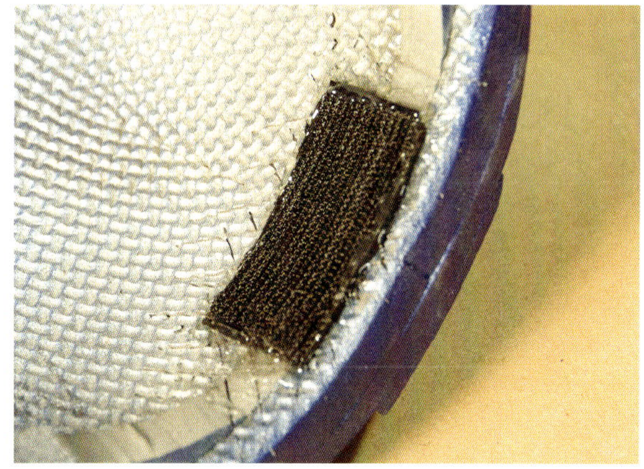

Undersuits are a supremely vital part of the foam armor making puzzle, so be sure to give yourself plenty of time to work on yours during the build process. If you put in the time, a good undersuit can set your armor apart from the crowd and help you along the path to cosplay badassery!

Strapping on Your Armor

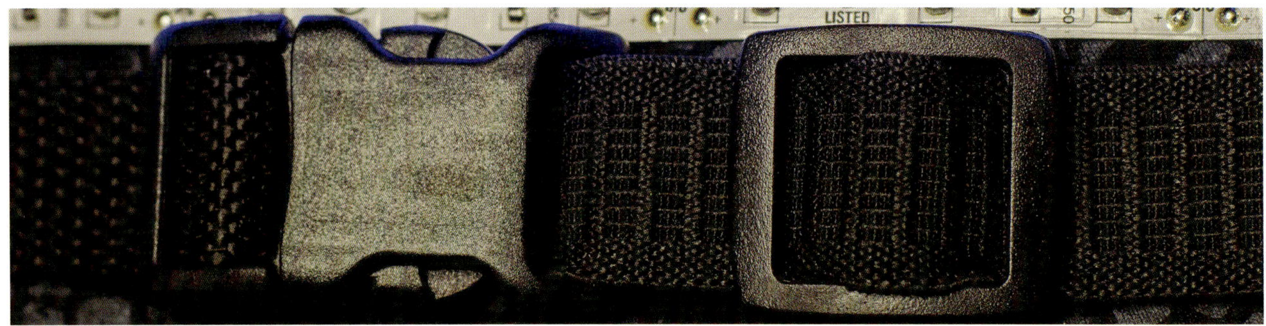

One of the most effective ways of attaching foam armor pieces to your body is with elastic and nylon webbing straps. These amazing materials can be ordered in bulk from the internet or picked up at your local craft and fabric stores. They are inexpensive, light weight, versatile, and easy to work with.

Let's get strapped!

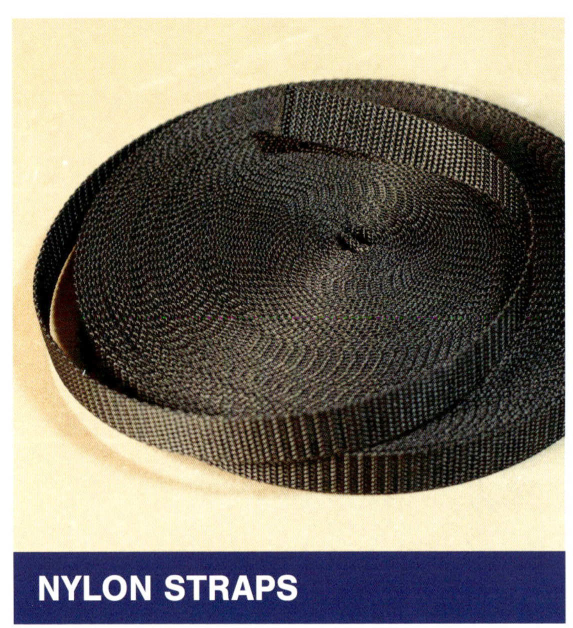

NYLON STRAPS

I like to order nylon webbing in bulk rolls. This way I always have a stock pile on hand for any costuming problems that need solving. I get them all in the same width, usually 3/4", so that all of the bulk hardware I buy will fit it. Buy whatever color you'll end up using the most, because it's really hard to change the color of nylon. Black is generally a good choice, but you may have to pick up something specific for your armor project.

Similarly, elastic is incredibly handy to have around. Some parts of your armor may need to slide on and be snug, so you'll want your straps to have a little bit of give. Again, I tend to order it in bulk in the same width as the webbing so that all of my buckles will work with it. Be sure to order heavy duty elastic. Some of it isn't meant to stand up to the all day abuse it'll see as part of a set of costume armor.

I usually end up applying elastic straps around my thigh armor, biceps, and sometimes chest pieces. You can build a piece with an armor strap that you simply slide a limb into, like on the biceps. This way, you don't require any additional snaps.

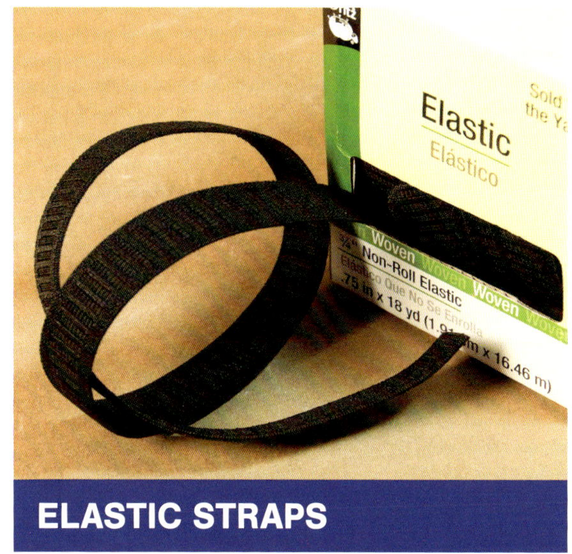

ELASTIC STRAPS

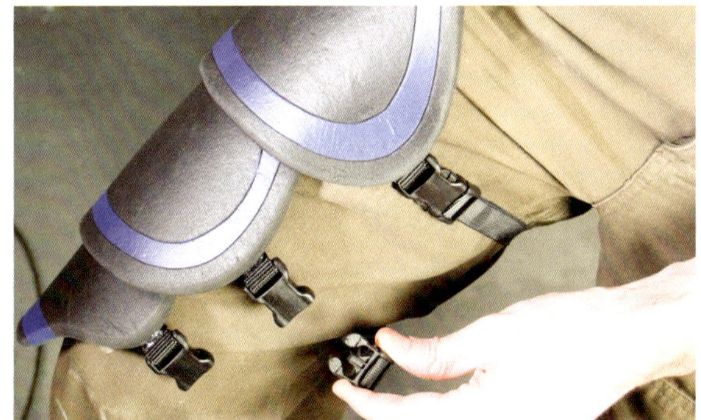

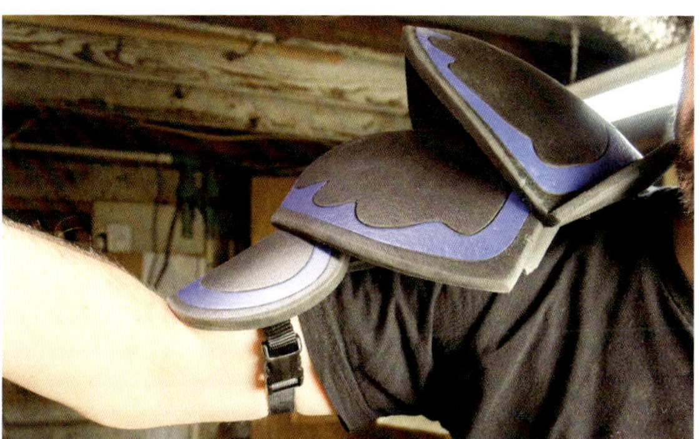

To cut your straps, a sturdy pair of scissors or a knife can be employed. The only thing that's vital here is that you cauterize the cut edges with flame or a heat gun. This will keep them from fraying.

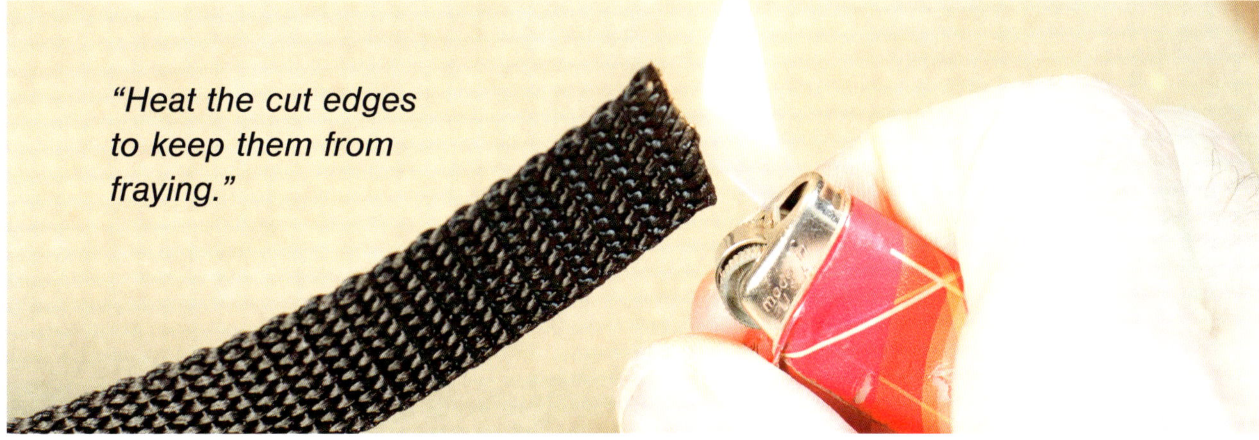

BUCKLES

To attach your strapping to itself, you'll need to pick up some buckles. The plastic, snapping kinds are extremely handy for costuming. They can be purchased in bulk for cheap. Also grab some slides in case you want to make your straps adjustable.

Buy Buckles, Slides, Nylon Webbing, and Elastic at your local craft stores or on the internet on Amazon or Strapworks.

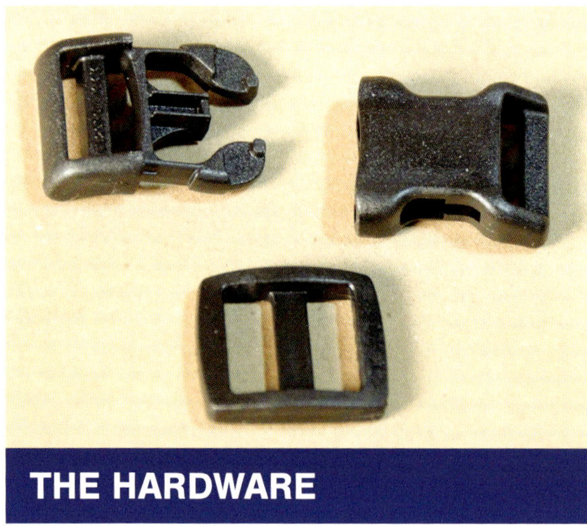

THE HARDWARE

I also like to keep a stock of some 2" wide nylon webbing to use around my waist. Belts tend to end up bearing a lot of weight in a set of armor, so you'll want to make sure it doesn't cut into your body when it's pulled tight, hence the additional width. Some really burly 2" wide plastic snap buckles and slides are necessary to keep these from falling to your ankles. The slides are use to accommodate any "seasonal girth variation."

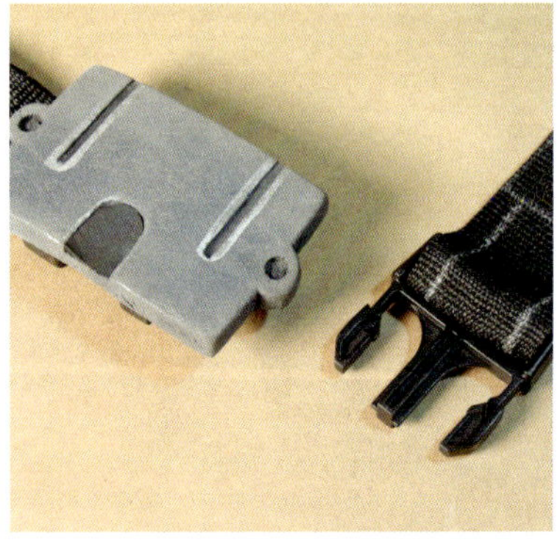

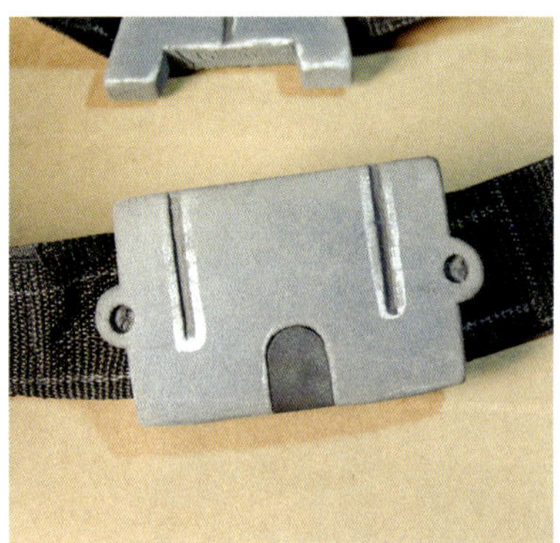

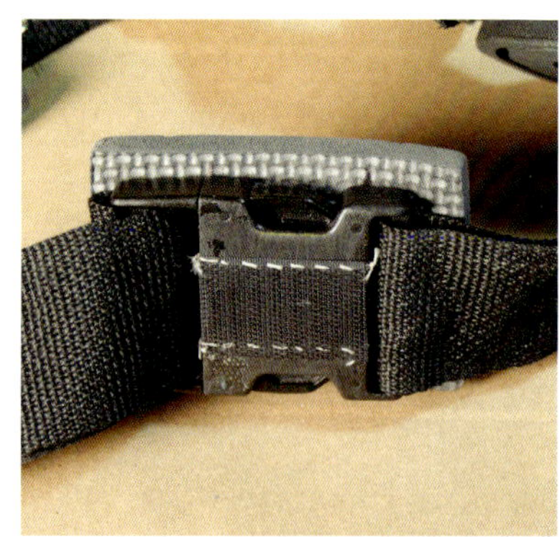

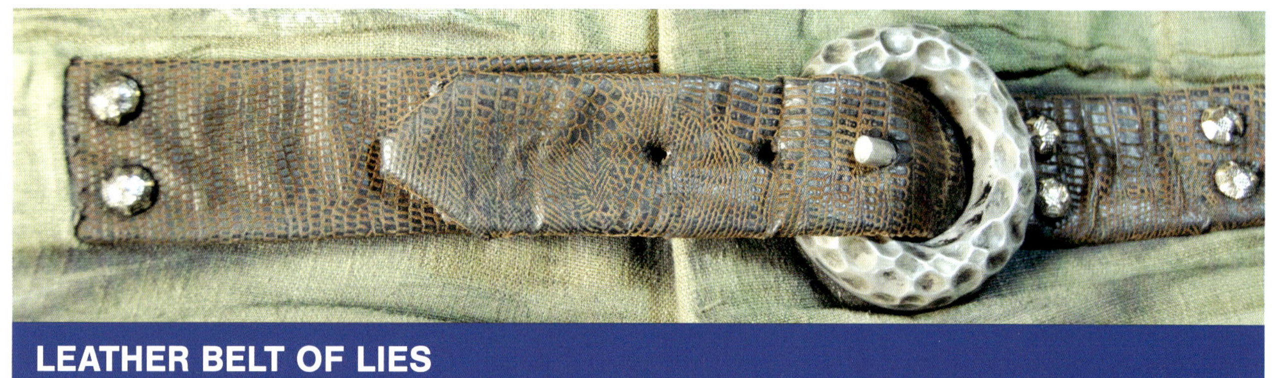

LEATHER BELT OF LIES

These large, plastic buckles can be a pain to hide on your armor, especially if your set is supposed to look medieval. One method is to craft a faux buckle (from foam, of course!) and glue it to the outside of the female buckle piece. Another solution is to put the buckle on the rear of your belt. This way your back armor or a cape can cover the functional piece of the belt.

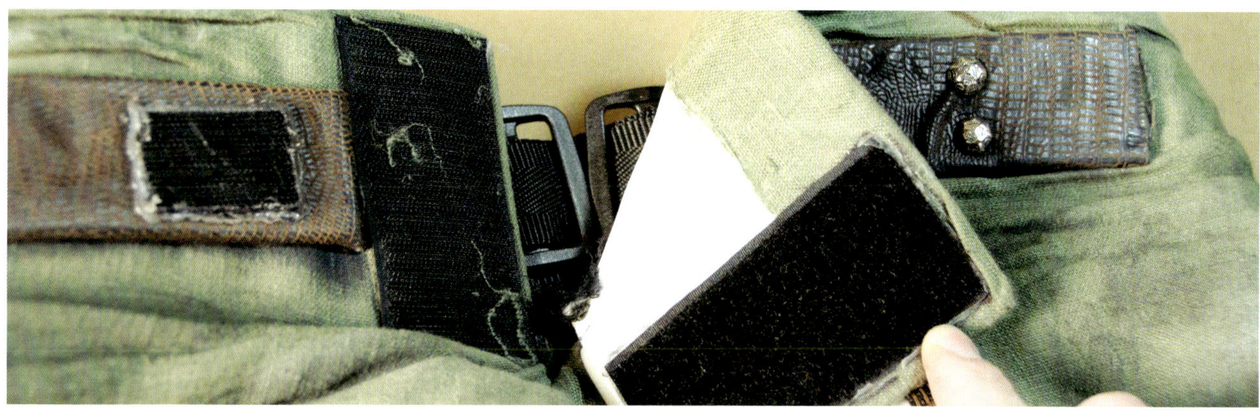

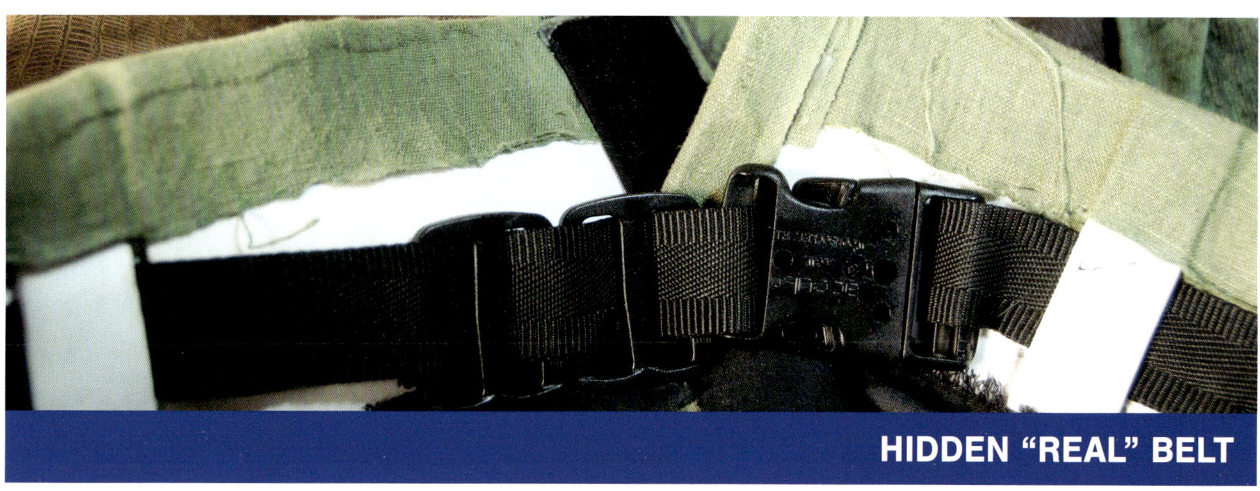

HIDDEN "REAL" BELT

Slides

Slides are used to make your strapping adjustable. This is crazy handy if more than one person is going to be wearing your armor. It's also handy if you, like me, tend to put on a spare 10lbs in the winter months. Common areas to utilize slides are the waist and chest. Use them in conjunction with snap buckles to create straps that'll be durable and useful for you and anyone close to your body size!

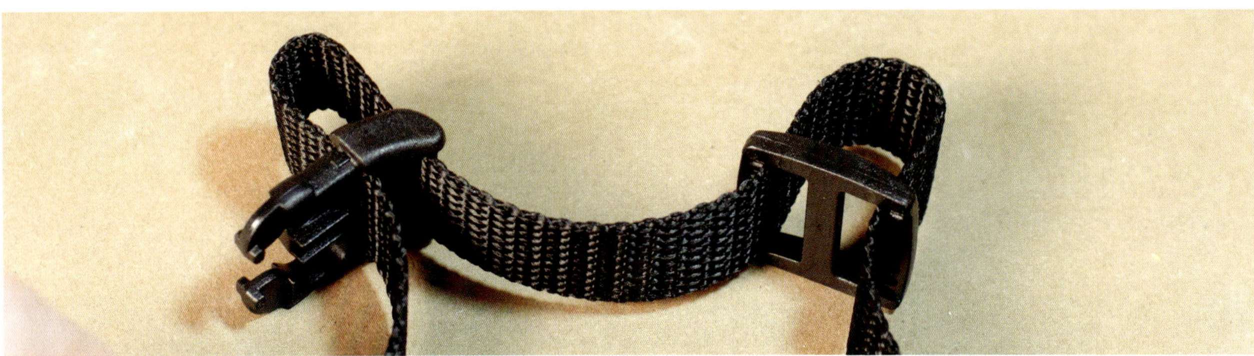

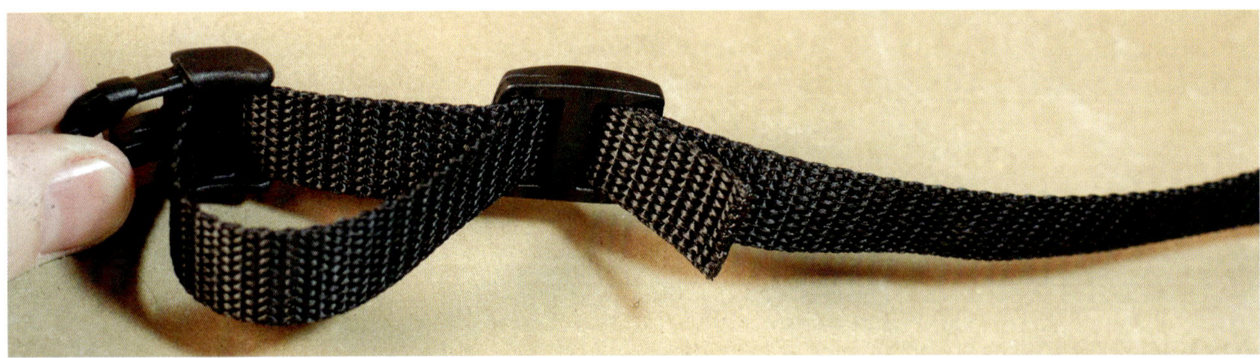

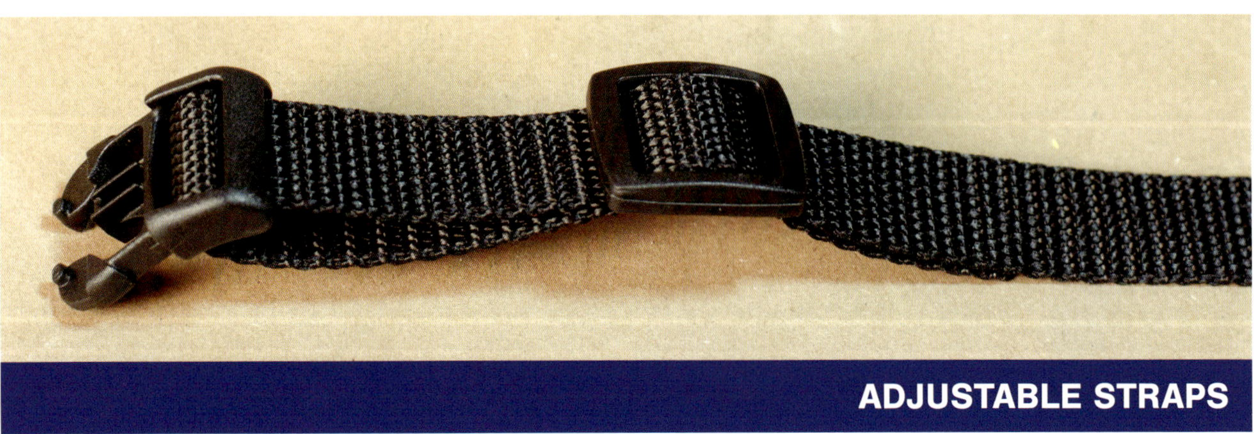

ADJUSTABLE STRAPS

ATTACHING STRAPS TO FOAM

My very favorite way to attach straps to foam is with hot glue. Usually, the textured side of your foam floor mats, the side that tends to be on the back side of your armor, is notoriously picky about what it likes to stick to. To make sure your straps don't ever come unglued, you'll want to give the foam a little extra gripping power.

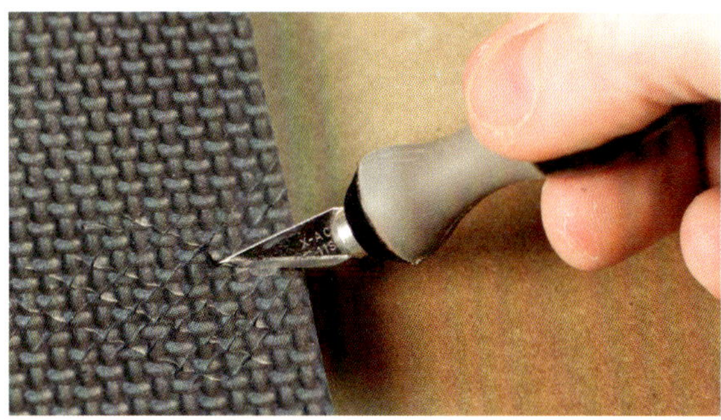

Take a sharp knife and score (partially cut) the area of foam where your straps will be glued. Then hit that area with your heat gun, revealing some nice grooves in the foam. These crevasses will drink up your hot glue, giving it something to grip on to! Bathe the area in hot glue and lay down your nylon webbing straps!

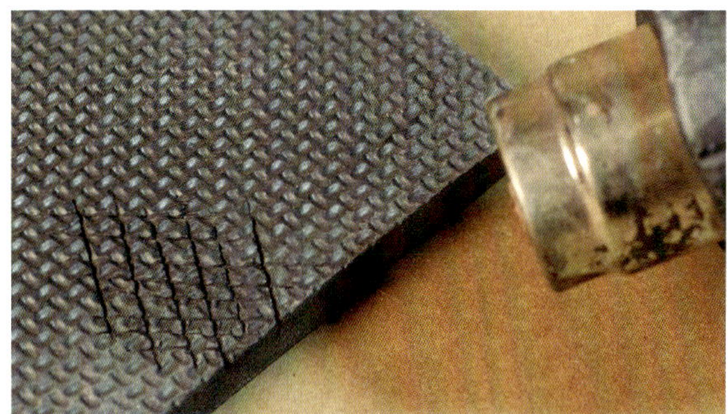

To really add some legit durability to your straps, you can hot glue the edges all the way around after they've been glued down to the foam. This will prevent the edges from peeling up after a lot of heavy use. I also prefer to put a bead of hot glue across the back portion of the strap near the edge of the foam armor piece. This is the area that will be most likely want to pull away from the foam when stressed.

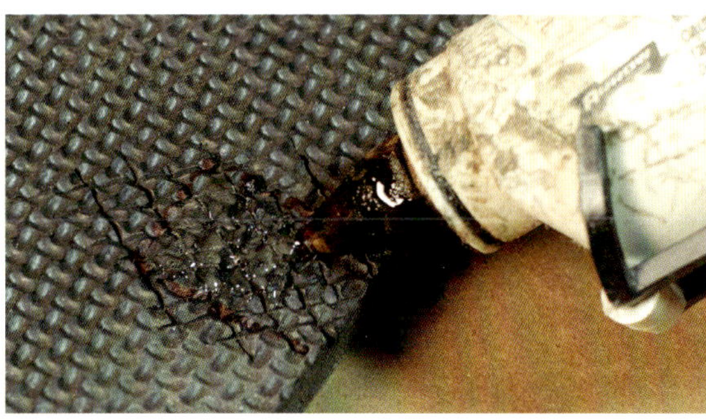

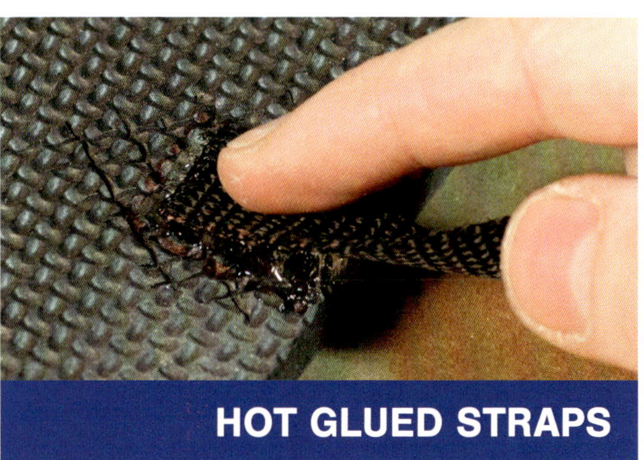

HOT GLUED STRAPS

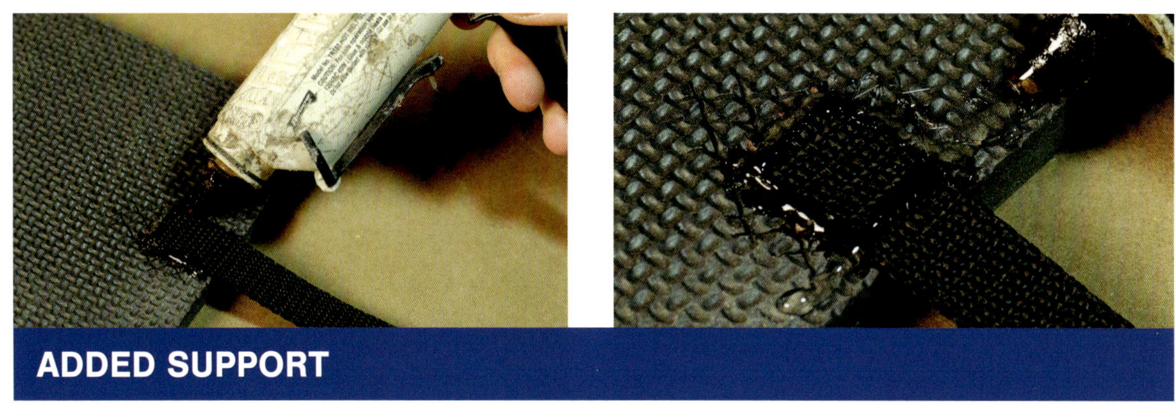

ADDED SUPPORT

Elastic can be kind of fickle to glue down. Since it stretches, over time it can stretch itself right out of the hot glue! To combat this, I prefer to sew a small length of nylon webbing to the portion of the elastic that is to be glued. This way, there is an area of the elastic that will not stretch. This is the area that will be glued to the foam.

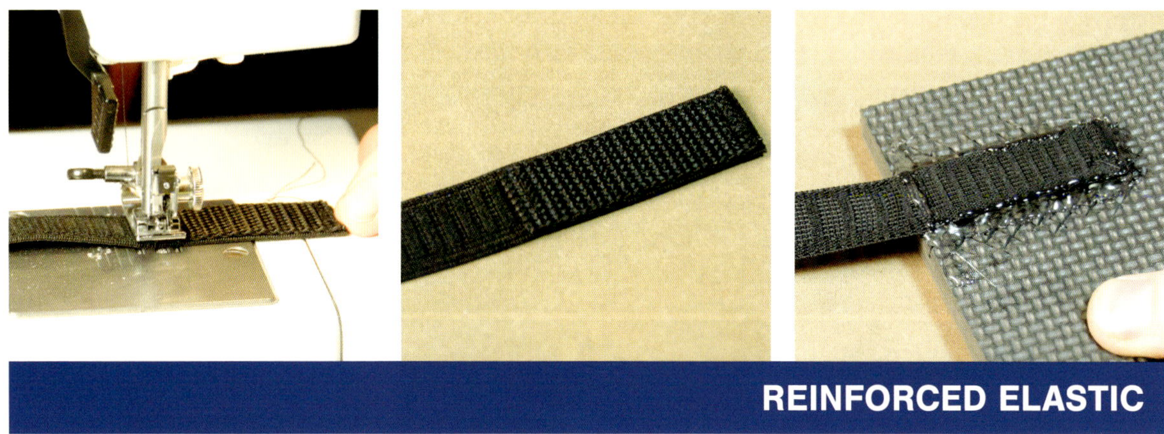

REINFORCED ELASTIC

Strapping Your Giant Shoulder Armor

If you really want to create armor that sets your silhouette apart from everyone else, you're probably going to make something with some really imposing shoulder armor! The problem is, the larger your pauldrons get, the more difficult it is to harness their sheer mass to your body. Snapping them to your undersuit simply will not do, as their weight will pull the cloth down your arms. For this, you will need to create some kind of a harness!

'DEM PAULDRONS

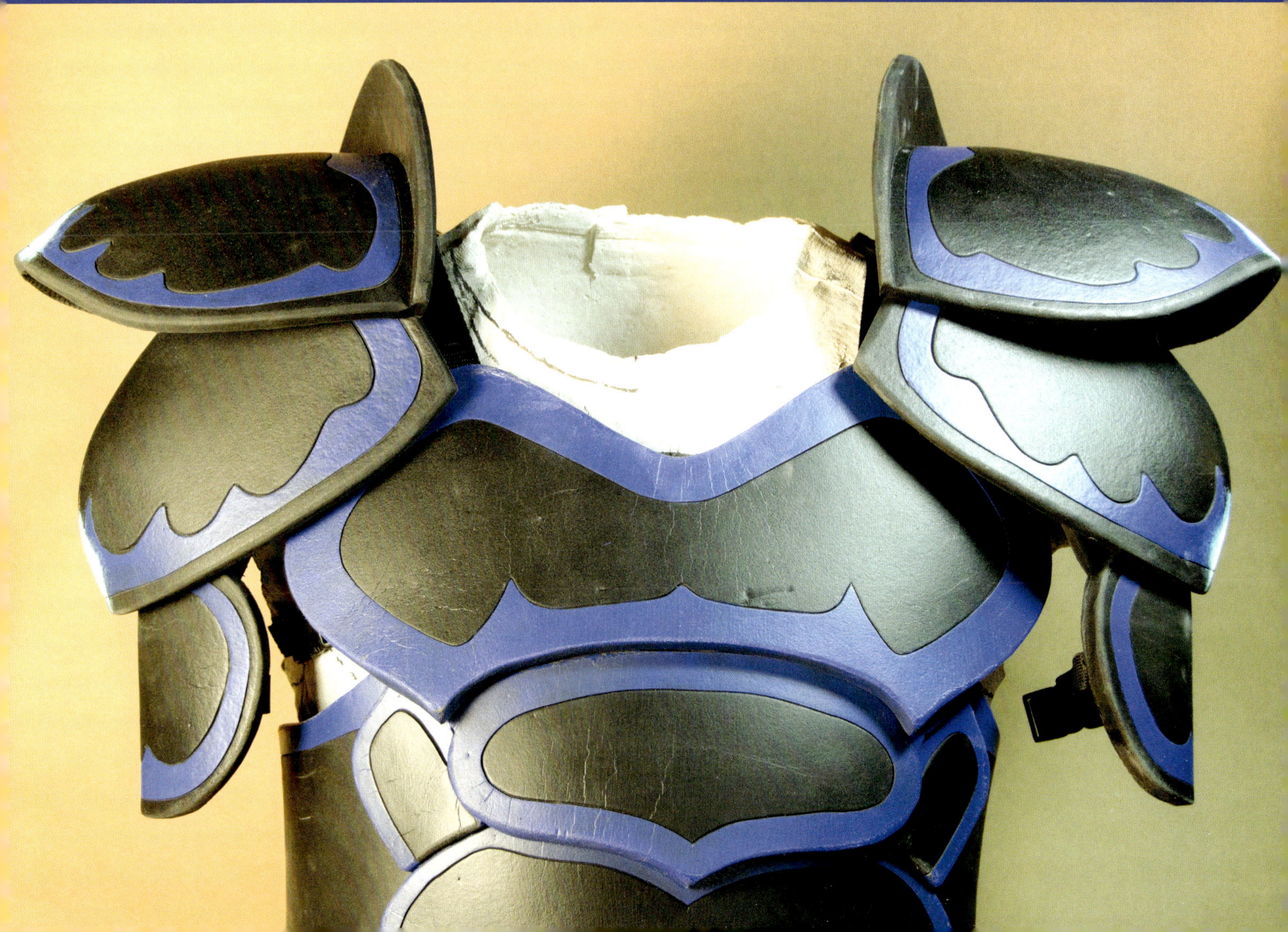

A good, functional, and durable harness can be built quickly with a series of hot glued nylon webbing straps. If you're super worried about durability, sew the straps together instead of gluing them. The key here is a strap that connects the shoulder straps together across the back of your neck. This way your pauldrons' weight will be distributed over your back and they will not be able to slide down your arms.

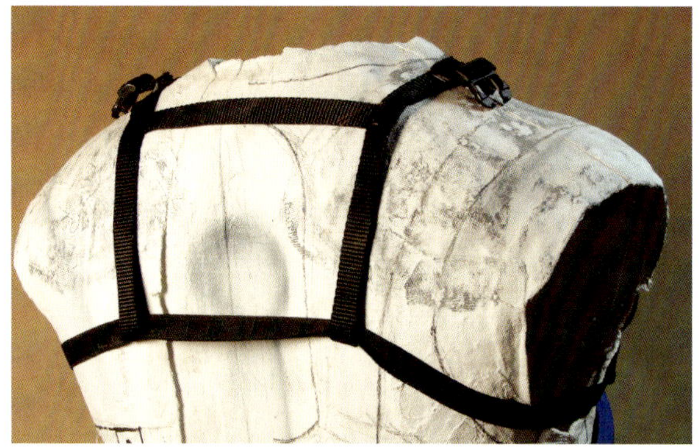

The front half of this harness is actually the foam armor. The strapping is the back half of the harness. You could, if the situation demanded it, make a harness completely out of straps and attach your armor to that.

In this case, the under arm and midsection horizontal straps are elastic. They stretch around the wearer's chest and belly and snap together with buckles, creating a tight fit.

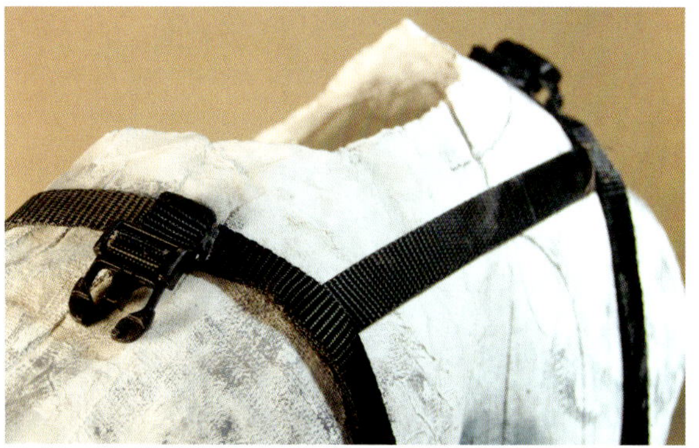

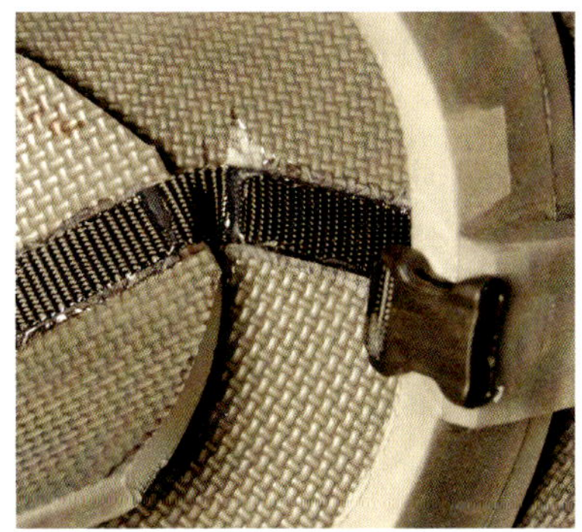

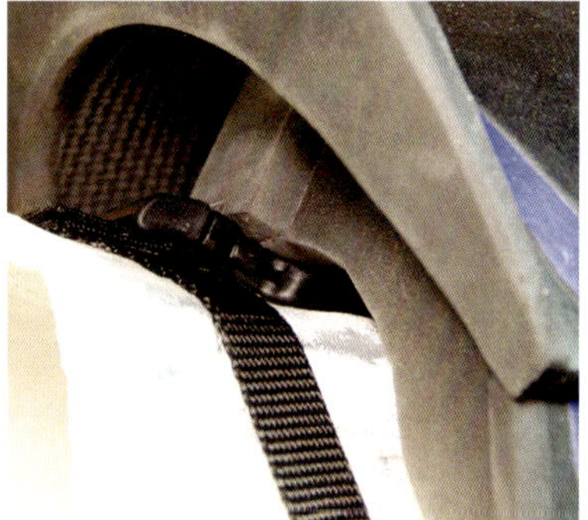

The pauldrons themselves can be attached to the straps with snaps, velcro, or more plastic buckles! This way, your massive shoulder armor will be removable for travel or when you need to go through doorways. I attached my World of Warcraft pauldrons with plastic buckles.

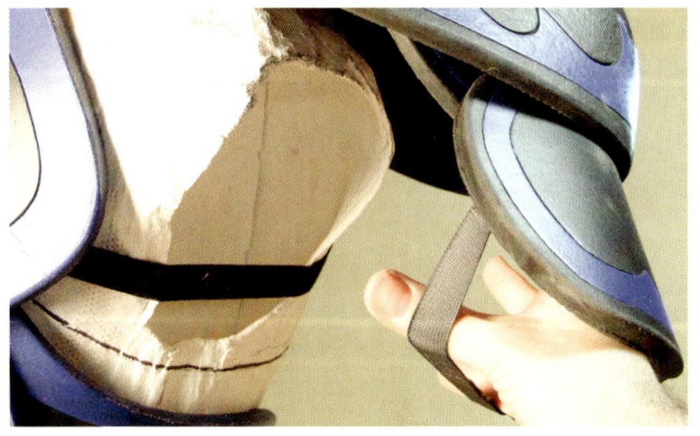

To keep the pauldrons from free floating around your shoulder, they can be attached to your upper arm with elastic straps.

"Real" Straps

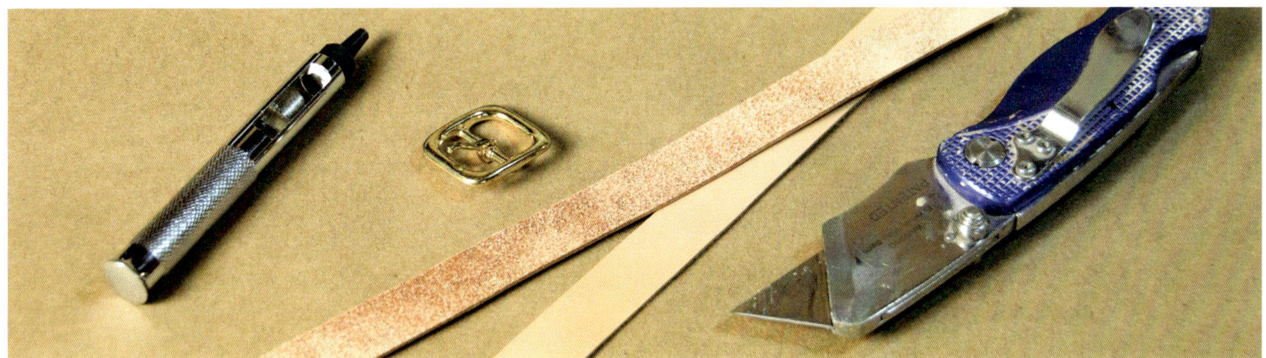

Many armor sets, especially the more fantastical ones, prefer to feature strapping, rather than obscuring it. Check your local area for stores that sell leatherworking supplies. Tandy Leather has many locations in the United States, but you may have local mom and pop stores too! If you don't have any, many craft stores have a leather working section. Of course, many of these materials can be purchased online too.

If your local store has one, check the scrap bin for small pieces that will suit your needs. Scraps are cheaper and usually work out well unless you need something long, like a belt. Another fantastic thing about leatherworking stores is they usually have an amazing selection of hardware at a great price. If your armor requires fancy buckles or other leather embellishments, you're going to have a field day at a leather working store!

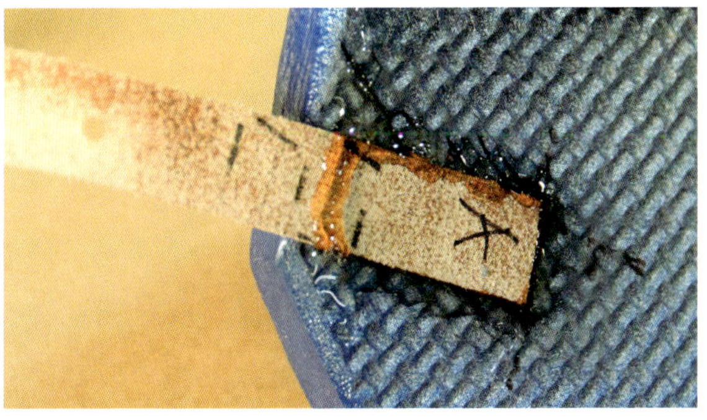

Cut your leather straps to the appropriate length and width for your costume. You'll also want to burnish them, punch holes, and dye them to your needs. Ask your leather working stores for the supplies and techniques you'll need to achieve your particular finish. Once they look good, you can adhere them to your armor. Leather can be glued to foam just like nylon webbing straps with hot glue!

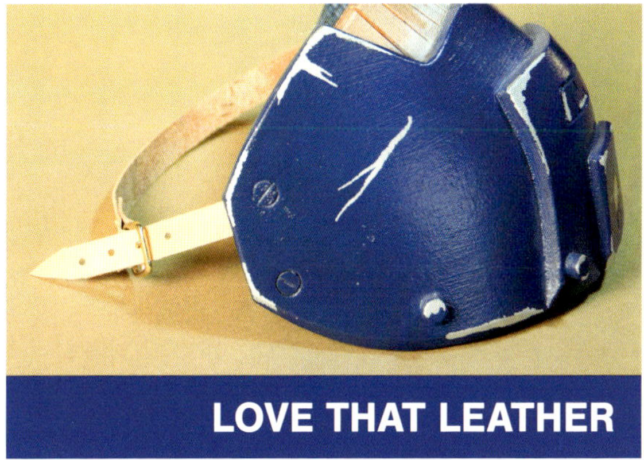

LOVE THAT LEATHER

Once your leather is glued to your foam, you can stitch on the buckles and use them as they were intended. How about that?!

STRAPPING: TRIAL AND ERROR

As you strap up your foam armor, remember that you're going to do a lot of adjusting to get it to fit correctly on your personal form. It's unlikely that you'll get it perfect on the first try, so think about only tacking your straps down with just a little hot glue the first time you try it on. Using a body form, like a plaster torso cast of yourself or a duct tape dummy, can be extremely helpful for adjusting your straps. Also leave plenty of extra strapping tailing off your pieces so that you can trim it if need be later on. Once your fit is perfect, then go back in and put the final hot glue on everything to lock it in. After many hours, hot glue burns, sweat, and tears, your armor is strapped!

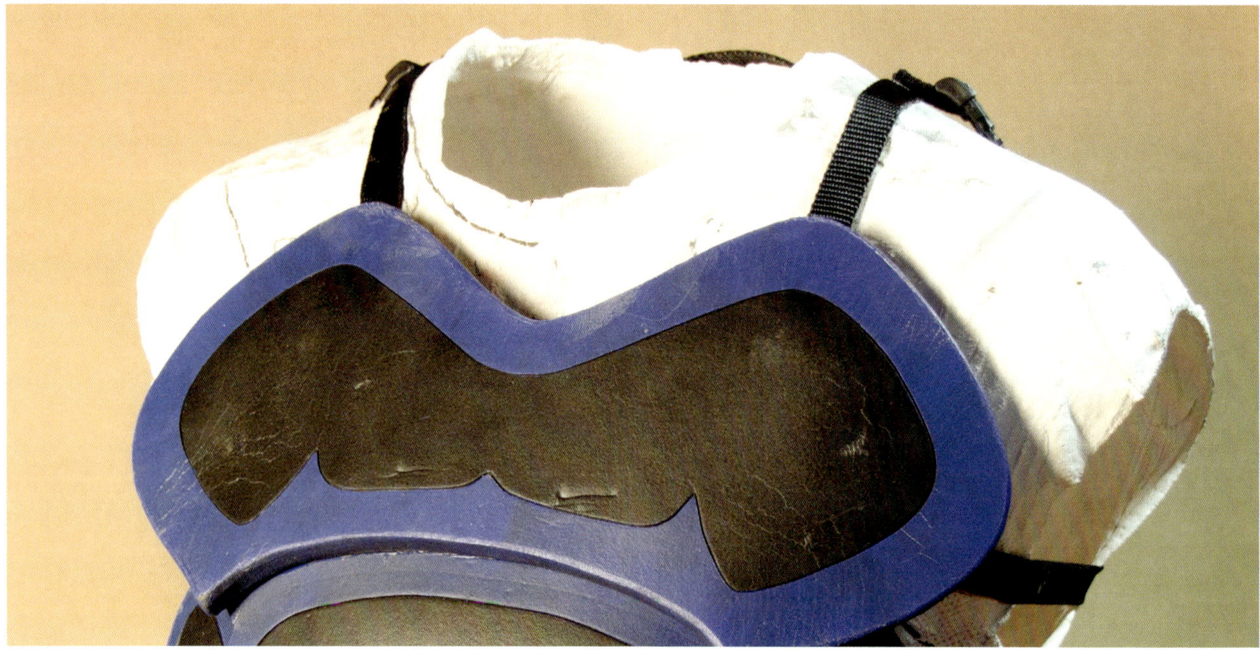

This plaster torso that I made of myself has been indispensable for fitting my armor straps. There are dozens of tutorials on how to make one available on YouTube. Look for "plaster bandage body casting" videos.

LIGHTS

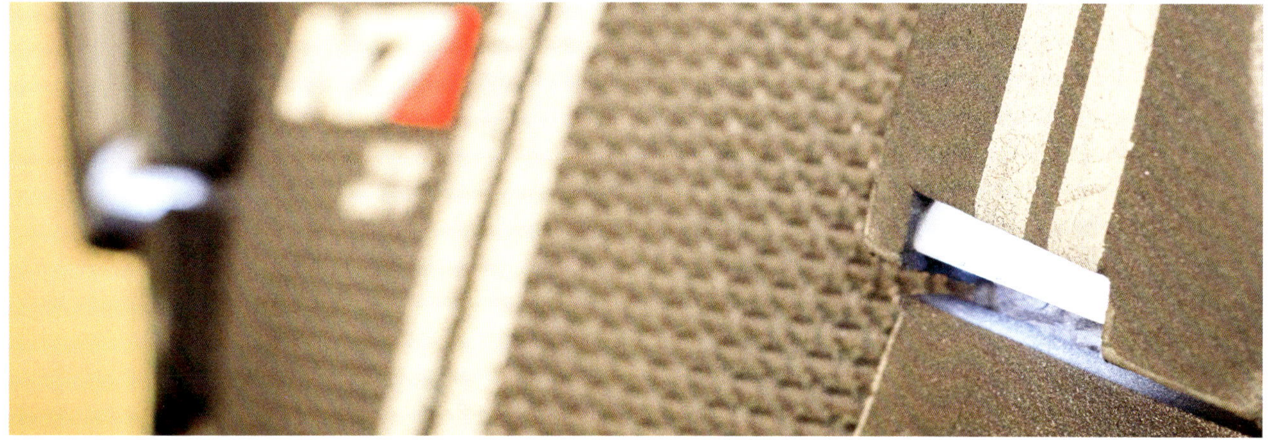

If there's one thing that'll make your armor really stand out in a dark crowd of costumes, it's lights! Many of the most impressive armor sets from fiction incorporate some kind of glowing effect that you'll want to try and emulate. Put on your electrical engineer hat, foamsmith, we're getting our glow on!

CREEPY... AWESOME

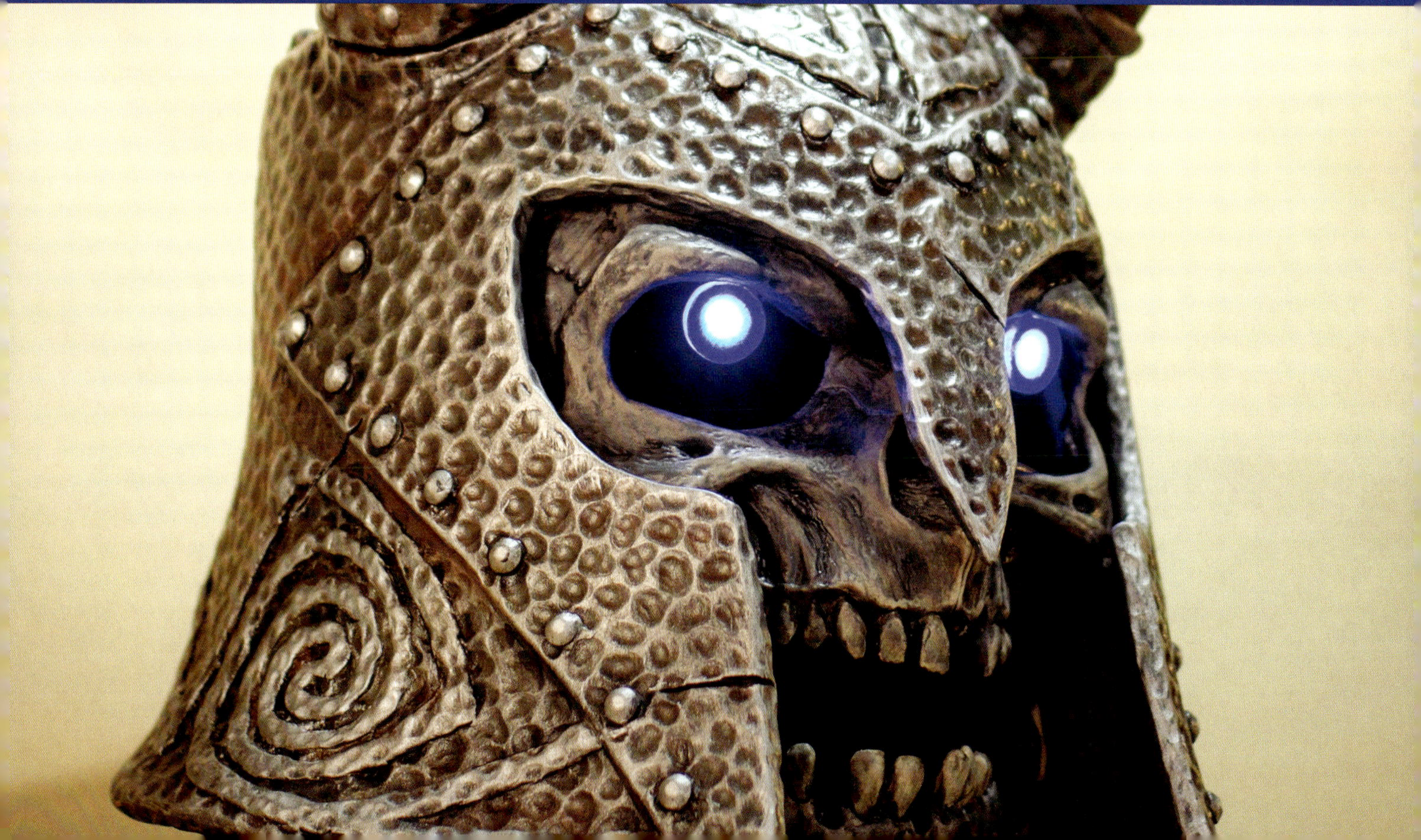

LEDs

More often than not, I go with LEDs for my illumination solutions. They are readily available at any local electronics store, though I prefer to order them in bulk from the internet. They require very little power to run and give off a wonderful amount of light in a variety of colors. LEDs also don't give off a lot of heat, so they're ideal when trying to keep cool in a big set of costume armor.

They come in several different varieties, colors, sizes, and shapes. You can even get RGB LEDs that change color, if you have the technical knowhow to make this magic happen! I really like 3v surface mount LEDS. They are teeny tiny, which is great for stowing them in hard to reach parts of a costume. I also really like the 12v LED strips. They are very handy when you need a bunch of LEDs in a row. I order my LEDs from SuperBrightLEDs and Amazon.

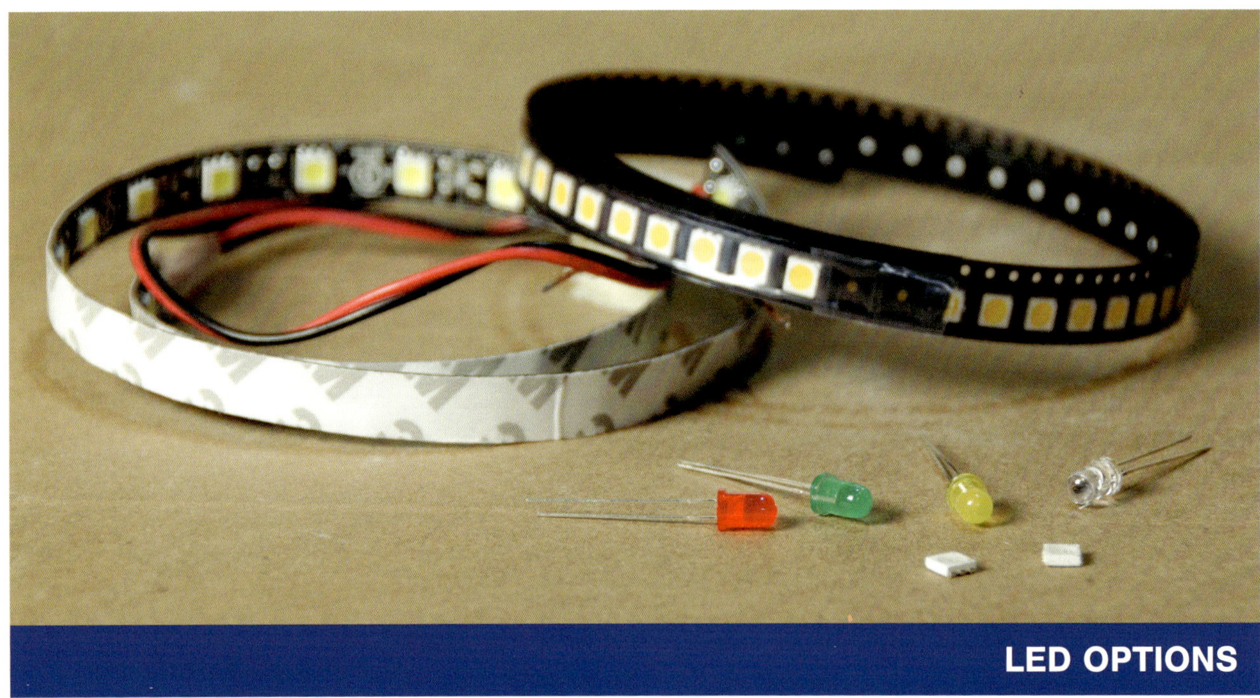

LED OPTIONS

Pre-Made LED Kits

It isn't always vital to put together your own lighting from component parts. In fact, for most beginners, the easiest way to get the best effect is to purchase pre-made lighting kits and modify them to your needs. These could be anything from bicycle safety lights, to finger tip rave lights, to strings of fairy lights, or the electronics out of children's toys. The sky's the limit and there are many stores you can browse for neat lighting kits, especially on the internet.

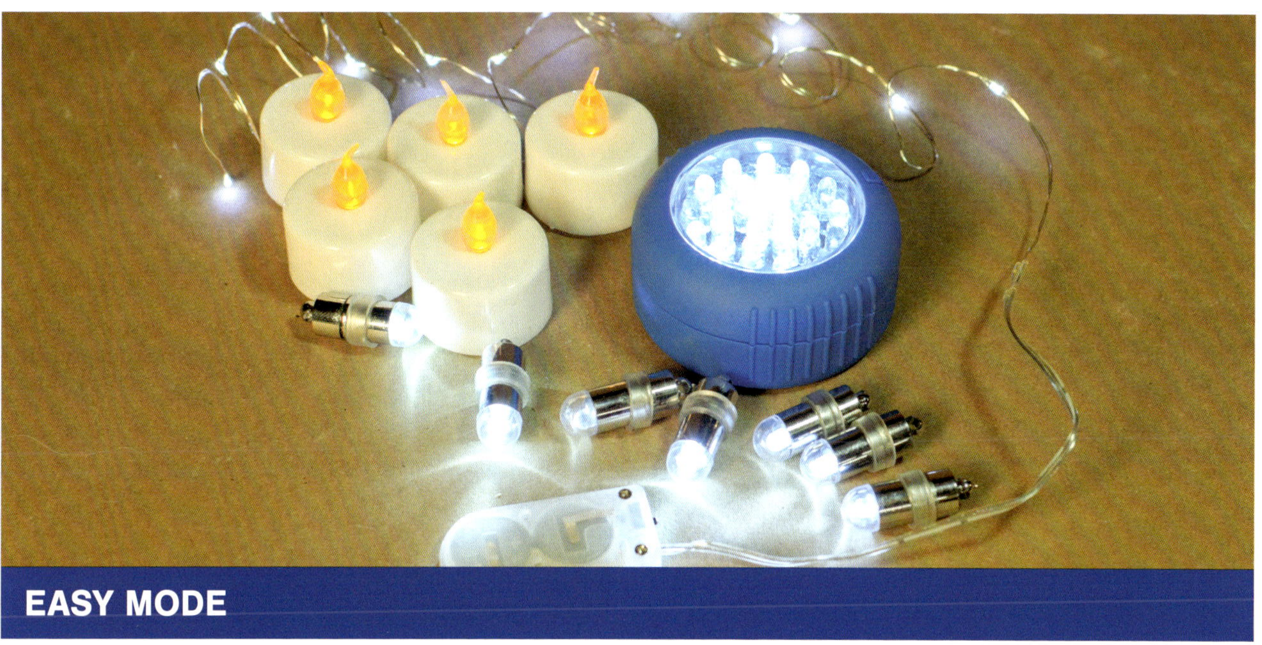

EASY MODE

For the absolute beginner, I highly recommend picking up some pre-made kits and playing with them a bit to become familiar with how they work. It is definitely the quickest, easiest, and cheapest way get shiny lights into your armor, though they can be a bit limited. Cheaper? Really? Yup! It requires fewer tools and component materials. You will be stunned to see how cheap some pre-assembled kits cost. A string of 12 LEDs, already wired to a battery holder, with a switch and two batteries cost just $8 on Amazon. To source the components myself would likely cost twice that.

Check your local craft and hobby stores for pre-made LED kits. Especially around Halloween!

LED Kit Examples

Moon Lights/Fairy Lights
These strings of LEDs are absolutely fantastic for getting started. They come in different lengths, depending on how many LEDs you might need. They can be strung out to use each LED individually, or bunched up all together if you need one big, bright spot.

Here are some ways to use Fairy Lights in your foam armor builds.

- Backlighting Any Semitransparent Surface
- Edge Lighting Etched Acrylic
- Single Lighting Gems

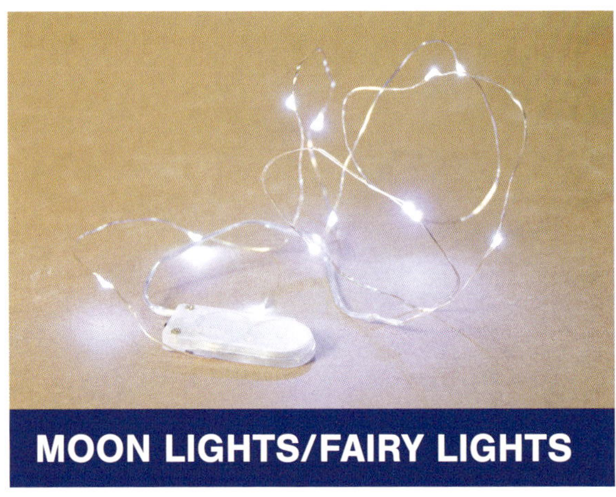

MOON LIGHTS/FAIRY LIGHTS

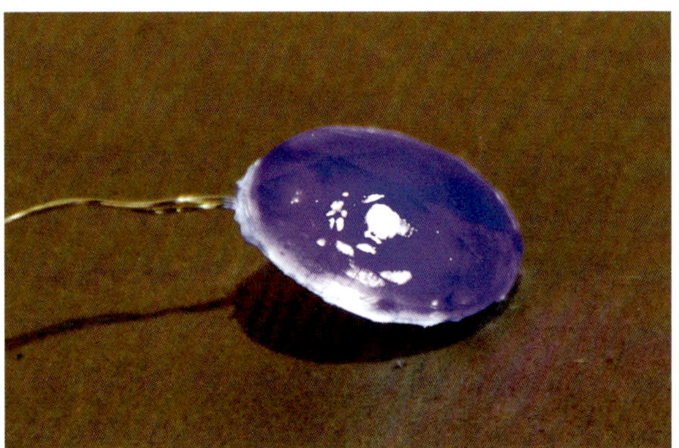

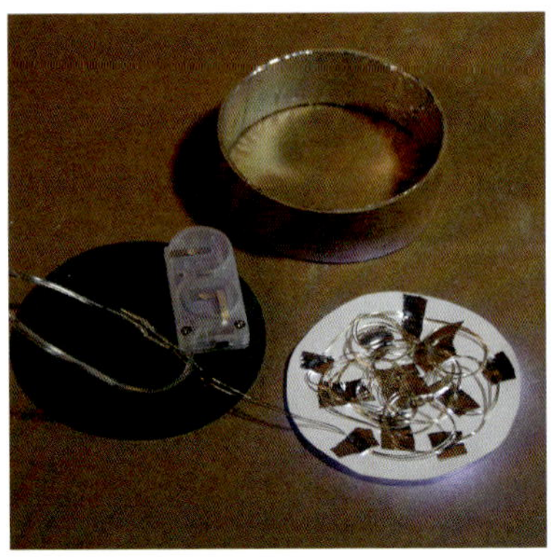

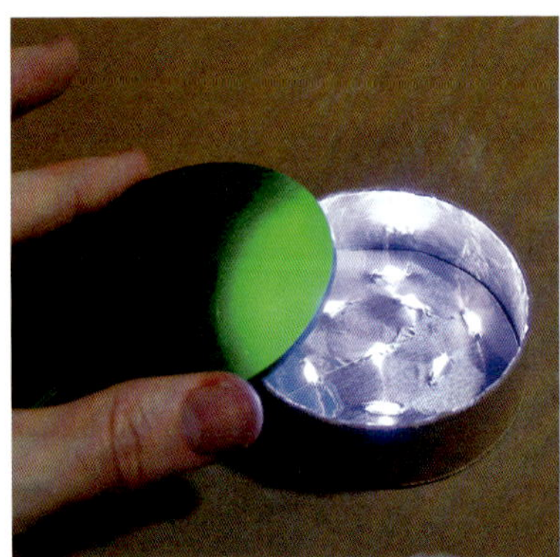

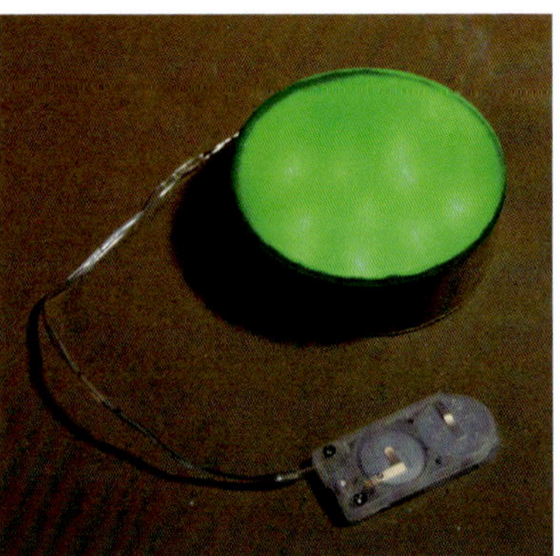

Round Magnet Lights

These super cheap lights are usually available at hardware stores for just a couple of bucks. If you're looking to pump out a lot of light, look no further! Making a large area glow bright is easily done with a diffused piece of plastic.

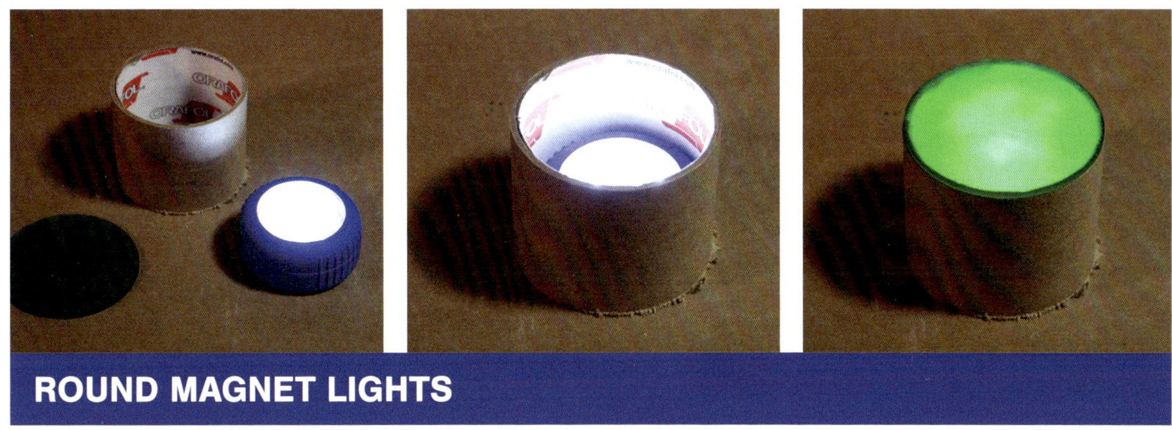
ROUND MAGNET LIGHTS

Individual Mini LED Lights

These pill sized lights are really handy! If you just need one little self contained light for a bright spot on your armor, go with these guys. If you use a lot of them all over your costume, you will have to turn them on and off all individually, so keep that in mind.

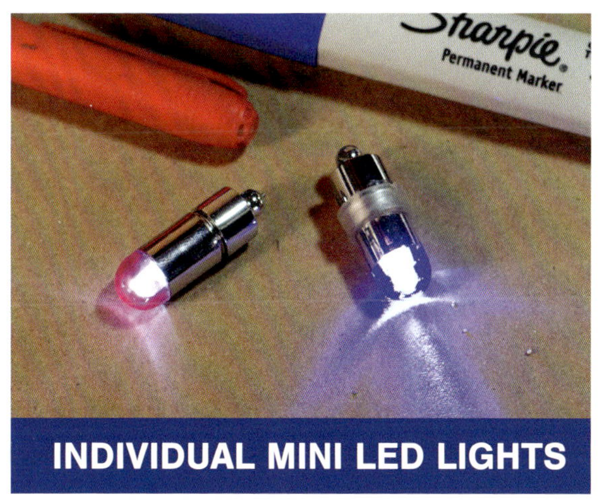

INDIVIDUAL MINI LED LIGHTS

The lights I bought were all white LEDs. To change the color of these lights, I simply drew over the outer light domes with permanent markers.

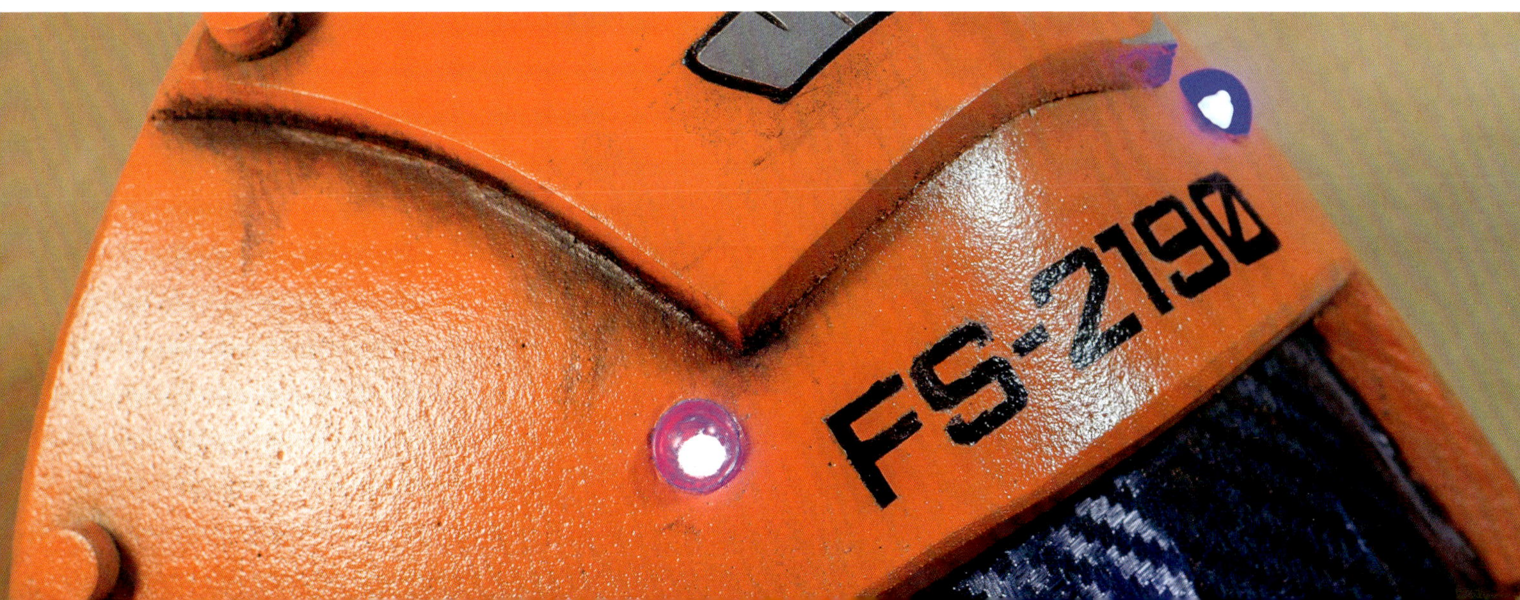

Flickering Tea Lights

You've probably seen these fancy little guys in your favorite restaurant being used as candles. What's really neat about them is that they pulse! If you're trying to simulate fire, or some kind of organic burning glow, these lights are perfect.

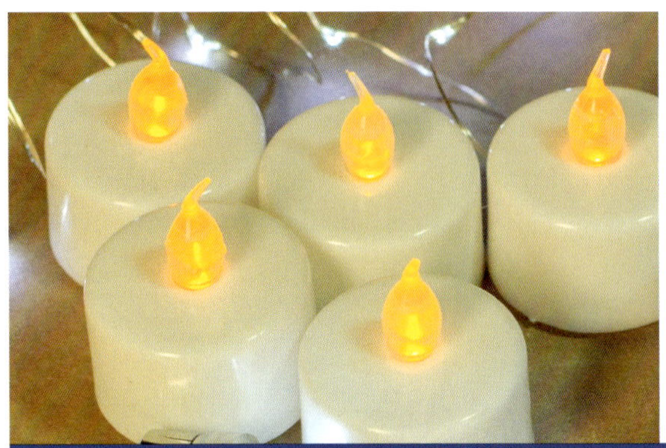

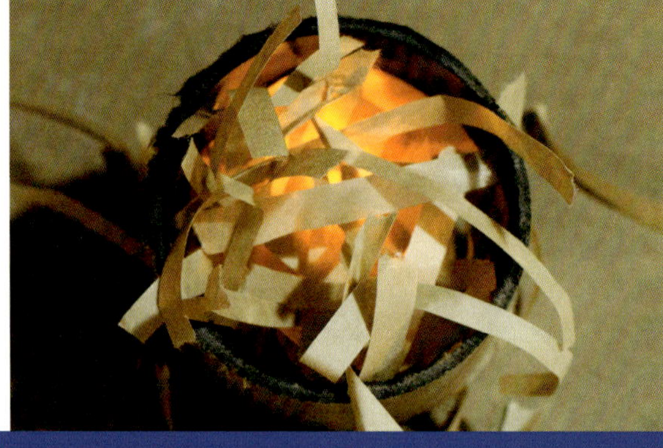

FLICKERING TEA LIGHTS

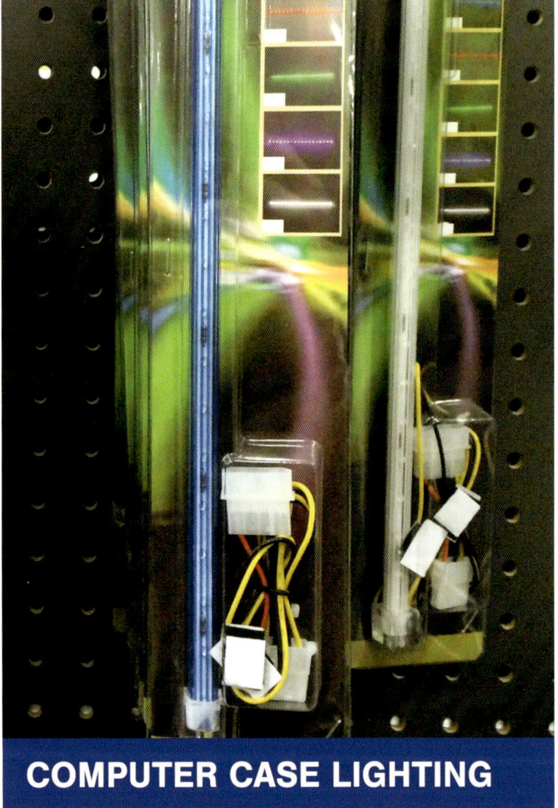

COMPUTER CASE LIGHTING

Automotive/Computer Case Lighting Kits

These are a little bit more expensive, but if you need a lot of light, look no further! They are usually designed to run on a 12 volt circuit, so be prepared to either run 8 AA or AAA batteries or some other specialty battery.

These examples only scratch the surface of what lighting solutions are available to you without a shred of electronics knowledge! Take some time to search for what's out there and experiment to see what works best for you!

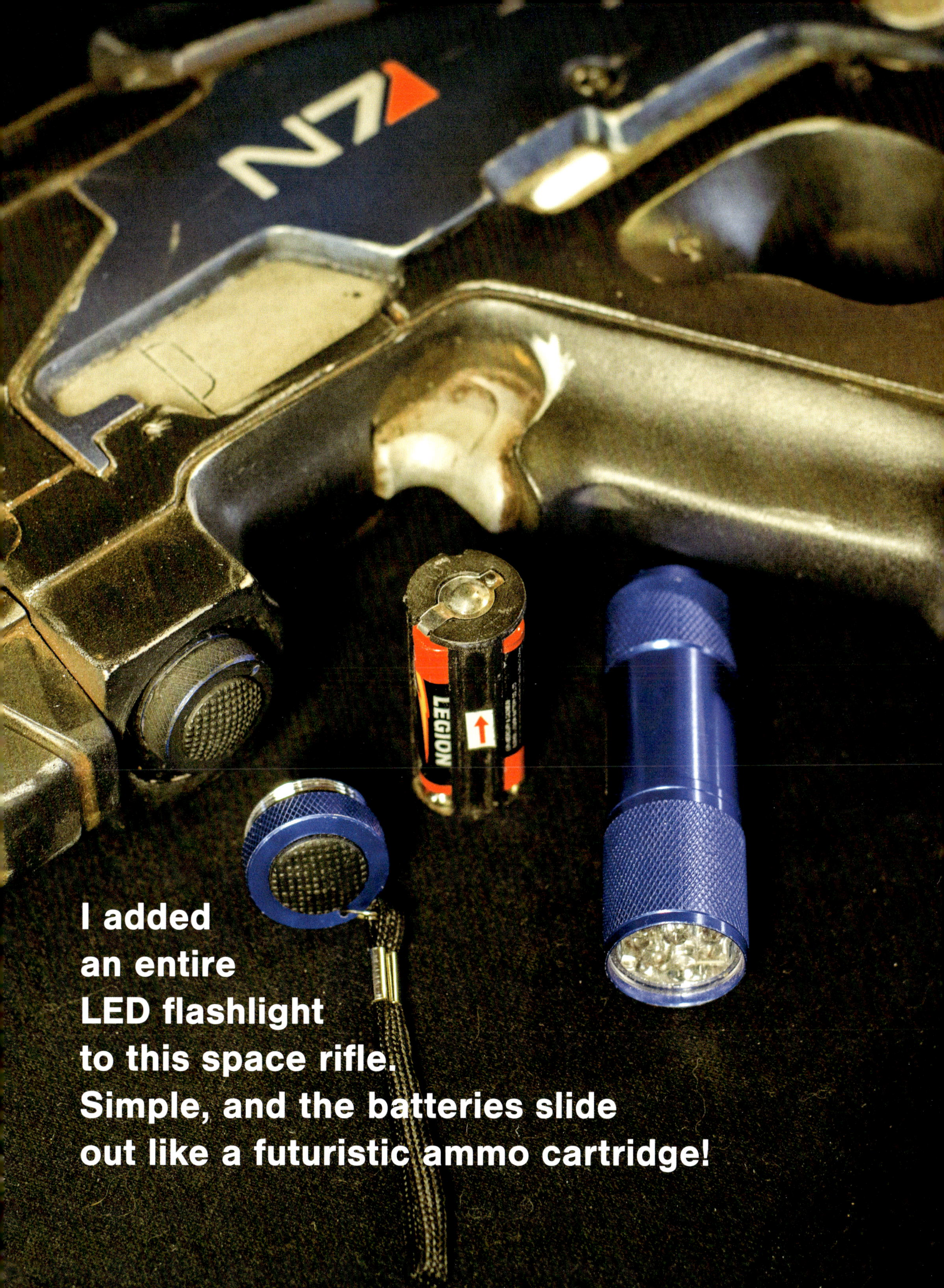
N7
LEGION
I added
an entire
LED flashlight
to this space rifle.
Simple, and the batteries slide
out like a futuristic ammo cartridge!

12 Volt LED Strips

Sometimes you need a lot of LEDs all in a row and the thought of wiring them all together makes you want to cry. Fortunately for us, it's possible to purchase long strips of pre assembled LEDs. These kits are extremely handy, but there are a couple of things you need to keep in mind. The LEDs are a pre-set distance away from one another. Also, they run on 12 volts. This means you're going to need a lot of power to get them glowing bright.

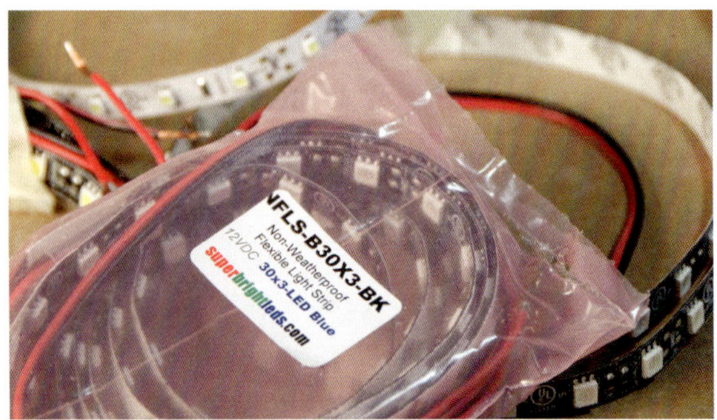

There are several easy solutions for powering these monstrous light strips. You could wire up 8 AA or AAA batteries, so long as you have the space in your costume to hide such a large package of batteries. You can also get your hands on a tiny 12v battery. Unfortunately, such a small battery will not last very long. Finally you could run the circuit on a 9v battery. The LEDs will not be as bright as possible, but they may be bright enough for your needs.

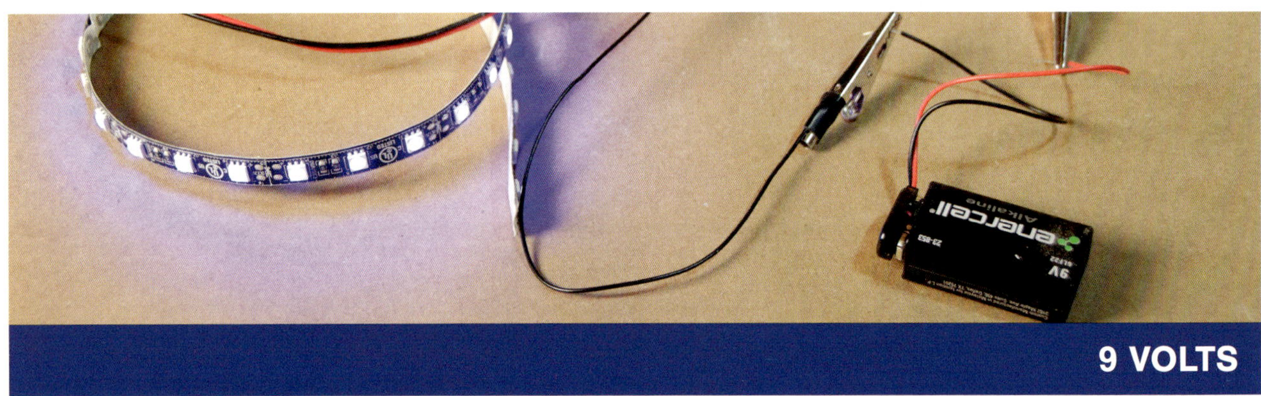

9 VOLTS

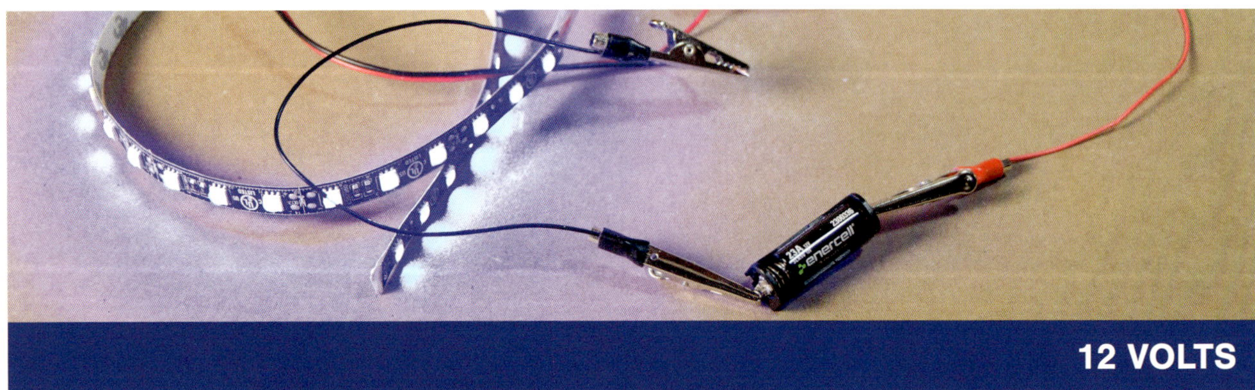

12 VOLTS

Scratch Built LED Circuits

So you want to get your hands dirty, eh? Wiring your own circuits is the next step towards getting your own very, super custom illumination. Here are some basic things you'll want to keep in mind before you plug in that soldering iron.

Series vs. Parallel Circuits

There are two different ways to run your lighting circuits: series and parallel. I tend to run most of my lighting circuits in parallel. This way, if one LED burns out, it doesn't interrupt power to the rest of the circuit, a la cheap Christmas lights. I also prefer parallel circuits because adding more lights does not affect the voltage requirements.

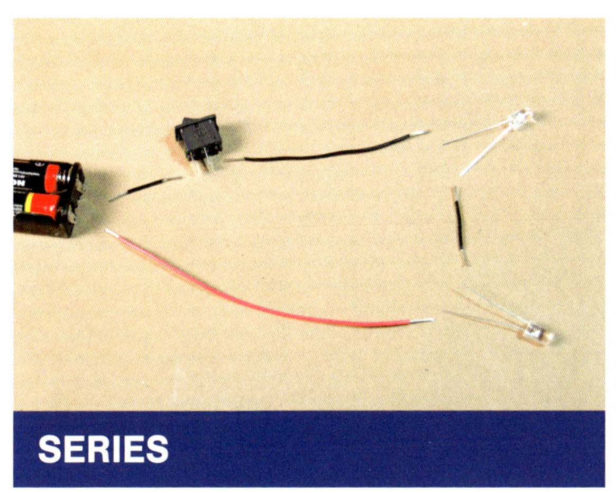

SERIES

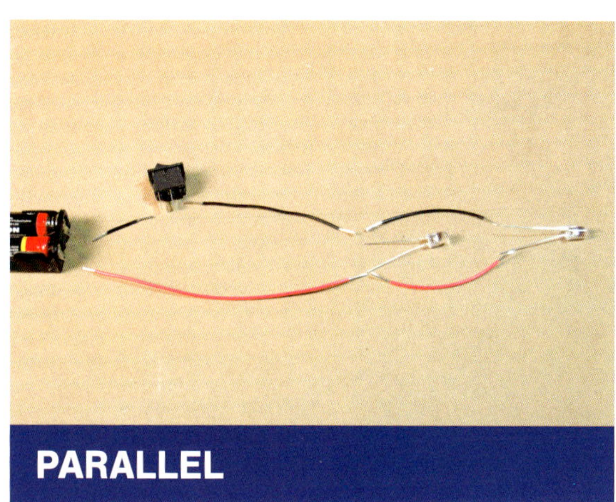

PARALLEL

Positive & Negative

Electrons only like to flow in one direction, so wiring lights and batteries in the proper order is pretty vital. LEDs have one positive and one negative lead. Be sure to wire them so that those leads connect to the corresponding terminal on your battery. Also remember that resistors should always be on the positive side of a circuit and switches can go on either side. Switches and resistors don't have a positive or negative pole, so either side of them can be attached in either direction.

On a battery holder, the red lead is the positive side and black is the negative. The color of wire you use is up to you, but sticking with this color scheme will remove any kind of guesswork later on when you're completing your circuit.

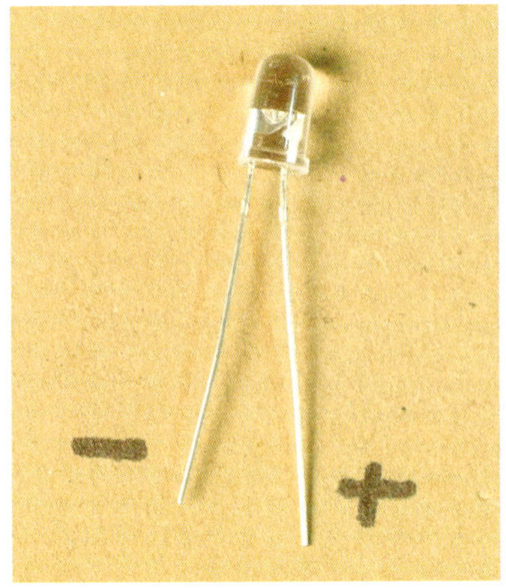

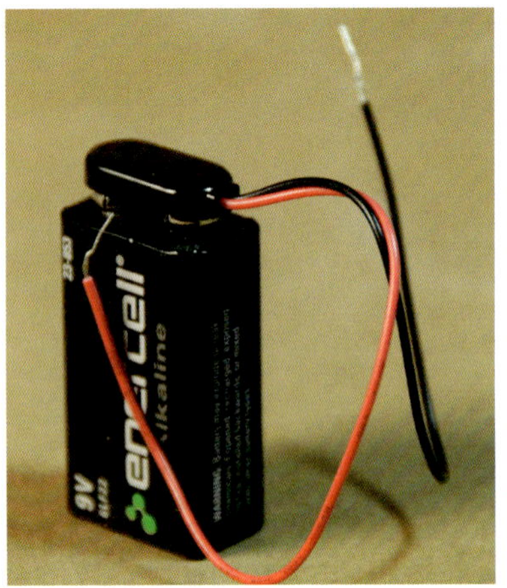

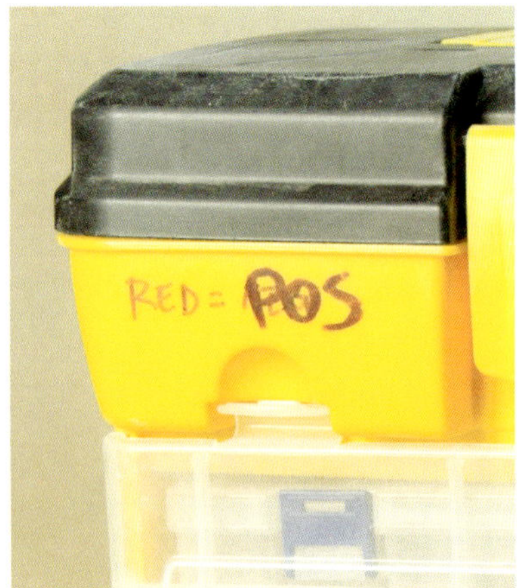

On LEDs, the longer lead is the positive lead. For wiring purposes, it pays to attach it to red wires as a reminder. That way you always know which terminal to connect it to on the battery.

Surface Mount LEDs will have something to indicate which side is which. In this case, the little triangle notes the negative side. They can be wired from behind, taking care to solder all three leads on each side.

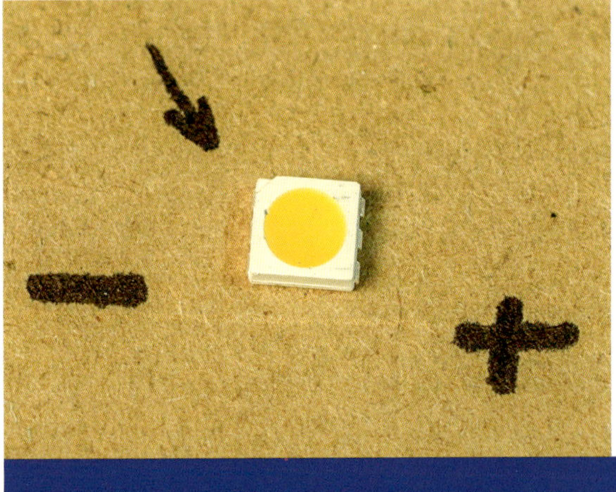

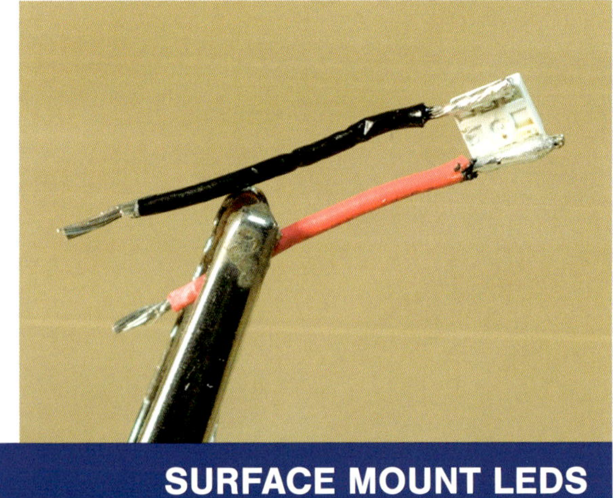

SURFACE MOUNT LEDS

ELECTRONICS TOOLS & SUPPLIES

If you're taking this route, there are some tools that are rather necessary to pick up before you get started.

- Soldering Iron/Stand
- Wire
- Solder
- Heat Shrink Tubing
- Wire Stripper/Cutter
- Electrical Tape
- Helping Hands
- Batteries
  AA / AAA / 2032 Coin / 9V
- Battery Holders
  AA/ AAA / 2032 Coin / 9V
- On/Off Switches
  Toggle / Slide
- Tool Box

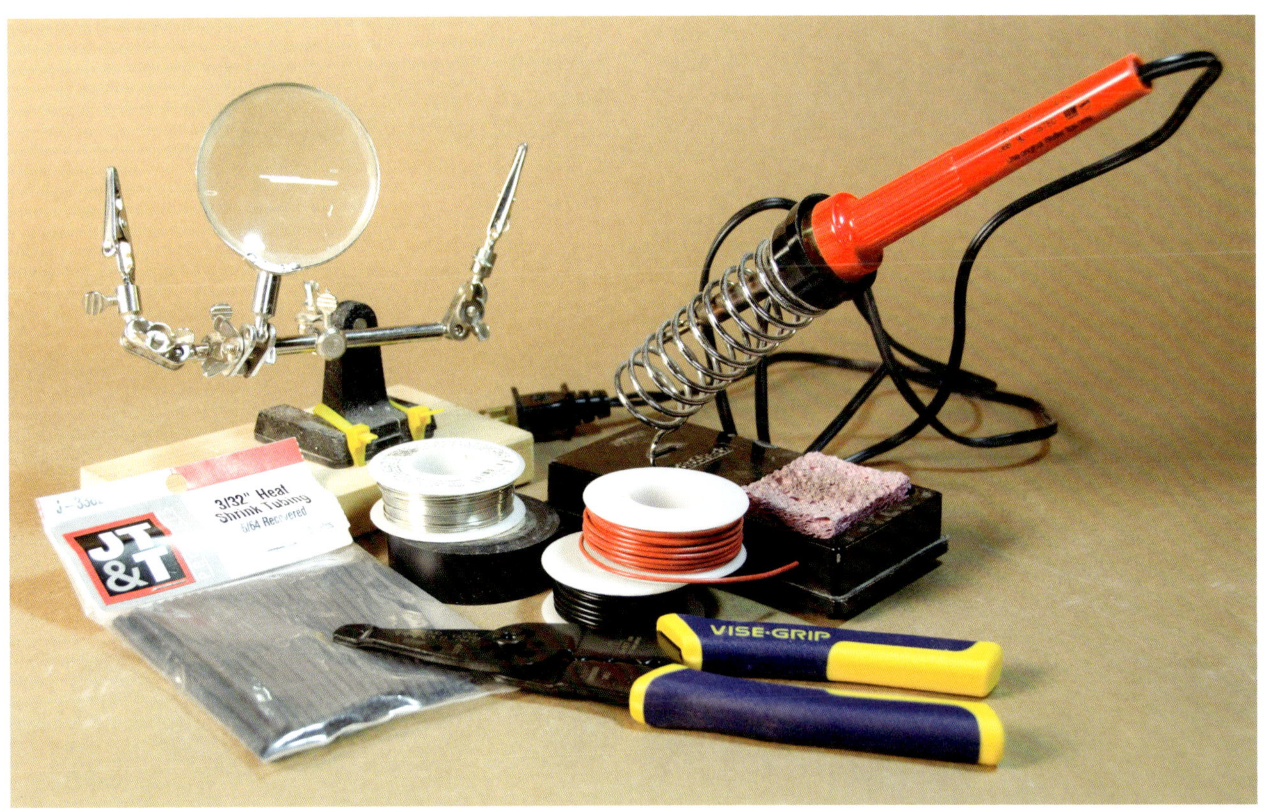

SOLDERING BASICS

You're going to have a difficult time doing any kind of electronics work without a soldering iron. They can be picked up for fairly cheap, though I do recommend spending the coin on a better one if you plan on doing lots of electronics work. You do not want a hot iron rolling around your desk, so you'll want to get yourself a nice stand with a sponge for holding the soldering iron and cleaning the solder off the tip between uses.

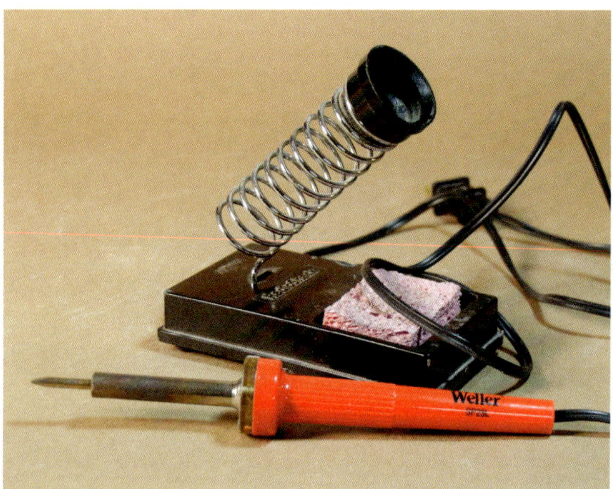

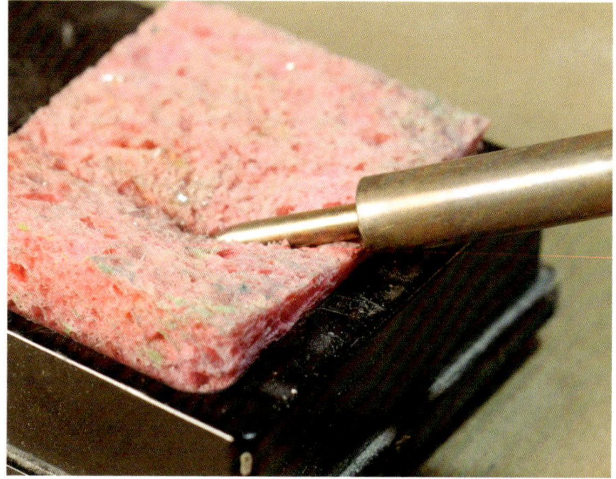

Before soldering, consider if you want to cover the connection with some heat shrink tubing (spoiler: you do). Usually you will want to slide on a tube before permanently soldering two wires or an LED together. With your tubing loosely in place, you can move on to soldering!

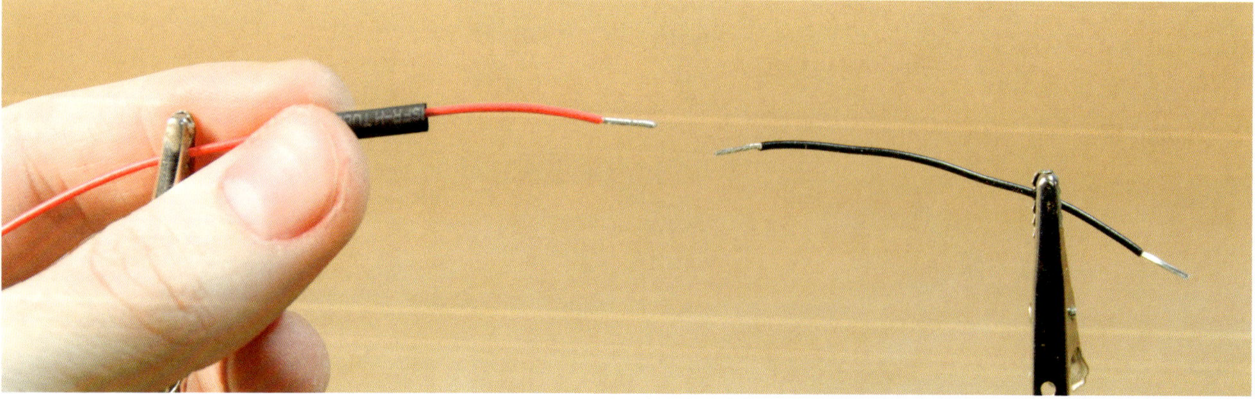

Soldering is used to either connect two wires together or a wire to an LED, battery, or switch. To do this, you'll want to first twist the exposed wire or LED ends together or hold them in place with a set of helping hands. Then, touch a little bit of solder to the tip of your hot soldering iron. This is known as "tinning the tip" and it helps transfer the heat of the iron to your wires. Next hold the tinned tip against the wires where you want to apply the connection. Then pull out a length of solder wire and touch it to the hot wire, not the soldering iron. If the wire is hot enough the solder will melt and connect your wires! Solder solidifies rather quickly, but remains hot for a little while, so don't go touching it right away.

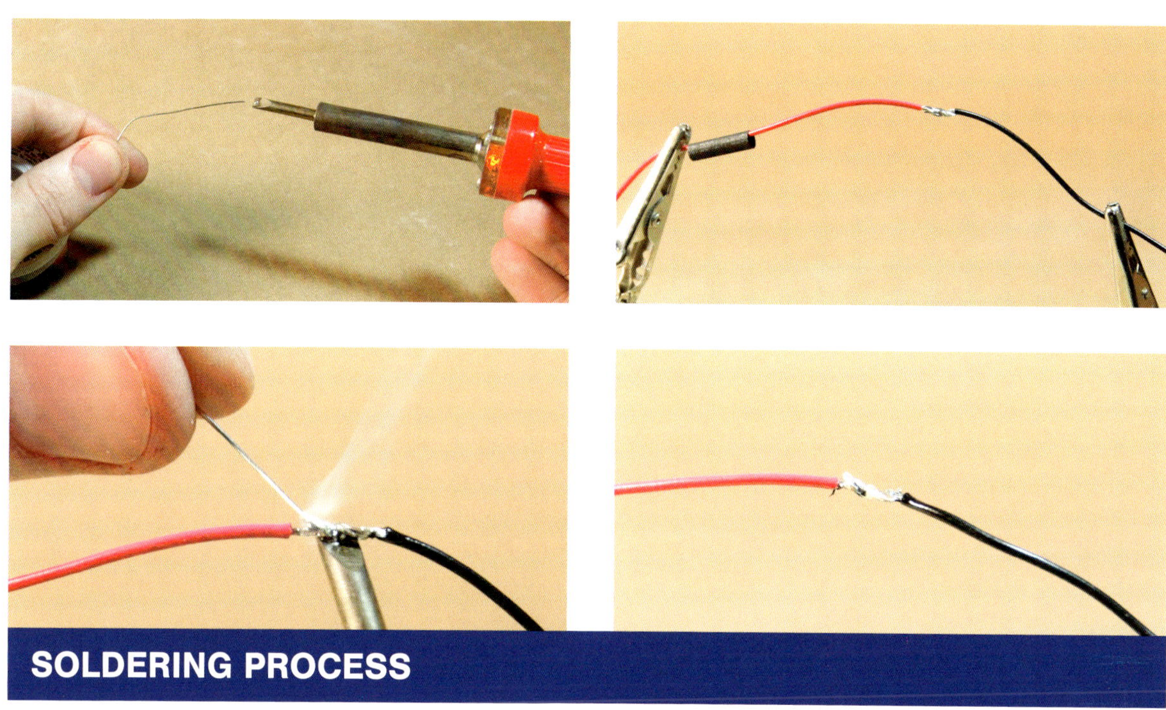

SOLDERING PROCESS

Now you're free to slide your heat shrink tubing over the solder and hit it with a lighter or heat gun to cinch it up. Congratulations, you've just done some soldering! Clean the tip of your iron on that handy sponge and move on to the next connection.

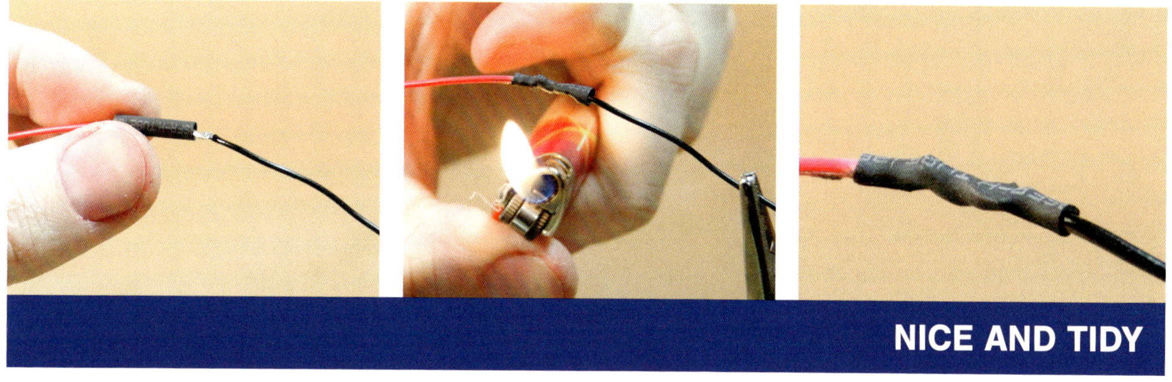

NICE AND TIDY

Troubleshooting Your Wiring

When I got started doing my own electronics, sometimes circuits would fail and lights wouldn't always work. This was usually because my soldering was pretty bad. This is where practice pays off. Take the time to get good at soldering and become very familiar with your tools. If a connection feels kind of wobbly, heat it with your soldering iron, take it apart and solder it again. Durability is a key factor in making good, reliable circuits that keep your armor lights running all convention long!

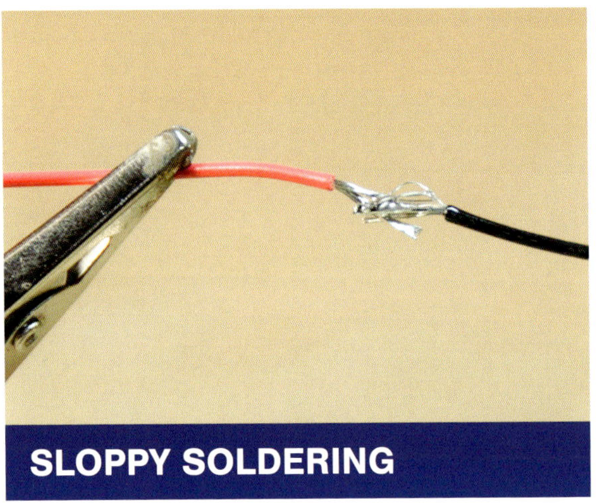

SLOPPY SOLDERING

Another issue that can keep your LEDs from lighting up is what's known as a "short". This is when there's an unwanted connection between a positive and negative wire. It will interrupt the flow of electrons and keep an LED from illuminating. If one (or all) of your lights refuses to glow, double check all of your wiring to see if you have any crossed wires. If you do, tidy them up with heat shrink tubing. In a pinch, a little hot glue can insulate an exposed short.

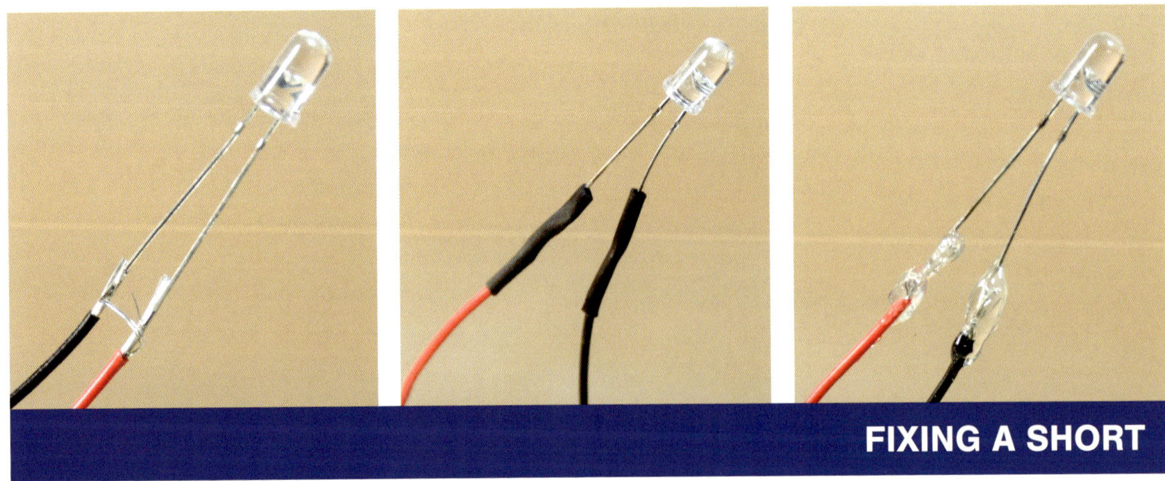

FIXING A SHORT

THE 3V, PARALLEL CIRCUIT

If you're ready to wire something completely from scratch, there are many variations that you can go with. I will be covering my favorite circuit, the 3V parallel circuit. I prefer this one because it doesn't require resistors, I always keep a healthy stock of 3V LEDs, and I really like how easy it is to hide those little 2032 coin batteries in my armor.

AA and AAA batteries are very common and they both run at 1.5v. If you have two of them in a battery holder wired in series, then your circuit is going to be spitting out 3 volts. Fortunately for us, 3v LEDs are extremely common! Since this is the case, I like to stock up on 3v LEDs, especially the tiny surface mounted ones. I'll buy a whole bunch of them in a wide range of colors so that I'm ready to put together custom lighting kits at a moment's notice.

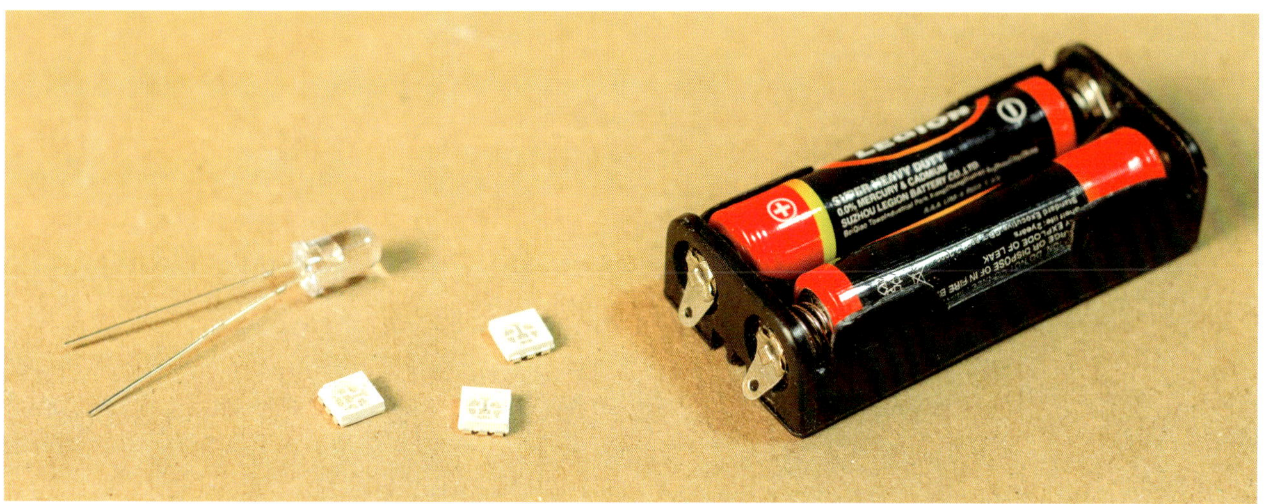

Some colors of LEDs (like red and yellow) don't come in 3V varieties, so I'll use white LEDs and color them based on the material they are shining through. More on that later.

Setting up a parallel circuit for this arrangement couldn't be simpler! You don't even need to add any resistors. Just throw a switch in there and boom! You've got yourself a running LED circuit.

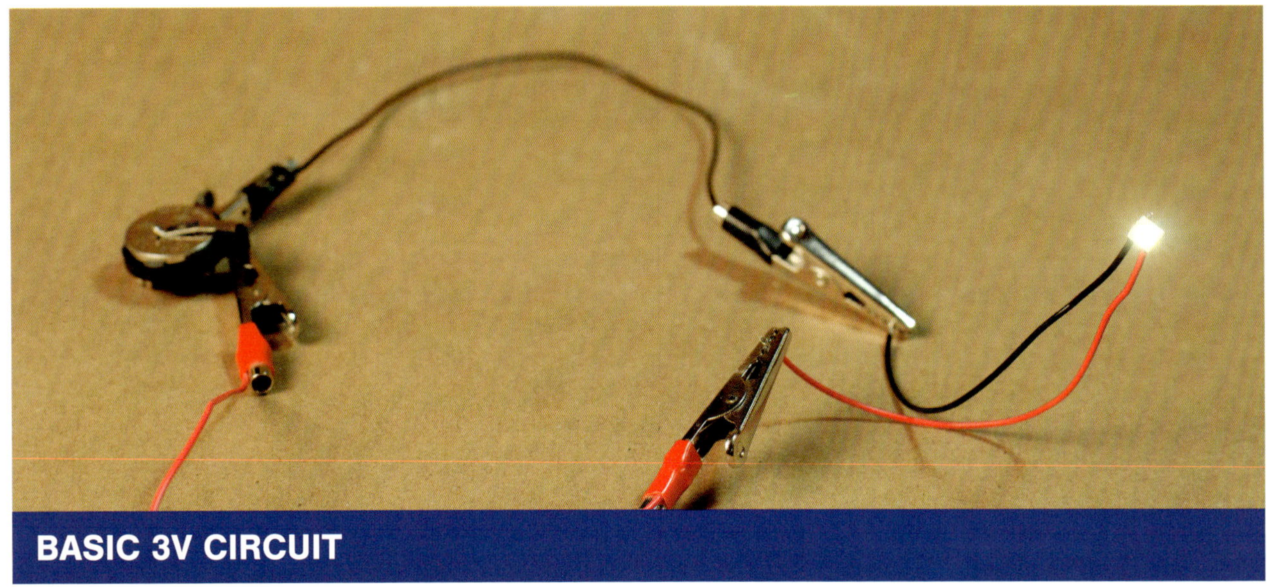

BASIC 3V CIRCUIT

To add multiple LEDs into a circuit, solder them together so that all of the same poles are connected to one another and the battery source. You can even just solder all of the leads from the LEDs in a chain if they need to be right next to each other.

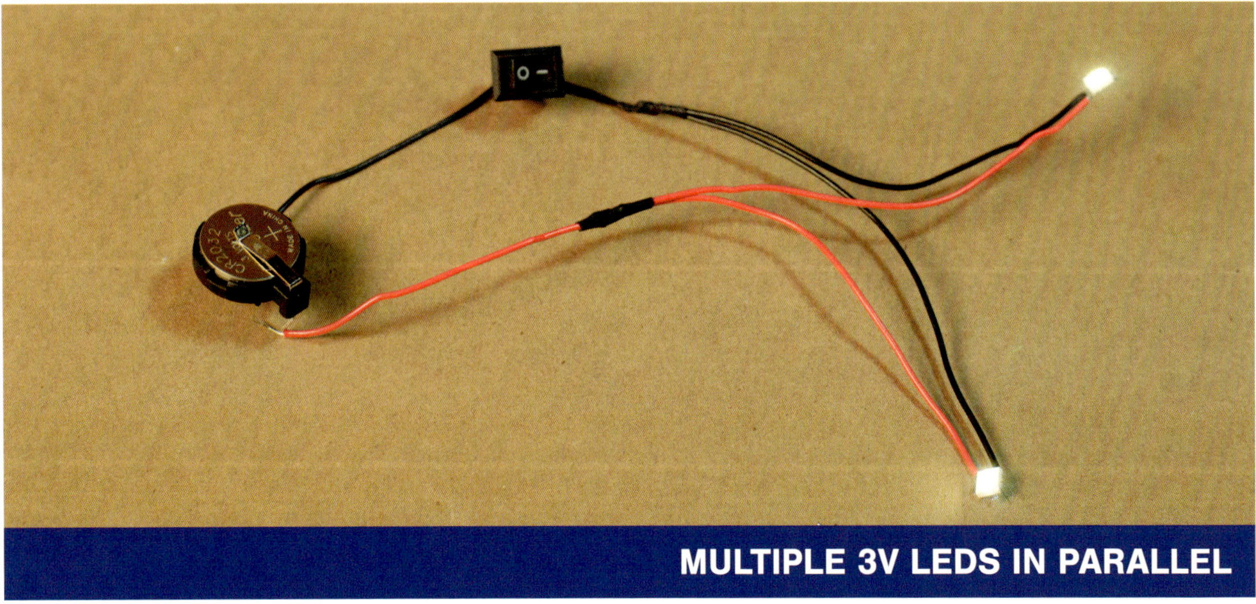

MULTIPLE 3V LEDS IN PARALLEL

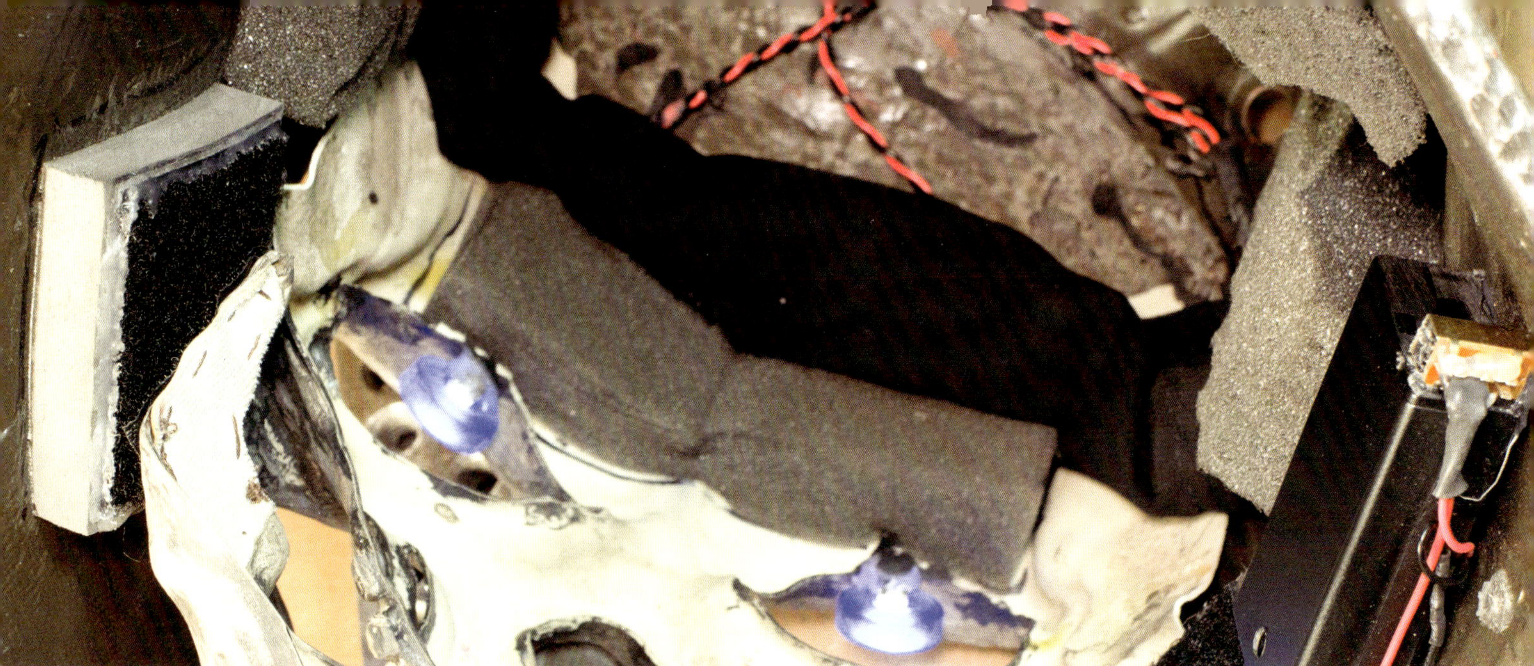

This is exactly the LED wiring I used for the glowing eyes in my Draugr helmet. So simple, yet so very effective.

If I need to set up a really small circuit, I'll use the 3v 2032 coin batteries. This is extremely useful if you don't have a lot of room in your armor to stow a big battery. Sometimes I won't even put a switch in one of these circuits. I'll just take the coin battery out of the holder to turn off the lights when not in use. This saves even more space. You can even run an LED just by bending the leads around either side of the coin battery and taping it in place!

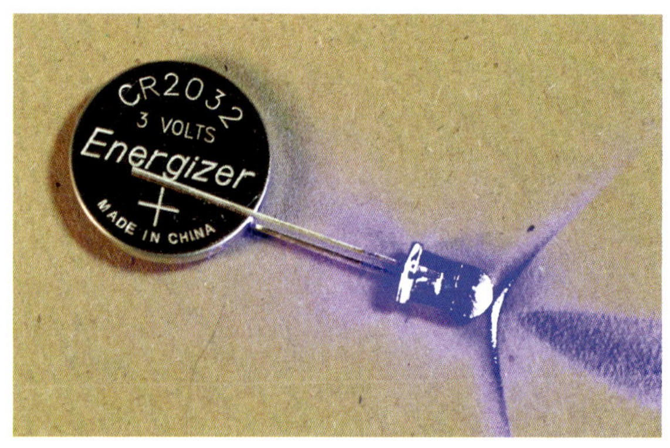

This 3v setup works very well if you're running just a couple of LEDs. For example, I've run the two lights in my Draugr helmet for several convention weekends on the same two AA batteries. However, if you run a lot of LEDs off of just two AA batteries, they will run out of juice pretty fast. It's worth doing some tests to see what kind of life you'll get out of your particular setup and, if need be, either bring extra (and/or rechargable) batteries with you to your costuming event (always a good idea) or consider running a different battery setup.

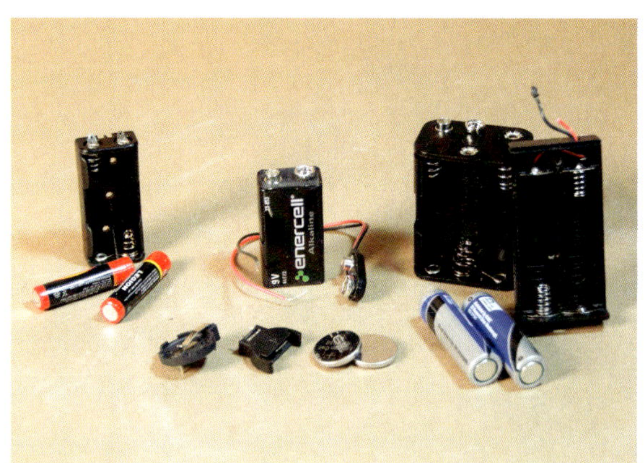

Custom Circuits & Resistors

You may find that 3 volts of juice simply isn't enough to keep your armor illuminated all day long. You could split up lights into more than one circuit. I actually prefer this method, especially if the lights end up on different parts of my armor. This way I don't end up with wires running across my body.

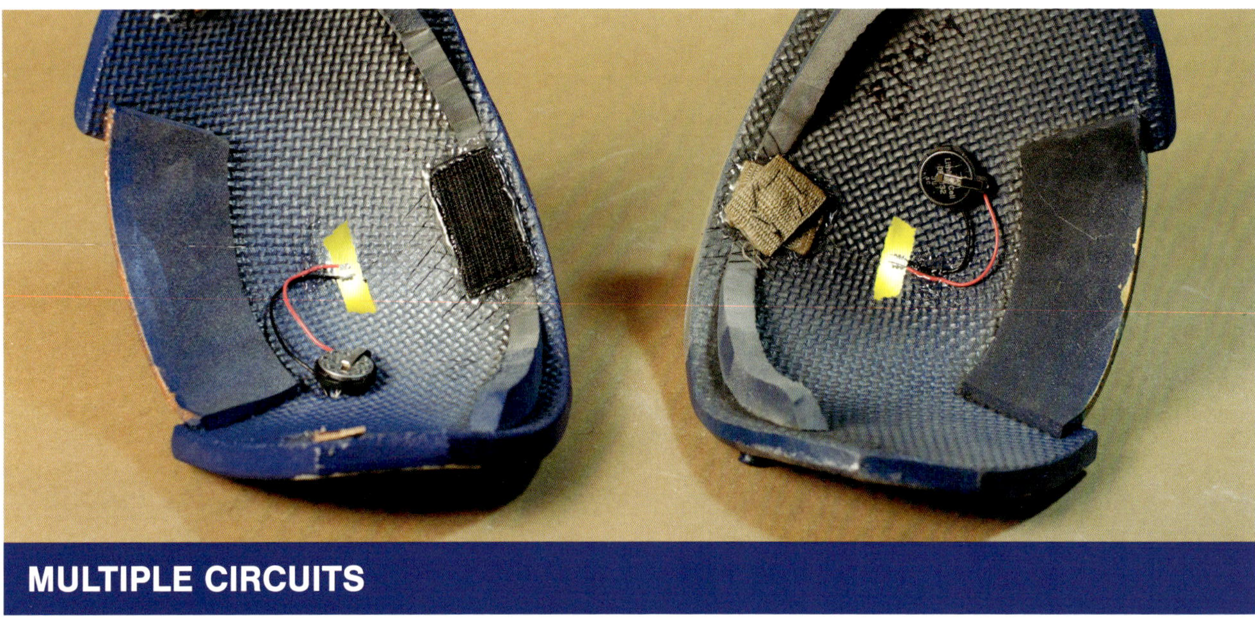

MULTIPLE CIRCUITS

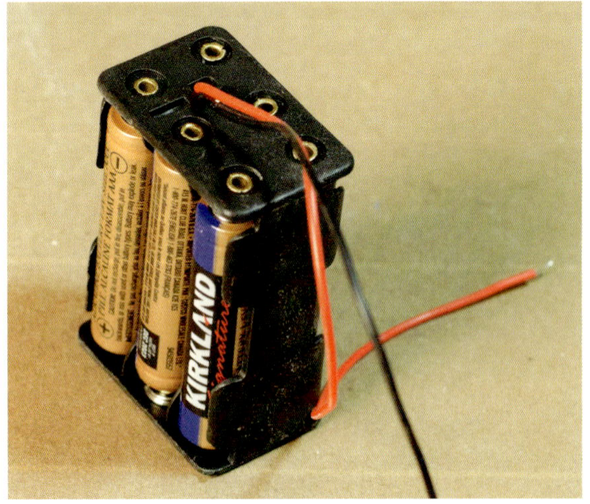

The other solution is to use a bigger battery. Using more battery power in your circuit means you can use more LEDs for a longer duration. This also means you'll be introducing more voltage into the mix. Without resistors, you're going to burn out those LEDs. This 6 AAA holder spits out 9 volts, three times what you need to run a 3v LED.

Search online for LED resistance calculators

In order to figure out what type of resistor to use, you'll need to do some math. Fear not! LED resistance calculators exist and are easy to use with just a couple of values. Here's an example.

Example Calculation for a 4.5V Battery (3 AAAs) and Red Through Hole LED

- Source Voltage (Battery): 4.5V
- Diode (LED) Forward Voltage: 2.2V
- Diode (LED) Forward Current (mA): 20 mA
- Resistor Required: 120 ohms, ⅛ watt

With the proper resistors in hand, you're ready to complete the circuit. Be sure to wire the resistor on the positive side of the circuit. Also remember that, so long as all of your LEDs are wired in parallel, that one resistor will take care of the entire circuit.

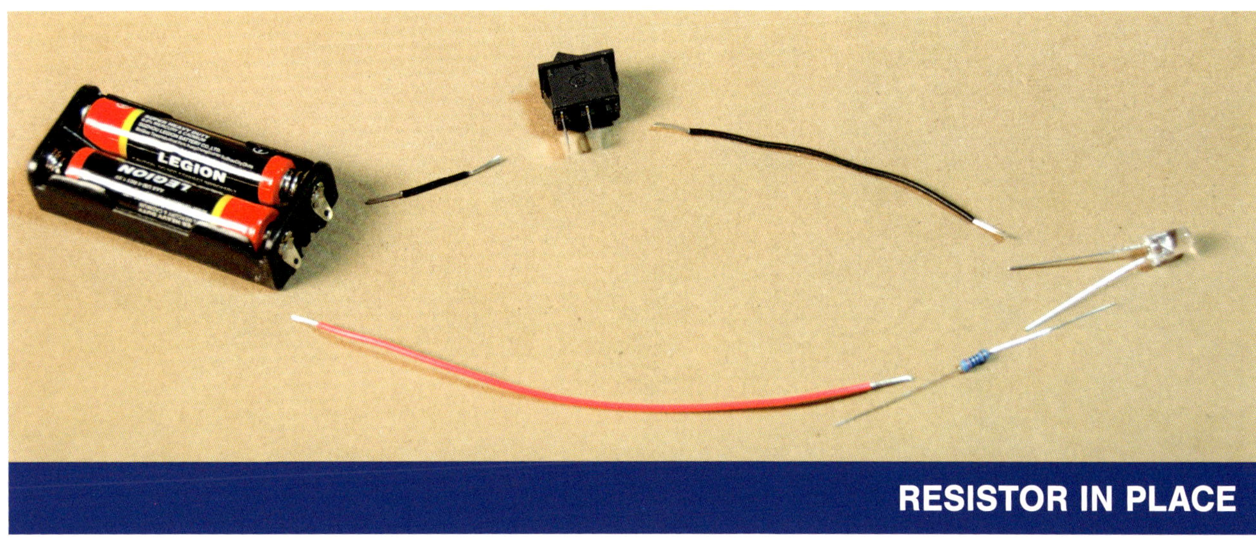

RESISTOR IN PLACE

To test my circuits before soldering, I have some wires that have alligator clips on them. These are utilized to temporarily make a little circuit and see how your lights work when they're installed. You simply clamp your clips onto your battery leads and then clamp the other ends onto your light leads.

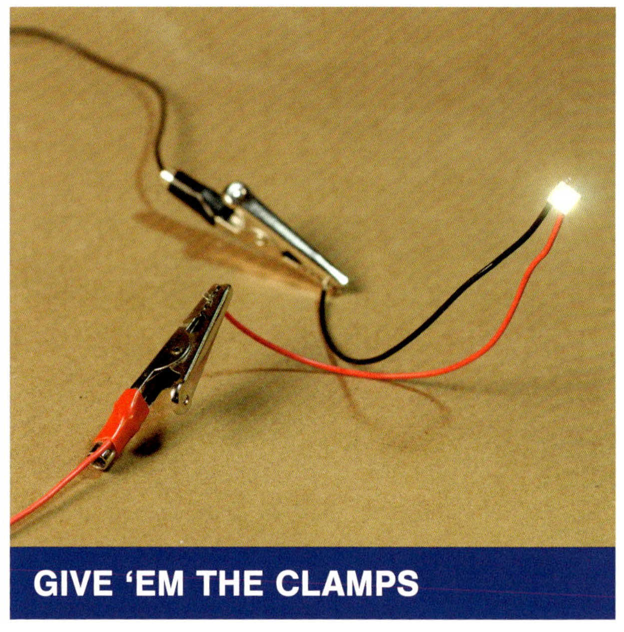

GIVE 'EM THE CLAMPS

Setting up complex circuits with many LEDs can be a long and complicated process. There are a myriad of ways to do it and each setup will be different depending on the specific needs of your costume armor. Drawing a diagram of your circuits before you start wiring can be extremely helpful, as well as a healthy dose of patience. If you get frustrated, remember that there are many communities online that specialize in electronics, so you aren't alone! Sparkfun and Adafruit are two great communities to check out!!

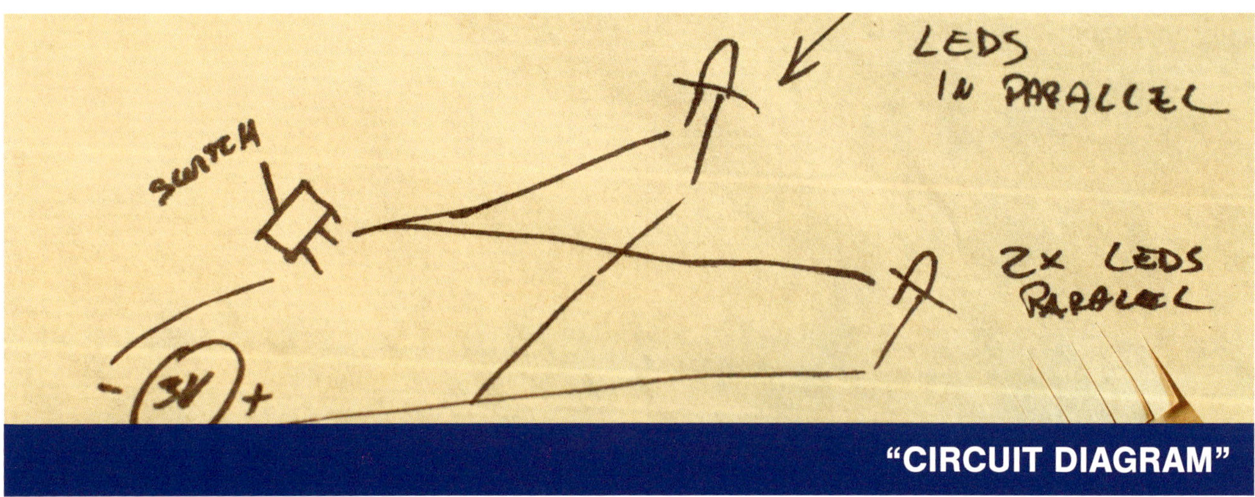

"CIRCUIT DIAGRAM"

Diffusing Your LED Lights

Most of the time, the desired lighting effect on a costume will not be just bare LEDs. To get a soft, glowing light effect, the bulbs will need to be diffused in some way. Here are a couple of examples of how to nail that perfect glow.

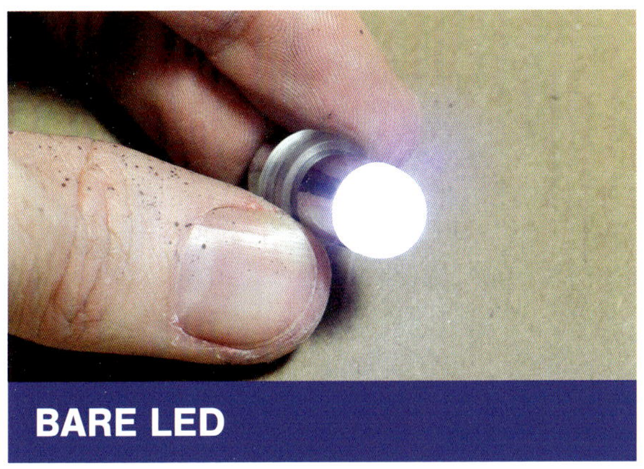

BARE LED

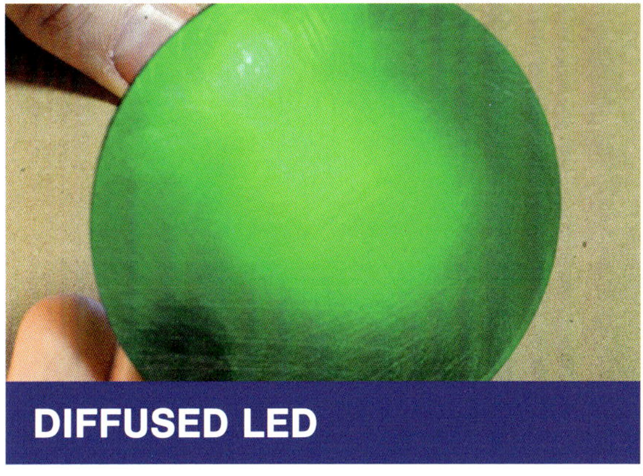

DIFFUSED LED

For most of your diffusion techniques, you'll be shining your LEDs through some type of material. You'll want to do a lot of experimenting with different materials to find what works best for you. I really like using thin sheets of plastic for this job. You can either buy stock sheets from a plastics supplier, or look around your house for things that can be repurposed for the job.

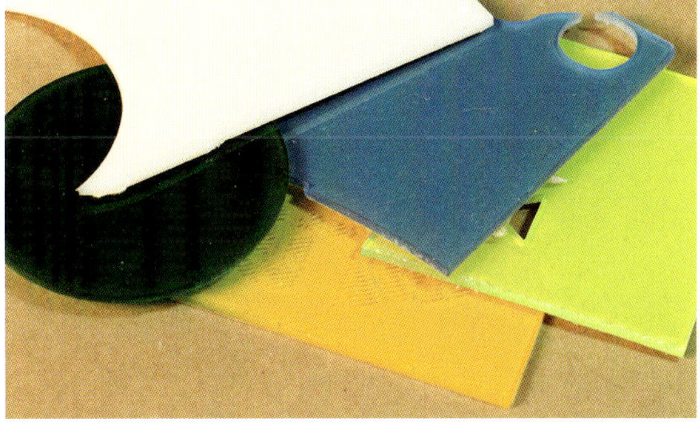

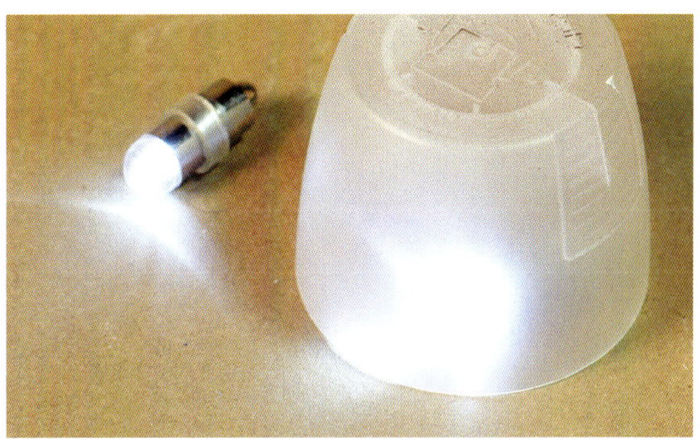

Whatever material you pick to diffuse your light, you probably want to sand the surface of it with a 220 grit sandpaper. By thoroughly scuffing up the surface, you're creating thousands of gouges that will scatter the light on its path away from the LED source.

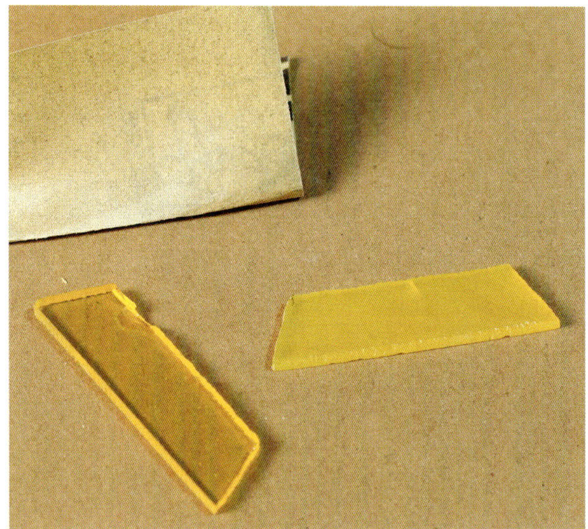

You'll also find that moving the LEDs away from the back surface of your diffusion material will have a dramatic effect on the "hot spots" that the bulbs can create. The further back you move the light source, the dimmer it gets, but it also get more diffused.

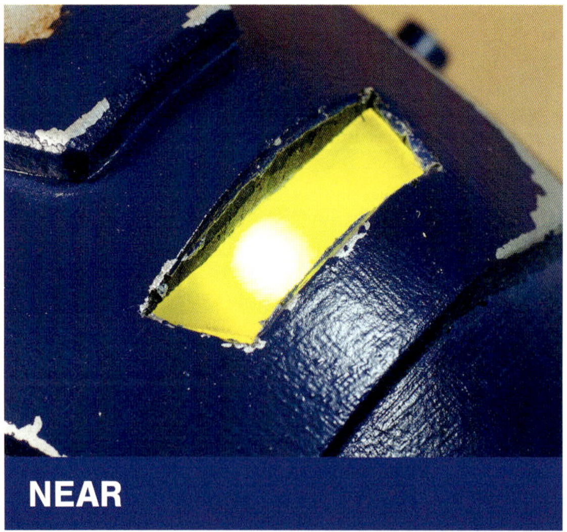

NEAR

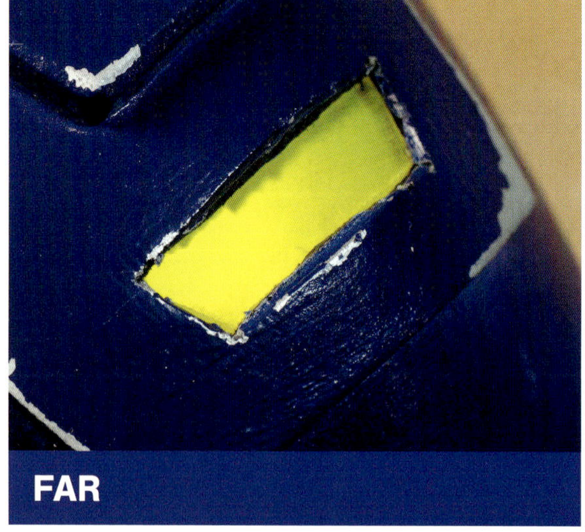

FAR

This method doesn't just have to be applied to flat surfaces. If you have some plastic gems or domes, you can get some really neat effects by back lighting them with LEDs too!

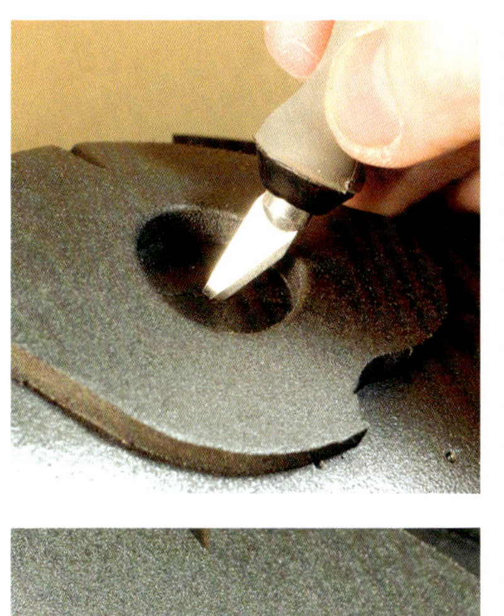

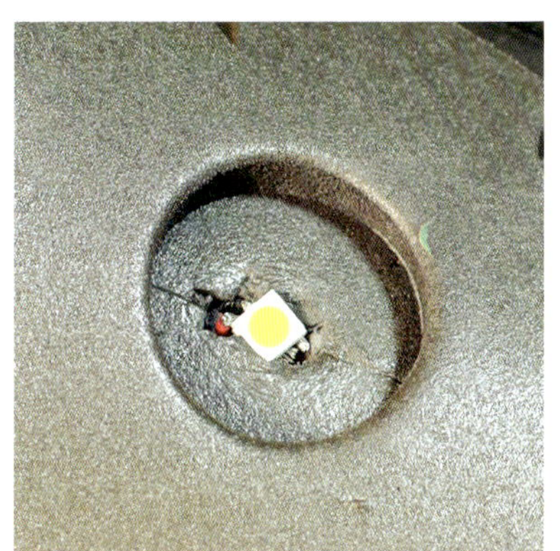

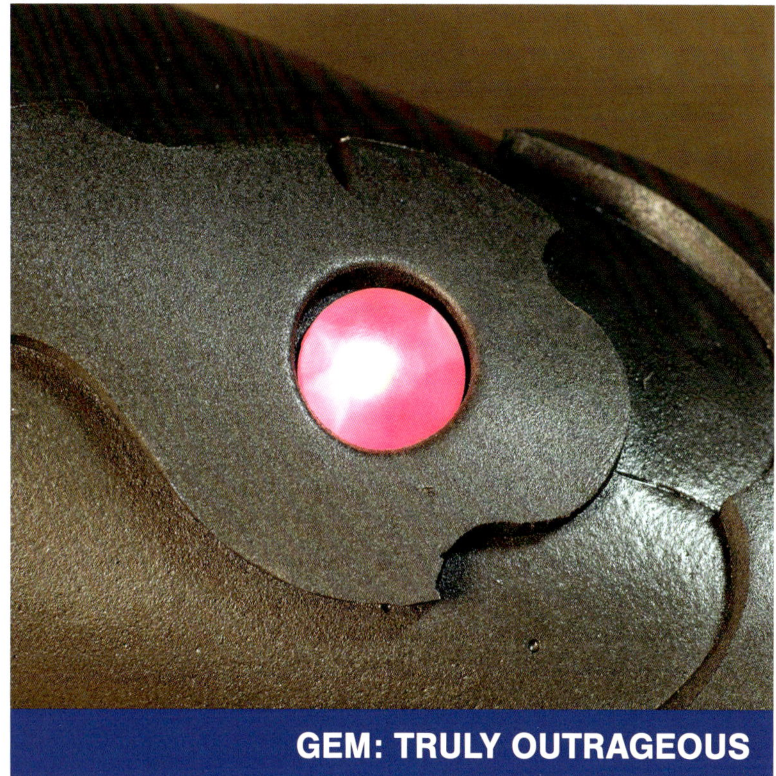

GEM: TRULY OUTRAGEOUS

You can also get some really neat custom effects by painting the back of your sanded diffusion surface. This way your paint scatters the light and you have the option of using a multitude of colors to achieve your specific look.

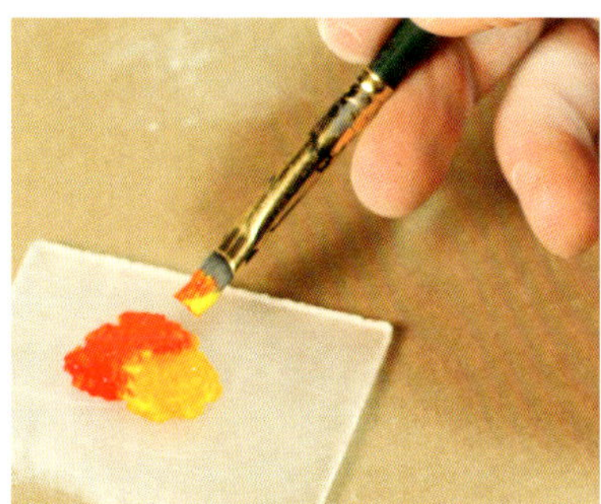

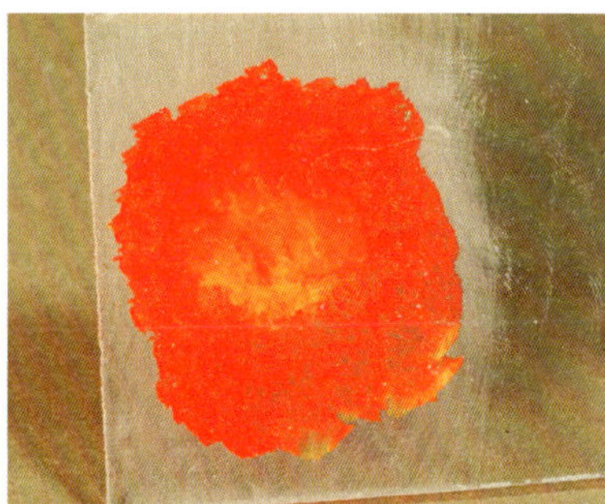

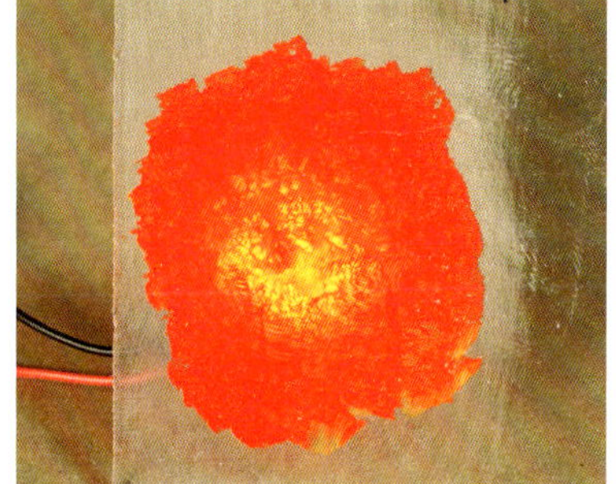

Edge Lighting

Sometimes you just don't have enough room to to put a bunch of LEDs and wires behind a surface on your armor. In this case you'll have to edge light your diffusion surface. This usually creates more hot spots in the glowing area, but it will get the job done.

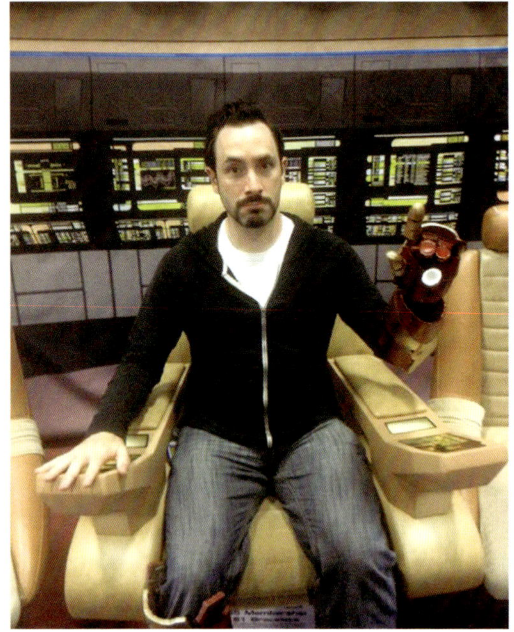

My Iron Man hand repulsor is an edge lit piece of white acrylic plastic.

While we're on the subject of edge lighting, you can get some really cool effects by edge lighting a transparent sheet of acrylic plastic that has designs etched into the surface. This is very effective for simulating visors, heads up displays, or digital readout displays.

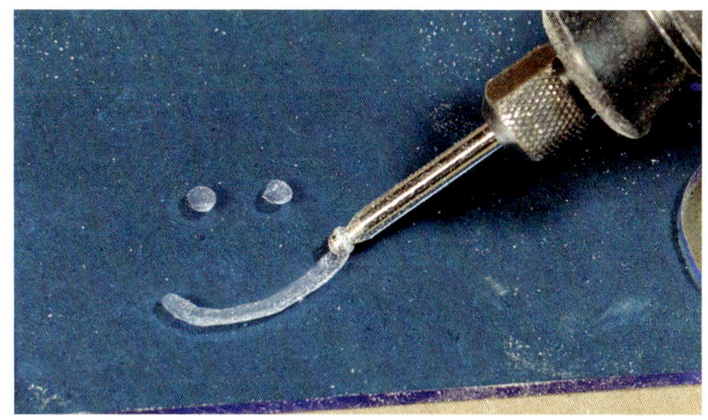

To etch your plastic, scratch the surface with a knife or an engraving bit on your rotary tool. The deeper you etch, the more apparent the lighting will be. Much like the sanding covered earlier, these scratches diffuse the light and create a nice glowing effect.

With your surface thoroughly etched, you can apply a strip of LEDs on any edge of the sheet and your etching will glow like magic! Since this is a very low profile solution, the LEDs are very easy to hide inside your armor.

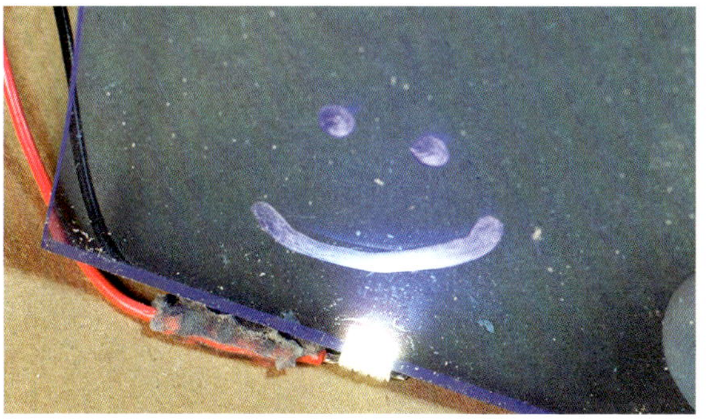

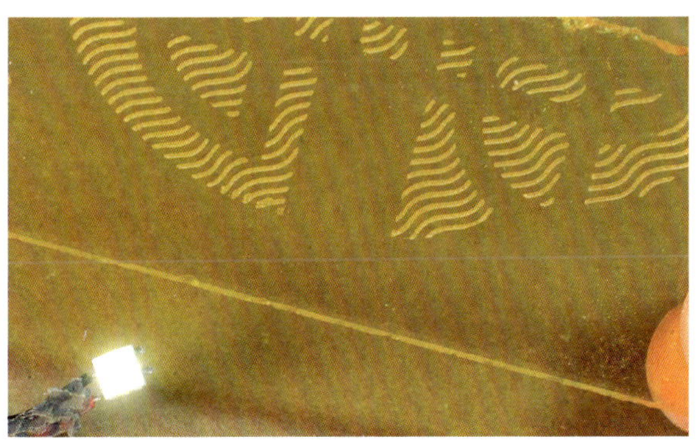

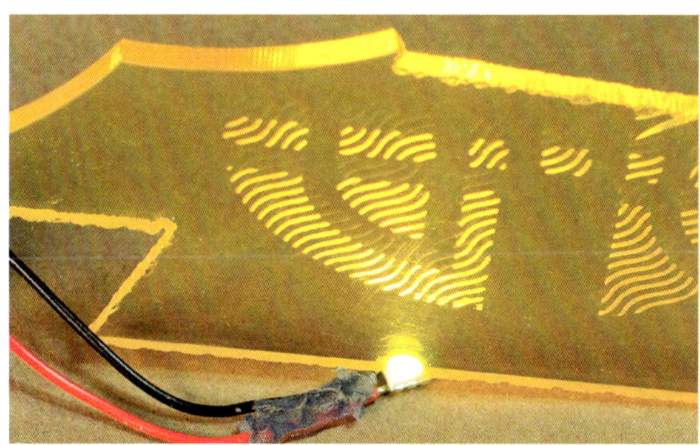

If you have access to a laser cutter/etcher, you can draw up complicated designs in a vector application, like Inkscape, and have them etched into a piece of acrylic! No laser handy? Use an online service like Ponoko or check your home town for local "maker spaces" or "hacker spaces."

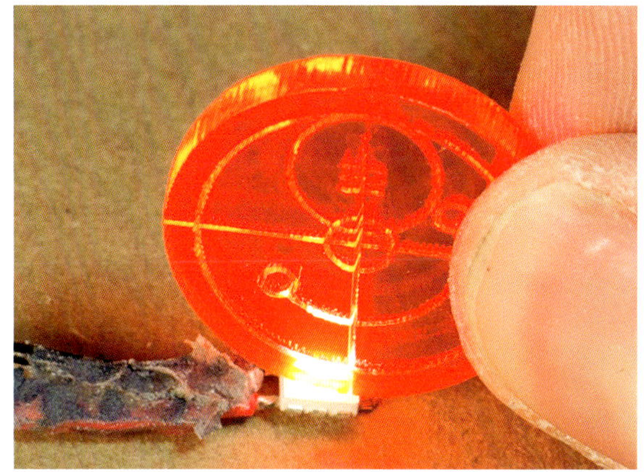

Installing Lights in Your Armor

Now that you've made some crazy cool glowing lights for your costume, it's time to install them into your armor! Hopefully, when you were patterning your foam bits, you left spaces to install your lights. If not, you can carve out recess for them using a sharp knife or your rotary tool.

If you've made some nice diffused plastic pieces for your lights, now would be a fantastic time to glue them in place. Try not to get any glue on the surface of the plastic as that will be seen through the plastic when it lights up. Just a little super glue on the sides will tack it in place.

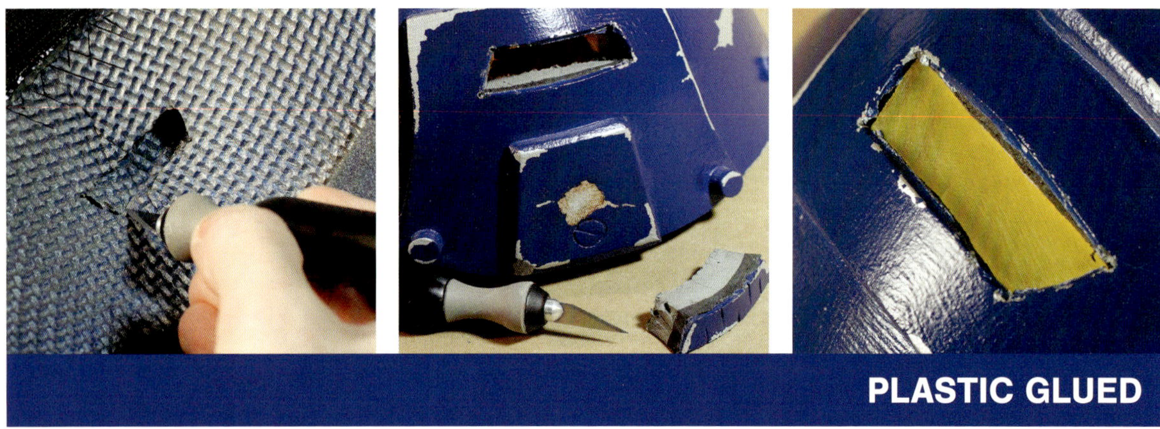

PLASTIC GLUED

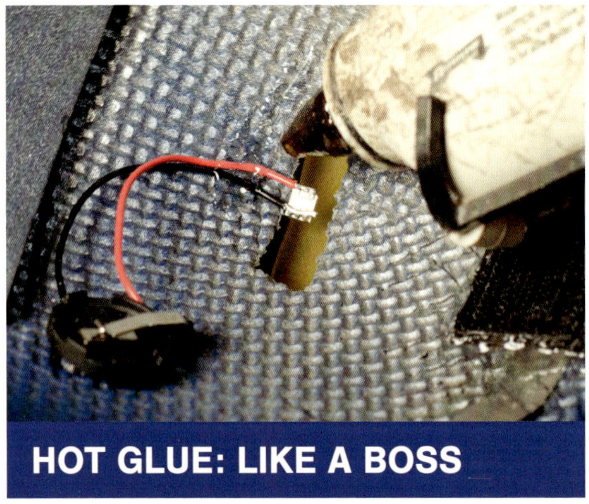

HOT GLUE: LIKE A BOSS

For your wiring adhesion needs, hot glue is king! Hot glue will hold wire and LEDs to foam like a champ. You can even use it to insulate any exposed wiring or leads if you're worried about moisture affecting their performance. Yes, your sweat can bugger your lights, so keep your wires protected!

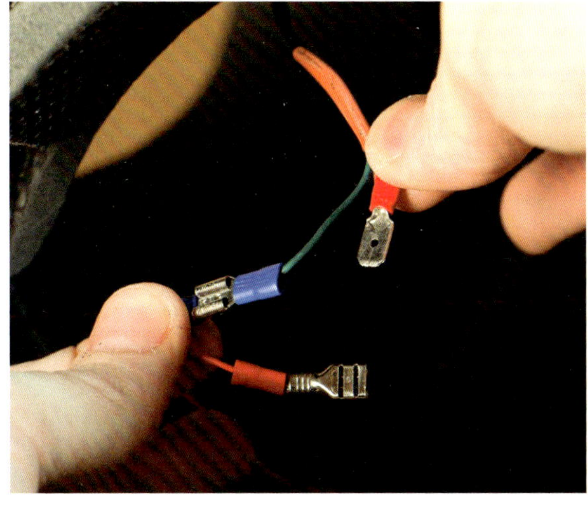

I prefer to glue my lighting arrays into place in my armor before permanently connecting all of the circuits inside the armor. In fact, it isn't even necessary to permanently attach them. You may want to end each array in a wiring connector so that they can be detached or replaced without re-soldering wires. This is especially handy if your armor comes apart into multiple pieces for transport or storage.

There are lights on the front and rear of my Mass Effect armor torso. I built the two pieces separate so they can come apart for transportation. The two lighting circuits come apart along with the armor.

You may also want to split up the lighting in your armor into multiple circuits. This way you won't need to run wires all around your body just to run everything off of one battery. This can also be helpful for troubleshooting if a circuit goes bad. This way if one circuit dies, your entire set of armor doesn't suddenly lose illumination. Also, if you end up running different parts of your lighting with different voltage power sources, you won't need to do any kind of complicated resistance wiring.

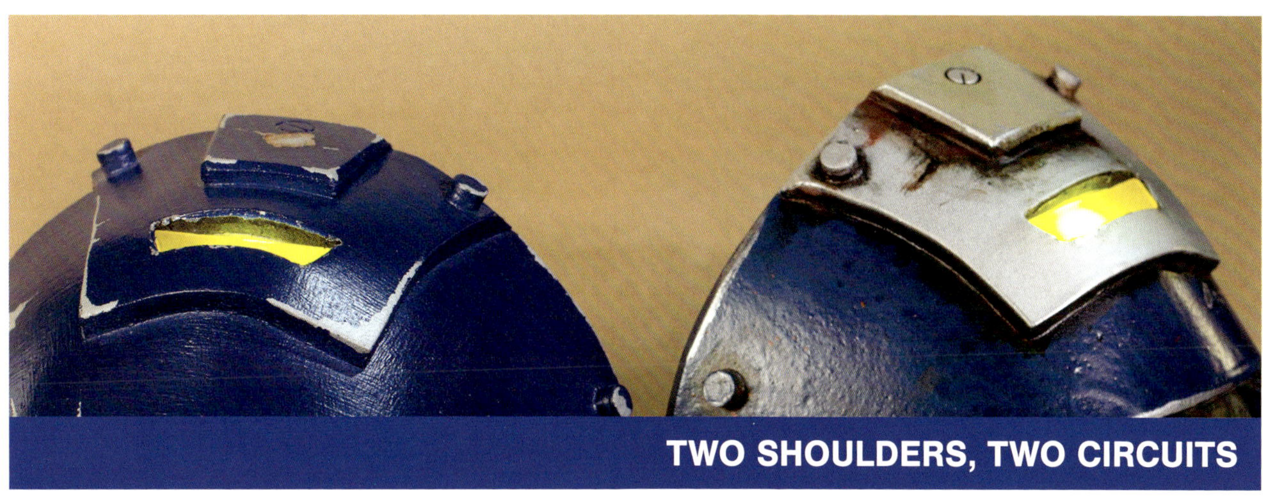

TWO SHOULDERS, TWO CIRCUITS

Stowing Batteries & Switches

Deciding where on your armor to put your switches and batteries will vary based on your space limitations, but there are a couple of things to keep in mind.

- Make sure you can reach your switch while in your armor in case you need to power down the lights at any point during a long con day.
- Being able to also reach the batteries while in costume is vital if you need to replace them midday.
- I usually end up wiring the switch right next to the battery, both physically and in the circuit. This way I know the switch will interrupt the entire circuit and they'll both be in an area that I can reach.

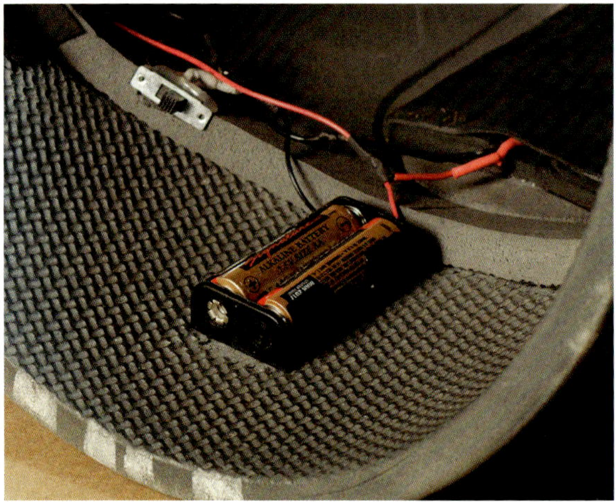

The switch and batteries for my Mass Effect armor hide behind my massive noggin.

The switch and batteries for my Draugr helmet are stowed under the lip of the helm. You'd only see them if you were lying on the ground looking straight up. And if that's the case, stop looking up my loin cloth, you perv!

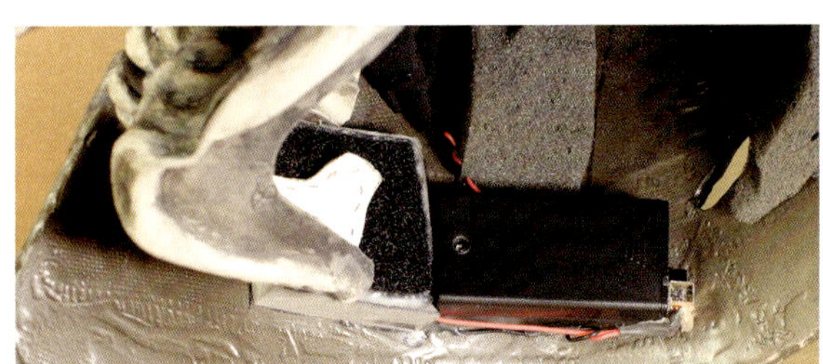

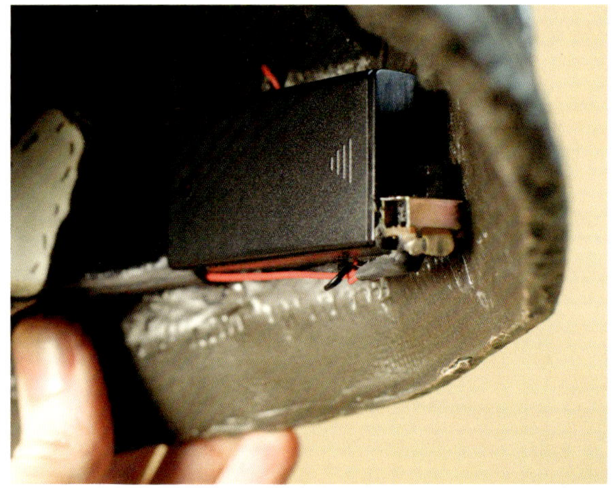

This book has only barely scratched surface of the vast possibilities available for lighting your costume. If you've nailed the basics and want to dive deeper, check out some of the electronics communities mentioned earlier to challenge yourself to do more. There are also nearly countless tutorials on YouTube that explain how to do more exciting lighting effects, so the sky's the limit!

Photographing Your Armor

This is it folks. The very end of the Foamsmith journey. It's been an exciting path and I'm thrilled that you came along for the ride with me! There's just one last thing to do with your amazing armor creation: Show it off.

Yes, you'll be taking your armored costumes to a Comic Con and yes, you'll be a total rock star in your amazing getup! Before you scurry off to be a total badass, you really should get some high quality photos of your incredible work. Here are a couple of tips to shoot your armor in a way that appropriately showcases your talents.

- If you can, hire a professional photographer to shoot you. There's a reason they get paid well for their work.

- If a pro is out of your price range, bribe a friend to help out. I have a photographer friend who is very good at what he does and he'll shoot my costumes in exchange for a case of beer. Everyone wins!

- Also look into modeling your armor for your local high school or college photography classes. They will be very excited to have your armor to shoot and you can exchange your time for the rights to use their photos.

- If you're shooting your own photos, remember that you can never have too much light. A bunch of cheap can lights from the hardware store can set your photography apart from under-lit, indoor bathroom photos.

- The camera doesn't make the shot. Good lighting and a cellphone camera is better than crappy lighting and a professional DSLR.

- No access to good lights? Take your armor outside and shoot under the biggest light in our solar system: the sun.

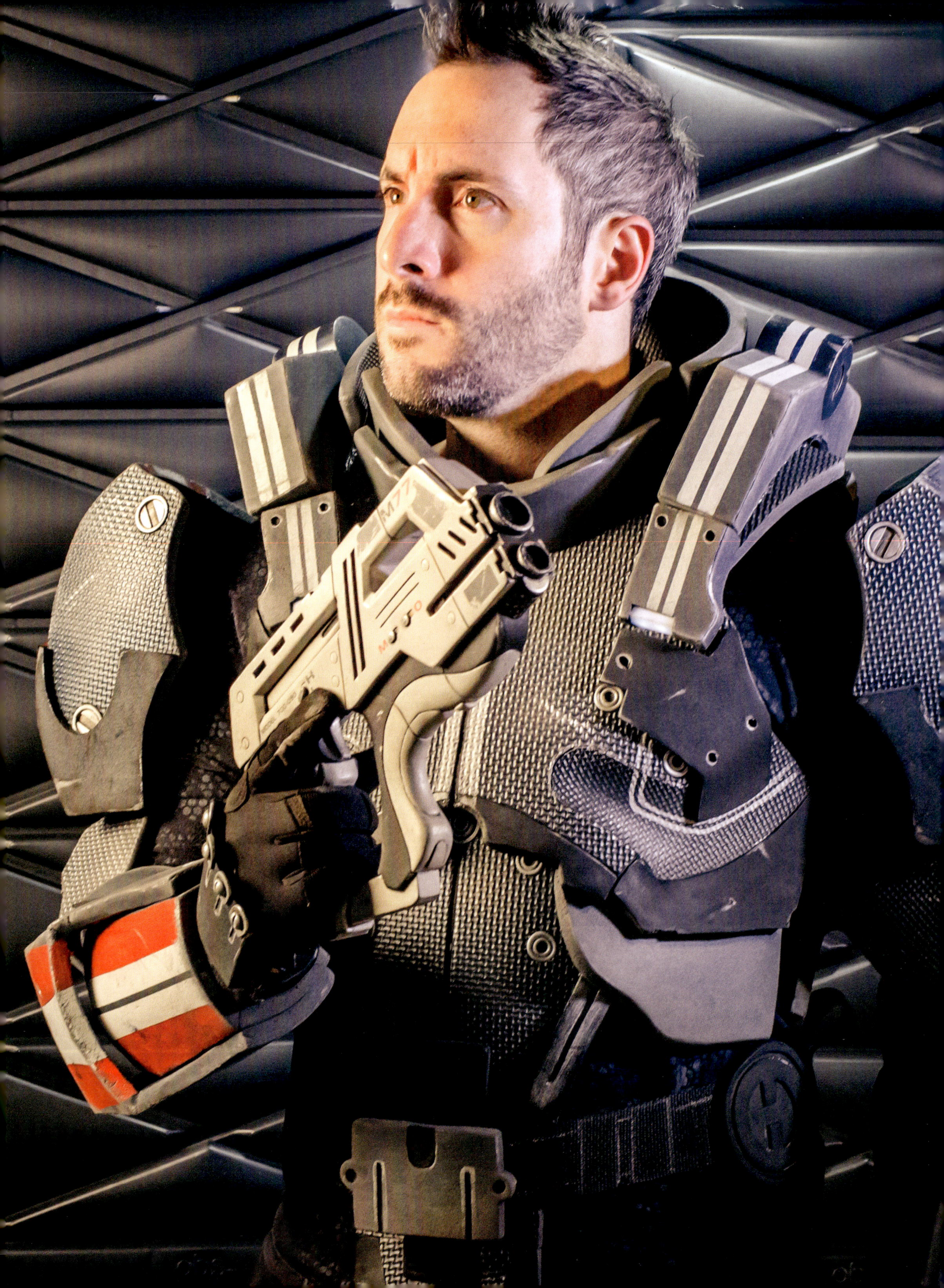
M77

FAREWELL, FOAMSMITH

I want to thank you for taking this journey with me. Expect more exciting foam armor making guides as additions to this book. I still have so much more to share with you, mighty foamsmith. I look forward to seeing what wonderful creations we make together.

-Bill

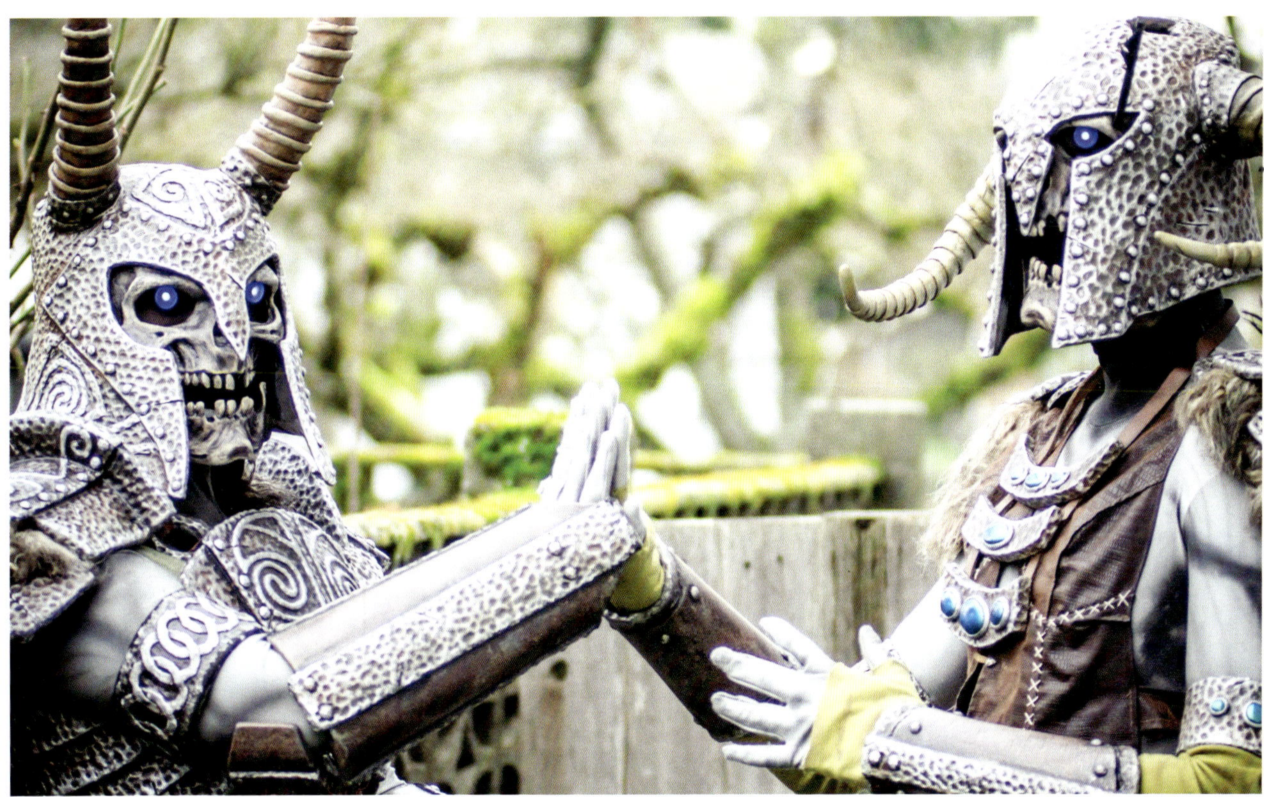

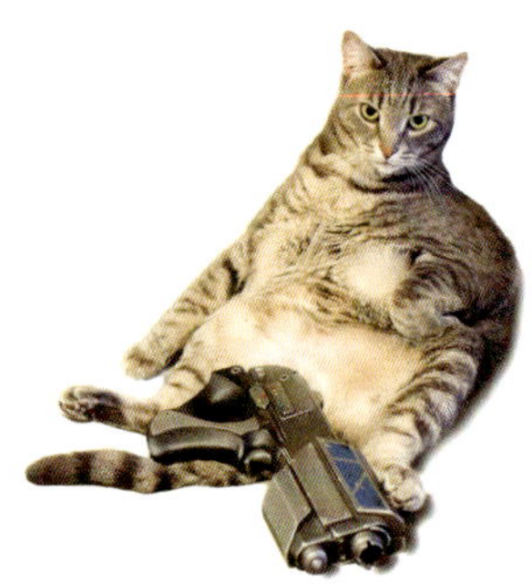

"I thank you too, human. Buying my slave's books keeps me fed."

- Buddhacat